First President

First President

A life of John Dube,
founding president of the ANC

by Heather Hughes

First published in southern Africa by Jacana Media (Pty) Ltd in 2011

10 Orange Street
Sunnyside
Auckland Park 2092
South Africa
+2711 628 3200
www.jacana.co.za

ISBN 978-1-77009-813-8

Job No. 001523

Cover design by publicide
Set in Ehrhardt 11/14pt
Printed and bound by Ultra Litho (Pty) Limited, Johannesburg

See a complete list of Jacana titles at www.jacana.co.za

Dedicated to Christina Brown, David Brown
and Mary Hughes with love and thanks

Contents

Acknowledgements

Through the long years of writing, my family has sacrificed much and been unspeakably patient, at times more hopeful than confident that one day it would be finished. My sorrow is that my father, Harry Hughes, did not live to see its completion. But it is to the living – my mother, Mary Hughes, partner David Brown (who discussed points of interpretation, sharpened my wits and willingly interrupted a busy schedule to locate vital documents) and wonderful daughter, Christina Brown – that this book is dedicated with love and gratitude.

I consider myself unbelievably fortunate to count Tim Couzens and Shula Marks as teachers and mentors. They have long been, and remain, towering figures in southern African studies, and have shown by example what 'community of scholars' is really all about. Their influence can be felt in the continuing work of the many academics, writers and policy-makers who were taught by them and benefited from their immense generosity. Tim's wise letters (penned, not typed) encouraging me to keep going will always be treasured. While conscious of the debt I owe them, for their own safety I hasten to distance them, as well as all my colleagues, informants, friends and relatives, from the contents of this book.

The Dube family, in particular Auntie Lulu Dube, Zenzele Dube and Langa Dube, have been gracious throughout this project, answering queries and providing encouragement. I thank them for their kindness. I owe a special thanks to Omar Badsha and Nasima Badsha: our friendship began at Phoenix Settlement, grew into many collaborative projects and has been an inspiration through many decades. From the moment Cherif Keita embarked on his own journey of discovery concerning the life of John Dube – the extraordinary connections he uncovered between Northfield,

Minnesota, and Inanda would make for a riveting detective story – he has generously shared his knowledge and research material. I thank him profoundly for his friendship and support. Similarly, Bob Edgar was amazingly generous in sending me materials that I could not directly access myself. Muzi Hadebe has willingly rescued me from translational and other blunders for a very long time, and I could not have managed without his advice and long conversations about Mafukuzela's life. Jane Starfield, Paul La Hausse, John Wright, Brian Willan, Peter Limb, Paddy Kearney, Dave Hemson, Christopher Merrett, Esther Sangweni, Julie Parle, Debby Gaitskell, Liz Gunner, Junerose Nala, John Daniel, John Lambert, Ashwin Desai and Jeff Guy have for a long time been committed to the sort of intellectual environment that has been a privilege to inhabit. The endnotes will reveal just how indebted I am to many of them.

The late Dr M.V. Gumede, local historian *extraordinaire*, received me many times in his wonderful Inanda home, willingly shared his copious library as well as his knowledge, wrote me many wonderful letters and put me in touch with several people who had known Dube. The Rev. B.K. Dludla likewise welcomed me to his home and indulged in hours of reminiscence. Grant Christison unhesitatingly sent me a copy of his thesis on Robert Grendon and allowed me to use what I needed, and Anil Nauriya sent me a copy of his work on Gandhi. Arthur Konigkramer received me warmly at the *Ilanga* offices in Durban and gave support wherever he could; news editor Mbongeni Khuzwayo took time off to tramp around Inanda graveyards with me, for which I am truly grateful. Alan Buff went to great lengths to identify Nokutela Dube's resting place in the Brixton Cemetery and may yet find it. Raymond Simangaliso Kumalo of the John Dube Foundation as well as Head of the School of Theology and Religion at the University of KwaZulu-Natal was constantly positive and helpful. Manning Marable offered encouragement from afar; his death came just as this volume was in its final stages. As a scholar whose work first initiated discussion on the role of John Dube in South Africa, all of us interested in the history of African nationalism in South Africa owe him an enormous debt.

Sheila Dlamini and Nongcobo Sangweni were accomplished interviewers in gathering oral evidence, while Mandla Ngcobo produced a highly skilled translation of *uShembe*. Nelisiwe Precious Ngcobo helped to search *Ilanga* while I got my Zulu in order; two of the people who made a huge difference in that regard were Jeff Thomas and the late A.B. Ngcobo. Surendra Bhana, Margaret Daymond, Uma Mesthrie-Dhupelia, Luli Callinicos, Wayne

Dooling, Christopher Saunders and David Attwell provided information and advice on, and opportunities to explore, John Dube and his role in history.

Many, many dedicated librarians have helped to deliver tomes of evidence to my desk or PDF files to my inbox, from various archives and collections: Bobbie Eldridge, Nellie Somers, Hloni Dlamini and Mwelela Cele at Killie Campbell, Pieter Nel in the Pietermaritzburg Depot of the National Archives, Melanie Geustyn at the National Library in Cape Town, Michele Pickover in Historical Papers Division at the William Cullen Library, University of the Witwatersrand, Herma van Niekerk of the Unisa archives, Bill Jerousek of the Oak Park Public Library, Rose Salmon and the acquisitions team at the Grand Central Warehouse Library, University of Lincoln, and staff at the SOAS library and in the reading rooms of the British Library (St Pancras and Colindale), National Archives at Kew, National Archives in Pretoria, Durban Depot of the National Archives, Rhodes House Oxford, the New York Public Library and Houghton Library at Harvard. There are also those countless and unthankable researchers who make ever more material available electronically: passenger lists, searchable old newspapers, photographs and other original historical documents, back issues of journals and so on. Carlos Alvarado, Richard Carr and Andy Norvock retrieved files after several computer crashes and Maureen Ille helped with computer access. The University of Lincoln funded a trip to South Africa from its Research Development Fund, and I am thankful to Ann Gray for facilitating this support.

Many friends and family members have helped this project along in a variety of ways: Coral Vinsen, Ela Gandhi, Rob Dyer, Korki Bird, Lynn Maree, Philip Daniel, Brigitte and Jurgen Brauninger, Martin and Jill Knight, John and Beatrice Brown, Liz Shephard and Ian Phillips. In Lincoln many individuals have supplied a much-appreciated collegiality: Bronia Hall, Martin Elliott-White, Linda Hitchin, Andy Daglish, Pam Locker, Andy Hagyard, Sue Watling, Mike Neary, Farhan Ahmed, Helen Farrell, Richard Voase, Martin Knight, Laura Donohoe and Debby Wilson. Across countries, the scholastic enthusiasm of Mwelela Cele, Farzanah Badsha, John Lumsden, Sine Heitmann, Martina Venus, Carolin Stamm and Kerstin Bock has been infectious. The unstinting support provided by Gilli Procter, Alison Lewis and Ian and Pam Barnes has been more important than they can imagine.

Russell Martin at Jacana has been the most supportive editor imaginable, correcting errors large and small despite a broken leg. Without his calm commitment, and the professionalism of the Jacana production team in meeting breathtakingly tight deadlines, this story would not have seen the light of day.

Heather Hughes
Lincoln
April 2011

Abbreviations

ABCFM	American Board of Commissioners for Foreign Missions
ABCSA	American Board of Commissioners Papers Relating to Southern Africa
AME	African Methodist Episcopal Church
ANC	African National Congress
ASAPS	Anti-Slavery and Aborigines' Protection Society
AZM	American Zulu Mission
AZMP	American Zulu Mission Papers
CNC	Chief Native Commissioner
CO	Colonial Office
DBN	Durban
DDNA	Durban Depot of the National Archives
HPCW	Historical Papers, William Cullen Library, University of the Witwatersrand
ICU	Industrial and Commercial Workers' Union
ISP	Inanda Seminary Papers
KCAL	Killie Campbell Africana Library, University of KwaZulu-Natal
KCAV	Killie Campbell Audio–Visual Project
GNLB	Government Native Labour Board (Director of Native Labour)
MNA	Minister for Native Affairs
NAD	Native Affairs Department
NAK	National Archives, Kew
NAP	National Archives, Pretoria
NC	Native Commissioner
NLCT	National Library, Cape Town

NRC	Natives Representative Council
NTS	Secretary for Native Affairs Correspondence Series
PDNA	Pietermaritzburg Depot of the National Archives
SAMP	Southern African Materials Project
SANC	South African Native Congress
SANNC	South African Native National Congress (the name of the ANC 1912–23)
SCA	Students' Christian Association
SNA	Secretary for Native Affairs
UNIA	Universal Negro Improvement Association
VM	Verulam Magistrate
YMCA	Young Men's Christian Association
ZCC	Zulu Congregational Church
ZTHC	Zulu Tribal History Competition

Introduction

Writing John Dube's biography

After a long and difficult illness, John Langalibalele Dube passed away at his hilltop home in Inanda during the early hours of 11 February 1946. His widow, Angelina – MaKhumalo to all who knew her – was preparing to observe the proper mourning rituals, as family, friends and followers began to arrive, many in disbelief that Mafukuzela was no more. There was much work to be done to make the house right: dusting, sweeping, washing and cooking. One close family friend voiced his concern to her that it would be fitting for Dube's study to be tidied up, what with all the dignitaries arriving to pay their respects. She readily agreed and gave him the key to discharge this task, while she and her kinswomen kept vigil over the body in the front room of the house.

The following morning, when the study was unlocked, it was found to be completely empty. All the books, files of correspondence, reports, speeches, sermons, newspapers – the accumulation of over half a century of public life – had vanished. Perhaps they were removed for safekeeping, perhaps they were destroyed. Perhaps they are still hidden away somewhere. When John and Angelina's last-surviving child, Auntie Lulu, told me this story, she could not remember the name of the friend responsible. Perhaps that is best, that the whole incident should remain shrouded in mystery. All that was left was a small selection of volumes from his library, among them *Annals of the American Pulpit*, *The Expositor's Bible*, Talley's *Negro Folk Rhymes*, William Holt's *I Haven't Unpacked*, S. Parkes Cadman's *Adventure of Happiness*, H. Grattan Guinness's *The New World of Central Africa* and R.L. Stephenson's *Treasure Island*.

The absence of this documentary record presents something of a challenge to anyone setting out to piece together an account of John Dube's life, beyond the bare outlines that are already well known. One experienced biographer, James Wolcott, has gone as far as to assert that if there are no diaries and other private papers, 'any biography is doomed to be a progress report, an interim statement'. Fortunately, John Dube did leave a documentary trail – nearly imperceptible in places, well marked in many others – precisely because of his aspirations to, and then achievement of, leadership in so many walks of life. Letters he wrote to other leading figures, evidence he presented before commissions, speeches he gave, reports he compiled and not least the many articles and books he wrote: some are published, many are scattered across archival collections on three continents. So there is some hope that a biography can be more than a progress statement.

It is important to be aware of the nature of the surviving evidence. Much of it was explicitly designed to be publicly consumed; there is little in the way of private reflection. It may be the case, therefore, that a biography of John Dube can be no more than 'the clothes and buttons of the man – the biography of the man himself cannot be written', as Mark Twain (Samuel L. Clemens) notes in his autobiography. There are some remarkably frank letters to sympathisers and detractors, but most of what we have is what Dube wanted us to see of his public persona. We also have some perceptive oral and written accounts of how family and associates saw him. As is so often the case, these tend to say more about their authors than their subject, but at the same time these sources disclose things that Dube may have wanted to keep hidden. This is all of great interest to a biographer. Nevertheless, the most important evidence in constructing his life must be that which he himself left behind.

When one's sources are relatively limited, one has to squeeze as much from them as one can: even documents and speeches designed with an audience in mind can hopefully reveal a great deal about private fears, hopes and preoccupations. Leading contemporary biographers such as Richard Holmes have shown how, if one immerses oneself sufficiently in the task, the most apparently simple statement can yield layers upon layers of significance. So, for example, in Dube's case, a guide to 'good manners' that he wrote in his fifties, *Ukuziphatha kahle* (1928), could well contain important clues about how he had tried to bring up his own children, quite apart from being an attempt to stem what he saw as a steady decline in public morals.

An objective body of evidence is one key thing – and it certainly is a key thing, part of what Michael Holroyd has called 'the rigorous documentation and exactitude of strict biographical method' – but what we do with it is another. Despite Hermione Lee's wry observation that the only rule about writing biography today is that there are no rules, there are several key issues concerning interpretation of evidence to confront, such as the attention we pay to a subject's private as well as public life, the relationship between subject and context, between subject and author, and the choice of biographical form itself.

We have come to expect that a biography will not just be about the public life of the subject, but will delve into the private, too. The biographer Janet Malcolm has put this best: 'Biography is the medium through which the remaining secrets of the dead are taken from them and dumped out in full view of the world. The biographer at work, indeed, is like the professional burglar, breaking into a house, rifling through certain drawers that he has good reason to think contain the jewellery and money, and triumphantly bearing his loot away.' It is the same quality that prompted the great German scholar Hans Magnus Enzensberger to describe the biographical subject as 'victim'. This voyeuristic quality of biography is perhaps the most compelling reason for its unabated popularity. While we are fascinated with fame, it is in the private dimensions of people's lives that they seem most like us. Once, bookshops scattered biographies alphabetically among the history, art, sport, literature and entertainment sections of their stock. Then they grouped them all together as 'biography'. Now, in some of them, this undifferentiated category is acquiring its own sub-genres: we can browse 'celebrity biography' and, most recently, something called 'painful lives'. Revelation of private, hidden detail is sometimes undertaken for its own sake, but more often indicates a changing preoccupation with how we understand other people's lives. Whereas writers used to want to account for what made a figure 'heroic' or 'great', concentrating on public achievement, they now seem more drawn to explanations of how domestic life – parentage, upbringing, and so on – has affected public profile, and what fame and trauma mean – not only to those who have high media profiles, but to ordinary people who dream of such a profile.

It is certainly the case that Freud's work on the influence of childhood on our lives has rendered it unthinkable to write or read a biography that starts with someone's adult achievements. Dube's childhood is significant not only because of this general point, but also because certain key events that shaped his life, such as his conversion to Christianity, happened in these years and he himself acknowledged their importance. This determination that nothing should be hidden, or at least nothing that we uncover in the course of our research should remain hidden, means that we have become used to a degree of candour unthinkable in Dube's time. While nineteenth-century subjects would have been mortified to have their private lives exposed to public comment, these very details – where they exist – can help us today to understand their public lives better. I have tried to suggest that in John Dube's case, several rather puzzling episodes, not least the confusing end to his presidency of the African National Congress in 1917, can be explained with reference to private preoccupations.

The trouble with all this is that it can reinforce the tendency, ever-present in biography, to exaggerate agency over structure, the single heroic figure over context and circumstance. This balance between individual life and social context used to mark the boundary line between biography-writing and conventional history-writing. One of the most eminent contemporary historians, David Cannadine, has written that 'while biographers are conscious of the things that make their subject unique, historians are more concerned with seeing individuals in the context of their times and class'. In fact professional biographers remain highly sceptical of historians' (and, worse, academic historians') ability to write biography. And some commentators argue that the distinctions between 'biography' and 'history' have become blurred, especially in the midst of so much debate as to whether we can know *anything* beyond ourselves – whether our 'times' (or historical context) are products of each individual imagination or experience, or whether there is something objective about the reality outside and around us.

On this point, I have followed Richard Holmes's optimistic view, that despite 'disabling self-doubt, the possibility and the desirability of knowing our fellow man and woman ... has remained extraordinarily constant. And biography has gradually become a prime instrument ... of that essentially human, courageous and curiously cheering epistemology.' So the matter of a balance between subject and context remains relevant. As a historian writing biography (and fascinated by the biographical genre), I have treated my task primarily as one of describing and explaining Dube's development as a public figure – how history made him, in other words, although I have also tried to assess the extent to which he 'made history'. His context was a particularly dramatic one, South Africa's own industrial revolution, which coincided almost exactly with his own life (1871–1946). It features hopefully in sufficient measure to make the narrative intelligible.

There are more idiosyncratic approaches to interpretation, including the consequences of writing about someone whose own notions of the objective world were so different from my own. John Dube's view entailed initiating 'grand designs and great projects' in order to engineer a form of social change driven by Christianity and market values, and an implicit belief in the onward march of human progress towards enlightenment. We would now call this 'conviction politics'. He was conscious of how radical his idea of social progress was, and therefore wanted to introduce it in a highly managed, disciplined way, under the auspices of those like himself who understood the modern values he wished to diffuse throughout society. His sense of modernity, moreover, included not only an intense pride in his race (and, increasingly, a defence of it under the onslaught of contemporary segregationist politics) but also a strictly hierarchical social order, a sort of meritocracy and aristocracy combined.

I am the product of a very different set of circumstances. I grew up white in apartheid South Africa, in a lower (but aspirant) middle-class, Christian home where the duty of 'service to others' was strongly encouraged (among my earliest memories are accompanying my father to deliver bags of second-hand clothing to Father Huddleston's mission in Sophiatown, and my mother to deliver food parcels to 'poor whites' in Jeppestown, Johannesburg). Yet I cut my political and intellectual teeth on the student Africanisation campaigns and charged ideological debates between liberals and Marxists in the 1970s and 1980s, and these changed my outlook substantially, not least by introducing me to the subversive possibilities of African history. My sense of 'the world out there' crystallised around ideas of nonracialism, gender equality, social justice, redistribution of resources and a growing scepticism that the narrative of history would necessarily have a happy ending, despite having experienced the momentous and heady days of 1994 and the arrival of the New South Africa. Through the dissolutions of postmodernity, I have maintained a sense of the narrative all the same, but of a deeply critical kind.

I began to write about John Dube through a combination of experiences. After completing postgraduate courses in African Studies, I taught African history and politics for a number of years, lived for a time in Inanda, completed a study of the Qadi chiefdom and, through research on Ohlange High School, spoke to many people who remembered him or revered his memory. I began to develop a fascination with this somewhat enigmatic figure, whose determination and political courage stood out. Early black South African politicians have been poorly served by the historical record; while there are a few landmark and truly wonderful biographies, so many other figures still await the recognition they fully deserve. So it was a question of starting the work because there was a gap to fill.

In form, this biography follows a generally narrative, 'womb-to-tomb' sequence. I wanted to try to present a sense of how his life was lived, as a way of capturing how participants experienced events as well as the interconnection between events. However, I was aware that this choice ran the risk of imposing a false sense of neatness and order. Hindsight is double-edged: in usefully telling us how the story ends, it risks overlooking contingency, the accidental wrong turnings and necessary deviations along the way. There were plenty of times in John Dube's life when it looked as if he would fail to make anything of his opportunities, or when illness would discourage him. I have tried to convey a sense of him confronting choices and making decisions, not just to report the outcomes of decisions.

Where does the title, *First President*, fit into this sequence? Luis Borges, the great Argentinean writer, mockingly referred to a particular kind of 'biography of Michelangelo that makes no mention of the works of Michelangelo' – the predisposition, that is, to focus so narrowly on one aspect of a subject's life that the overall significance is lost. This may not be treated as a problem if the subject's life and works are already well represented in the biographical literature. But it is certainly more problematic in cases where so little is already known. One of the remarkable things about Dube was the breadth of his achievement: he founded Ohlange, a school with a trailblazing vision that is still open for education; *Ilanga lase Natal*, a newspaper that has managed to survive the vagaries of economic and political uncertainty; the first novel in Zulu, *Insila kaShaka*, which was recently reissued as a Penguin Classic; and as an ordained Congregational minister, he played a leading role in church affairs in the early twentieth century. And these are just *some* of the activities to which he harnessed his considerable energies. Yet from the moment that Nelson Mandela chose Ohlange as the place to cast his vote in the 1994 election, and to pay homage at Dube's graveside with the words 'Mr President, South Africa is now free', Dube's pre-eminence as the founding president of the African National Congress was sealed. Here was one remarkable president reaching back across time to another, symbolising the completion of a long and difficult mission. In a sense, then, the title not only refers to one of Dube's most important offices and draws attention to his dedication to the making of a common South African political culture, but also captures two historic moments, one in 1912 and the other in 1994, underlining the point that biography is about past as well as present. The intention is not to privilege Dube's political activities over the others but to provide a way into the totality of his life's work.

All the ingredients that go into the writing of a biography mean that while every care is taken in the making, the result is nevertheless selective and provisional. It is constrained by the author's outlook, and it is constrained by available evidence. Other authors will have different perspectives; more evidence will surely come to light, and so future biographies of Dube will be different from this one. May there be many more. Not that this is the first attempt by any means. A number of figures close to Dube in his lifetime were sufficiently intrigued by or admiring of him to want to undertake biographies. Probably the earliest is that of G.G. Nxaba, related to Dube by marriage, whose writings on various subjects are scattered in various archival collections, but none of them is published. (There is clearly much further work for biographers and historians here.) R.R.R. Dhlomo, who edited *Ilanga* for two decades, was attempting to write a biography of Dube in the 1960s but, as he explained, under very trying conditions: 'no typewriter, and by candlelight'. Both wished to focus attention on Dube's considerable achievements, stressing the adversity he had had to overcome to realise greatness. It was a theme they themselves felt keenly.

More recent studies have generally taken the view that there was a clear trajectory to his public life: John Dube started out a fiery young radical, and became increasingly reactionary, ending up politically emasculated. The first sustained monograph was Manning Marable's PhD thesis, which argued that John Dube had sacrificed his cause of winning political rights for African people to his pursuit of recognition and that ultimately he let down the struggle. Eddie Roux, who taught for a time at Ohlange, dismissed the middle-aged Dube as a 'traitor'. Hunt Davis concluded that Dube's admiration for Booker Washington shaped not only his educational efforts but his contacts with white liberals, themselves impressed with the Washingtonian legacy. Shula Marks came to the conclusion that he had been outflanked by his times: he was unable to deal with the urban radicalism that bubbled up in the years after the First World War, and responded by adopting a narrowly ethnic approach that accorded with segregationist thinking and served to undermine class solidarity. While acknowledging a very great debt to this body of work, I have read and interpreted the evidence a bit differently, arguing that there were both radical and conservative elements in Dube's make-up all the way through his life and that each was more, or less, pronounced in different situations and at different times.

Most chapters are written around a particular phase or incident in his life (his first experience of America, for example, or his role in the Bhambatha Rebellion). I have been mindful, however, of the very important point made long ago by William Gerhardie that the divisions that we imagine make so much sense are in reality quite arbitrary: 'he who does not see that the segments into which we cut up life are revelations, not of truth, but of our particular defect of sight, has not begun to think'. There is rather more emphasis on his earlier years, for two reasons. The undoubtedly important contributions he made to public life from the 1920s were based on a political style already developed and a reputation already earned; what this style and reputation consisted of has been as carefully traced as possible. Further, his later roles have been the focus of much fine scholarship, as noted above, and are therefore already better known.

Everyone who has written on the history of the African middle class in South Africa has faced difficulties of terminology. For La Hausse, the 'bewildering range of terms ... captures the profoundly contradictory and mediated identity' of this group. Limb reminds us that it was a petty bourgeoisie lacking effective access to the means of production, an elite without power or the vote, an intelligentsia without academies or publishing houses. Indeed, behind all his public leadership roles and responsibilities was Dube's constant preoccupation with finding enough money to keep Ohlange going. In the nineteenth and early twentieth centuries, this class was small and marked by the attributes of formal education and Christianity, revealing its origins on mission stations rather than in commercial opportunity or industrial transformation. Yet its members were highly articulate and their influence was far greater than their small numbers would suggest. It was a class, moreover, whose development was blocked by a dominant settler society unwilling to accommodate it. Until recently, what most studies emphasised was the isolation of the African middle class from traditionalist as well as white society and the urban African masses. Research is now revealing the multiple connections and shifting social composition of this group, and this biography similarly suggests the heterogeneity and fluidity, not only of membership but also of the many and varied associations across classes and between 'insiders' and 'outsiders'. Dube's own family exemplifies the point.

I have used the term 'middle class' as a reminder of this fluidity. Like Norman Nembula, one of James Stuart's informants, I 'did not like the word *ikolwa* as the name of a class', partly because it 'fixes' it in a way that runs counter to this sense of fluidity, partly because it was a term that the Natal government used in an attempt to 'retribalise' Christian communities, which people like Dube resisted. Some of the other terms in contemporary use, like *izemtiti* (those who had exemption certificates), were often used disapprovingly, which hardly seems fitting when the subject of a biography is one of them.[1]

From the late nineteenth century, the term 'location' generally referred to areas designated for African occupation in towns, and rural ones were called 'reserves' – except (as in so many other matters) in Natal. Here, 'locations' meant the tracts of land in rural areas recognised by the state as under the control of chiefs; reserves were those similarly occupied but under the control of missionaries – and therefore also housed a growing number of Christian communities. Only from roughly the 1920s did 'location' apply to urban settings in Natal. Hopefully, context will help to clarify usage of these terms.

It is virtually impossible to standardise usage of places and people's names; I have tried to follow the rule of thumb that place names adopt the most recent orthography (except for very well-known ones that may deviate in form), whereas personal names follow contemporary orthography (so 'Nokutela', rather than 'Nokuthela'), except where convention has set a norm – thus, Martin Lutuli, but Albert Luthuli. As far as collective names are concerned, the usage here has been to drop prefixes except in cases where this seemed necessary to make sense: so 'the Zulu' for Zulu people, but *amaQadi omhlophe* (as a designation for 'white Qadi'). Similarly, 'Zulu' has been used for the language, on the grounds that this is an acceptable usage in English and conforms to the way all others are treated (German, rather than Deutsch, and so on).

The endnotes are an uneasy compromise between not having any at all and having one for each reference, and like most compromises will probably not please anyone. I have tried to group notes in a way that makes sense and is readable; since there is no section at the end containing references, an effort has been made to indicate the nature of primary sources and the location of documents as clearly as possible.

1

The inside people and the outside people

One January day in 1849 a woman called Mayembe descended on the small, isolated mission station of Daniel and Lucy Lindley in the Mzinyathi valley in Natal, seeking protection from angry relatives. Her young son, Ukakonina, was with her; his older sister had remained behind and would be fetched later. Ukakonina was driving eight head of cattle, five that Mayembe had purchased from the sale of corn, and three that the boy's father had given him at birth. They hoped these cattle would help them to make a new start. Mayembe had already shown interest in Christianity but was now cutting off her known, traditionalist life completely. This must have seemed a miracle to the Lindleys, the breakthrough they had been longing for these two years of labouring among the Qadi people. They did have a tiny band of followers and helpers, but these were more like a household than a congregation. Now they decided to found a church. It would grow into one of the most important in Natal, and Ukakonina would one day become its first African pastor, better known as James, John Dube's father.

Mayembe's arrival caused 'quite a stir' in the neighbourhood, as Daniel Lindley noted with characteristic understatement. She was not the stray misfit or uprooted outcast, the waif or wanderer commonly thought to have been the first to join the Christian church in south-eastern Africa. On the contrary: she was a person of considerable status, an *inkosikazi*, the widow of the late Chief Dube, a most notable and respected chief of the Qadi. She had lived among his people, undisturbed in her widowhood, for some 12 years. Mayembe had not been Dube's principal wife and her son was therefore not directly in line for the chiefship. Now, however, a young relative by the name of Mqhawe was being installed as the next chief. In an early assertion of authority, possibly because he was bothered by all her talk of Christianity, he was insisting that she marry one of her late husband's brothers – according to the custom known as *ukungena*, the levirate. She would have none of it. She had great things planned for this son of hers, Ukakonina, 'Like his mother', and clearly felt that they would have a more promising future in the church than with a new husband. So she had fled to the Lindleys.

This event was played out a very long way, in time and place, from Mayembe's short married life. The 'small chaos of broken twisted ridges' among which the Lindleys had established their modest station was located in what would one day be known as the Valley of a Thousand Hills, some 30 kilometres north of the settlement of Port Natal – a great distance from the Qadi ancestral lands far away to the north in the Zulu country, across the Thukela River. In the twentieth century, poets would elide these places, Natal and Zululand, in richly symbolic gestures. But in a time when travelling on foot was the only form of mobility, the story of Qadi migration southwards had an almost biblical quality to it, of terror, dispersal, wandering, and finally of regrouping and prospering. Precisely because Dube's was a chiefly family, there are many traces of it in the extant traditions, as spoken and as committed to paper, and as recorded by the Qadi as well as external observers.[1]

The Qadi had been living in the wide Thukela valley along the banks of a tributary, the Nsuze, since at least the eighteenth century. They had done well there, with access to good grazing and crop lands, control of significant river crossings and surrounded by thick forest that supplied fuel and building materials. They called this territory Eziqalabeni, 'Place of the hardwood trees'. Before Shaka's rise to power, they had been a minor lineage (they took their name from *iqadi*, a junior wife in a chiefly homestead) within the mighty Ngcobo polity, but Shaka had dismantled the Ngcobo in his drive for Zulu domination. While the ruling lineage, the Nyuswa, bore the brunt of the Zulu attack, the Qadi took a different political course and made their peace with the king. As their traditions put it, 'Amaqadi people say "Ngcobo" only; we do not say "Nyuswa".' To this day, Ngcobo remains the chosen name of the Qadi ruling line.

Dube had become chief in Shaka's time and was by all accounts a prudent ruler. He made great efforts to secure the chiefdom's integrity under the next and rather more irascible king, Dingane, who murdered Shaka in 1828. For close on a decade, Dube had been successful in this aim. He could not have anticipated anything more than an opportunity to confirm his loyalty when in the autumn of 1837 Dingane ordered the Qadi men to cut down trees and carry them to the royal court for building work. There are many versions of what happened next, but we should let John Dube tell his, since it is the one episode of his own Qadi history he recorded in any detail.

My grandfather was a powerful Zulu chief; so powerful that he excited the jealousy and hatred of the king. This was because he was kind and just to his subjects, while the king was very cruel. Hence many people flocked to the support of my grandfather, and had he so desired, he could have taken his followers and defeated the king, and assumed the ruling power. The king knew this; so he said to himself: 'Unless I do something Dube and his men will come some day and overthrow me and he will be king.' So he sought to accomplish by treachery what he dare not attempt by force. It is the custom of our people, in a heathen state, to live in kraals, which are surrounded by fences made by driving poles into the ground, and intertwining bushes between them. The king commanded to have such a fence built for himself and sent to my grandfather to contribute some of his best men for the accomplishment of the work. My grandfather suspecting no treachery sent many of his best warriors. When they came before the king, he commanded them to lay down their arms and weapons, and go into the forest to procure trees and bushes. They did so. Around this wood the king had placed large numbers of his men in ambush, and when the last one of my grandfather's followers had entered the forest, the king's men fell upon them and killed them. Others of the warriors of the king were sent to my grandfather's home, and in the absence of his best supporters, succeeded in killing him and many of his friends and kindred.

We can picture John Dube as a small boy sitting at his father's feet with his siblings, listening to this tale and being instructed in its moral lessons, in much the same way that every Qadi child would be told it for generations. His version provides us not only with a graphic account of the event, but also with an insight into his own sense of how he belonged in the story. It is based on talks he gave while accompanying American missionaries on fundraising tours in the United States in the late 1880s, still in his teens, homesick and desperately short of cash. He was invariably the most popular speaker on the platform. We can well imagine the mixture of fear, awe and sympathy his audiences would have felt at that description, 'a powerful Zulu chief'; it had been only a decade since the Zulu had astonished the world by inflicting defeat on the British, before being militarily crushed themselves.

But his story involved far more than asking for money. He called his grandfather a Zulu rather than a Qadi chief, because all through his adult life he thought of himself as Zulu, despite this terrible incident. The Qadi had after all been incorporated into the kingdom quite early on in Shaka's reign and subsequent generations believed very strongly that Dube and

Shaka had been close allies, even that the Qadi men in Shaka's army had been instrumental in the final defeat of his oldest and most formidable rival, Zwide of the Ndwandwe, in 1826. Shaka and Dube had suffered a similar fate at the hands of this aberrant new king, Dingane, too. Much later in the nineteenth century, Chief Mqhawe made strenuous efforts to relocate the Qadi back to the Nsuze because of land hunger in Natal: once the Zulu army had been neutralised and the threat of a Zulu invasion of Natal had been removed, people could reassert cultural and political affiliations. For John Dube, this meant highlighting the achievements of the old kingdom, which in his view had reached a level of sophistication – centralised authority, geographic reach, economic organisation and military might – that he was intensely proud of. Even though he often had harsh words for its heathen, 'benighted' ways, there were seeds in his very origins that he could transplant into the new world of Christian civilisation. There was also a more deeply personal sense of connection bound up in this story: unlike most early Christian converts, he was never entirely cut off from his pre-Christian past. In fact, as we shall see, at critical periods in his career he was to depend utterly on his chiefly relations for support and was on very close terms with them.

Such was the trauma of this exit from their ancestral lands in the Thukela valley that Qadi traditions are particularly voluble on the matter of Dingane's attack on them. What is notable about the basic message running through them all – the defenceless, unsuspecting Qadi, loyally performing their duty, being mercilessly attacked by a tyrannical and irrational king – is its striking similarity to accounts of the same king's much smaller-scale attack on another group of unsuspecting and unarmed victims, lured into the king's enclosure on a false pretext, just one year later. This attack is far better known because of its place in a white nationalist mythology that would be forced onto the consciousness of generations of South African school children: Dingane's massacre of the Retief party of Voortrekkers in 1838. In fact the very first written account of the Qadi killings, by Henry Francis Fynn, noted the parallel between the two attacks: the later one had turned the first into history too. It is clearly more than the scale of treachery or the size of a disaster that mobilises such myths.[2]

The Qadi survivors, including Mayembe and her two small children and led by Dabeka, Dube's son and heir, scattered southwards. They settled in coastal forest on the northern banks of the Mgeni River near to its mouth, some three kilometres from Port Natal. British agents and adventurers, hopeful of making their fortunes out of trade with the Zulu, had carved this base for themselves from the luxuriant subtropical undergrowth in 1824, on the only navigable inlet along the entire south-eastern coast. When the Qadi arrived 13 years later, there were about 40 whites at the Port, together with their retinues of African servants and clients. Early sketches show them inhabiting an assemblage of both 'upright' houses and thatched huts arranged in homestead formation.

As was the practice with other immigrant groups, the Qadi men were drafted into a militia that the traders had organised; relations with the Zulu king were always unpredictable. In reporting the arrival of the Qadi in May 1837 and their request for protection, the Port Commandant, Alexander Biggar, expressed 'serious apprehensions … that it may afford a pretext for the Zulu chief, Dingane, to carry into execution his long and often threatened intention of attacking and invading this settlement'. These fears were real enough, as Zulu power south of the Thukela had not yet been broken, and it would be another year before the Boers arriving from the Cape would assume republican control over Natal. The militia successfully raided Zulu villages in early 1838, capturing about 500 women and children and 4,000 head of cattle, of which participants would have been rewarded with a share.

After Dingane's killing of the Retief party in April 1838, the 1,500 men of this militia marched out again on an expedition against the Zulu king, possibly hoping for the reward of cattle once more. Led by John Cane, an early trader at the Port whose maverick tendencies had caused much of the tension between Dingane and the settlement, a few were armed with guns but most had only 'pig-skin shields and spears, many of them so old they used walking sticks'. As they departed, onlookers (including Daniel Lindley) tried to deter them. The fate of the expedition was related long afterwards, possibly by an eyewitness: 'Many were killed, being blocked by the drift; many threw themselves into the Tugela and were drowned. Twelve whites died, and all the coloureds except a few. Many blacks were killed, only a few being able to escape. They reached Thekwini [Port Natal] … singly, all with the same report: "You see me, the only survivor." And such was the battle of Dlokweni.' John Cane was among those killed, leaving his children, including Nancy and Christian, orphans. Their late mother, Rachel, frequently described in accounts as a 'Hottentot woman' (probably meaning of mixed race), had commanded both respect and authority at the Port in its very early days. Nancy was taken in by the Lindleys and in time became their interpreter at Inanda.

Also among the dead was Dabeka kaDube. Twice, then, in as many years, the Qadi had suffered defeat, dispersal, the untimely deaths of their hereditary chiefs and the loss of a large number of men at the hands of the

Zulu army. They were displaced yet again during the Zulu attack on Port Natal in the wake of the Dlokweni battle. These were bitter experiences, which shaped their attitude towards the Boer republican and British colonial authorities in Natal and the still-independent Zulu kingdom beyond its borders. Dabeka's heir, Mqhawe, had been born in the late 1820s and was still too young to become chief, so one Madlukana acted as regent in his stead, assisted by surviving homestead heads who had been close to the chief in the Thukela valley.

The Qadi had pressing concerns, especially the accumulation of cattle, and finding adequate land for grazing and cropping, in order to regain some measure of ordinary life. Much effort was put into the acquisition of cattle so that, among other things, *lobolo* arrangements could be normalised. The upheavals of the previous decade had led to the suspension of customary arrangements: there was rather more dependence on *promises* of the completion of *lobolo* transfers after marriage than parents of children of marriageable age would have liked. In other words, marriages occurred without a husband's family transferring any cattle, or far fewer than were habitually the case, to his wife's father's homestead, the rest being left to some later date. While this enabled even cattle-poor young men to effect marriages, fathers of marriageable girls for their part would not have felt very secure in this arrangement, especially if they also needed to supply sons of similar age with their own *lobolo* cattle. (It is also possible that grain could have been substituted for cattle, as was happening elsewhere at the time. Maize in Natal fetched high prices from the 1840s to the late 1860s.) These disruptions affected chiefly houses as well as commoners: Mqhawe complained in the 1880s that he was still completing cattle transfers for his mother's *lobolo*. He considered cattle to be fundamentally important for ensuring lasting social harmony; his testimony to the 1881 Native Affairs Commission was one of the most expressive on this issue: 'Our children are our own blood, and in nursing our children we admit that we are nursing the cattle.'

While most methods of building up herds were now costly and time-consuming, two events in the early 1840s provided the Qadi with a dramatic turning point in their fortunes. Firstly, in 1842 the British took control of the area that the Boers had proclaimed a republic in 1838; it was formally annexed to the Cape in May 1844 and became a separate colony the following year. Because the Qadi had arrived before the British, they were regarded as indigenous inhabitants rather than refugees, an important distinction in that it accorded their chief a superior status in the developing colonial administrative hierarchy and enabled the chiefdom to gain easier access to land. Secondly, a new Zulu king, Mpande, was making every attempt to secure his position north of the Thukela. One of those whom he considered a threat was Mawa, an aunt of Shaka's. She was still a power in the land and a close ally of her brother Gqugqu, who had a possibly stronger genealogical claim than Mpande to the kingship. Gqugqu's death in 1843 provided Mpande with the opportunity to move against Mawa, who fled with a large herd of royal cattle – enough, as officials in the capital gasped, to 'cover the site of Pieter Maritzburg' – and a considerable number of followers, estimated at 2,000 to 3,000 strong.

Mawa and her entourage crossed into Natal and reached the Mdhloti River, where they were stopped by the British Commandant at Port Natal. Mpande sent a messenger to the new British colonial administration in Pietermaritzburg in a fruitless attempt to demand the return of the cattle. Instead, Kofiyana kaMbengana was instructed to seize them for the British. Kofiyana had fled from Shaka with the Tshabeni chiefdom; Fynn had 'brought them out of the bushes' and made Kofiyana one of his *izinduna*. He became an important source of information and support to the colonial authorities, called by them their government *induna*. (One of the earliest artistic impressions of Port Natal was Thomas Bowler's 1845 watercolour 'View from Kofiana's kraal'.) The Qadi, who were on close terms with Kofiyana and who assisted in the enterprise, benefited greatly from this booty: 'it is with those cattle that we had established ourselves, we of the white men's country', as Madikane Cele, Mqhawe's *inceku* (or steward), put it. While acquisition of these cattle might have seemed like a kind of compensation for all the hardship the Zulu monarch had inflicted upon them, how acutely aware they must have been that without the protection of the 'white men's country', these stolen cattle of the Zulu country, and more besides, would be severely at risk.[3]

Now in a more favourable position to rebuild their polity, the Qadi needed suitable land on which to raise their herds and their children. The British were just beginning to assert control over their new colony and claims to land had yet to be tested. The Qadi moved upstream beyond the old and mostly abandoned Boer farms of Piesang Rivier, Groeneberg and Inanda to the Mzinyathi River, a tributary of the Mgeni. This area had recently been proclaimed Crown land and had apparently been known previously as Mhladlangwenya ('Spine of the crocodile'), an apt evocation of the rocky outcrops there. The Qadi renamed it Mkhuphulangwenya, 'Raiser of the crocodile'. It is their heartland to this day.

The Mzinyathi valley, down which the river flows like a central artery, is where the 'tossed, riven, cut, cleft' hills begin to flatten into the undulating coastal evergreen belt. Dense forest then covered wide strips of either bank, a ready source of fuel wood and building materials, as well as game. As a boy in the 1860s, the local farmer George Armstrong accompanied Qadi huntsmen and always returned with good-quality buckskin, which they could sell for 2s apiece. Rainfall was relatively high and, though falling mostly in the summer months, was distributed throughout the agricultural cycle, leaving only a short, dry winter period. The soil was suited to the staples of sorghum and, increasingly, maize, as well as vegetables. Sweet grasses which could support year-round grazing probably predominated in the mid-nineteenth century; only later did these give way to mixed sweet and sour types as a result of heavy use. Ridges and hills gave commanding views of the valley. When Mqhawe became chief a few years later, he established his own principal homestead, Ekumanazeni, 'Place of quibbling', on one of the ridges to the east of the Mzinyathi. Senior kin and councillors like Madikane Cele built theirs within easy walking distance of the chief's. So desirable was the valley that in 1904, even after the damage of 60 years of colonial land policy, the report of the Mission Reserve Superintendent concluded that it was, in effect, too good for African occupation.[4]

Those, like the Qadi, 'of the white men's country' were developing new expressions for their situation, one that they perceived (for the moment, at any rate) to be preferable to the years of disruption they had had to endure. The Qadi are one of a number of chiefdoms that have long been described as 'Lala'. Some have thought of Lala as a matter of blood ties, reinforced by a linguistic peculiarity, the *tekeza* or *tekela* dialect. Others have proposed a distinction based on craft or culture, such as iron-working. As skilled craftsmen whose wares were highly valued, smiths were often debased in social terms as a form of close control; thus, *ilala* became a derogatory term to describe outsiders or those unable to support themselves. Yet others have argued that Lala was an ideological category, encompassing those who had been incorporated into the rising Zulu state as inferior underlings. Madikane himself graphically described how Shaka 'used to insult us and frighten us by saying that we did not have the cunning to invent things out of nothing, like lawyers. He said that we Lala could not do it.'

The rich evidence that has become more readily available in recent years points to a further possibility for the meaning of Lala. If one compiles a list from the Stuart archive of all those chiefdoms and fragments of chiefdoms who regarded themselves as Lala, a bewilderingly large and seemingly random variety is the result. Yet this very variety is the key: they are all fragments, and possibly larger sections, of virtually all of the peoples who fled, or chose to move, south at some point during the rise to dominance of the Zulu kingdom; that is, they found themselves in an area over which the British came to exercise control. It is highly likely therefore that Lala became a term by which those 'seeking protection' from a southern rival authority (first the traders at Port Natal, then the Boers, then the British) referred to themselves. Bishop Colenso's dictionary entry for Lala, 'Common name for a person belonging to many tribes which were driven south of the Tugela by Tshaka, whose dialect is very harsh', would support such an interpretation.

In the sense that this held out the hope of re-establishing chiefly authority, rebuilding herds and replanting crops in relative peace, Lala carried positive connotations to its bearers. As Madikane put it, 'in the time of Mpande we in Natal had good fortune. The English came, and times were easy, and there was happiness.' This was in sharp contrast to the derisive term used by the Zulu rulers against the haemorrhaging of people from the kingdom to Natal: *amakhafula*, 'those spat out'. It is significant that Madikane's testimony, alone among the surviving traditions, plays down the whole episode of Dingane's attack on the Qadi and makes much more of the chiefdom's later achievements in Natal. Perhaps it was the people who had suffered most in earlier disasters who were most willing to submit themselves to an alternative form of rule. To colonial overlords, the flip side of this meaning of Lala – neutralised, conquered, subject – would have been attractive too. Thus Joseph Kirkman described the broken remnants of the fighting force marching out of Port Natal against Dingane in 1838 as 'Amalala', and the missionary Joseph Shooter could write with approval in 1857 of the way in which the 'Amalala seem to treat their wives', in contrast to the cruel treatment meted out by (steadfastly anti-Christian) Zulu men to their spouses.

To those polities such as the Qadi, confronted with the dismembering of protective political bonds, the 'scattering of nations' associated with Zulu state formation seemed an unnatural time, when dogs and birds talked to people. While old networks were destroyed, experiences of war and disruption are also powerful shapers of new associations. Lala was an ingredient of the consciousness of those setting up again in Natal from the 1830s. It had to do with their experiences in the Zulu kingdom, their ejection from it, their subsequent attitudes towards it, their hopes for a better deal from the authorities south of the Thukela, and perhaps their longer-term hopes of a return some day to their ancestral lands. While Lala as an ideological category had its origins in state formation to the north, it was imported and reworked to positive ends as an 'improving' consciousness in the different state setting of colonial Natal. It accorded well, moreover, with early colonial administrative policy, as elaborated by Theophilus Shepstone, of allowing chiefs fairly wide latitude in the exercise of authority.

John Dube's 'outside' background was thus made up of three main kinds of affiliation: Zulu, Qadi and Lala. There were dramatic changes occurring in all of the societies of south-eastern Africa through the nineteenth century, due to the titanic struggles between different states, indigenous and foreign, to consolidate and advance their interests, so that such forms of association tended to be dynamic, their meanings altering with circumstance. By the time he became conscious of such things, his apprehension of being Zulu, or Qadi, or Lala, was perhaps very different from what these had meant to his grandfather or father. Yet there were continuities as well as disruptions, and the continuities would in time enable him to build effective support structures.

In addition to these horizontal forms of belonging was the equally important matter of status. From his earliest writings, we are left in no doubt that John Dube was keenly conscious of having been born into an advantageous position, into a chiefly family, stretching back many generations: he was always able to recall a long list of Qadi chiefs: Njila, Bebe, Ngotoma, Silwane, Dube, Dabeka, Mqhawe, Mandlakayise. From his 'outside' background came a strong sense of both the entitlement and the responsibility to lead. Moreover, it was important to him that his forebears had used their positions well, had achieved something of value. It was what they *did*, as much as who they *were*. This belief in the leader's sense of duty was at the heart of his recounting his grandfather's fate at the hands of Dingane. At once a very ancient and a most modern ideal, benign kingship was to lie at the heart of much of his own sense of achievement.[5]

There were nine founding members of Daniel Lindley's church in that January of 1849. Aside from Mayembe and her son (who was just old enough to count as a member), there were Nancy Cane, Joel Hawes, John Mavuma, George Champion, Jonas Mfeka and the Lindleys. They and their families would form the nucleus of a small, close-knit community of converts, or *amakholwa* ('believers') as many have called them, of which the Dubes would emerge as the leading family. The longevity of many would ensure stability and a sense of cumulative achievement: Mayembe, Joel Hawes and John

Mavuma would all live another half a century, dying within a year of each other in the late 1890s.

Joel Hawes and John Mavuma, like Mayembe, had grown up in the Qadi chiefdom. Hawes had lived under Chief Dube in the Thukela valley, done military service, and already had a family when he fled with other survivors after the 1837 massacre. There is no record of his previous name; the Lindleys gave him his Christian one in honour of the Connecticut minister who had married them (and who also baptised Harriet Beecher Stowe). The Inanda Joel caused great distress both to his family and to his church, when in a lapsed moment he took a second wife some time after 1849. She apparently gave him so much trouble that he returned to his first wife, Keziah, and to the congregational fold, thereafter leading an unimpeachable existence. Two of their sons, Benjamin and Thomas, were early African pastors of the American Zulu Mission (AZM), as the local operation of the American Board came to be called.

John Mavuma had fought under Shaka and had been a bodyguard and executioner of Dingane. He had himself been condemned to die at the time of the attack on the Qadi but managed somehow to escape. Lindley had baptised him some time before 1849, when he was in his forties. He and his wife, Kombozi, led what the missionaries described as 'exemplary Christian lives'; he was constantly troubled by thoughts of the number of men he had killed. In the 1860s he indicated that he wished to be a missionary but was considered too elderly by then. In the 1870s, he took himself off to live at Bishopstowe, the Colensos' mission near Pietermaritzburg; there were strong links between the two stations, despite the differences in denomination. His son David continued to live at Inanda with his wife, Mkosi, pillars of the local community. Their daughter, Nomasonto, was a classmate of John Dube.

As noted earlier, Nancy Cane had been adopted into the Lindley household as a child. Daniel Lindley had a very good grasp of Zulu, but he always preached in English and Nancy would translate. So it was really from her that the curious in the Mzinyathi valley first heard about Christian belief. Nancy to some and Nanise to others, she was in many ways the bridge between the spoken world and that of books, full of their 'unfathomable glyphs'. Her brother Christian remembered with reverence that she had 'a box full of books'; the only photograph we have of her shows her holding a book, echoing his memory. Early missionaries are often credited with translating the Bible into vernacular languages, while few record the contributions of those, like Nancy, who were paid assistants in this process. In the early 1850s, she eloped with a Mosotho by the name of Edward Ndamane. It was all very romantic: he 'came in the dead of night, on horseback himself, and leading another horse for the dark lady of his love, and carried her off in triumph'. Ndamane was very possibly as unsettled in his background as Nancy had been in hers, yet he lacked her ability and means to adjust and adapt. He turned out to be a drunkard and they ended up living separate lives, she in Inanda helping with mission work and he with a section of the Qadi near Botha's Hill. They had no children. The Lindleys' son Bryant described Nancy as 'one of the finest and most able women I have ever met'.

George Champion, whose original name was Patayi Mhlongo, had been taken in by the Lindleys when his eponymous guardian returned to America after a number of years' mission work in southern Africa. He lived at Inanda until 1866, when he accompanied one of the Lindley daughters to New Guelderland, near Stanger. His son A.W.G. Champion, born to his second wife in 1893, was to be a fierce political rival of John Dube from the 1920s. We know very little of Jonas Mfeka, save that his son would be among the most prominent of Inanda farmers and community leaders in the twentieth century, and a daughter, Deliwe, was also an early classmate of John Dube. On her conversion to Christianity in 1849, Mayembe took the name Dalida, a variant of the Old Testament Delilah. So memorable was this act in the life of the young convert community that over the following years several Inanda families named their daughters Dalitha, Talitha, Dalida or Daleka, in her honour.

The new generation would be as remarkable as their namesake. One, Dalida Seme, an elder sister of the more famous Pixley kaIsaka, became a missionary at Inhambane in Mozambique. Another, Talitha Hawes (Joel and Keziah's granddaughter), would achieve the remarkable feat of saving enough money by the early 1880s to pay for her passage to New York, to fulfil her dream of studying in America, even more remarkable in the light of the fact that she was physically disabled. She was decisively dissuaded by her teachers. She had already distinguished herself as the translator of one book of the Bible into Zulu – the brief but intensely lyrical Song of Solomon.[6] Ukakonina took the Christian name James, after two of Christ's disciples, and thereafter would be James in his Christian life and Ukakonina in his extensive dealings with the Qadi chiefdom. James spent most of his days in the early 1850s in the Lindley household, imbibing literacy and a dogmatic Christian tradition of piety and thrift. It was a demanding yet nurturing environment, the Lindleys' utter sense of conviction shaping every waking minute.

Daniel was the product of Midwest frontier revivalism, Lucy of the more urbane milieu of the Eastern Seaboard. Both were anti-slavery and Republican (then the more liberal of the two main political parties), and earnest in their commitment to an ascetic, morally improving creed. What leavened their particular approach and distinguished them from most of their peers (and contributed in no small measure to the rather unusual set of relationships that developed at Inanda) was a sense of humour and willingness to learn from those around them. They had come to southern Africa on behalf of the American Board of Commissioners for Foreign Missions, thinking that they would soon convert kings and princes, and their subjects would all follow suit, and Africa would be the Continent of Light in a matter of years. But Africa was not Hawaii (where this method had achieved some success). No sooner had they arrived in the mid-1830s than they were buffeted by the series of raids, counter-raids, displacement and destruction caused variously by the Zulu rise to power and the Boers moving eastwards, away from the Cape, in search of their own promised republic. Not only had it been a hard blow to come to terms with the slow, individual approach to conversion; they also reluctantly acknowledged that unless some power, necessarily an imperial one, brought a degree of political stability to south-eastern Africa, there could be no mission field. This demonstrated something else about the Lindleys: they were eminently pragmatic individuals, managing to hold strong views and yet not to rock the American Board boat.

From 1838, they ministered to the Boers in Natal, only returning to mission work proper in 1845, after Britain had annexed Natal. By the time they founded their church four years later, therefore, they had been in Africa for 13 years. Daniel was also closely involved in setting out the land policy of the new Colony. He supported the demarcation of so-called locations, on which Africans might be guaranteed communal land rights rather than be turned into landless labourers for the white settlers who were steadily trickling in. His Mzinyathi mission station, as well as the Qadi and several other chiefdoms, all found themselves well inside the new 480-square-kilometre Inanda Location. He had not actually seen many of the tracts that he and other commissioners enclosed in 1847; when he did, he was angered at their generally poor quality.

The Lindleys were helped in their instructional task by Martha, the second eldest of their 'tribe of Dan', as the children called the family, and by Nancy. These were the teachers whom James knew best in his earliest days of learning to be a Christian. There was as yet no proper school room, so the busy Lindley kitchen served the purpose for the small number of children requiring not only the formalities of reading, writing and arithmetic but also socialisation into Christian childhood, what the Lindleys called 'the alphabet of civilisation'. This was no easy task, since their parents had grown up in a different cultural world and lacked knowledge of acceptable Christian children's games, songs, stories and habits. A convert at a Methodist mission in Verulam, not far from Inanda, summed up something of the sense of parental helplessness in this situation: 'We have given up our Native dancing, and attend tea meetings and the like … The boys and girls have no games; they have given up our Native games; the boys do play at marbles sometimes …' This was one of the reasons that Lucy Lindley established a Maternal Association immediately, in 1849 – to assist mothers in the process of proper Christian upbringing.

The converts built themselves 'upright' houses on land that Lindley allocated to them around his mission house – they were tucked into the valley, where some flattish land was to be had, but not in great quantities. At first, dwellings were of wood, mud and thatch, humble yet exceedingly orderly. On his brief visit to Inanda in the early 1850s, Bishop Colenso reported that the converts' cottages were 'as good as those of many an English settler' – in fact he mistook one of them for the Lindleys' on his arrival. (It was with these same converts that he conducted one of his famous discussions about the concept of an *Unkulunkulu*, or 'God of all things'.) Later, their industriousness enabled station residents to be more comfortable inside brick and corrugated iron. Each house had a garden plot for growing vegetables and cereals and keeping small stock, such as chickens and goats. Cattle were herded on common land. Life was patterned by the requirement that everyone meet their own sustenance needs; though no one went without food or clothing or shelter, frugality was a necessary element of life, partly for financial and partly for moral reasons.

They did all aspire to grow a little better-off, though, materially as well as morally. Moral well-being was encouraged through the holding of daily prayers at home and attendance at church on the Sabbath. The main avenues for material betterment were the sale of produce, transport riding, and running local trading stores – and more often than not it was a combination of several activities, using as much family labour as they could muster. Nearly all of these activities required investment, in ploughs rather than hoes, in oxen and wagons and in stock, and it was hard work accumulating the necessary capital. Daniel Lindley was only too willing to assist in the ordering and importation of converts' requirements, but they had to pay for the goods themselves. Some converts wanted to be able to own their plots. Elsewhere there were experiments, but this was not an option that was ever seriously entertained during Lindley's tenure at Inanda.

James Dube did not let his mother down. Making careful use of their cattle wealth, he acquired both plough and wagon, and as he grew to adulthood, he emerged as a well-to-do transport rider, employing some of the other station men. He collected and delivered goods for a number of local farmers and storekeepers, black and white. His customers would later include such leading colonists as George Armstrong and Marshall Campbell – he was known to many in the Natal colonial elite and highly respected by them. He was reputed to have loaned £1,000 to a white man. An immensely impressive figure, both in physique and in personality, he was over six feet tall with a booming voice and magnetic presence. Lindley described him as having 'perfect symmetry' – he would later gain rather too much weight for this to apply – and as 'a true man, a wise man, inside and outside a noble man … It is rare that a stranger sees him without asking, "Who is that fine-looking man?"'

Marsh Isaac, Pixley Seme's father, had arrived on the mission in the 1850s with his wife, Eliza. He was also well established in transport riding. Years later, Pixley Seme would claim that he was a cousin to John Dube. This may indeed have been a blood tie, or possibly one that was created out of common local interests, like many kin relationships since time immemorial. It is possible that their fathers were in business together, and close enough for them to feel a family-like bond. Jordan Ngubane, who knew both men well, claimed that Seme was a commoner of Tonga extraction and that Pixley and John would treat each other through their adult lives as 'home-boys', which is almost as good as kin. Pixley would call other members of the Qadi elite his cousins, too.

Another improving spirit who came to live on the mission at this time was Klaas Goba, also a Qadi, whose original name was Magandlela and whose Christian name suggests he had previously worked for the Boers. He too was a transport rider and as keen as James to better himself. Klaas and his wife, Maweli, were married by Lindley in 1854, and produced 11 children, including Helen, who was in the first intake at Inanda Seminary when it opened in 1869; Cetywayo, who became a minister; and Gracie, who was born in the same year as John Dube and later went to Inhambane as a missionary with Dalida Seme. The Goba and Dube families would be locked in various kinds of rivalry for decades to come.

It was not long before household heads like James Dube, Klaas Goba and Marsh Isaac were agitating for better grazing and agricultural land, away from the topographical constrictions of the Mzinyathi valley. Lindley was sympathetic to their needs, though also aware of the dilemma it raised, as he made clear in a letter: 'The men, especially, have waked up to something like energetic, persevering industry. The result of this is that some of them are obtaining worldly substance so fast as to make me fear they may lose sight of the true riches.' James was surely uppermost in his thoughts as he wrote this – he most clearly typified the connection between Christian conversion and commercial opportunity.

Lindley was also gravely concerned about the attitude of the Natal Governor, Benjamin Pine, who was threatening to break up African location lands in order to release labour for new white colonists: 500 had settled at Verulam, on an assisted emigration scheme, and were somewhat ambitiously aiming to supply the Lancashire mills with cotton. For all these reasons, Lindley arranged for the entire station – his own household and 17 convert families – to relocate in 1857 to 'Inanda New Station', carved out of the south-eastern corner of Inanda Location. Still overlooking the Mzinyathi (which continued to supply the settlement's water needs) but some way downstream, the new station was established on a wide ridge-top, where the land was open and suited to enterprise. Along the lines of other missions in Natal, the kernel of the station was the 500-acre glebe, belonging to the mission body. The mission house, church, school, converts' houses and gardens were located here. This was surrounded by a bigger Mission Reserve – technically remaining Crown land, but administered by a board of trustees of the mission as if it were a sort of parish. This was where day schools and outstations would gradually appear. The Inanda Mission Reserve, some 11,500 acres in extent and containing approximately 1,500 people, incorporated a good proportion of the Qadi homesteads, including the chiefs', which had been settled in the valley since the chiefdom's arrival in the 1840s. Some of the more successful entrepreneurs attached to the mission, like James, rented private land adjoining the Mission Reserve to accommodate the expansion of their farming and related operations.[7]

At about the time of the move to the new station, James Dube married Namazi Shangase, whose Christian name was Elizabeth. Frustratingly little is known of her background. She may have been from the Tshangase chiefdom, which bordered the Qadi in the Inanda Location; indeed, there was much intermarriage between them. She may even have been an early 'run-away' – escaping to the mission from an unwanted marriage. John Dube did note that his mother had grown up in the Lindley household, so it seems she had known James a long time. Lucy Lindley always had a small number of African girls living in the mission house, learning to cook, clean, sew, read and write. After the birth of her children, Elizabeth was known on the mission as MaShangase, an 'outside' convention of naming imported into the Christian community, and lived to see the outbreak of the First World War in 1914.

It is hard to find exact details about James and Elizabeth's wedding for the same reason that it is almost impossible to piece together an accurate record of the names and ages of all the Dube children: the church records were destroyed in a fire, and James never applied for exemption from Native Law, which process would have recorded the children's details. We do know that James and Elizabeth's first-born was a daughter, Nomagugu. There were at least three more girls, Victoria, Esther and Hleziphi, before their first son was born. He was christened Africa; it was to be a prophetic name. It is noteworthy that the Dubes never engaged in the practice, so common in early convert communities, of naming children after missionaries. They showed an altogether more independent flair. As if to stress the maintenance of 'inside' as well as 'outside' links, Dube children were often given a Christian as well as a traditional name, and some, like Africa, were given names that broke with Christian convention altogether.

The children attended the station primary school, and the girls were among the first to attend Inanda Seminary, the girls' high school that the Lindleys fought so hard to establish in 1869. It was in fact the first of its kind in southern Africa, an all-female boarding school, or 'complete Christian home' as the missionaries styled it, for the daughters of converts. Here, the approximately 20 girls in the first few years were taught reading, writing, arithmetic, geography, Bible study and sewing. In an effort to teach the skills of self-sufficiency (but equally to cut down costs), the girls were also expected to grow their own food, fetch water and clean the dormitories and classrooms. The Seminary's first and very long-serving head was the redoubtable Mary Edwards, who became a friend and supporter of both the Dube family and Chief Mqhawe.[8]

Through the 1860s the Inanda station built on its reputation for success, Daniel Lindley frequently making observations like 'some of our best men are so deep in worldly affairs that I hardly see how they can creep out from under the load they are now carrying' and 'everything that runs on wheels is now away from my station earning something'. Inanda seemed unaffected by the recession that crippled much economic activity in the Colony in the mid–1860s. An indication of the wealth contained within this community was demonstrated in 1862, when the church burned down. Funding to replace it came entirely from within, and it was a 'commodious edifice' that they built. Again, when a violent storm destroyed the new structure in 1873, the Inanda converts raised from their number the £400 required to rebuild yet again.

This hectic entrepreneurialism was also of intense interest to Mqhawe. Ever since Mayembe had absconded (as he saw it), relations with the mission had been tense. The Qadi had closed ranks around their chief at the time, and this meant a drastic fall-off in the number attending Sunday services. That Lindley was now 'bishop' over the same territory where Mqhawe was chief hardly seemed an auspicious basis on which to improve relations. For example, it was now the missionary's, rather than the chief's, prerogative to grant permission for newcomers to settle on the reserve. Yet by the mid-1860s Mqhawe was coming to listen to Sunday services, along with the 170 or so others who now regularly attended, and to ask for a teacher. He also sought the help of both James Dube and Daniel Lindley in acquiring ploughs, horses, clothing and other outward signs of well-being. 'I am getting a large African wagon made,' wrote Lindley, 'nominally for myself, really for the chief at his request. The other day he brought £70, mostly in gold, to deposit with me to pay for the wagon when finished.' Lindley was not the envious sort, but he was still somewhat awestruck when on a trip to Durban (as Port Natal was now known) with Mqhawe, the chief 'bought three good coats, three pairs of trousers, two vests, a shirt, a pair of braces and a *clothes brush*. He rode a horse I would much like to own, and with us were sixteen Natives, all on horseback ...'

Mqhawe thereafter enjoyed extremely cordial relations with the mission. Over the years until his death in 1906, he would enlist many of its residents as chiefly functionaries in pursuit of Qadi interests. James Dube, as Ukakonina, rejoined the chiefly inner circle and was much respected by ordinary Qadi. He sat on the board of management of the Qadi farm near Pietermaritzburg, which Mqhawe purchased in 1875. Mary Edwards wrote letters to the government and testified before official commissions in Mqhawe's defence. Daniel Lindley, as we have seen, helped him to acquire the trappings of modernity and, far from undermining the chief's authority, did what he could to protect Qadi land rights on the Mission Reserve. He routinely consulted the chief, for example, about applicants wishing to move into the Mission Reserve. In recognition of the services they performed for the chief, Edwards and Lindley were among a select group that became known as *amaQadi omhlophe*, 'white Qadi'.

Through the 1860s, James Dube not only reconnected with his 'outside' past and oversaw a successful business, both of which contributed to and fed on a web of supportive local relationships in Inanda. He was also placed in charge of the mission day school and (after some soul-searching) agreed to undergo training for the pastorate. In line with American Zulu Mission policy of moving the local church towards self-sufficiency, there was now a Home Missionary Society, an association of African converts on all the AZM stations, which was responsible for selecting and supporting preachers and pastors; its annual meeting was often hosted at Inanda. It was meant to foreshadow the emergence of a fully self-supporting church in Natal. A male theological seminary had also been founded. At first, it moved around to wherever there was a suitable missionary willing to tutor candidates. Though many deacons and preachers had been trained, there was great hesitance in taking what seemed to be the very radical step of ordaining African pastors. After a quarter of a century of mission work, there was still not a single one. At length in the late 1860s, a few men were selected to undergo training at Esidumbeni, under David Rood. The first to be ordained was Nguzana Mngadi (who became Rufus Anderson) at Umzumbe Mission, on the south coast of Natal, in May 1870. Next was Umsingaphansi Nyuswa of Imfume, also on the south coast, in June.

James Dube's turn came six months later, on 17 December 1870, a historic event for his family and for the Inanda church. His ordination was a dignified yet simple ceremony, with several missionaries from other stations in Natal and the African pastors Anderson and Nyuswa all taking part. There was much emotion. Daniel Lindley regarded it as the crowning moment of his missionary career. 'It was with the hearty approval of our whole mission that he has been ordained, and we have a strong hope that he will prove himself to be a workman of whom we shall never be ashamed,' he wrote in his report of the occasion, adding, 'This is the gladdest day of my life. I never anticipated beholding such a sight as this.' It was not only the symbolic high point of his Christian mission, but also an indication of the settling into maturity of the rural middle class that he had encouraged into being. If Elizabeth Dube attended, she would have been heavily pregnant. For just two months later, she would give birth to their second son.[9]

The python and the buffalo

John Langalibalele Dube was born at Inanda on 11 February 1871 – at least, this was the date he himself used as an adult. It was in all likelihood a retrospective approximation worked out with his mother (in relation to James's ordination, perhaps), since the church records had been destroyed in the 1873 storm. He did occasionally give other dates, but he fixed this as his official one when such things came to be required on passports and other legal documents. It was more than a matter of pragmatism: having a particular date of birth was the essence of that peculiarly modern quality, an individual identity.

His names, one Christian and one traditional, are significant. John, a contracted form of the Hebrew for 'God is merciful', was an immensely important name in the early Christian church: there was John the Baptist, the precursor of Christ; John the Apostle; and John the Evangelist, associated with the New Testament gospel of St John. It became favoured by royalty in the Christian world. 'John' must have seemed most suitable for a son born to the leading family in this momentous period in the life of the early Inanda church. It was already a well-established Christian name at Inanda and possibly this influenced their choice, too. Yet with James's ordination still fresh in everyone's memory, there was something especially deliberate in the parents choosing not to name their son after a missionary.

His second name, Langalibalele, 'Scorching sun', recorded his parents' admiration for the elderly Chief Langalibalele of the Hlubi. In the early part of the nineteenth century, the Hlubi had faced even more terrible upheaval than the Qadi. They had been a strong chiefdom, settled in what is now northern KwaZulu-Natal, but they had experienced a number of deadly succession disputes just at the time of intense rivalry between the more powerful Zulu, Mthethwa and Ndwandwe polities. Defeat and flight set in motion a trail of displacement across the Hlubi area; it was what they called *izwekufa*, 'death of the nation'. After years of uncertainty under Zulu authority, they had crossed into Natal in 1848.

Both the Hlubi and the Qadi were Lala, speaking the *tekeza* dialect, and both had gambled on British protection bringing peace and stability. Though located a very long distance from each other, there had been contact between the two chiefdoms, and one of Mqhawe's wives was a Hlubi. On a more personal level, Langalibalele's and James's lives had followed certain parallels: James had fled with his mother as a very young child, just as Langalibalele had experienced *izwekufa* as a boy. Like James, Langalibalele was of high birth but not directly in line to the chiefship. Unlike James, however, he found himself chief after a later round of succession disputes. It was he who had ushered the Hlubi into Natal; they had been permitted to settle on lands under the Drakensberg, where it was thought they might prove a useful buffer between the surviving San and white farmers, from whom the San tended to raid cattle. Langalibalele had successfully rebuilt the chiefdom in Natal, acquiring some 40 wives and a reputation as a rainmaker. Like James's close kinsman Mqhawe, he was a hereditary chief, which carried far higher status than those chiefs appointed by the 'Supreme Chief', the Governor of Natal. Langalibalele also demonstrated a great deal of autonomy, a mix of rejection and cooperation, in his dealings with the colonial government: he was 'not inclined to be submissive to an authority which he sensed as weak'. Perhaps this was a quality that James and Elizabeth hoped their son would emulate.

The early signs were not promising that he would even survive babyhood. For the first two years of his life, John Langalibalele was ill much of the time, struggling for existence and spending long periods in the mission house being nursed by Lucy Lindley and his mother. It is difficult to work out what might have been the cause of John's illness. Daniel Lindley diagnosed 'inflammation of the lungs', accompanied by high fever, so that the young child tossed restlessly through day and night. He treated the condition with a poultice. Perhaps John had contracted rheumatic fever. Whatever it was, it would recur and bring him down on several subsequent occasions. His health did improve greatly through his childhood, though. The earliest photograph of him, which still hangs proudly in the living room of the family home at Inanda, shows a smiling, chubby-cheeked, contented child aged about four.

While his mother watched over him anxiously, life went on in its predictable pattern around them. James Dube delighted everyone in his new role. As Lindley wrote,

Thus far the results of this ordination have exceeded my highest expectations. Mr Dube is a live man, well endowed intellectually and personally, has a heart for his work, is amiable, discreet, and has much independence of thought and action. With all these good qualities he commands the respect and confidence of all who know him. While he shows that he is alive to the responsibilities of his new position, I see no sign that he is in the least lifted up with pride or that he will fall into the condemnation of the devil. It has gratified me very much to learn from him how well he appears to know the spiritual condition of everyone, converted and unconverted, under his pastoral care.

He added that in the half-year since the ordination, the church had gained 11 new members. The Dube family business continued to thrive, too: though James's salary was set at £24 per annum, he never took any money from the Home Missionary Society – he supported himself entirely by his oxen and wagons. The young John clearly grew up in a household that was both well thought of and well-to-do.[1]

It has often been noted that John Dube's life was bracketed by the momentous events that came to be called South Africa's mineral revolution. In the year of his birth, what turned out to be diamonds were unearthed on an obscure hillside farm in Griqualand, away to the arid interior, and alluvial gold was discovered in the eastern Transvaal, sparking a gold rush. There were already upwards of 10,000 diamond diggers along the Vaal River, having responded to rumours of vast alluvial deposits there, but now they turned their attention to the Griqualand farm, gouging out what would eventually be the Kimberley Big Hole. Deep and rich seams of gold would also be found in the interior, but not for a few years yet.

These two subterranean treasures, gold and diamonds, would propel the subcontinent towards its own take-off to modern industrial development. John Dube himself would never have to experience the whole complexity of being shaken from the known, organic routines of the countryside and travelling great distances to live and labour in dangerous, alienating conditions dictated by the rules and rewards of strangers. His life choices would certainly be shaped by the demands of the new industrial world, though. But before that became clear, it did seem as if the most immediate threats to the orderly lives of Inanda residents would stem from transformations in the countryside itself.

Ever since the 1840s, Natal's white settlers had been bent on discovering some crop that would make them and the Colony rich. After several failed experiments, including arrowroot, tea, coffee, cotton (the Verulam settlers had not, after all, been able to supply Lancashire) and sesame seed, sugar seemed to hold the greatest future; this would be Natal's 'green gold'. The planters faced major difficulties in achieving their own take-off, however, of which the paucity of indigenous labour was the most pressing. Natal Africans still had enough access to land – in locations as well as on private farms abandoned to speculators after the various schemes collapsed – not to be tempted by the wages or type of work in sugar farming. Not all planters faced this problem, but those who did managed to persuade the colonial government to organise the importation of bonded labour from another British possession, India. The first Indian workers arrived in 1860; by the time the scheme ended half a century later, over 150,000 would have disembarked in Natal. They were joined by so-called passenger Indians, better-off traders and professionals who came to Natal on their own account to supply the needs of their labouring compatriots.

Indian workers were indentured for an initial period of five years, after which they could return to India, re-indenture, or work on their own account in their new land. Most took this last option either by migrating to the towns or by taking to small-scale commercial farming, or market gardening. First they rented land and, gradually, with the help of credit from 'passengers' (if frequently on exceedingly onerous terms), they purchased their own smallholdings.

Inanda Mission Station was very close to the centre of production of the Colony's green gold. From 1864 to 1874, the number of acres under sugar in the Inanda Division of the Colony (occupying the belt between the Inanda Mission Reserve and Location to the interior and the sea) rose from 5,000 to over 12,000 and the two largest mills were sited here. Indian workers in consequence were also concentrated here: by the 1880s, an estimated 14,000 were living in the Division, of whom 6,000 were under indenture and 8,000 were 'free'. As early as 1866, small Indian growers had spread quite close to the mission, displacing African tenants on many of the private farms in the area, and it was not long before the Inanda magistrate was reporting that Indians 'were the real agriculturalists of this Division ... But for them, maize would be at famine price, and vegetables would be strangers to our table.'

While all this might be cause for optimism among settler communities, it represented something altogether more ominous to Daniel Lindley. He especially deprecated the arrival of Indian workers: 'the great majority of these imported labourers will never return to their native land ... they are indescribably wicked, and seem to me hopelessly lost, now and forever ...

I look upon these Indians as a growing cloud on our social horizon.' The tolerant, even liberal, attitude that typified his approach to life in most other respects was quite absent from his feelings on this subject. He was not alone at Inanda. Mary Edwards took the precautionary step of buying up a large block of land out of her own pocket to forestall the construction of barracks for Indian workers anywhere in the vicinity of Inanda Seminary.

It is hard to know how far such sentiments spread among African convert families, though there are indications that at Inanda at least, a pronounced anti-Indian attitude was beginning to emerge. It would touch John Dube and become something of a motif in his adult life. Much of this attitude arose out of different 'cultures of production': the intense self-exploitation that Indian farming families seemed prepared to endure, and the fact that Indians possessed no cattle, for example. An African convert living at Verulam observed that 'Three Coolies could live in a space that one Kaffir would want. Natives like cattle; Coolies do not.' That was why, he added, Africans would be 'elbowed out of the country' by Indians. This was a key reason that Indians were considered impossible to assimilate and why a wide social distance came to be observed by these two groups. White settlers, landlords and officials drove their own wedges between them, for example in imposing differential rental agreements on Indian and African tenants that were stacked against Africans' interests and in urging African agriculturalists not to deal with Indian traders.

While Inanda converts did not face any immediate threat from Indian growers, there was increasing anxiety about access to land. In order to safeguard their positions, they began requesting some sort of security of tenure. The American Zulu Mission (AZM), which had sold off plots on other stations, was set against the idea of alienating land at Inanda – probably because of the likelihood of Indians becoming future buyers. They did not wish to lose control over who was living in their midst. Converts could not have been pleased at either prospect, of never acquiring property rights or of acquiring them only to lose them to competitors.

The quickening tempo of change beyond Inanda did not seem to offer much succour, either. The young John Dube's namesake, Chief Langalibalele, was engulfed in a series of catastrophic events in 1873 that were closely watched from the mission. Many Hlubi men were now trekking to the diamond diggings, acquiring a reputation as hard workers and helping to make the chiefdom strong once more. A favoured possession of returning migrants, almost a badge of status, was a gun. The Natal authorities, always anxious about such things, had many years before passed a law requiring all firearms to be registered. However, their fear was matched by their incapacity for enforcing such a requirement, so it was not implemented for a long time.

Then at the beginning of 1873, the local magistrate suddenly ordered Chief Langalibalele to send all Hlubi men in possession of guns to attend his office to register them. The chief was at this time distracted by the recent death of one of his brothers and the prescribed rituals that had to be performed. In any case, he probably would not have been able to insist on his men obeying such an order. So he procrastinated. As a result, the Secretary for Native Affairs summoned him to Pietermaritzburg to explain himself, a hugely arrogant gesture, designed to belittle Langalibalele; he delayed again, torn between resistance and compliance. Already deeply suspicious of this influential chiefdom – the Hlubi had on occasion refused to pay taxes as a form of protest – the colonial government decided it was time to move against it. Plans were put in motion to arrest and charge Langalibalele with treason.

As the year progressed, there was a rising sense of alarm in the chiefdom that it would be 'eaten up'. By November, panic had reached a pitch as the Hlubi scattered and Langalibalele fled into the mountains with several hundred followers and thousands of cattle. A small colonial force pursued him. During a skirmish on the pass, five members of this force were killed, three of them white. It was the first time since the British had taken control of Natal that white lives were lost in direct action to subdue its African inhabitants. Martial law was imposed and Langalibalele declared an outlaw. In the 'flushing out' operations that followed, up to 200 ordinary Hlubi were killed. Realising that he would find no peace in the mountain kingdom of Basutoland, Langalibalele gave himself up and was escorted back to Pietermaritzburg to face trial. In a 'mockery of justice', and despite the strenuous efforts of the Bishop of Natal, John Colenso, the chief was permanently banished from Natal, hundreds of Hlubi were fined or imprisoned, and their cattle and lands confiscated. The Hlubi chiefdom effectively ceased to exist.

Early on, soon after the original order to Langalibalele to register guns, Mqhawe seriously considered joining up with Langalibalele in a show of defiance at such an unreasonable and deliberately provocative gesture. It was popular lore among elderly Qadi still in the 1980s that the two chiefs had been preparing for joint action in 1873. Langalibalele was even supposed to have dispatched one Gamela to Mqhawe to organise preparations for war. Word that something was afoot reached Daniel Lindley at the time, possibly through James: it is inconceivable that they would not have discussed the matter, given the closeness between James and Mqhawe, and the respect James had for Langalibalele. Lindley decided to visit Mqhawe to talk him out of a course of action that would spell disaster for the Qadi. Accompanied by Joseph Fleetwood, a settler who supported the mission, 'he pointed out, most emphatically, that, though the white people in Natal were few in comparison with the natives, they came from a land where an unlimited supply of soldiers could be brought out in a few months. The chief promised to remain quiet and see what would happen to Langalibalele. When they were leaving the chief said, "You are the only two men to whom I would have listened."'[2]

Long before the Hlubi chief's fate became clear, a more immediate event left the Inanda converts feeling somewhat exposed. In April 1873 the Lindleys retired to the United States, having provided the mission's stability for a quarter of a century. There was a highly emotional ceremony at Inanda on 5 April, with several valedictions by the leading men. Thomas Hawes, son of the founding church member Joel Hawes and by now himself a pastor, gave the main speech. There were by that time five African pastors in the AZM; all were present. The station's residents had collected a handsome sum of money to send the Lindleys on their way, to which James had liberally contributed.

John was too young to be conscious of the deep sadness felt at Inanda by the Lindleys' departure, though he referred to it several times in later years. His father was left in charge of the mission, although a new American missionary was appointed to Inanda to assist in the background: he was Stephen Clapp Pixley, whose major contribution to mission work was biblical translation. His name was to live on for a more prominent reason, as it was he after whom Pixley kaIsaka Seme (born in 1881) was named. Stephen Pixley's approach to mission work was rather less flexible than Lindley's. He regarded Mqhawe as an 'intemperate heathen man' and was not in favour of close relations between 'inside' and 'outside' parishioners. For the next few years, James Dube and Mary Edwards continued to be the main contacts between the Qadi chief and the mission.

Then calamity struck inside the Dube family itself: on the morning of 10 November 1877, James very suddenly died. He had become ill with dysentery four days earlier, but despite strenuous efforts 'the man who had been the strength and head of this station' and who was barely 40 years of age, could not be saved. The mission residents were devastated: 'we feel as though we have lost a brother beloved and will mourn for him as when one mourneth for his mother,' Pixley wrote emotionally in a long and distracted letter on the day of James's death. Hundreds attended the funeral, most of them filled with disbelief that he was gone. Many fell down, wailing 'Ubaba wami, ufile!' ('My father, you are dead!'). He was buried in the cemetery, close to the church where he had presided for almost seven years. Those anguished words of lament were later carved on his headstone.

James had not made a will. Nor had he applied for exemption, a mechanism that had been introduced in the 1860s for African Christians who wished to release themselves from the operation of the colonial code called Native Law. Many had refused to apply because of a fear that it would undermine family ties; James had signed a petition to this effect in 1875. Legally, then, he was still under the direct authority of Mqhawe. The chief used the opportunity to try one last time to recover the cattle that Dalida had taken with her all those years before. Pixley, determined that the chief be kept right away from James's property, approached the Secretary for Native Affairs on behalf of Elizabeth. The outcome was that she was able to keep her husband's accumulated wealth to bring up their nine children, all the sons still minors. Besides Charles, who was just a baby, John had three brothers, Africa, William and Thupana. Their mother would, in time, send three of the boys (Charles, John and William) abroad to be educated.

James had been a larger-than-life figure, and now that they were left without him, there must have been enormous pressure on the sons, especially Africa as the oldest, to be leaders and exemplars like him. The prevailing expectation for daughters (in spite of evidence that some at least did hold aspirations for a different life) was that they would become helpmates of successful husbands, not public figures in their own right. It was on the sons that all hopes settled, and clearly education was a key to realising such hopes.

John Langalibalele was three months off his seventh birthday when his father died, and had begun attending the station primary school. It was AZM policy that children ought to read and write in Zulu before they learnt English; accordingly, the primary curriculum was almost wholly taught through the medium of Zulu. Apart from elementary school textbooks, nearly the whole of the New Testament was by then available in Zulu, and one of the AZM's newer missionaries, the Rev. Seth Stone, had written a few tracts and a general work on history, and had composed some new hymns in Zulu. In addition, the AZM bought in products of the 'writing machine' of other denominations, such as Henry Callaway's collection of Zulu folktales, *Izinganekwane*, and Colenso's translation of *The pilgrim's progress*. This was the diet of reading matter on which the mission's young pupils were fed. For the first few years of his formal education, therefore, John encountered a great deal of pious religious text in Zulu, but very little in English.

His place in the orderly pattern of work and worship at the mission largely consisted of attending school during the week and Sunday school on the Sabbath, completing daily chores and saying prayers, sometimes playing with his friends, though there was little time for frivolity. Sometimes the young John accompanied Chief Mqhawe and his men on hunting expeditions – hunting was to be one of his life-long passions. His elder sisters probably took some responsibility for the small ones when they were not in lessons at the Seminary. Esther in particular had a playful sense of humour and liked little adventures. She wrote to a friend about how she and her classmates had gone on an outing to Sugar Mountain, explaining how this hill had acquired its name: 'One day Mrs Edwards gave the girls a holiday and they went there. She gave each one some sugar in a paper. When they got there two girls quarrelled about the sugar so we gave it the name.' Esther never travelled abroad herself, though possibly would have liked to do so – she was corresponding with white friends in the United States in the 1880s.[3]

If there had been distant warning in the Langalibalele affair in 1873 that African polities would not be allowed to resist the march of economic transformation, there was a much louder reminder closer to home at the end of the decade. British dreams of a subcontinent reorganised to support an endogenous capitalist development based on diamonds – an agricultural sector wrenched from its ponderous ways to supply food, a communications and transport system thrusting inland from the coastal ports, and the release of a plentiful and cheap labour supply through more forceful pressure on Africans to earn wages – were becoming less fanciful and more possible as the 1870s wore on. Yet there were many obstacles in Britain's way to realising such a goal, and its first attempts to draw all the kingdoms, republics and colonies of southern Africa under one confederated British umbrella were not promising.

In 1877 Theophilus Shepstone (lately retired from his post as Natal's Secretary for Native Affairs) had been sent to annex the Transvaal Republic for Britain. He was not at all welcomed in the Transvaal. In an attempt to win Boer support, he thought he might be able to settle a border dispute with the Zulu in the Boers' favour. In attempting to do so, he displayed little sympathy towards those he had claimed to know so well, with the Zulu effectively accusing him of treachery. All in all, the annexation of the Transvaal turned out to be a fiasco; the Boers took it back (admittedly with conditions attached) after the Battle of Majuba in 1881.

Yet the border dispute was to prove most useful when the next target in Britain's grand design came into focus: the still-independent Zulu kingdom. It had long been perceived as a threat to white settler interests, mostly because it was deemed politically unfathomable and economically damaging, locking up as it did much-needed labour as well as vast swathes of fertile land. Through 1878 the British High Commissioner, Bartle Frere, did all he could to find a pretext for war with the Zulu king, Cetshwayo. Late in the year, Frere announced the final outcome of the border dispute to a Zulu delegation, adding a number of demands which had nothing whatever to do with the border issue and which were impossible for the Zulu king to comply with at all.

The Inanda community anxiously watched preparations for the inevitable war. As troops and supplies rumbled northwards from Durban, local farmers were called on to provide food and owners of oxen and wagons to provide transport. Men prepared to be called on to fight. A sense of foreboding filled people's thoughts, and even the young were affected. A pupil attending Inanda Seminary remembered it very vividly in this rare surviving school essay:

> When we were at home my Father told us to go and light a lamp in the house, for we were in the kitchen, then I was afraid to go alone, but my Father scolded me and told me to go, so I went very fast, and looking round me all the way to see what was coming after me.
>
> Just as soon as I was in the house, I was looking for matches. I looked through the window and saw some soldiers coming. I lighted the lamp very quickly. They came to the door, just when I was ready to scream, I saw my Father coming, and I was very glad.
>
> My father asked them to go away. Some of the people asked the soldiers what they were going to Zululand for, and they said, 'Tina hamba Cetywayo' ('We are going after Cetywayo').

It may be that the seven-year-old John Dube also registered something of this uneasy mood. Many around him were directly caught up in the conflict. In response to a call for troops, Mqhawe told the resident magistrate at Verulam in early November that he thought he could muster 10 to 20 men for the newly formed Natal Native Contingent. Later in the month, he was ordered to call out 500. His only hope of meeting such a target was to enlist himself, and he became an officer of the Second Battalion of the Second Regiment (later reorganised as the Fifth Battalion). Though they were somewhat slow in coming forward, the full requisition of Qadi men, many of them from the Inanda Mission Reserve, did respond.

In the coming months, Mqhawe distinguished himself by his zeal and courage. He and his men saw battle on the two campaigns in which they participated, in January 1879 (the aim of which was to reach Ulundi, but the Zulu victory at Isandhlwana sent the force scurrying back to Natal) and again in March to relieve Eshowe. Before they disbanded, Mqhawe addressed his Qadi troops, reminding them of Dingane's 1837 slaughter and adding, 'Tonight we dance on these Zulu hills, and none can make us afraid.' Yet the Qadi foot soldiers did not really want to fight and many deserted. They may very well have felt that the decision long years before to seek the protection of the British had been vindicated, and that justice had been done at last in defeating the Zulu, but they wanted to be at home in case of the rumoured Zulu attack on Natal.

The Inanda converts on the whole stayed out of the fighting; they did not sign up for special units, as did the men from the Wesleyan mission at Edendale, near Pietermaritzburg. Rather, they were busy with their wagons, carrying supplies towards the Zululand border. Whatever their feelings about the war, Pixley, now the resident missionary at Inanda, supported it wholeheartedly. John Dube would later endorse Pixley's view that Cetshwayo had brought the war upon himself, that the Zulu king had moreover demonstrated fateful weakness, in contrast to the qualities that his father James had displayed. Whatever the wider implications of such a view, the upholding of his father's impeccable memory was of utmost importance for a young man about to embark on his own quest for perfection.[4]

Meanwhile, there was still an education to complete. In 1881 Elizabeth sent John to Adams College (named in memory of Newton Adams, who had been in the first party of American missionaries with the Lindleys in the 1830s), where Africa was already a boarder. It was what their father would have wanted; the peripatetic forerunner of Adams had educated him. Now permanently located at Amanzimtoti on the Natal south coast, it had become the leading AZM centre for the education of young men. Over the following decades many distinguished teachers, pastors and other African leaders were trained there.

John Dube was 10 years old when he enrolled at Adams. He had never been away from the protective confines of the Inanda mission for any length of time, and we do not know whether this first great journey induced feelings of fear or excitement. It was a form of 'estrangement': not only was he being subjected to a concerted attempt to reinforce in him the cultural norms of his Christian community, but he was being deliberately removed from his home environment so that the missionaries would have a better chance of success. John and his brother would have walked the eight kilometres to the nearest railway station at Phoenix. Travelling third class, on an open carriage

– more like a truck, with benches for seating – they would have changed on to the Isipingo train at Durban central station. He had probably never seen Durban before. The town was then a low-slung, leafy settlement, laid out in an orderly grid that stretched northwards from the harbour. The streets were wide and unpaved – there would be complaints about the sand for years to come – and there was some suburban development creeping up the Berea. A few solid-looking stone buildings, mostly shops and hotels, rose to two storeys. One or two grander buildings, symbolic of a more settled colonial phase, had lately been completed or were under construction: a courthouse, post office, station and town hall.

After disembarking at Isipingo, there were still eight kilometres to walk to Adams. The boys' school was situated within a busy mission station complex, in a sturdy brick building constructed in 1873. It housed a central hall cum dining room, classrooms, library, dormitories and kitchen. For its time, it was extremely well equipped, with desks, books and laboratory equipment imported from America. At its opening, it was described in rapturous terms: 'The fair proportions of the whole crown a grassy hill which slopes gently towards the river in three directions, thus securing abundance of air, dryness, and beauty of situation, and, by consequence, healthfulness.' A second building would be added in 1885 to commemorate 50 years of the AZM in Natal. There were about 40 pupils on the register in the 1880s, from various AZM stations up and down Natal.

A missionary newly arrived from the United States, the Rev. Herbert D. Goodenough, assumed the headship in John's first year. He and his fellow teacher, Laura Day, presided over a highly regulated regime, and it was this that impinged far more on the boys' experience of school life than the bricks, mortar and 'healthfulness' of the place. They would have to be up, washed, dressed, have had their breakfast and prepared for the first bell at 8.30 am, when a neatness check of the dormitories was conducted. Classes on weekdays commenced at 8.45 am. In the afternoon, there was a session of manual work before lessons recommenced in the evening, including a period for homework, finishing at 8.30 pm. A prayer meeting was held before bed. Twice-weekly military drill had recently been introduced. On some evenings, one or other of the societies – the Literary Society, the Society for Christian Endeavour or the Missionary Society – would meet, or there would be a music class. On other evenings there would be informal discussion, sometimes based on a biblical quotation or an article from the mission paper *Isigidimi samaXhosa*. *Isigidimi* was produced at Lovedale, the leading missionary training institution in the Eastern Cape (much admired by Goodenough), and John Tengo Jabavu had lately become its editor. Jabavu was soon to become better known as founder-editor of *Imvo Zabantsundu*, the first newspaper in southern Africa owned and controlled by Africans. Even within the more restrictive editorial policy of *Isigidimi*, however, he included a great deal of commentary on Cape politics and those liberal white politicians who supported the African franchise. It may well be that these issues were discussed at Adams. In this way, the boys were introduced to the world of an already well-established African intelligentsia based at the Cape.

The two hours of daily manual work (three on Saturdays) were expected of every boy. It mostly took the form of cleaning and gardening, but there were also opportunities to learn printing, blacksmithing and carpentry – Goodenough was a passionate believer in what was known as industrial education and lost little time in strengthening this side of the school. Those boys whose families were not able to afford the fees had to work an extra hour daily, and certain tasks, such as sweeping the stairs and corridors, were reserved for them. There was a clear and institutionalised distinction between 'working' and 'non-working' boys. We may assume the Dube boys were in the latter category. For both categories, the experience was considered important in inculcating respect for physical labour and habits of regularity. In addition to these timetabled sessions, boys also assisted in cooking and washing up in the kitchen and did their own laundry on Tuesday afternoons. Monitors and stewards were appointed from among them to ensure compliance with the rules. Infringements were punished by a 'native court', sitting every Friday evening, which imposed further periods of manual work. John well remembered the court, and the boys who sat as judges, chosen 'for faithfulness and integrity'; he also noted pointedly that they not only acted as judges but also reported offenders!

The curriculum was delivered over a six-year period, from Standards 2 to 7. The subjects that John Dube most readily recalled in his account of these years were chemistry, algebra and geometry, although arithmetic, geography, physiology, history, biblical history, and English grammar and composition were also studied. He also remembered that one of the school rules was that no Zulu could be spoken between 6 am and 1 pm. Because his command (or, as he saw it, lack of command) of English was to be an embarrassment to him later on, he did intimate that insufficient attention had been paid to the speaking of English.

Sundays were mostly taken up with religious instruction. After breakfast, there was a prayer meeting, followed by the singing of hymns and recitation of texts. The boys were then split into smaller groups for Bible class. This was all before the mid-morning chapel service. After lunch, there was Sunday school in the classrooms, before another evening prayer meeting. This minutely organised weekly cycle was what the missionaries deemed necessary not only to educate African boys but also to lead them towards self-confessed Christian belief. It was not enough that they came from Christian homes; they must find and proclaim the faith for themselves as they approached the age of responsibility. Few of the boys had reached this state; John certainly had not.

Not only was this John's first experience of living away from home, but his first experience also of relative privation. Twenty of the 21 meals of the week consisted of mealie meal (corn) porridge, with sugar. Goodenough proudly reported that it was the sugar that set the school food above what white employers in Natal gave their workers, who got nothing at all with their porridge. The only change to this monotony was Sunday lunch, consisting of beef and rice. Then, as on countless later occasions, it was food that caused most grievance and trouble at African boarding schools, and Adams was no exception: there were to be two serious 'sugar rebellions' during John Dube's time at Adams.

The first occurred soon after Goodenough arrived. What touched it off was a pocket of sugar for the mealie meal that was particularly dark and bitter; the boys registered their disgust by sitting in 'sullen silence' and refusing to eat anything at all. Goodenough tried to reason with them, and to undertake to get acceptable sugar the following day, but eight boys packed their bags and in 'the most insulting way' waved their sticks at him as they left. It is unknown whether either of the Dube brothers was among them, but it is unlikely that John, as a very new pupil, would have been. Those who did go home were only allowed back after payment of a fine.

John and Africa were both implicated in another serious incident in October 1882 and food again featured as one of the factors prompting their involvement. It was the first anniversary of Goodenough's tenure as head, and on this day he uncovered what he shuddered to describe as the depths of 'moral rottenness of this people'. It started with the theft of food from teachers' food safes and rooms. In the course of isolating boys for interrogation in order to identify the culprits, Goodenough and his co-accusers stumbled on a number of other goings-on completely at odds with puritan propriety: boys were sneaking out to visit girls at night, some were taking snuff, and several were stealing fruit from trees and eggs from hens in the neighbourhood. They were more than a small knot of troublemakers: half the boys in the school seemed to be involved. Goodenough convened a special Court of Investigation, consisting of several missionaries (including Mary Edwards, who was paying a visit from Inanda Seminary), which, in a process of hearings over three days, found 17 boys guilty of various offences. What emerged from the questioning was that snuff-taking and visiting girls had been going on for years; it was only the theft of food that was recent. One boy was sent off to face charges before the Durban magistrate; the others were all dealt with at school.

Africa and John were among the accused. The charges against Africa were that he visited one Zayo, the female servant of a resident missionary, and they conducted *ukuhlobonga* (external sexual intercourse) on four occasions; that he stole beef from the Goodenoughs' pantry and ate it with his friends; that he stole oranges and ate stolen eggs. For the first offence he was sentenced to perform extra manual work for two weeks with the option of a £1 fine; for the other transgressions he was fined another £1. John was found guilty of stealing oranges 'many times', eating oranges and eggs stolen by other boys, using snuff continually through term-time and giving snuff to other small boys (it was noted in the proceedings that he was a 'small boy' himself), and of being 'a persistent and bold-faced liar': clearly he had held out under questioning, protesting his innocence of the charges. This was a quality he would display at school again. For stealing and eating stolen produce he was fined 10s, and he was whipped and made to dig ditches for taking snuff.

A few months later, Goodenough reported that the school roll was much reduced, as several of the boys with fines to pay were unable to do so: 'there is a great financial depression all over South Africa. Many of the natives have been getting in debt to the white men who are pressing them unmercifully for the money, charging interest at the rate of 60% ... I need very much a small fund out of which to help boys whose fathers are unable or unwilling to pay fees.' Families might have been financially squeezed, but it was also obvious that many pupils had been deeply unhappy about conditions in the school, especially regarding discipline and food, and were registering their rejection of the Adams regime. Goodenough, to be expected, did not see any aspect of their conduct as legitimate. His view was that all Zulus were 'liars and fornicators ... the people are down deep in the mire of African heathenism and we have to begin at the lowest foundations in helping them to rise towards God ... you can scarcely conceive how weak the majority of our professing Christians are.' Both Dube boys, yet to prove their worth, were still principally known as the 'sons of James Dube, the Inanda preacher'. They had failed woefully to measure up to that revered reputation.

The pressure of Christian conformity proved too onerous and unattractive to Africa, who left Adams and reverted to a life of traditionalism back in Inanda. He successfully claimed inheritance of some of James's possessions as the eldest son, married and settled in a homestead on the Mission Reserve, where he was described as 'a steady, well-behaved young man'. Along with other traditionalist farmers, he suffered his share of land hunger, with his wife becoming embroiled in a drawn-out dispute with a neighbour over access to garden land. Eventually Africa was appointed the principal *induna* (chiefly functionary) of the Qadi on the Mission Reserve under Mandlakayise, Mqhawe's heir. He did come to occupy a position of authority, then, but not at all of the kind that his parents had imagined for him.[5]

John soldiered on at school. Despite possible feelings of resentment at his treatment by the court, this was still in many ways a privileged existence and a necessary passage to greater things. The earliest known first-hand memories of what he was like as a person date from these years at Adams. When Manning Marable was collecting material for his study of John Dube in the 1970s, he was able to obtain a unique recollection from an aged Congregational minister, the Rev. Gideon Mvakwendlu Sivetye, who had been at Adams with Dube and continued to be a close associate of his throughout their careers. Sivetye remembered the schoolboy John as thoughtful, even ponderous, rather than sharp and quick-witted; withdrawn and self-contained, rather than sparkling and sociable. Trying to fathom him was a bit 'like a python trying to swallow a buffalo, even though dead or already shot by somebody'. This evocative image points to other traits in Dube's character: his singlemindedness, persistence and dogged determination, which would underpin his emergence as a leader. 'He aimed high and got what he wanted,' recalled Sivetye. He concentrated not only on his studies but also on his self-image, to 'cultivate an air of handsomeness, charm and a sonorous voice which made it easy to be heard'. One imagines that he was also cultivating suitably impressive things to say with his sonorous voice – perhaps observations on religious or moral questions.

His reserve, growing self-confidence and focus must have stood him in good stead through the middle years of high school. He does not appear to have got into serious trouble again until his senior year, 1886, and this time the incident proved to be a turning point in his life. Again the spark was inedible sugar for the dreary mealie meal, which he had now been eating, day in and day out, for six long years. It was a diet that by now had made him a bit chubby.

One Monday in November, a monitor reported to Goodenough that the boys were refusing to eat a new batch of sugar that they considered inferior. Goodenough was in feisty mood: 'I was thoroughly angry and told him they would get no other from me and if any of them complained to me about it they would "get hurt". No-one did complain, neither did they eat the sugar.' By Wednesday morning, the boys – who still had not eaten the sugar – had decided to leave school en masse. Goodenough got to hear of their intentions and marched into the dining room to address them. He told them that no Christian boy would run away for such a trivial reason, and that even if they left, their families would be charged fees for the whole term. Thirteen boys left anyway, and the others said they would leave the following day.

Goodenough called what he described as a 'Council of War'. His dilemma was that he had lately received notification from the government that all schools in receipt of a grant must be able to show that they were in session during all the days that they claimed were term-time, and that such a requirement would be adhered to very strictly. Faced with the *de facto* closure of the school if the boys all went home, Goodenough would be in breach of this requirement, and he intensely disliked breaking rules. After consultations with other missionaries late into the night, he softened his line towards the remaining boys in the morning. If they were prepared to pay a small amount extra, or work extra hours, he could get them better sugar. Four more left that day, including the two sons of Thomas Hawes of Inanda (the same who had given the main speech at the Lindleys' departure). Goodenough felt particularly let down by one of them, Benjamin, whom he said he had trusted, and who had shown signs of a 'genuinely Christian life'. Circumstantial evidence suggests that John Dube also went home. Half the school had gone. Then, fortuitously, a visitor arrived at Adams. He was a Mr Butler, Pietermaritzburg lawyer and successful preacher, whose upbeat, evangelistic message had resulted in many conversions. Over the next days, in an attempt at spiritual revival, he held services in the chapel and saw boys one by one; in this way, it would seem that no more boys departed. Within a fortnight, the others began to trickle back.

Tension continued, however, as there was still the matter of punishment looming. Goodenough decided to be very firm – conciliation sent out the wrong message, of weakness and indecision – and accordingly divided (or in fact doubled) the boys' offence into 'guilt' and 'evil results'. The guilt of insubordination was dealt with by a whipping, alternatively one and a half extra hours of early morning manual work for three weeks. Most boys chose the work, even though 'as the mornings are cold it is really no fun'. The 'evil results' referred to what he saw as parental failures of duty. Had their sons been brought up more strictly, they would never have dared to run home, he reasoned. Accordingly, 5s were demanded of each boy's family. So this was a kind of punishment for parents.

Some of the returning boys showed spirited signs of indignation ('cheek', Goodenough called it) at the severity of these penalties, insisting they had done nothing wrong. He told them that he would interview each of them individually after their three weeks of labour, to see if it had done anything to change their minds. Those who still refused to admit their guilt were made to clean out the toilets, 'a work they have a special prejudice against.' At this point, he called on his friend and fellow missionary, William C. Wilcox, to help him interview the boys. Wilcox was to be a huge figure in John Dube's life from that moment.

Goodenough and Wilcox had studied together at Oberlin College, Ohio, and arrived in South Africa together in 1881. Wilcox was based at Adams for a time then, and taught the boys music and other subjects. Although they remained close, he and Goodenough had very different approaches to mission work in Africa. Where Goodenough saw only darkness and the need for severe discipline to overcome it, Wilcox saw opportunity and the potential for mutual responsibility. Goodenough felt honour-bound by the rules of the American Zulu Mission; Wilcox was often questioning them. Goodenough was patient, even dogged, in his determination to Christianise the heathen, and reluctant to relinquish control of the process; Wilcox preferred to arrive in a promising new place, plant an idea, support it to the full, and then leave the rest to local converts who had been awakened to the possibilities. He expected his message to resonate with immediate results. Wilcox's vision for Africa was of a whole continent thrumming with lively, hard-working, independent Christian communities who shouldered obligations and shared rewards. In short, he was more radical than most of his contemporaries in his approach to belief and conversion, stressing a cooperative social dimension of Christian teaching and living. Tall and solemn with 'deep-set eyes and a Mark Twain moustache', he was a man of impressive intellect and strong personality, with an ability to infect people with enthusiasm for his numerous schemes. He would earn the praise name Mbuyabathwa, 'Prickly plant'.

He and his wife, Ida, had been in Natal only two years when they were given AZM permission to begin a new East Central Africa Mission at Inhambane on the eastern coast of Mozambique. They spent some time at Inanda making preparations (the connection may have been that he and Pixley were both extremely good linguists and were conferring about translation and the production of dictionaries and grammars). While at Inanda, Wilcox persuaded two of the Dubes' close family friends, Dalida Seme and Lucy Mbambo, both graduates of Inanda Seminary, to accompany them and another white missionary couple, Mr and Mrs Richards, to Inhambane. Dalida and Lucy stayed six years. Two other young women from Inanda, Selina Mdima and Grace Goba, would join the East Central Africa Mission in the 1890s. In this way, Inanda rather remarkably produced African women missionaries ready to venture into new fields far from home.

More than that: it was through such African women missionaries that a network of information was spread more widely in the subcontinent about the lives, experiences and attitudes of African Americans. For at Inhambane they worked alongside three African American missionaries who had been sent out by the American Board to assist Wilcox at his specific request. They were Benjamin Forsyth Ousley, Henrietta Bailey Ousley and (later on) Nancy Jones. The Ousleys had both been born into slavery; all three were graduates of Fisk University and, in addition, Benjamin Ousley had studied theology at Oberlin. The little group encountered various kinds of resistance to their work – soon after their arrival, they were attacked by the local chief, Mzila, and lost most of their possessions, and Henrietta Ousley and Nancy Jones would write many reports in which they regretted the reluctance of local women to receive their Christian message.

What this experience did for Wilcox was to confirm his belief in the need for an entirely different approach to mission work than the one that the AZM had practised for half a century. He called his model a 'Faith Plan'. It involved setting up missionary settlements based explicitly on 'industrial' activity – trades, or milling, or farming – that would be self-supporting from the start. Accordingly, in late 1886, he applied to withdraw not only from Inhambane but from the AZM, so that he could return to America to raise funds for his initiative. Despite his sometimes sharp criticism of the AZM, he was greatly respected by his colleagues and, even though they were sceptical of his Faith Plan, they did all they could to keep him in the fold. They offered him the latitude to carry out his scheme under their auspices, with financial support and a paid assistant, and to compensate him for his losses at Inhambane. They urged him to rethink, but in any case to return to Inhambane in the company of Herbert Goodenough, to review and wind up his work there. Wilcox was at Adams, considering his future, writing up a grammar and doing a small amount of teaching, when he found himself called upon to help return the school to an atmosphere of normality.

His own account of what happened next was written many years after the event. One of the boys who had been 'cheeky' was John Dube. Wilcox claimed that Dube had been in a fight which he (Dube) said another boy had started, and as a result refused to apologise; this may or may not have been bound up with the recent sugar rebellion and his conduct through that. In any event, Wilcox brought him around to the position that he ought to show humility and apologise – this was his first great test in Christian forgiveness, since he had indicated he would like to be a Christian. Wilcox read him a passage from Matthew 5, 23–24: 'If you are offering your gift at the altar and there remember that your brother has something against you, leave your gift there in front of the altar. First go and be reconciled to your brother; then come and offer your gift.'

Dube struggled with the idea, then did as Wilcox suggested. The result was a revelation: he was filled with lightness and relief. It was the moment he definitely became a Christian. It was a moment, too, that shaped everything he did for the rest of his life, and he never doubted that he had made the right decision – his was a total conversion. Though in future years he might wonder about the commitment of some Christians to their faith, he never after this moment, as far as we can tell, ever questioned his own. Conversion was more than a religious turning point; it was an intellectual one, too. Although young John Dube had grown up in a Christian home, this moment committed him as an active practitioner and propagator of the worldview that his parents and teachers had held up before him. Wilcox's forceful influence cannot be underestimated. He seemed to understand the deepest needs of the young man, to care unreservedly for him, and to be able to persuade him to change his ways utterly. Yet what was probably most attractive to the young Dube was Wilcox's refreshing social attitude – more expansive, trusting, *liberating*. He was the father-figure Dube had missed for a decade. His epiphany would bind him to Wilcox forever. His mother, Elizabeth, who must have begun to despair that any of her sons would follow in their father's footsteps, would surely have been deeply grateful to Wilcox.

Wilcox had been struggling with ideas, too, and had decided that his future course was to return to the United States to raise funds for an independent missionary effort in southern Africa. Accordingly he sent his letter of resignation to the AZM and made preparations to decamp. Dube's time at Adams was coming to an end and perhaps he wished both to stay in close touch with his new mentor and to continue his studies: what better solution than to go abroad? Elizabeth begged Wilcox to take John to America.

Initially, he refused: it was not on the whole considered desirable to encourage mission boys to travel so far from home. At length, however, he agreed. John probably felt that he was embarking on the greatest adventure imaginable. It would turn out to be far more difficult than he could ever have supposed.[6]

An encounter with ice cream

The 1880s were very early for someone like John Dube to aspire to study abroad. It was really only after a number of choral tours by black South African and American choirs in the 1890s that the transatlantic educational flow between these two regions would begin. Yet we have seen that he was not the first to dream such dreams. Talitha Hawes of Inanda had hoped so much to study in America that she had saved her fare several years earlier, and already someone known to John Dube had actually done it.

He was John M. Nembula, and the likeness between his family story and that of the Dubes is extraordinary. His grandmother, Mbulazi Makhanya, had been the widow of a chief of the Qwabe, another of the strong Thukela valley chiefdoms displaced in the Zulu rise to prominence. A number of Qwabe, including Mbulazi, had settled south of Port Natal, at Mlazi. This was where Dr Newton Adams had established the very first American Zulu Mission station in Natal. He had laboured almost a decade before he made his first convert in 1846: the very same Mbulazi. (This also made her the first convert of the AZM in Natal.) She and her son Nembula had already lived for some time in the Adams household. Nembula was about 20 when he too became a Christian in 1848. Ultimately he was ordained, as the Rev. Ira Adams Nembula, in 1872, two years after James Dube.

Ira had a son called John, who was born probably in the late 1850s or early 1860s. Like his namesake in the Dube family, he was a third-generation Christian, son of a pastor and grandson of a chief. He had also studied at Adams. In 1879 John Nembula moved to Inanda to become Pixley's assistant in the work of biblical translation, and must have become acquainted with the Dubes. Two years later, when the manuscript of the completed Zulu Bible was ready for printing, he accompanied Pixley to America; perhaps this was the inspiration for Talitha Hawes. The published Bible was received back in Natal in 1883, and was the cause for much celebration at all the AZM stations.

It is not clear whether Nembula remained in the United States or returned there later, but in the mid-1880s he was studying to be a medical missionary at the Chicago Medical College. Even though he had a sponsor, the American Medical Missionary Society, he had to work to support himself through college. At times he despaired of being able to complete the course because of the pressing need to earn his keep. With four months to graduation in March 1887, a benefactor loaned him $50, which he worked to repay once he had qualified. Later in the year, after a visit to Oberlin College, he returned to his home at Adams Mission, the first black South African graduate of an American college and the first African doctor in Natal.

Since there were no facilities for further study in South Africa for them, America was the natural destination for these early African students. Although they had grown up in Victorian Natal, and AZM missionaries did work to inculcate an imperial loyalty in them, their consciousness was shaped far more by American than British ideas. Through their upbringing, they had been enveloped in an American missionary worldview: everything from Christian morality to classroom desks crossed the sea from America. Moreover, all the white people who had been most immediate and influential in John Dube's life thus far, and whom he most admired, were American – their outlook was what he imbibed. They were to a person not only ardent puritans, but also northern Republicans who welcomed the end of slavery (one of Lindley's sons had fought for the Union in the Civil War), admired Frederick Douglass, mourned Abraham Lincoln's untimely death, supported reconstruction, and believed in Christian improvement and industrial education on both sides of the Atlantic, as a means to participation in the 'Golden Age' for black Americans and as a means to incorporation into civil society for black South Africans (admittedly still many decades off, most of them thought). In addition to all this, American colleges seemed to beckon all-comers in a way that British universities did not. Whereas there already existed a strong ethos of 'higher learning for all' in America, an equally strong sense of exclusivity still pervaded institutions of higher learning in Britain: they remained the preserve of a small elite of aristocrats and professionals.

Elizabeth Dube promised the large sum of 30 gold sovereigns (equivalent to £30) to support John's plans. It would be sufficient to get him to America, but no more than that. The Rev. William Wilcox impressed on him that he would have to work to get himself through his studies, just as John Nembula had done. The missionary tried to persuade John to apply to Hampton

Institute in Virginia. It was a sensible enough suggestion. From the start, Hampton had been a black college, founded in 1868 by the legendary General Samuel Chapman Armstrong (who had commanded black Union troops during the Civil War), with the support of the American Missionary Society and the Freedmen's Bureau, the government organisation set up to assist ex-slaves to adapt to their new status. Its curriculum emphasised practical, industrial training in such skills as bricklaying, farming and domestic work. Its most illustrious graduate to date had been Booker T. Washington, who had recently established his own college, Tuskegee Normal and Industrial Institute in Alabama, modelled on Hampton. Hampton thus embodied all the ideals that Wilcox wished to promote in Africa. Furthermore, it would have provided a supportive environment for his teenage protégé, and possibly also a shield against racial discrimination.

The determination that had already become so noticeable in John Dube's character disposed him otherwise. He refused to consider Hampton. He was bent on Oberlin, where his hero had studied. Benjamin Ousley, the African American missionary at Inhambane about whom Dube had doubtless heard, was another graduate. Moreover, it was located in Ohio, the same state that had produced both Daniel Lindley and Mary Edwards. There was another, more personal reason that Dube chose Oberlin. He may well have felt that the years of manual labour at Adams had improved him morally, training his head as well as his heart and hands. But at this juncture in his life, he did not imagine that 'practical education' applied to *him*. He had loftier ambitions than bricklaying, or even teaching bricklaying: he wished to be a doctor. John Nembula was very possibly his role model here. It was with this expectation in his head that he prepared to set off to America.[1]

Oberlin had been an outcome of the same impulse that had sent Lindley and his fellow missionaries to Africa, the religious revival known as the second Great Awakening. Two evangelists, John Shipherd and Philo Stewart, had founded their institution in 1833 as a place of Christian example and learning. Its aim was to train missionaries who would carry the 'American way of life' – simple faith, hard work and individual initiative – westwards over the plains, as the frontier moved ever closer to the Pacific Ocean. It admitted both men and women (though women could not proceed from preparatory to college level until 1837) and in 1835 it became the first American college to open its doors to all races. Although it remained overwhelmingly white, until the Civil War it had been a centre of anti-slavery activity and a key point on the Underground Railroad, the route that escaping black slaves took to freedom in Canada. By the mid-nineteenth century, then, this remote institution in 'the hottest, coldest, wettest, flattest part of the state of Ohio' had won national renown as a symbol of social tolerance.

Oberlin was not, however, insulated against the seeping segregation and discrimination that came to characterise American society in the decades after the Civil War. Lincoln might have abolished slavery by the 13th Amendment, and the North might have planned an ambitious reconstruction of the South. Yet by the late 1870s, a new President (also from Ohio) was withdrawing troops from the South and allowing the old planter class to retrieve some measure of political power. Institutionalised segregation in the Southern states became a reality and was beginning to poison relations between the races in the North as well. By the 1880s, Oberlin's tradition of open educational access was under strain on two fronts. Firstly, incidents of discrimination by white students against their black peers were becoming frequent, much to the disappointment of the college leadership. Secondly, the college had abandoned its founding principle of requiring all students to perform manual labour to defray their educational costs. Now manual labour was required only of students whose families could not afford the fees and other maintenance costs. Openness was thus compromised on both racial and class grounds. During his student days there, Wilcox would have known of such developments, but he proved unable to dissuade John Dube from entering his alma mater.

The furthest Dube had ever travelled had been to Adams, all of 50 kilometres distant. He had known no existence other than the sheltered one of the AZM mission station, where missionaries mediated virtually all outside influences. They were considered liberal in their views, as we have seen; nevertheless (or perhaps 'in addition', such was liberalism at that time), nearly all of them treated African people as an inferior race because of their heathen state. They applauded and encouraged the newly converted, though most were convinced that Christianity would take generations to bed down as the norm. In the meantime they kept a strict social distance on their stations. (One of the reasons that James Dube had been so highly regarded is that he did not *look* wholly African. His appearance was often the subject of favourable comment: 'It is only a good eye that will see a faint trace of the African type in his speaking face,' Lindley once noted.)

Yet the whole point of the missionaries' labours was their conviction that there was hope, that they could elevate Africans to a level similar to, if not quite the same as, whites. Their attitude was thus one of benign domination, coaxing their charges to abandon sinful ways of darkness and turn towards civilisation and the assumption of responsibility. Accordingly, everything that they did was presented as being in the best interests not of themselves but of their converts: it was what set them apart from colonial administrators and settlers. For their part, however much African Christians might have jibbed and chafed against everyday relations of inferiority and superiority, they could not deny that the missionaries had sacrificed a great deal to bring them the light. Now that he was sailing thousands of kilometres from home, John Dube would discover just how protective and deceptively simple this world had been. This was the biggest adventure of his life, but it was also very risky. Although for the moment he still had Wilcox as a guide, he was finally travelling outside the clutches of missionary paternalism.[2]

There was a deep and well-founded fear of the sea among most Zulu speakers, who knew its treacherous conditions along their stretch of south-east African coast. Consequently they thought of its creatures as unclean and certainly not fit to eat, and found it extremely hard to imagine that anyone who disappeared over the edge of it would ever be able to get back. Yet missionaries came and went, and so had John Nembula; perhaps this lessened the foreboding for John Dube and his family a little. The small party sailed from Durban to Cape Town, and on to London, towards the middle of 1887. Union Line and Castle Line had a joint contract to operate the 'mail run' on this route, each line departing in alternate weeks; they had to complete the voyage in a maximum of 42 days. Unlike the northern Atlantic, this was not a major emigrant route and passenger accommodation was on a relatively small scale: about 200 passengers in two classes on most ships.

London was then the biggest city in the world, containing some five million people. John Dube had never before seen so many together, waves of them flowing inwards from the boroughs and suburbs in the morning, and then outwards again in the evening. This was truly a mass society, presenting all the novel challenges of supplying food and water, keeping order, preventing disease, disposing of waste and the dead. It was also an inquisitive, curious society: daily and weekly newspapers sold in the hundreds of thousands, disseminating ideas and information to a huge audience, and there was a wide variety of museums, libraries, zoos and concert halls to cater for every taste. Any number of chapels and sects had established themselves here, trying to save souls from the evils of the urban morass; there was always more squalor and deprivation than prosperity and refinement. By the 1880s, these religious bodies had persuaded most leading politicians to embrace the cause of temperance, something with which the AZM and its followers fully identified.

The city had sprawled and spilled all over the place, so that it was impossible to walk from one end of it to the other in a day. This was very largely due to revolutions in transport. Horse-drawn buses and trams clogged the streets; palaces to industrial genius such as St Pancras and Paddington railway stations vied with cathedrals for dominance of the skyline. The railway reached below earth, too: the first underground line, the Metropolitan, had been constructed between Paddington and Farringdon in 1862 and carried millions of passengers in its first year. By the year of John Dube's visit, it could be remarked, 'everyone today went Underground'.

This metropolis also of course lay at the hub of the biggest empire in the world, the same one in a distant, insignificant, rural corner of which John Dube had grown up. Never before had so many instruments of rule been so geographically concentrated: it was the seat of both national and imperial government, official residence of the monarch-empress, heart of a business and financial establishment with global reach, and the centre of legal, scientific, artistic and literary achievement. The year 1887 was a highly significant one for empire. In April, all the colonies' prime ministers and governors had attended the first Colonial Conference in the capital. And it was the queen-empress's golden jubilee. Dube and the Wilcoxes had just missed the climax of celebrations on 21 and 22 June (the day, coincidentally, that Zululand was formally annexed to Britain). Queen Victoria had been the centrepiece of a vast procession through London, representing every bit of flummery and finery from across the empire; 30,000 children had gathered in Hyde Park and each one received a commemorative mug. If the mass age was going to be about spectacle, then this had been the most elaborate yet. Londoners had loved it. The whole nation in fact was still basking in the patriotic afterglow of it all.

John was overwhelmed by London: 'I was so amazed at what the white people were doing, that it all seemed like a dream to me,' he wrote. Of the tall buildings, he later said, 'I asked the missionary what those big piles were, and he said they were houses. I could not see why the white men piled their houses on top of each other ... the next day I had my first experience in an elevator. I followed him through a grated door and a young man pulled a string and we shot up in the air. I was scared so much that I fell on my knees.' Such a mixture of wonderment and bewilderment was the initial impression of many a first-time visitor. Even decades later, a new West Indian immigrant would write home, 'Boy, London is a confusing place, a complication of traffic and geography.'

They were bound for Boston, because it was still cheaper to get there than to New York. Their steamship, the Cunard Line *Pavonia*, departed from Liverpool on 19 July 1887. It had accommodation for 200 first-class and

1,500 third-class, or steerage, passengers. Steerage was a large space below decks, fitted out with bunk-type berths, crowded, noisy and unpleasant. Seasickness was a major problem and it was 'impossible to get away from the sight, sound and stench of each other's distress'. There was no possibility of privacy and one had to guard one's possessions as best one could. Most of Dube's fellow steerage passengers boarded at Queenstown (later Cobh) in southern Ireland. He was thus witness to the great surge of Irish emigration that had begun with the 1840s potato famine, and peaked again in the 1880s, when up to half of each generation made for America. Fortunately for him, the emigrants of the 1880s were more orderly and better clothed than the desperate, starving peasants of earlier years, and the advantage of steam power to everyone, especially in steerage, was that the ocean crossing was relatively short – they docked in Boston on 30 July.

Boston was just a tenth of London's size. Two-thirds of its population was either foreign-born or first-generation Americans, and mostly of Irish extraction: many of those disembarking from Queenstown had stayed put, lacking the means to go any further. In the middle decades of the nineteenth century, it had ceased to be a predominantly seafaring town of sailors, shipbuilders and maritime traders and dramatically expanded its manufacturing capacity. The city also had a reputation for invention. Alexander Graham Bell had first successfully used his telephone here in 1876, and Elihu Thomson had developed all sorts of electrical applications, for welding, lighting, street railways and X-rays. Thomas Alva Edison had begun his career here, working on a voting machine and telegraph devices, as had one of America's best-known black inventors, Lewis Latimer. Motor cars were still some way off, but a prototype of the electric car was unveiled in the city in 1887. To support all this activity, an 'inventing business' proliferated – legal firms arranging patents, machine shops to test new devices, and the establishment of the premier institutions of Lawrence Scientific School at Harvard University and the Massachusetts Institute of Technology. Boston thus had an air about it of expectancy, novelty and opportunity.[3]

It was therefore fitting that it should have been in a Boston hotel that John Dube had what he later called 'a peculiar experience': 'Ice-cream was served. It looked and smelt delicious, and I thought what a lovely pudding that must be. I took a spoonful of it, and then jumped out of my chair, almost upsetting the table at which were seated several persons who thought I was insane. I had never in all my life tasted anything so cold. I did not know that anything could be so cold. I was angry at the waiter whom I thought had played on me a "Yankee trick".' We may gauge from this story how very ascetic his diet had been up to that moment, yet there is greater significance in its recollection. Dube, nearly always rather starched and proud about his public demeanour, only ever told this one story at his own expense, an indication of his youthful humour. It reveals the shock as well as the delight he felt – 'I have since learned to be very fond of ice-cream,' he added – in becoming acquainted not just with this cold, sweet substance but also with a very fast-paced new world. The intense sensations that the taste of ice cream produced, not to mention the reactions of onlookers and his hasty admonition of the waiter, would sum up much of his engagement with modernity in the years to come. It was almost as if the incident had played on his consciousness as the one most emblematic of his encounter with America. He related it a few years later, before his return to Natal, in his pamphlet *A talk upon my native land*. It appears in the middle of an entirely unconnected subject, a long and rather tedious account of the climate of Natal, which reads painfully as if it had been extracted from a guidebook for new settlers. It stands out there, as it must have done for him when it occurred, like a very sore thumb.

Oberlin, remote in earlier decades, was now only an hour's train ride south-west of Cleveland, the centre of America's fast-expanding oil industry. When Dube arrived in the summer of 1887, very little remained of his 30 sovereigns, and Wilcox had his own needs to attend to. So for the first time, he was left to his own devices, and felt immediately vulnerable. 'There I was in a strange land among strange people, but with very little knowledge of the English language,' he reflected. We have an extraordinary insight into how he tried to improve his English. Two months after arrival, he was seated quietly in the courthouse in Cleveland, trying hard to follow the formal proceedings and tangled legal arguments. The judge was struck by the 'bright eyes and expressive countenance', as well as the engaging smile, of this dark-skinned, muscular young man, and asked John about himself. John gave a brief resumé of his family background, telling the judge that he belonged to a 'Zulu family of high rank'. He recounted James's contact with the missionaries and explained his own aspirations to get a good education. He was already working in Oberlin on night shifts and Saturdays, he said, and attending school during the day.

His first job was on a road gang – he later described it as 'the hardest day's work I ever had in my life'. It made him ill and it was not long before he was sacked. Then he found work as a Pullman porter. Pullmans were overnight sleeper trains that had carried travellers between American cities since the 1860s. The job of porter was from the first defined in racial and gender terms, for it was performed by black men (in the same way that coloured men came to be the 'bedding boys' on South African trains in the twentieth century). The work was demanding, making beds and being constantly on call to attend to passengers' every need throughout the night, including shining shoes and pressing suits. Though they were poorly paid and without any form of employment protection, Pullman porters came to symbolise the adventure of train travel. Many minstrel-show songs were composed about them, some displaying open racism. A fairly harmless one from the 1880s went as follows:

> He is always just as neat and just as tidy
> As you could wish to see,
> And he never is the slightest out of temper,
> Unless you make too free;
> Remember he's the most important man
> Upon the train by far,
> Life's journey is a weary without
> The porter in the Pullman car.

There is no record of where Dube travelled, how he was treated or how long he survived as a Pullman porter, but this was probably short-lived, as were other menial stints sweeping the floor in a barber's shop and cleaning in a printing business.

These jobs were his first taste of contact with whites as employers and customers. It is hard to escape the thought that a young black man in such lowly positions and with faltering English would have been subjected to a certain amount of discriminatory treatment. On this specific issue Dube was silent, but he did write of these experiences that they made him 'very homesick and wished I had never gone away from home'. He may of course have been aiming at the sympathy vote in his audience (this was also part of a platform performance), but his style always tended more towards the artlessly earnest than the artfully ironic. In any case, one can well understand his sentiments: he had never had to endure anything as harsh as this before. Once again, his determination to succeed must have been virtually all that prevented him from returning to Inanda.

He was rescued, after a fashion, by Eliza Foster, the wife of Oberlin's distinguished Professor of Church History, Frank H. Foster. She was the daughter of Aldin Grout, who had been in the same missionary group bound for Natal as the Lindleys, and had been born and grew up at the north-coast mission station of Groutville. She had known James Dube well. She was able to find John employment on the college campus, running errands and performing chores for wealthy white students. Yet again he was set on a lower level not only by his lack of money but also by his colour. She was able to speak with him in Zulu too, which was a welcome relief to him, 'like medicine': he had become intensely self-conscious of his English, having been discouraged by children making fun of his mistakes. This issue of language competence would always be a sensitive one with him.[4]

After a year of scrimping and saving, John Dube was finally able to enrol as a student himself in late 1888, in the Preparatory Department. The campus was at the centre of the neat town, laid out in its orderly right-angled pattern. Oberlin College was just entering its 'Stone Age', a period of construction of several new edifices out of local sandstone. Three impressive buildings, Peters Hall, Talcott Hall and Baldwin Cottage, all bursting 'in a bold profusion of towers and bays and tall punched windows', had just been completed. This was a campus that was acquiring a decidedly established, as well as establishment, air.

These were also the very last years of the long presidency of James Harris Fairchild. He had been a student at Oberlin in the 1830s, had joined the teaching staff, and then had become president in 1866. He was a sort of 'moral father' of the College, personifying the connection (now increasingly tenuous) with its antebellum past. There was concern that when this cord was broken, Oberlin would change beyond recognition. Students of Dube's generation had no real knowledge of the days of hiding escaped slaves and promoting black freedom; as we have seen, discrimination was a growing issue on campus. There had been racial incidents concerning seating arrangements at meals, rooming together, and exclusion from literary societies. Fairchild himself had recently voiced the fear that the old Christian values on which Oberlin had been founded were being submerged in a more aggressive, self-seeking attitude towards the acquisition of knowledge.

Black students were always in a tiny minority at Oberlin – five or six per cent out of a population of some 1,300 students during Dube's time there. Most were based in the Preparatory Department and most left college without graduating. Feeling somewhat isolated, they tended to turn to the black churches in town for support and fellowship, though John Dube was able to draw on his connection with the Fosters instead. They introduced him to Oberlin's Second Congregational Church, and to their nephew Frank Foster, who was in the Preparatory Department at the same time as him.

The curriculum to which they were subjected was intensely traditional: Greek and Latin, including five hours of Cicero's *Orations* every week, moral philosophy and mathematics. The subjects were much the same in the senior year, except Cicero was replaced by Ovid and Virgil. Worlds away as this might have been for the new student, it did offer him the opportunity to deepen his knowledge and skills of the dramatic art of public speaking. He would have learned of Cicero's distinction between the three genres of rhetoric: judicial ('the art of accusing and defending'), demonstrative (for ceremonial occasions) and, most usefully, deliberative, 'the art of persuading and dissuading' – that is, oratory for parliamentary and popular politics. He may also have learned that Cicero himself had not been born into the ruling class of ancient Rome; he had used his formidable rhetorical skill in the law courts to work his way up to become first a senator (75 BC) and then consul (63 BC).

John Dube's name appears in the Oberlin General Catalogue as a student enrolled in the Preparatory Department from 1888 to 1890. We know very little about his living arrangements (whether he lived in college or private accommodation, for example) or day-to-day experiences during this period. Eliza Foster seems to have kept certain members of the American Board informed of Dube's position: he was visited by Sidney Strong, based in the Boston headquarters, and the retired missionary David Rood, the same one who had prepared James for ordination (and was also Pixley's brother-in-law). Rood was impressed with his progress: 'Those acquainted with him gave me an excellent report in regard to him. His conduct in every respect was commendable, and his standing in his classes creditable.' Rood added that Dube and Eliza Foster had both assisted him with revisions for a new edition of the Zulu New Testament, which must have furnished the young student with a small income.

In order to support himself, he worked at least one summer stint on the Fosters' farm. He also visited William Wilcox, who by mid-1888 was based in a smart summer resort in Keene Valley in the Adirondack Mountains of New York State, already a retreat for the wealthier residents of East Coast cities. As such, it was fertile ground for missionary fundraising. Wilcox had acquired a hand press, and Dube set up the type and did the printing for him. He seems to have accompanied Wilcox on a speaking tour sometime in 1889; emboldened after having listened to him, he asked the missionary if he might speak himself. 'I told him to prepare his lecture and see what he could do,' recalled Wilcox. 'I was so impressed with it that I appointed a special afternoon meeting which was crowded with curious city people. They were simply amazed to hear a seventeen-year-old Negro boy speak like a veteran of the platform.' One listener who was deeply impressed was Olivia Phelps-

Stokes, a member of the influential philanthropic family that already had connections with Inanda Seminary.

All the years of training his sonorous voice, of struggling to conquer spoken English, of rehearsing the appropriate tone and of holding his audience's attention – in short, of developing a forceful oratorical style – at last seemed to work in his favour. What a transformation from the brooding schoolboy who had exuded anything but dynamism just a few years before! And it was Wilcox who brought him to the platform, as he had brought him to Christianity. Usefully, this further stage in John Dube's career was accompanied by material reward. On the basis of his performance, he acquired a patron, a wealthy 'influential lady' who arranged various speaking engagements for the young 'veteran'. From the middle of 1890, he travelled in the Catskills, Finger Lakes and Great Lakes areas, with the purpose of raising the necessary funds to return to Oberlin.[5]

We have some insight into the subject matter of his talks from the composite version that he prepared for publication, a pamphlet entitled *A talk upon my native land*. It is an assemblage of personal reminiscence, Zulu history, accounts of missionary endeavour in Africa, descriptions of Natal, and appeals for support in spreading Christianity among the heathen. As a previous biographer points out, it is significant as an early example of an African perspective on such matters, even had its author not gone on to any greater achievement. Indeed, it can be read as a statement of Dube's outlook on life at that time, even though its 'authorial intent' was to raise funds: there is no reason to suspect he dissembled. Since he rarely related personal stories and recollections in his later writings and no letters from these years survive, it is an extremely valuable source. The Qadi massacre, Pixley's long object lesson on the contrast between his father James and Cetshwayo, the encounter with ice cream – all are contained in this brief document, alongside a potted history of African migration and linguistic development, an account of Natal's export crops, an explanation for the rise of Shaka, and praise for the effects of Christianity on his kinsmen.

In fact there are two separate editions of it. Printed by the same company, the one, *A talk upon my native land*, is rough and ready in style, whereas the other, *A familiar talk upon my native land and some things found there*, is more polished, more considered, better argued. It seems reasonable to suppose that the former was very largely Dube's own effort. It tends to wander at will between disparate topics and contains more about his early life. Tellingly, it contains no reference whatever to industrial education, either in the reminiscences of his days at Adams – which proudly note the academic nature of the syllabus and painfully recall the operation of the 'native court' and English-language rule – or in his prescriptions for success in the mission field. Instead, there are general statements about his belief in the power of Christianity to turn crude heathens into smartly dressed and professionally trained citizens: 'Most of those who graduate from the boarding-schools become teachers and preachers among their own people.'

Though there are extensive overlaps in content between the two editions, the major changes to *A familiar talk*, seemingly by the editorial hand of Wilcox and possibly other missionaries, are in the more logical arrangement of material and the inclusion of a closely argued case for mission work in Africa. The stress is now on the importance of industrial education. In mission schools, we are told, Africans are prepared not only as teachers but also in 'many other enterprises which are of great importance to their civilized state. There are printing offices, carpenter shops, shoemaking, and blacksmith shops … By working at this trade three hours every afternoon, they are able to pay most of their expenses, and have the advantage of knowing a trade besides.' It also includes three testimonials from prominent Congregationalist figures (two professors, of whom Frank Foster was one, and David Rood). The updated edition not only renders the whole document more serviceable for fundraising purposes but adds an 'official' line about the direction of missionary endeavour.

Both versions contain the same three illustrations. As the frontispiece, there is a studio photograph of a solemn, confident, young John Dube, formally attired in stiff collars and dark tie, jacket buttoned, staring intently at some object over the photographer's right shoulder. There is also a drawing of James Dube in a long coat hard at work at his desk, pausing for a moment in his labours to look up, his features notably unAfrican, and another drawing of Cetshwayo, dignified if bulky in a Western suit and wide-brimmed hat, seeming to gaze down from a slightly elevated position. This last image is somewhat at odds with the textual description of a bloodthirsty tyrant who refused to better the condition of his people. In fact all three speak of the heavy duties and responsibilities, even burdens, of high-ranking leadership, whether king or Christian. Barely into his twenties, John Dube was very consciously inserting himself into an illustrious line. *A talk upon my native land* would receive wide exposure when W.E.B. Du Bois selected it to feature in the 'Exhibit of American Negroes' for the 1900 World's Fair in Paris.[6]

Even as he was preparing his pamphlet for publication, Dube already knew that his plans to return to college level at Oberlin would be frustrated. In late 1891 he had become extremely ill again and decided that his best course was to return home. The money he had raised would at least pay his fare. His disappointment must have been very great: he did not have a degree, not in medicine or in any other subject. His older brother, Africa, had failed to make the grade. Now, even though for different reasons, it seemed as if he too had fallen short of expectation. After spending most of 1892 recuperating at Inanda, he appealed to the AZM for employment. Opportunities were severely limited for a person in his position, more worldly-wise and educated to a higher level than most African converts. Another drawback was that even in this familiar environment, he was still no more notable than 'the son of the late highly respected pastor James Dube'. He was given a post attached to Adams Mission in February 1893.

Adams by now had established an outstation in the heart of Durban, a rapidly growing urban centre. In response to the gold rush on the Reef, the port was undergoing extensive modernisation and the railway line already reached beyond the Transvaal border. As the main point of arrival for immigrants and the wide range of construction, consumer and technological goods bound for Johannesburg, Durban was doing well as a merchant entrepôt, even if it still had a distinctly parochial quality about it. In the early 1890s, its population was around 30,000, some 12,500 whites, 5,500 Indians and 12,000 Africans. The African population was overwhelmingly male and made up of manual workers, employed in the port, on other public works and as servants. Most of them lived in informal accommodation behind shops and in suburban backyards.

Increasingly, young men from the mission stations were also heading for the city in search of work. Though most had had some form of practical education, they preferred to rely on their academic classroom training, finding their way into low-level clerical jobs. The AZM was extremely concerned about their welfare in Durban, where they were 'beset by new and manifold temptations'. Accordingly, it had recently opened a small chapel in Beatrice Street, in the main African and Indian quarter of the city, where there were a number of eating houses and other facilities and a lively trade in all sorts of goods, from fresh and live produce to agricultural implements, animal skins and cheap books. The AZM reported great interest in its work: 'the chapel is regularly crowded, some often having to go home for lack of room.'

John Dube's main responsibility in Beatrice Street was to preach: here was a chance to practise and perfect his platform ability. His duties began on Saturday evenings, when he held classes as well as a music rehearsal for Sunday service. He conducted a prayer meeting early on Sunday mornings, before preaching at the main services in the late morning and afternoon. Eighteen congregants had already been admitted to full church membership; all of them were male with no family in Durban. Dube was reported to have entered his work among them 'enthusiastically and with success'.

As if to confirm his status as a young man of respectable position, doing well and intending to go far, he obtained exemption from Native Law in June 1893. The objections to this process that his father James had expressed, namely that it would divide generations within families, had been removed in 1880. After that date, all unmarried children of a successful applicant, and all children born after exemption had been granted, would also be exempted from the 'operation of Native Law'. Women could only be included in an application of a male guardian, either father or husband. Many male converts tried for exemption as an affirmation of achievement, even though it did not relieve them from the legal confusion that resulted. By the time of Dube's application, some 1,300 exemptions had been granted. With the arrival of Responsible Government the following year, notably fewer applicants would be admitted to this select 'club', and by the end of the decade the door would be all but closed. From the 1890s, converts could buy a lapel badge in either bronze or silver to show that the wearer was exempted; many refused to purchase these in protest at the increasing difficulties being experienced by applicants.

Though tailored to the prosaic requirements of colonial officialdom, exemption application forms are an important source of information about converts, not least because they were responsible for filling them in – they had to show they were literate – and could therefore leave a trace of how they wished to be perceived. Applicants generally gave more than one occupation, and nearly always one of these was 'farmer', a term carefully chosen to distinguish them from 'native cultivators' – in other words, signalling commercial rather than subsistence activity. John Dube gave his address as Adams Mission Station and his sole occupation as 'preacher'. He declared that he had no property, that he could read and write English and Zulu, that he had been born 'under chief Mqawe' and had been his subject until arriving at Adams, and that he now wished 'to be governed by civil laws, because I am civilised'. He signed an oath of allegiance to Queen Victoria and was declared by the magistrate to be a 'fit and proper person to receive Letters of Exemption'.

In addition to his duties in town, he spent short periods assisting at the Groutville and Maphumulo stations of the AZM too. Despite his praiseworthy efforts, in his new post as well as attaining exempted status, he was, as he soon discovered, expendable. By the year-end he had been told that his services were no longer required. Clearly it was extremely difficult to get on in the way that he had hoped. For whatever reason, the AZM was not showing the same satisfaction with, and trust in, him as it had done towards his father. It may have been that he came across as too confident for his years, or that the AZM was facing financial difficulties, but there was also the fact that he did not fit the new sense of a model convert. For over a decade now, while he had been at Adams and Oberlin, the AZM's so-called Umsunduze Rules had formalised an inflexibly puritanical attitude to customs such as *lobolo* and imbibing alcohol. These practices had never been acceptable, of course, but whereas an earlier generation of missionaries had preached pragmatism and persuasion, a newer one was pushing a harder line: converts needed to be isolated from all heathen influence. What would be encouraged was a sort of Christianised pseudo-tribalism, a sense of solidarity, hierarchically ordered and presided over by a Christian 'chief', whose authority would be unquestioned.

The AZM had ready administrative and legal assistance in the form of the Native Administration Act of 1875, the general intention of which had been to strengthen a 'tribal tradition' in the governance of Africans in Natal. Among other measures, provision had been made for the appointment of *izinduna*, or headmen, from among the ranks of station converts. This legislation, reinforced by Umsunduze, meant that instead of African converts being gradually incorporated into a common colonial society, they were being encouraged to look upon themselves as polities akin to 'tribes', reflected in the official use of the term *Amakholwa*, 'in the same way as any other tribal or clan name then current'. Some converts would not accept being sealed off like this, and drifted away to town, as we have seen.

Stephen Pixley, who had become resident missionary at Inanda after James's death, was enthusiastic in the application of this new approach and lost no time in appointing the first *induna* to the Inanda station, Klaas Goba. His jurisdiction as headman (which included hearing civil cases and charging fees and fines) was confined to the mission glebe, where some 100 families of converts had their homes and land. He began styling himself 'Chief Klaas', a position recently validated by Law 19 of 1891, the Natal Code, although the curiously self-contradictory debate about whether an 'exempted Native' could actually hold the position of chief continued. (He always wore his bronze exemption medal, though.) As befitting his elevated position, he felt that the whole Mission Reserve should be brought under his control.

Although formally the responsibility of the mission, Mqhawe had in practice exercised chiefly authority over this land for 50 years. He had allocated land, heard cases, collected fines and taxes. Now Pixley and Klaas together were testing him severely, threatening not only his authority but some at least of his income. Without any consultation, Pixley had started allowing newcomers onto reserve land and allotting them gardens already cultivated by Mqhawe's followers, provided they acknowledged Klaas as their chief. He had tried to confiscate a garden from one of Mqhawe's people for the use of his station 'policeman' (as Pixley called him – a man who was also used by Klaas) as a reward for reporting drunkenness among Qadi on the reserve to the Verulam magistrate. And he was encouraging Mqhawe's followers to *ukuvalelisa* – that is, to pay a 'leaving' fee to Mqhawe and to join Klaas. This way, men could evade *isibhalo*, the deeply unpopular system of forced labour instituted by the Natal authorities for the construction of public works.

There were strong and multiple ties between converts, and they did feel similarly on such points as the desire for private lots of land, yet this tension caused several families to polarise into one or other camp. Members of some of the leading families – the Mdimas, Celes, Mavumas, Semes and Dubes – had given support to Mqhawe in various ways, such as acting as his scribes, and looked on Klaas as a wholly unwanted imposition. (Of course there was also the indomitable Mary Edwards, long a champion of Mqhawe's interests, who wrote letters to the government and gave evidence to commissions on his behalf.) Pixley cannot have been willing to find a formal role for one whom he regarded as too closely tied to Mqhawe, when John returned to Inanda at the end of 1893. [7]

This was clearly frustrating for him. Perhaps he consulted his mentor William Wilcox (who in 1891 had returned to Natal, once more having made his peace with the AZM, and was based at Maphumulo) on his options; perhaps Wilcox advised him to strike out on his own. Such advice would certainly have reflected Dube's impatience with the AZM. Perhaps he had already been offered the prospect of independent mission work, and to accept would be highly risky. The line between bravery and foolhardiness could not have been thinner. But this is what he decided to do.

Although Mqhawe had never become a Christian himself, he had for decades drawn on those mission resources that he considered would strengthen the chiefdom. He had bought wagons, ploughs and much else with Lindley's help, welcomed as many 'kraal schools' as could be staffed by trained teachers, and sent several of his children to the mission's own schools. He had become concerned, however, that those of his subjects who had relocated to the Qadi farm Incwadi, near Pietermaritzburg, were being neglected. Any of them who wanted an education had to travel back to Inanda for it, and he thought it was time to establish facilities for them locally. Accordingly, what he had in mind for his young kinsman John Dube was the establishment of a proper mission at Incwadi. Mqhawe would not have missed the nice inversion of roles: that he, a non-Christian, could unilaterally send out missionaries to the heathen, something that Pixley and Klaas Goba did not have the power to do. And the new missionary could exercise authority over his parish independently of AZM (or any other mission) supervision. Here was John Dube's opportunity to prove his worth to others.

Before he left for Incwadi, he and Nokutela Mdima were married in the Inanda church, in January 1894. Their lives had long been intertwined in the small world of the AZM. Nokutela's mother had been converted to Christianity by David Rood and her father, Simon, had been at the men's seminary with James. Her uncle Maziyana was the chaplain of Inanda Seminary, and Nokutela and John were close to his children Selina, Richard, Willett and Simelinkonza. Nokutela later explained that her name derived from a meaning of *ukuthela*, to pay taxes. At the age of eight, in 1880, she had walked the 50 kilometres to Inanda Seminary from Adams Mission, where her family was then living. They all relocated to Inanda sometime in the later 1880s. Amazingly, one early school essay of hers survives – a first attempt in English, a language that the girls then only ever spoke in the classroom. It was sent to the *Rice County Journal*, in Northfield, Minnesota, by Ida Wilcox, wife of William Wilcox, as part of a regular series of letters on her missionary experiences in southern Africa. Unusually, she names the author: it is striking how infrequently missionaries *did* name their converts in reports and correspondence. Thanks to Ida Wilcox, we have this fragment of a direct connection with the young Nokutela, aged about 13, from her essay called 'My Home':

> We live in Africa, there are many people here. Some are good, and some are wicked. They know how to read. There are a great many who have waggons, oxen, goats, sheep and some other things. Some are rich and some are poor. Those who are poor are jealous for the things of those who are rich. Their food are these, mealies, potatoes and other things. There are a few who are diligent, their houses look so clean and nice; and some are bad. In our homes we sleep down upon mats, and some people buy beds to sleep.

After completion of her schooling, Nokutela taught for a time at one of the day schools that Mary Edwards had started up at Amatata, among the people of Chief Kamanga. Her cousin Selina had also been schooled at the Seminary and by the mid-1890s was in Gazaland in southern Mozambique with Grace Goba, engaged in work for the East Central Africa Mission that the Wilcoxes had begun. Another cousin, Ntoyi, was Mary Edwards's assistant at Inanda; the two of them were planning to open a hostel for African women in Durban. Nokutela had returned to teach at the Seminary for the past couple of years; now it was her turn, following her close kin, to be a missionary. A photograph of her taken not many years after their marriage shows an attractive, open face with bright eyes and an engaging smile; an American journalist would describe her as 'young, with blazing black eyes, smooth brown skin and handsome regular features. She speaks good English with a deliberation that is charming and in the softest voice in the world. Her manner is grace itself.' Whereas John would later seem to lose his good humour and feel constantly weighed down by his responsibilities, Nokutela would bear hers with cheerfulness, a welcome foil to his gravity.

The Dubes set off at once in a wagon belonging to John Mdima, a brother of Nokutela's, who had been at Adams with John Dube and had completed his schooling at Lovedale, the most prestigious school for Africans in the Eastern Cape; he would become a key member of the Dubes' most trusted circle over the following decades. They were bound for their new life at Incwadi, a rare opportunity in the hardening racial atmosphere of 1890s Natal. (Mdima and his wife would join them the following year, when he too lost his post in the AZM, owing to the poor financial state of the mission.) The 9,000-acre Qadi farm lay on the Mkhomazi River to the west of Pietermaritzburg, in country that was more open and undulating than the Mzinyathi valley. About 300 homesteads were located there. On their arrival, Nokutela later recalled, 'Our hearts went up in prayer to God as we looked and saw nothing but kraals with no sign of Christian civilisation' (possibly slightly exaggerated, given that there were already graduates of the Seminary among the local people). It is hardly surprising that their own conduct adhered so closely to that of the American missionaries, despite their desire for autonomy from them. They raised initial interest through preaching on Sundays, and their first services attracted curious crowds of up to 200. Their priorities, of establishing a day school and setting up classes to teach women how to look after 'civilised' homes and families, were soon achieved.

Where they departed markedly from the white missionary model was the rapidity with which the Dubes won converts: within a year, the missionaries had over 100 children in the school rooms they had built, and a congregation of 27, for whom a small church was constructed. To this day, the original church site is known as Amelika, in remembrance of the fact that the first superintendent of work had acquired his learning there. On top of all these achievements, they planned an industrial institution for those completing primary school. A few years earlier this element of the missionary model had seemed relatively insignificant in Dube's thinking but he now endorsed it enthusiastically. Perhaps he relied increasingly on his previous experience of schooling, once he had become a teacher himself. Perhaps he was drawn to Wilcox's ideas more strongly than before, now that his mentor was relatively close by and experimenting with his own industrial approach. Perhaps it was a pragmatic response to what he considered would be to converts' economic advantage.

Whatever the reasons, the Dubes' successes and plans cost money, and for the moment at least there would be no industrial department. The resources available to them – possibly some funding remaining from the lectures in America, or from Mqhawe – could support developments at Incwadi for a limited time only. Mary Edwards had long been petitioning the government (unsuccessfully) on Mqhawe's behalf for the establishment of a school at Incwadi. She and her long-time trusted assistant, Fidelia Phelps, must have agreed to exercise some oversight of the Dubes' work, since it was in their names that government grants, in the form of two teachers' salaries, were finally forthcoming from 1895. So this Incwadi initiative was not quite as independent as it seemed. In reality, the old chief and the Dubes would not have done anything to upset or alienate their missionary friends at Inanda, in particular Mary Edwards, by threatening to operate completely outside their control. The Incwadi mission might have raised eyebrows but no serious accusations of secession.[8]

John Dube made his first foray into public political debate while based at Incwadi. In May 1894 a letter of his was published in the paper *Inkanyiso*, concerning the treatment of Africans in magistrates' courts. He reported that certain magistrates were demeaning Africans by forcing them to crawl on hands and knees before them. What was even worse was that 'Native Christians … are not excluded in this practice, and should they attempt to walk on their feet like men, policemen are ordered to force them to kneel down'. It was his first open expression of a grievance that would trouble the African middle class increasingly as the years passed: racial abuse at the hands of whites, aggravated by their being lumped together with African heathens and workers. It was what may be called indiscriminate discrimination. Other correspondents were quick to confirm the problem and support his stance. He followed up this letter with contributions on 18 May and 22 June, both on a similar theme of whites' hypocritical treatment of Africans: claiming they were too lazy to work, yet refusing to offer apprenticeship schemes for fear of competition. These were the very issues that most concerned the members of Funamalungelo, an organisation that had been formed in 1888 precisely to campaign for the rights of exempted Africans.

The Dubes took advantage of their proximity to Pietermaritzburg to acquaint themselves with two important missionary enterprises there: St Alban's College and Ekukhanyeni. The Anglicans had founded St Alban's in 1880, primarily as a training institution for African priests and teachers. Headed by the Rev. Francis Green, it was also where *Inkanyiso* was produced. One person then employed there to teach printing was Magema Fuze. He and Dube were kin: Fuze was the son of a chief whose lineage had been a minor one (like the Qadi) in the old Ngcobo polity, and had been scattered even before the Qadi. He had grown up in his father's homestead before being permitted to attend school at Ekukhanyeni, Bishop Colenso's mission, in the 1850s. Though a devout Christian, he retained extensive connections with and deep sympathy for his 'outside' background. Dube and Fuze therefore shared this ability to move easily both within and between two worlds. John must have been impressed with St Alban's, for he was to employ several of the staff himself in years to come. The Natal authorities for their part had long disliked such centres for encouraging too much book learning and too much open expression of grievance. Once they had acquired Responsible Government, they moved rapidly to pass legislation necessary to curb such operations. St Alban's was their prime target and it was forced to close in the year 1896.

Ekukhanyeni was now the base of the remarkable daughters of Bishop Colenso, Harriette and Agnes, who had carried on the work begun by their father after his death in 1883. They were the 'other Anglicans', the Bishop having been excommunicated in the 1860s for his widely published argument that the Bible could not be the literal word of God (an argument that had begun in conversations with his assistant, William Ngidi). Colenso had embarked on a long and bitter struggle against the injustice of colonial rule in 1873, when he had censured the vindictive excesses of the Natal authorities towards Dube's namesake, Chief Langalibalele. His exposure of the wrongs done to Cetshwayo after the 1879 war isolated him even further from prevailing colonial attitudes. By the 1890s, a circle of 'Ekukhanyeni letter-writers' had emerged, who maintained a lively flow of information and opinion across a wide network of converts, particularly concerning the unjust treatment of the uSuthu, supporters of the Zulu royal house. Magema Fuze, William Ngidi and Harriette Colenso were all influential members. Dube was in touch with these prolific letter-writers and had other personal ties with Ekukhanyeni, too. John Mavuma, who had been one of the founders of the Inanda church with his grandmother Dalida, had lived there for some years, as had several residents of one of Inanda's outstations at Tafamasi, including William Ngidi himself.[9]

Then in late 1895, a vacancy arose at Inanda which John Dube found irresistible. Stephen Pixley was finally retiring as pastor, having been in Natal for nearly 40 years and in charge at Inanda almost half that time. Only three men had held the post in the half-century since its inception – Lindley, John's father James and Pixley. Alongside Adams, Inanda was the most prestigious station in the AZM. Dube's problem was that although he had gained valuable experience in Beatrice Street and at Incwadi, he was not ordained. There were several possible candidates for the post but only one other serious contender, and he *was* properly qualified. He was Cetywayo Goba, preacher at the Umsunduze station and son of Chief Klaas. Predictably, Klaas objected to Dube's candidacy, not only on grounds of family solidarity but because he knew that a victory for Dube would strengthen Mqhawe's influence on the station. The prospect also went against a belief held deeply by both Gobas that, as Klaas expressed it, 'The opinion of the Natives living on the glebe, nearly all of whom are kolwas, is that there should be a white missionary over the black missionary in case of any difficulty.' Cetywayo echoed, 'The Natives here very much prefer a resident white missionary.' Dube had dangerously shown himself willing to dispense with white tutelage.

The contest made an already tense atmosphere even worse. Dube supporters circulated rumours that Cetywayo's sister Grace, a teacher at the Seminary, was trying to poison girls; families on the station 'ranged themselves into two political parties' and stopped speaking to each other. Apparently concerned about the growing sense of division, John Dube himself appeared unannounced one Sunday in October and asked to preach; he spoke of the healing powers of the Holy Spirit. Afterwards Maziyana Mdima tried to ease matters by appealing to the congregation to put their differences aside. The ballot was held in early 1896, the result of which was close: 109 votes to Dube and 98 to Goba. Pixley, with the backing of the AZM, requested that both candidates step down. Goba complied; Dube refused. There was deadlock until the conference of the AZM declared the ballot null and void on technicalities: it found that many had voted who had not been eligible to do so, and that Dube was rather too young and in any case not qualified. The 'Dube party' refused to accept defeat and formed a committee to confirm their man as the new pastor; they even pledged to pay his salary.

This course threatened an open schism in the AZM, which on reflection both John Dube and his committee (and probably the ailing Chief Mqhawe) considered overly hasty and drastic. Accordingly, the Dube supporters changed tactics. Instead of using funds for a salary, they agreed to pay for John and Nokutela to return to America for proper training. For the meantime, then, John Dube would not step into his father's shoes. All Pixley in his bitterness ('the spiritual life of the church was lost and all our hopes for a year of prosperity were blasted') could do was to write to the American Board advising them not to assist him financially because he was probably planning to work independently of the AZM.

While this contest was in progress, Dube also organised his first petition. At a meeting in Durban in early 1896, he drew up a letter to the chairman of the AZM, the Rev. Charles Kilbon, requesting that Mary Edwards be placed in charge of a home for African girls in Durban: 'we thankfully realize and acknowledge her influence among those interested in her work for our comfort as natives.' It was clearly a matter of concern to the African middle class that unattached young women were coming to Durban; the perceived risks to them, both moral and social, as well as the sense of patriarchal loss to their guardians, were great indeed. There were 53 other signatories to the letter from many mission stations across Natal, not just AZM ones. Aside from Dube himself, 18 were from Inanda, including one Pixley Isaac; he had not yet Africanised his name to Pixley kaIsaka Seme (and was rather young to be signing petitions). Many of the names would recur as they became more organised politically in the years to come. Moreover, this is a very early and striking intimation of John Dube's aspirations to speak for all educated Africans in the Colony. Funamalungelo had been active for some eight years but it was based up-country at Edendale and Driefontein, seemingly a very long way from the more urban concerns of coastal-based Africans, especially in Durban.

It may have been at this time, as a result of his studies abroad, work at Incwadi, bid for the Inanda position and early petitioning, that John Dube acquired his praise name, Mafukuzela. This has been rendered into English as 'Energetic and industrious' by some authorities, while others have it as 'Trailblazer'. Both of these capture something of his energy and impact. Yet despite his high ambitions, his initial attempts to break into

respectable positions of leadership after his return from America had not
been characterised by unblemished success. He was now in his mid-twenties.
Though he had clearly made an impression on African converts across Natal,
it must have seemed puzzling to him that he could not do the same within
the AZM, on those white people who had seemed to be so dedicated to his
upliftment before. They appeared unable to accommodate a young, capable
and ambitious black man, who after all was committed to the very same goals
as they were. Impatient and self-assured he may have been, he had shown
a certain preference for autonomy and could clearly draw on other forms
of support. Years later, he recalled that at this point in his life he believed
the missionaries hated him and wanted to put him down. Even so, he was
reluctant to veer off the path of acceptance in the church; there was simply
too much to lose. There he was, then, with his burden on his back, waiting at
the wicker gate. When *would* Good-will come and let him through?[10]

4

Preparing for Africa's redemption

A story in the *New York Tribune* on 1 November 1896 announced that 'Mr and Mrs John Lindley Dube, two natives from Zululand', would shortly be welcomed into the Lewis Avenue Congregational Church in Brooklyn. The item was accompanied by a sketch of the couple, the epitome of refinement: John sported handle-bar moustaches and double-breasted coat, Nokutela was enveloped in a capacious ankle-length dress of dark stuff. The adjustment in their name was perhaps to make things easier for their hosts, and perhaps to make obvious their connection to a revered figure. Their declared objective was to equip themselves more effectively as missionaries to the heathen. John would study for the pastorate and Nokutela would enrol for a home-making course. This sounded humble enough, but their three-year stay would turn out to be of momentous significance: it would provide the 'intellectual rationale' for virtually the rest of Dube's long career.

The Dubes had probably left Natal sometime in April 1896, and were among the 607 passengers on the *St Paul*, which departed Southampton on 30 May for New York. John would have been galled to know he had been classified as a 'labourer', most likely because he and Nokutela were travelling in steerage: most other male steerage passengers were given the same occupation and women steerage passengers were merely noted as 'wife'. On arrival in the United States, they travelled to accumulate further funds for their stay. It was no longer uncommon to encounter African men on the fundraising circuit, but Nokutela, as an African woman, was still a rarity. In what was to become a familiar pattern, John spoke with great force about their mission work at Incwadi, and Nokutela sang – by all accounts, her singing was as captivating as her husband's oratory. They enthralled audiences wherever they went.

Back in Brooklyn by November, they were house guests in Brooklyn

Heights, an elite white suburb on the East River looking towards Manhattan's Greenwich Village, until they found lodgings in the Bedford–Stuyvesant area, where there was an established African American community. They lived at two addresses at least, Halsey Street and 639 Herkimer Street. They arrived just as winter was setting in; one of their abiding memories would be that 'water becomes so hard that men can walk on it'. It was a season of holidays and celebration on the streets, if not in the churches. The Christmas Tree Society would organise a huge tree in one of Brooklyn's theatres and hold a feast for all the city's poor children: it was quite a spectacle, usually spilling out into the street. For their part, most Protestant churches did not then hold special services, believing that the exact date of Christ's birth was unknowable.

In reality, Brooklyn was an assemblage of historic towns – among them Flatbush, Bushwick, Gravesend, New Utrecht, Flatlands and Brooklyn itself – that had grown together into one, which was why the streets did not line up in an orderly grid pattern. By the mid-1890s, a network of trolley lines had enabled Brooklyn to expand dramatically; workers no longer had to live in the neighbourhood of their workplace. And Brooklyn, having reached the limits of the old Kings County, could grow no bigger unless it amalgamated with another big neighbour. Brooklyn and New York became a single city in 1898, 15 years after they had been joined by the Brooklyn Bridge.

Brooklyn's almost one million inhabitants were made up of several immigrant groups: Dutch, British, French, Irish, German, Italian, Jewish East European, Polish, Scandinavian. The African American population had been free since the 1820s, although they were excluded from most of the city's thousands of industries until the twentieth century. They were the targets of periodic riots, as vulnerable workers struggled to hold on to some future for themselves. In the 1860s, for example, Irish workers had attacked the tobacco factories where African Americans were employed, and African American houses had been sacked in anti-draft demonstrations, as white conscripts feared losing out on their return from Civil War duty. Despite such trials, an African American middle class had been active in establishing church and educational facilities in Brooklyn and supported any number of literary societies.

The Dubes were by no means the first Zulu speakers to have lived in the area (or the first Dubes – there was a whole clutch of them, this being a reasonably common French surname too). In the aftermath of the Anglo-Zulu War, entertainers and impresarios on both sides of the Atlantic had sought to capitalise on international interest in the 'mighty tribe' that had defeated the imperial troops at Isandhlwana; there had long been audiences for this type of ethnological show business. In 1881, Bunnell's Dime Museum in Brooklyn had proudly exhibited a 'Zulu Chief and his Pretty Bride'. This supposed chief was supported by other (also supposed) Zulu warriors, one of whom unfortunately took his act a step too far and as a result appeared in court charged with assaulting a boy with his spear. Another, 'Quongo Umkosana', had married locally and taken the name Thomas Murphy. He claimed to have fought at the Battle of Isandhlwana, been involved in the action that killed the Prince Imperial, and to have been captured at the end of the war, shipped to Cape Town and freed. He had made his way to America via England, and once there joined the Dime Museum display. He had lived in Brooklyn ever since, doing odd jobs.

John and Nokutela enrolled at an unassuming but highly regarded establishment at 131 Waverly Avenue, in the Fort Greene area, wedged between Brooklyn's main thoroughfare, Fulton Street, and the Navy Yard. Looking just like the other respectable, three-storey brownstones on the street, this was the Union Missionary Training Institute. Lucy Osborn, a missionary with strong connections to India, had founded the Institute as an interdenominational training facility in Niagara in the early 1880s. It relocated to Philadelphia for a time before opening in Brooklyn in 1890. Osborn was assisted by a vice-principal, Hester Alway, and a small paid staff; most of the lecturers were pastors at Brooklyn's Congregational, Presbyterian and Baptist churches and professors at other colleges and gave their time voluntarily.

Priding itself on its homely character, the Institute attracted promising students who possessed neither the finances nor the qualifications to enter the more prestigious seminaries. There were between 30 and 45 in any one year and came from a wide range of countries – Bulgaria, India, Armenia, China, Japan, Korea, Persia, Australia and Britain, as well as the United States; Lucy Osborn's background meant that connections with Asia were far stronger than those with Africa. Most students lived in single-sex dormitories, although there was never quite enough accommodation and some (like the Dubes) were obliged to find lodging elsewhere. They undertook all the day-to-day chores of shopping, cooking, cleaning, laundry and so on themselves, according to a seemingly very strict gender division: men, Alway declared, were incapable of starching and ironing linen properly. By the late 1890s, the Institute had sent over 60 missionaries out to foreign fields, as well as acting as a feeder for other colleges and universities.

Students spent their preparatory year of the three-year programme on the Institute's 140-acre farm at Hackettstown, New Jersey. Alongside theology and biblical interpretation, their course covered agricultural methods, chemistry, moral science, rhetoric and general history. The farm also supplied the Institute with fresh produce. It is possible that the Dubes visited there, but they seem to have enrolled into the second year: this was permissible for those with adequate prior qualifications. Nokutela's chosen course was music education, while John's training as a missionary would be followed by preparation for ordination. John's senior years covered the subjects of Bible study, moral science, church history, theology, comparative religion and ethics, history of missions and missionary countries, elocution and medicine: in an early attempt to train 'barefoot doctors', there was strong emphasis on hygiene, physiology, obstetrics and elementary healing. All students were expected to participate in gymnastic exercises daily. The Dubes impressed the staff greatly and became star attractions in the Institute's own fundraising efforts, depending entirely as it did on donations from well-wishers. 'God will provide' was its motto. There was a meeting every Monday night to pray for funds and an annual reception for the same purpose.[1]

This was also a time for the Dubes to follow, and participate in, the swirling debates about relations between black and white in American society, in particular the dilemmas facing African Americans. Many in the South had known slavery as children and were now adults in a world of freedom, which they had tasted but not fully enjoyed, and which after the failure of Reconstruction seemed to be slipping away from them again. This generation was grappling with issues such as how – or whether – to accommodate to the new realities and how – or even whether – to demand full citizenship. Some thought it might be better to find a future in their ancestral land, as a solution both to their inferior position in American society and to Africa's in the world.

On the other side of the Atlantic, Dube had for some time been exploring the general question of Africans' social progress. Convinced that Christianity must be an essential accompaniment on the long journey towards modernity, he also wished to assert the role of talented indigenous leadership in showing the way. Everything so far in his adult life seemed directed towards this end: his attempts to prepare himself at Oberlin, his speaking tours, his work in the AZM and at Incwadi, his bid for the Inanda pastorate. During this American visit, he would find the guidance and inspiration he needed.

In 1895 Booker Taliafero Washington of Tuskegee Institute, Alabama, had delivered a speech to a Southern, predominantly white, audience at the Cotton States and International Exposition in Atlanta. It was a brief speech

– Washington was another powerful orator who could use brevity to great effect – but it catapulted him to national prominence, for in it he appeared to endorse the view that segregation was to some extent tolerable and that African Americans should leave politics alone. He used a formulation that came to be famous to some, scandalous to others: 'In all things that are purely social, we can be as separate as the fingers, yet one as the hand in all things essential to mutual progress.' Blacks, he argued, could accommodate themselves to white paternalism, building a better life for themselves in whatever enclaves could, judiciously and without fuss, be carved out of prevailing social practices and attitudes. Central to Washington's message was the need for an entrepreneurial spirit and strong, middle-class leadership: 'the wisest of my race understand that the agitation of questions of social equality is the extremest folly.'

As his biographer has noted, there was nothing new in the Atlanta speech; 'the Wizard of Tuskegee' had been advocating this very approach for years. Born into slavery in Virginia in 1857, Booker T. Washington had worked in the West Virginian coal mines after the Civil War. He heard by chance of Hampton and, determined to experience it at first hand, started out to find it, walking, hitching rides, sleeping rough. It was everything he had hoped for: 'I was surrounded by an atmosphere of business, Christian influence, and a spirit of self-help that seemed to have awakened every faculty in me.' Soon after graduating, he became head of a tiny shack school at Tuskegee, which he proceeded to turn into a model black-run industrial institution. By the mid-1890s, with state aid and donations from well-wishers, Tuskegee proudly boasted 30 buildings, an experimental 1,400-acre farm, 79 staff members and 800 students. Washington used his own life story as the template for his philosophy, which he described as 'education of mind, skill of hand, Christian character, ideas of thrift, economy, and push, a spirit of independence'. He was dismissive of the kind of book learning that bore no relation to vocational endeavour.

Conditions outside Tuskegee and across the South were, however, bleak. In one of his speeches, Dube noted that he and Nokutela witnessed plantation life first hand on their travels, and were shocked by the poverty in which many African Americans were living. Widespread immiseration followed the collapse of cotton prices; segregation was intensifying in this age of Jim Crow, and with it an escalation of anti-black violence, filling many African Americans with foreboding. W.E.B. Du Bois explained Washington's rise to prominence precisely in these terms: 'a sense of doubt and hesitation overtook the freedmen's sons – then it was that his leading began.' Here he was, advising his fellow African Americans to accommodate to the new realities and to turn away from an insistence on political equality. His address became known as the 'Atlanta compromise'; whites as well as most other African American leaders (among them Du Bois, later to offer a radical alternative) applauded it. Suddenly 'Tuskegee' was on everyone's lips and Washington was in demand as a speaker and role model. As if to reinforce the dramatic shift in all this, Frederick Douglass, a giant of the struggle for political equality, had died earlier in the same year. Until his death in 1915, Washington's dominance as the voice of gradualism and moderation was assured. The President himself wrote to him to thank him. Several wealthy Americans, among them Andrew Carnegie, became benefactors of Tuskegee and ensured its long-term prosperity as an independent establishment. Even rulers in distant colonial empires would breathe a sigh of relief that sense could prevail in this tricky area of 'race relations'.

If Dube had known of Washington's work at Tuskegee before, it was only after the 1895 address and resulting fame that he seems to have been drawn towards this example as a possible solution to his own questions. The following year, Washington published 'The awakening of the Negro', an inspirational piece on Tuskegee's philosophy and influence, which Dube must also have read. He quickly identified with this figure who managed simultaneously to define the education and progress of African Americans as his life's work, to command the attention and admiration of leading and influential whites and blacks and, in consequence of these two achievements, to reach a position of pre-eminence in American public life. It was precisely the combination he had been trying to find for himself since his return to South Africa after Oberlin. (Dube was not to be the only black South African leader who dreamed of being able to speak with such authority: his political associate R.V. Selope Thema would one day declare, 'I wanted to be able to speak before European audiences on behalf of my people, as he [Washington] did on behalf of the Negroes … This became the burning passion of my life.')

In the spring of 1897, Washington was in Brooklyn on a speaking tour and to inspect local industrial schools. On the evening of 7 March, he addressed a packed audience in the Lafayette Avenue Presbyterian Church. 'In the elevation of a race, as well as of an individual, it is necessary that we throw as much responsibility on the race itself as possible,' he declared. This fierce dedication to self-help held powerful appeal, embracing as it did an intense pride in his race and a source of inspiration for the future. In a deeply divided society, even in the most adverse circumstances, there was always hope of eventual success if a subordinated people determined that their destiny was in their own hands.

Dube missed this opportunity to hear Washington, though he would have heard and read reports the following morning. Instead, he had written earlier in the day to express his regrets. 'I am very much interested in just the same work that you are for my people the Zulus of So. Africa,' wrote the superintendent of the Incwadi Mission Station, 'but I am engaged for the evening and cannot possibly see you.' Washington, always intensely status-conscious and now relishing his new position as national spokesman, must have wondered at the precociousness of this obscure correspondent who not only addressed him as an equal but even slightly rebuffed him. Dube explained that a friend called Mrs Mitchell (probably Sarah Mitchell, daughter of Daniel and Lucy Lindley) had informed him about Tuskegee and Washington's work there and indicated that he intended to build an industrial school on his return to Natal. He wanted to visit both Tuskegee and Hampton, he said, and would be available to meet Washington anywhere in New York over the following days.

It is not clear whether Washington and John did meet then, but in late May he and Nokutela made the pilgrimage to Tuskegee for the first time, probably as part of their tours to raise funds for their studies and missionary work. Washington introduced them at the commencement ceremony. It was an intensely proud moment. John delivered an address in which he praised Washington and outlined the urgent need for similar work among his own people. It was so well received that he almost became the centre of attraction at the ceremony. Owing to popular demand, he delivered another address on campus a few days later, for which he was able to charge a small amount for entry. His topic was 'Home life in Zululand'; he discussed Zulu traditions but alluded to Cecil Rhodes's destructive campaign in Matabeleland too.

On their way back to Brooklyn, they attended commencement at Hampton, not only Washington's alma mater but also the college that Wilcox had wanted John to attend a decade earlier. On this occasion, he spoke of his chiefly background in terms similar to those expressed in *A talk on my native land*, and described his accomplishments at Incwadi. After criticising white missionaries for not doing more to help Africa (he exempted only Daniel Lindley), he touched on a theme that would become close to his heart, the need for African Americans to return to Africa to assist in the work of uplifting that continent. His forceful Christian rhetoric impressed: 'I long for the day when the "Sun of Righteousness shall rise with healing in his wings", and when on every hilltop shall be a school-house and a church. Then shall we say to Africa, "Arise and shine, for thy light has come, and the glory of the Lord has risen upon thee." May the sons and daughters of Hampton have a part in bringing about this great day.' Dube went even further, claiming that 'If the Negro is ever really to have a country it will be Africa, because it is his God-given country'. The clear suggestion was that once Africans were educated and Christian, they could expect entitlement to certain rights. His speech was published in the *Southern Workman*, Hampton's newspaper, in July. Dube followed this up with a request to Washington for an endorsement of his work. It was not forthcoming at this stage, perhaps because Washington did not feel that Dube had yet proved himself sufficiently.[2]

The parallels between Booker T. Washington and John L. Dube were to be so striking over the course of their separate careers that Dube would in time become known variously as the Booker Washington of Natal, of the Zulus or of South Africa, and would frequently declare his deep indebtedness to Washington's ideals. The parallels were so strong, in fact, that Dube's wider engagement with African American thought in these years has been overlooked. A clue here is the figure with whom he chose to correspond on his theme of African American help in Africa: John Edward Bruce, a leading Washington-based intellectual. Bruce was a distinguished journalist who commanded a national readership of his prolific output. He was also instrumental in developing a black history movement, was an accomplished playwright and poet who wrote one of the earliest crime novels to feature a black sleuth, and was an enthusiastic supporter of Pan-Africanism who ended up as one of Marcus Garvey's key supporters.

Born in Maryland in 1851, Bruce had experienced slavery as a child; his father had been sold on when he was three and never managed to re-establish contact. He had grown up in Washington DC, where his mother and he both took various jobs as servants, cooks and waiters. His education was patchy and he was largely (and proudly) self-taught. At an early age, he began writing for newspapers and later established several of his own, though he struggled to make a living as a journalist and always had to find ways of supplementing his income. Committed to full incorporation into American life for African Americans, he was an active member of the Republican Party. He believed that the interests of his race would best be served by the encouragement of 'black thinking' – what would later be termed psychological decolonisation.

Bruce deeply admired the most famous African American leader of the nineteenth century, Frederick Douglass, but his immediate mentors were three other towering figures of that earlier generation of black leadership:

Martin Delaney, Alexander Crummell and Edward Blyden. Delaney had been born into slavery in 1812; his father had purchased the family's freedom in 1823. A graduate of Harvard Medical School and later a tireless campaigner for abolition as well as emigration, Delaney was made a major in the Union army during the Civil War, after which he worked for the Freedmen's Bureau. Alexander Crummell was born to an ex-slave in New York in 1819. He travelled to England for his education and was a graduate of the University of Cambridge. As an ordained minister, he spent 20 years in Liberia as a missionary of the Protestant Episcopal Church. He then returned to the United States, where he established a parish in Washington and taught at Howard University. Edward Wilmot Blyden had been born in the West Indies in 1832 and emigrated to Liberia in 1850. Also an ordained minister, he held leading posts in the Liberian government, including Secretary of State and ambassador to Britain, and in the country's education system. Together with Crummell, he attempted to establish the institutional basis for a national Liberian church. Through his publications (for which Bruce acted as his US agent), Blyden was the best-known African leader in America, and on his various tours there – the last was in 1895 – he always attracted large audiences.

All three were prolific and influential writers, publicising their ideas through a vast array of pamphlets, collected sermons and newspaper stories, as well as through longer tracts. Their writings served not only to assert Africans' role in human progress but to conjure up, in a way that had not been done before, the very notion of 'Africa' and 'Africans' as a unified place and a united people. While outsiders had long held a notion of the continent as a relatively homogeneous (and essentially backward) entity, thinkers like Blyden and his associates were the first of African origin to appropriate the idea of African unity as a more positive construct for progress. In a sense they 'were able to perceive Africa because of their very removal from it'. Intercontinental travel and physical removal were thus fundamental to shaping notions of racial unity, progress and eventually self-determination.

Not only did these men influence Bruce; he also knew them personally. While each held complex views that often seemed in 'creative conflict', there were also certain common themes in their thinking. It would be wrong to portray them as opposed to Washington in all matters; rather, they represented a tendency in thinking that diverged in certain ways from his, most notably on the issues of industrial education, political engagement and relations with whites. All of them shared, though, an intense race pride. Taking as their inspiration the words of verse 31 of Psalm 68, 'Ethiopia shall soon stretch out her hands to God', they elaborated their history of human progress, privileging within it the peoples of Africa, and positing that a special genius lived on in those of African descent everywhere. (Towards the end of the century Ethiopia's symbolic significance increased, as the only part of Africa not colonised by Europe.) These were early stirrings of a consciousness that would grow into an intercontinental Pan-Africanist movement of solidarity of oppressed black peoples in the twentieth century. Until about 1914, the more familiar term for Pan-Africanism *was* Ethiopianism. It would also provide a powerful fillip to nationalist movements for independence from colonial rule, especially in Africa.

Washington's race pride led him to stress self-reliance and accommodation to the status quo until such time as African Americans had equipped themselves for citizenship. The emphasis was on acquiescence and submission to the political authority of the day, no matter how exclusionary or unequal: this was perhaps even more important than the role of industrial education in his thought. By contrast, Bruce and his associates would have none of this accommodation. They favoured political action and engagement as a way of hurrying the process of social equality for all, through party politics, government office, campaign organisations and a robust independent press. They were not anti-white; rather, they were confident of the correctness of 'conserving the race', of acting in solidarity as a separate nation, and asserting their rights as such. As Crummell asked, where would they otherwise find friends, 'circles for society', or 'cheerful intercourse'?

Their race pride, accordingly, extended to a rejection of assimilation and intermarriage. Blyden had written witheringly about the mixed-race elite of Liberia and Crummell believed he had been hounded back to America by them. Bruce for his part developed a strong dislike of Washington DC's 'black aristocracy' – the so-called upper tens, who through intermarriage tended to be quite light-skinned and, according to Bruce, showed contempt for darker-skinned African Americans. He was outraged at Douglass's second marriage to a white woman in 1884; he penned a story called 'The mistake of his life'. Booker Washington was also somewhat disapproving – and they all wished to overlook the fact that Douglass had a white father.

Their view of African talent led them to develop a capacious, inclusive view of human progress towards civilisation, which for them was by no means exclusively, or even primarily, the white man's burden. Yet here a certain awkwardness crept in: while their ancestral land had been the origin of human civilisation, progress seemed to have faltered and even ceased there; continental Africans seemed to them less advanced than they themselves were. Crummell, whose father had been born in West Africa before being taken captive as a slave, had a closer connection to his African background than most of his contemporaries, and had high praise for it. And Bruce was one of the few intellectuals of his time who believed that indigenous cultures would play an important role in social development. Even so, it did seem to all these men that Africa would require outside stimulus to make up the deficit. Moreover, as devout Christians, they held that Christianity would underpin this effort – and it would not be the 'falsehood', as Bruce called it, that legitimated white domination in the United States or colonial rule in Africa (although it has to be added that Crummell preached the virtues of colonialism). They all accorded a unique role to African Americans in the modernisation, or redemption, of Africa. Indeed, for Blyden, 'slavery had been ordained by Providence to prepare African Americans for the task of redeeming their ancestral continent'. Even Bruce – the most vociferous advocate of civil rights for all, regardless of colour – accepted that slavery had integrated African Americans into modern society, which was a condition of full citizenship.

In line with their commitment to uplifting Africa, they readily endorsed the notion of industrial education there, but their opinions differed about its purpose in America. The long-established tradition of industrial education as a means to advancement had attracted heightened interest after the Civil War; Hampton was a leading example. By the early 1890s, however, when Booker Washington held it up as the only solution to African American acceptance and progress, leaders like Bruce and Crummell were firmly of the opinion that industrial education was disempowering because it was so heavily dependent on white philanthropy. More than that: in the American context, *intellect* ought to be the dominant mode of development, far more important than the acquisition of skills for economic self-sufficiency. To turn Washington's example on its head, it was an admirable thing for ragged African American boys to want to learn French and dream of becoming citizens of the big world beyond their hovels.

Whether wedded to industrial education or to advancement by intellect, all these thinkers believed deeply in the necessity of middle-class leadership, or 'civilisation from the top down'. The masses required careful tutelage, at a pace and of a type to be determined by their educated betters. A system of education was the important thing; what was promoted in the syllabus was a secondary matter. To be orderly, progress must be based on the reproduction of a social hierarchy, of which they formed the apex: this was a position that carried both privilege and responsibility. It meant not only leading by example, but the necessity of speaking out on behalf of the poor and ignorant, although this did not imply any sense of equality. Crummell's role in founding the American Negro Academy stemmed largely from his determination to consolidate this middle class: 'men who will come together for purposes, so pure, so elevating, so beneficent, as the cultivation of mind, with the view of meeting the uses and the needs of our benighted people.' Perhaps except for Bruce, they did not have much faith in the idea of democracy – there was still too far to go in civilising the lower orders.[3]

It is highly significant that Dube should have chosen to write to Bruce. He had very possibly encountered Bruce's work while at Oberlin, for in 1887 Bruce had published his first articles on African American history in the *Cleveland Gazette*, a black-owned weekly strenuously opposed to any form of racial discrimination. (If the *Gazette* did not reach Oberlin, Dube would have reached Cleveland, during his time as a Pullman porter.) He chose this occasion to detail the contribution of the 180,000 African American soldiers who had fought in the Civil War, a topic he felt had been overlooked by other writers. The series was hugely popular and launched his career as a historian.

Dube gave his letter a title, 'A Zulu's message to Afro-Americans'; perhaps he hoped Bruce would publish it. Strongly echoing Blyden, he noted that 'God has wonderfully prepared the Afro-American, through years of bondage by a civilised nation'. If African Americans thought themselves more advanced than their African counterparts, so did African leaders like Dube. Indeed, the progress of African Americans was proof that African people, scattered over the globe, would not be downtrodden for all time. Yet Dube was not completely overawed by their achievement: 'there are still in America thousands of Afro-Americans who need the Christianizing and civilizing influences of America as much as we', he felt. He identified the qualities which Africa needed, echoing the 'civilization from the top down' theme: 'we need leaders who are [not only] mentally superior, but who understand agricultural and industrial methods of work.' He went on to lament the lack of awareness of Africa's needs he had encountered, claiming that African Americans were as ready to spend money on fripperies as whites, whereas they ought to be supporting mission work in Africa. There was no place for such petty materialist gratification. His solution was that all schools and colleges ought to offer courses on Africa, so that African Americans would be better informed about their continent of origin. He ended by referring to the useful role that black soldiers had played in the service of 'Uncle Sam', clearly indicating his familiarity with this theme in Bruce's writing.

Perhaps most tellingly of all, his letter-headed paper, giving both his Incwadi and Brooklyn addresses, prominently incorporated the seal of Ethiopia. In this single gesture, on his specially printed stationery, he made clear his affiliation to the Ethiopian ideas of Blyden, Crummell, Delaney and Bruce; he was announcing his identification with the ambitious programme that was so much associated with them. This is the strongest evidence we have of Dube's own race pride, affirmation of African culture and commitment to racial unity at this time. Here was a declaration of his determination to assert the rights of Africans and to lean on his own people to redeem Africa, rather than on the white missionary world of the American Zulu Mission, or even of the Congregationalists of Brooklyn (though this would prove impossible). Viewing Africa from across the Atlantic, he too could see a communion between the people he knew in Natal and those scattered over the entire vast continent.

Dube might very well have found a congenial home in Tuskegee, yet he was also drawn to a rather different philosophical house. It was not only the complicated social and political environment of Natal in future years that would throw up contradictions in his public position. These also stemmed from a tension between two tendencies in African American thought: the more moderate, pragmatic approach of Washington and the more intellectual, politically engaged ideals of Bruce and his associates. In the earliest years of the twentieth century, other black South African leaders, too, would express admiration for Washington yet be drawn towards Bruce's example, notably Solomon Plaatje. Ultimately, though, these leaders shared a deep conviction that the status quo needed to be stretched and pulled to accommodate their aspirations, rather than turned upside down. Moreover, their aspirations were clearly defined in terms of status: while industrial education might be the way forward for the majority, the needs of the middle class could not necessarily be contained in such a way. As Dube's own case had shown, the responsibilities and frustrations of the intellectual class were a different matter from the masses waiting for conversion and redemption.[4]

If Dube promoted African American help in the civilisation of Africa, he stopped short of supporting wholesale emigration, not only because of his belief that some were ill equipped ('it would not do to send ignorant negroes to Africa,' he later wrote). His position was a great deal more restrained than the populist 'Back to Africa' movements that had arisen from the 1870s, especially in the South, whose most forceful promoter was Henry McNeal Turner of the African Methodist Episcopal Church (AME). In Brooklyn, however, Dube's path soon crossed someone's who *did* fly the flag for such a movement. He was an English missionary based in Nyasaland, Joseph Booth, and he had with him his first convert, John Chilembwe.

Born in Derbyshire in 1851, Booth had been self-taught and had come to missionary life after a string of different jobs and a period abroad in New Zealand and Australia, during which time he launched a successful business. Its sale would fund much of his initial activity at the Zambezi Industrial Mission at Mtsidi, Nyasaland, where he based himself from 1892. Since that time, Booth had been an eccentric and independent spirit. His heady mix of fundamentalist religious views (he was an ardent sabbatarian, and would later be responsible for introducing the Watch Tower movement to sub-Saharan Africa) and political radicalism (he denounced imperialism as a retrograde step in Africa's development) meant that he came into conflict almost at once with both established missionary societies and colonial authorities. This, combined with his somewhat impatient personality, made life difficult for him as well as for his financial backers, and he was more often than not on the move seeking new sources of support, as one missionary body after another cut its links with him.

Booth had lately attempted to set up an ambitious African Christian Union in Durban, in September 1896. He had missed the Dubes, already in America, but did manage to attract John Nembula as a supporter. The Union's prospectus was vocal in its condemnation of the wrongs done to Africa by European powers and claimed that the damage would only be eradicated when all the continent's converts united in a single 'African Christian Nation'. This would come about through the efforts of converts themselves, through 'gift, loan or personal service' – and the basis of the Nation would be secured by the purchase of vast blocks of land up and down the continent where farming, mining and manufacturing could be independently undertaken. But his vision went much further. Booth was an early populariser of the slogan 'Africa for the African' – he believed not only that African Americans should return to their land of origin, but that the United States government ought to support their passages. All this from an excitable stranger must have seemed at best bewildering and at worst wildly messianic to Durban's African intelligentsia, struggling for respectability in a difficult social and political climate, and the African Christian Union found little support among them.

In the wake of this failure, Booth decided to take John Chilembwe to America, partly to find new avenues of funding and partly to secure a proper training for this promising convert. Chilembwe had come to Booth's mission soon after its establishment, offering himself as a servant to the Booth household, and was baptised in 1893. He had acted ever since as the missionary's general assistant and interpreter. Chilembwe was probably slightly older than Dube but, like him, was an imposing figure and a commanding presence. He was an accomplished *kalimba* (harp) player and hunter, had been extremely diligent at school, and showed a care and responsibility towards both converts and heathens that were specially remarked upon by observers. He would make history in 1915, as leader of an uprising against colonial rule in Nyasaland that would bear his name and cost him his life.

Booth made much of their association with the Dubes, claiming that they were 'together in Brooklyn, all on the same errand – all pleading for the commencement of Native Independent Missions'. On the face of it, this is precisely what they were all doing. But there were differences in orientation and emphasis, as already suggested, so that the Dubes did not make nearly as much of the association as Booth did. Booth contacted Washington (very likely at Dube's suggestion) and sent him the African Christian Union prospectus, but nothing further came of it. In any event, they did not make common cause for long: soon Chilembwe began his training at the Virginia Theological Seminary and College at Lynchburg, Virginia, an institution run by the Negro Baptist Convention. During his training there, he would break decisively with Booth, who returned to Nyasaland with funding from the Seventh Day Baptist Church of Plainfield.[5]

The Dubes participated to the full in church life. Their main home, the Lewis Avenue Congregational Church, had started out as the Grace Presbyterian Church in 1877. As a result of internal dissension, the first pastor had departed and the congregation had applied for membership of the Congregational Union in 1880. Work on a new building in the 'Modern Gothic' style, with a seating capacity of 1,200, had been completed in 1894 at a cost of $62,000. Its pastor since then had been the Rev. Dr Robert J. Kent, who was so impressed by the Dubes during their time in Brooklyn that he would be instrumental in supporting their future work in Natal. One of a growing number of Congregational churchmen who were interpreting the Bible less literally and embracing social activism more openly (including the ordination of women), Kent was a prominent Republican sympathiser. He had achieved a certain local fame during elections in November 1893, when he and a group of observers travelled down to Gravesend to ensure that voting was free and fair. A local henchman by the name of John Y. McKane did his best to obstruct their work, claiming that no outside observers were required. One of his associates accused the Kent party of being nothing more than 'ragamuffins, ruffians and drunkards'. Kent was knocked down as the fracas got physical, and an injunction was served on McKane. The subsequent court case was widely reported in the local press. Just before the Dubes' arrival, Kent had also launched a new campaign to 'Make Brooklyn dry' and was taking a leading role in reuniting the Congregational churches of Brooklyn and Manhattan, after a 20-year split.

Kent's church was extremely active in the local community. One of the customs he considered important was the annual presentation of Bibles to children who had been baptised there and had reached the age of seven; it underlined the sanctity of marriage and family. Funds were regularly collected for sick and wounded sailors and soldiers on active service abroad whose families were church members. A special project of the congregation's came to fruition during the Dubes' membership, the opening of a new parish centre, Ariston House, at 304 Lewis Avenue on 13 December 1897. It became the home of the Ariston League, a men's dining club that met monthly to discuss topical issues. Membership was open to all men contributing to church funds; Louis Stoiber, another prominent Dube supporter in years to come, was on the organising committee.

All the Brooklyn churches had busy programmes of events every Sunday, featuring local as well as visiting speakers; pamphlets were distributed door to door giving details of Sunday evening lecture series. People regularly attended each other's churches to hear famous and favourite speakers. If one browsed the list for just a small selection of churches, one could, on a single Sunday in early 1898, hear a blind evangelist, Fanny Crosby, tell the story of her life in the Puritan Congregational Church, or a lecture on 'How the Bible has come down to us' in St Marks, Adelphi Street, or a sermon on 'Jesus the life-bringer' in St John's Methodist Episcopal Church, or 'David and his cripple guest' at the Reformed Church on the Heights – or John L. Dube's address and Nokutela Dube's rendition of Zulu hymns to a missionary meeting at the Reformed Episcopal Church of the Reconciliation. Of course there were regular morning and evening services in all of them too, though sermons were an important element in drawing congregations: pastors were considered ineffectual if they were not good orators. Among prominent figures to be heard on Brooklyn's church circuit in the late 1890s were Booker Washington; Parkes Cadman, the leading church spokesman on the media; and Charles Stanton, author of *In His Steps*, the Congregationalist publishing sensation of 1896.[6]

The Dubes corresponded frequently with friends and family back home to tell them of their experiences and life in America. They also did all they could to assist relatives and members of their close Inanda network to pursue their studies in America, or at least to experience American life: the task of Africa's redemption should involve a two-way traffic of learning and ideas. By the late 1890s, the number of black South Africans who travelled abroad, primarily to the United Kingdom and America, was growing noticeably, although still tiny. Some were on organised tours (such as the African Choir), some were seeking education and some religious affiliation. Several African Americans had visited South Africa, too, even though historically they had no connection with this part of the continent. Compelled by a common sense of oppression, they too were seeking 'spiritual answers and explanations about the nature and reasons for white domination'.

John's younger brother Charles Lentallus had by now completed his schooling at Zwartkop and Adams. He had taught at various establishments across Natal, including Umvoti and Umhlatuzana, and had also spent some time at Incwadi, probably at his older brother's behest. There was a small group of black South Africans studying at the AME's Wilberforce University near Xenia, Ohio, who must have been known to the Dubes in Brooklyn. They had come to be there largely through the efforts and connections of Charlotte Manye, a member of the African Choir that had toured Canada and the United States earlier in the decade. She had been amazed by the opportunities available for study in America, and Bishop Derrick of the AME had arranged for her to enrol for a BSc at Wilberforce. She would shortly facilitate the entry of the AME into South Africa, through an uncle, Mangena Mokone. Fellow students at Wilberforce included James and Adelaide Tantsi, children of J.Z. Tantsi, one of the first black South Africans ordained as minister in the AME (which he was later to leave), Marshall Maxeke, Henry Msikinya and Edward Magaya. All of them were from the Eastern Cape.

John Dube, mindful of his own feelings of isolation while a student at Oberlin, perhaps considered that Charles would benefit from 'home' company of a sort, in a black institution that was self-consciously elitist. Further, Wilberforce was a liberal arts college, stressing intellectual achievement, even though it did possess a large industrial and even a military department by the 1890s. Accordingly, John arranged for Charles's entry there in 1898. He enrolled with another Eastern Cape student, Theodore Kakaza, and though he had an instant set of associates, he did not find it an easy experience. He was homesick, suffered financial hardship and struggled with his studies. He had to complete preparatory courses, as John had done at Oberlin, before he was able to enrol for his BA degree proper in 1900.

The Dubes also acted as hosts to several other Inanda kin. Among them were John Mdima and at least one of the Seme boys – frequently also called by the surname Isaac – who went to study theology at Benedict College, South Carolina. Pixley Isaac, a precocious boy 10 years younger than John, was the son of Kuwana and Eliza Isaac; his elder sisters, Dalida and Lucy, had both spent time with the East Central Africa Mission. He had attended the Inanda primary school and Adams, where, besides his normal lessons, he had learned photography. He was quick-witted, intelligent and excelled at his studies, and greatly impressed the resident missionary at Inanda, Stephen Pixley (after whom he was named), who offered to assist in his further education. The Dubes undertook to assist him too, and the 16-year-old Seme arrived in Brooklyn in early 1898.

In what was already a familiar pattern, he first had to work to secure funding and improve his English before enrolling as a full-time student. He was with the Dubes for some months, travelled on to Boston to visit Stephen Pixley, who was on furlough from Inanda, and then found a job as a bellboy at the Northfield Hotel, in north-western Massachusetts. Stephen Pixley applied for his admission to Mount Hermon School, undertaking to pay the $100 fees for the first year. The young Pixley began his studies there in September 1898. Dube completed part of the application form, naming himself and Louis Stoiber as Seme's guardians. It was a difficult financial business keeping Seme in school: he worked during vacations, and Dube approached various philanthropists to help. Stephen Pixley sent money to cover part of the second year. He graduated in 1902, some time after the Dubes had returned to Natal, and went on to Columbia University.

Yet another kinsman who crossed the sea at this time was Mqhawe's son and heir, Mandlakayise, by his chief wife Ntozethu, daughter of Chief Phakade of the Chunu. Mqhawe had sent some of his children to the Inanda schools for education, but not Mandlakayise. Neither was he a Christian, and he lived with the rest of the chiefly family at Maqadini, in the hills surrounding the mission station. Mandlakayise was a few years older than John and had taken two wives, the first in 1892. Mqhawe was concerned that he would not be fit to lead the Qadi unless he acquired some learning. The Qadi people paid for his American trip: Mqhawe ordered each ordinary homestead to contribute 2s 6d, and each headman 5s. This could not have been a welcome imposition just at the time that homestead heads were desperately trying to rebuild their herds after the ravages of rinderpest.

Mandlakayise slipped out of Natal in the company of Mabhelubhelu Cele, son of the venerable Madikane Cele. Madikane was the same age as Mqhawe and had played a leading role in rebuilding the chiefdom at Inanda. He had always been Mqhawe's *inceku* – his closest confidant, adviser, steward; in the olden days he would probably have been killed or banished when Mqhawe became chief, so as not to pose a threat. He had overseen all the arrangements for each of Mqhawe's several marriages; he had taken messages to the colonial government office on Mqhawe's behalf; he had advised Mqhawe every time a new crisis with the colonial authorities threatened the Qadi. Quite late in his life, Madikane decided to become a Christian and spent some time at school at Adams, learning to read and write with the children. He had sent his headring and best beast to Mqhawe as a sign of his transformation and asked two of his three wives and their children to live away from him. At the invitation of a neighbouring chief, Bhulushe, he set up a small mission church in Amatata, also in the hills beyond Inanda. Yet the extraordinary thing is that he continued as before in his role as Mqhawe's *inceku*. And it seems that Mabhelubhelu, a son of one of the wives who 'went away', was meant to perform a similar role in the next generation.

The two kinsmen, Mandlakayise and Mabhelubhelu, travelled to England with a female African American missionary whose identity is not known. They thought of the sea as a great waste; they could not believe they would ever reach Inanda again. In England, they found it hard to think of Zulu words to describe the marvels they saw, like lifts: 'houses inside houses'. They arrived in Brooklyn in late 1897, and were installed in lodgings near to the Dubes, in the Bedford–Stuyvesant district. They complained bitterly about the cold and the way that their boots hurt, and felt hemmed in by their shirts and suits. They struggled with the idea of eating turkey, a particular problem at Thanksgiving, and flatly refused to try fish. And the only way they could explain the movement of Brooklyn trolley cars was that they were possessed by spirits. The ostensible purpose of their trip was to learn trades, so that they could help at Incwadi; they spent some time at least at Slater Academy in North Carolina.

Mandlakayise returned to Natal only in 1904. His father was by then very old and ill, and conspicuously unwilling to cooperate with officialdom in these last years of his life. He procrastinated over court cases and the supply of men for *isibhalo* (forced) labour on public works and was fined several times. He refused to comply with the census regulations of 1904, and said he would not be enumerating the Qadi, until warned by the nervous local magistrate that he was behaving just like Langalibalele 20 years earlier. The magistrate believed that Mandlakayise was behind all this, commenting that he was 'the most reserved and unapproachable Native, of any social position, that I have met'. Moreover, Mandlakayise had apparently become a naturalised subject of the United States; this must have been rare indeed for a chief's heir in colonial Africa. There was nothing whatever in Native Law to cope with it. The only thing to do was to pretend that it had not happened. Mabhelubhelu was still studying in 1907 (this was the 'Bea Mabelubelu Dube', about whom Pixley Seme wrote to Booker Washington in that year). He never returned from America. One of his brothers, Qandeyana, would shortly join him there – a visit also arranged by the Dubes.[7]

Not only was 1898 a busy year for visitors: on 25 May, John Dube was one of seven students to graduate from the Union Missionary Training Institute, at a special ceremony in the Hanson Place Baptist Church. His fellow graduates were Margareta Franz of Germany, Rose Hill and A. Sharp of Ontario, Katherine Richer from Indiana, and Helen Root and O. La Dona Deavitt of New York State. Each one had some part in the ceremony; Dube gave the valedictory on the topic 'Christianity, the world's hope'. Nokutela sang Zulu hymns.

Over the following 10 months, their main goal was to raise funds ahead of their return to Natal. Their target was an ambitious $15,000, to build an industrial department and dormitories at Incwadi. They managed to reach $4,600 and, to achieve it, had to appear on very many platforms, John speaking and Nokutela singing – and, increasingly, speaking herself. They were even able to illustrate their talks with stereopticon views of African life. Many of these engagements were in the Brooklyn churches, but they travelled more widely too. In September 1898 they were at the Rev. Howard Cornell's Presbyterian Church, Seneca Castle, New York State. This was not too far from Keene Valley, where Dube had been with Wilcox a decade earlier, and perhaps he returned there to seek out old contacts and new funding. They also spoke in Northfield, Massachusetts, where Olivia Phelps–Stokes heard them. They also did their best to increase their profiles in the press, and gave a number of interviews and wrote articles themselves. John and Nokutela published separate accounts of their first efforts in the mission field and their visions for the Incwadi of the future. John's 'Zululand and the Zulus' was published in *Missionary Review of the World*, edited since 1887 by the prolific Christian writer and influential thinker on missions Arthur Tappan Pierson (named after the prominent abolitionist Arthur Tappan). Through the 1890s, Pierson and his son Delavan, the managing editor, had turned *Missionary Review* into the foremost nondenominational missions journal in America and a mouthpiece for ecumenical evangelicalism. It would provide Dube with a ready platform for years to come. Nokutela wrote a piece called 'The story of my life'. Through these various printed contributions, it is also possible to catch a glimpse of the content of their platform performances. All their efforts helped to extend the script of the story that John had begun in *A talk on my native land*, and laid the basis for what would become the 'official version' of their lives and work: these themes would recur over the following decades.

From being identified as 'grandson of a Zulu chief' in 1896 on their arrival, John had become 'son of a Zulu prince', 'son of a Zulu chieftain' or even 'member of the Zulu royal family' by 1899, in the months before their departure. This description readily conveyed his high-born status and close relationship to Chief Mqhawe: he noted many times that the chief had pledged 500 acres at Incwadi for the new industrial plant. Shame on the sceptical Christians! It was also a point of importance to stress his grandmother Mayembe's pre-eminence as the *first* convert at Inanda and similarly James's position as the *first* African pastor of Inanda. Not only was this a matter of sequence but of pre-eminence too. Once again a sense of unassailable status is underlined, this time from the mission-station side of things: it is what made Dube 'doubly elite'.

By contrast, Nokutela was described as a 'native Zulu', who had been born into savagery, 'on the dirt floor of a kraal, like all Zulu babies': her closeness to ordinary Zulu people was what came across. Perhaps this was a way of exploiting popular knowledge of 'Zulus' in order to personify the sharp and dramatic contrast between heathen life and civilisation, and to underline how challenging the mission task would be. The marriage, both literal and figurative, between high-born and commoner would ensure success of the Christian cause and prefigure the future of African society. They were both at pains to show how deeply committed they were to mission work, as Zulus who had made the leap to Christianity, itself no easy feat: there were temptations at every point on the way. The redemption of Africa, or at least of Natal, was a conviction that had seized them, and they could not shake it off.

John was strident in his criticism of white settler rule and missionary activity in Africa, continuing the theme of his letter to *Inkanyiso*. This was of course a period during which imperial wars of conquest were still being waged up and down the continent in the wake of the partition of Africa between various European powers a decade earlier; his perspective on the process now stretched far beyond his immediate experience of Natal and Zululand. Asked soon after his arrival in 1896 about the Matabeleland uprising, he had responded, 'This has been caused by the treatment given to the natives by the English. Rhodes and the other officials of the [British]

South Africa Company, we have found by fearful experience, are trying to put all they can in their pockets by killing and plundering us. I am afraid that, unless the company changes its methods of treating the natives, there will be war for many years to come.' (Booker Washington was similarly scathing of Rhodes's methods: 'What is the crime of these heathen? Why are they thus shot down – mowed down by the acre? Simply because God has given them land that some-one else wants to possess.') Dube would also have known of an insult Rhodes had delivered to Wilcox and Benjamin Ousley, the African American missionary assisting him at Inhambane, in 1894. The pair had met Rhodes in Cape Town; he had refused to shake Ousley's hand. Wilcox was deeply contemptuous of Rhodes thereafter. All in all, Dube thought, white rulers were setting a shocking example to the conquered; they possessed no enlightened self-interest whatever in their failure to civilise Africans. He seemed at this stage to make no distinction between metropolitan rulers and settler administrations: they were equally culpable.

On missionaries, he had asserted similarly that 'no white man will teach the natives any useful trade'. In a neat inversion of Social Darwinist thinking, he reasoned that 'Africa is the white man's grave' and that was why, in the Christianisation of Africa, he intended to 'use the teaching and preaching of native schoolmasters and preachers'. This was not merely a matter of physical preparedness for the task, however: unlike white missionaries, educated Africans treated heathens with respect, and so (he argued) were simply more successful in this work. He pointed, too, to the obverse of this argument: 'If the Zulus could see their own sons and daughters actually making and doing the great things which they now think only white men can do and which have made him appear to them as a superior being, they would respect the religion which could so exalt them.' Whites were not superior; people merely *thought* they were; they merely *appeared* so. With determination, Africans could prove their equality. So much of his motivation for wanting to succeed in the establishment of a training institution is summed up in this observation. And so much of his frustration with modernity lay in the contrariety of theory and practice: the trouble was not with Christian civilisation but with those who called themselves Christians and then behaved in a most unchristian-like manner.

He had found the white people he met in America, he said, the antithesis of those in Africa: 'they have given me money and ploughs, carpenters' tools, household and toilet articles, planes and sewing machines.' The clear suggestion here was that white donors in America *trusted* him: inspired by his declared intentions, they had given willingly, without setting conditions. However, he did find irksome the suspicion he encountered in some of the mission boards, which were wary of independent mission work and seemed to think the funds were for personal aggrandisement. He underlined both his suspicion of colonial rulers and his gratitude to white American donors in a last statement before departure: 'There is a saying in my country that "the last honest white man is dead", but I shall have a different story to tell when I return. I shall tell them that I have found the white men very kind …'

For her part, Nokutela was rather reserved about white Americans: for all their civilisation, they did not seem altogether happy. She declared, 'I do not like your women. They are very busy – always engaged – but they do no work as my Zulu women do. They must be taken care of too well or they complain. They hurt their bodies with their clothes, and they will not bother with children. They are of no use in the house and they have too many clothes … every day they go shopping, and always for something to wear … I do not wish the Zulus to become like that.' Both John and Nokutela saw as part of their mission the elevation of the status of women, but they clearly rejected both this new dependence and rampant consumerism, a sort of 'false progress'.[8]

On 10 March 1899 Dube was finally ordained in the Lewis Avenue church. In the afternoon, an examination council convened, at which 15 Brooklyn churches were represented. Dr Kent commended the Dubes highly, stressing the love and trust that the congregation felt towards them. Dr Butler, his theology teacher at the Institute, praised Dube's acute mind and grasp of the finer points of biblical interpretation. His psychology teacher, Mr Overton, announced that Dube had obtained 96 per cent in the final examination. Dube was asked to present his credentials, and gave a short resumé of his life, noting his grandmother's conversion under Lindley, his father's ordination, the bad company he had kept at school until his own conversion, his attempts to prepare himself for service at Oberlin and his work at Incwadi. He told them, 'The Zulus believe that God created the world and all things in it, but when he came down to earth and saw man, and how wicked he was, he flew up into the clouds and no man has had communication with God since. I want to teach my people that man can communicate with God through Christ.' The council endorsed Kent's recommendation that Dube be ordained. After a celebratory supper in Ariston House, there was a special ordination service at which the findings of the council were read, Kent preached a sermon and Arthur Tappan Pierson gave Dube the charge. His training had at last been completed. From now on, he would be 'the Rev. John Dube'.

Kent had been so inspired by the Dubes' devotion and determination that he offered to organise a committee not only to manage the funds they had raised (much of which came from local sources), but to organise further fundraising to support the work at Incwadi. He and Louis Stoiber were central figures in this effort. Apart from being extremely active in the Lewis Avenue church, Stoiber owned a woollen manufacture business and was a generous supporter of connections with Africa – he helped Pixley Seme greatly through his years at Columbia. He was also deeply committed to charity work for the poor of New York. He was chief attorney in the New York Legal Aid Office and a director of the Legal Aid Society, heading as well as financially supporting the Brooklyn branch. He and Kent attended a special dinner in 1898 marking 22 years of the Society's work in New York, at which the president, Arthur von Briesen, noted that some 90,000 'poor and afflicted' citizens, wronged by their employers, had been given assistance by the Society. Such activism was typical of devout Congregationalists, dedicated not only to making this world a better Christian place, but to augmenting their chances of salvation in the next.

The American Committee, as it came to be known, was at first composed of congregants of the Lewis Avenue church; apart from Kent and Stoiber, other early members were Delavan Leonard Pierson, son of Arthur Tappan Pierson; S.E. Strimson; shipping magnate Frank M. Sutton; and Thomas B. Kniffen, a glassware merchant. It soon broadened out to include several prominent church people in Brooklyn and beyond, including the Rev. Dr James Farrar of the First Reformed Church, who had caused a minor sensation by declaring that he could do without his annual salary of $6,000 and would try to live on $500 instead, and Howard Cornell of Seneca Castle. A third was Byron Horton, superintendent of the prestigious Packard Commercial School in New York (its graduation ceremonies were held in the Carnegie Music Hall, with guest speakers such as the Attorney-General) and author of several business books, including *The new Packard commercial arithmetic*. Horton was from an eminently entrepreneurial family: his cousin James Madison Horton was a well-known ice cream manufacturer. His wife, Elizabeth, acted as secretary to the American Committee. For many years to come, members of the committee would do all they could to support the Dubes in their efforts to build an industrial training institution in Natal.

John Dube was finally returning to Natal with a substantial qualification, an impressive amount of money for his work of redeeming Africa, and many contacts in progressive, sophisticated African America and mission-oriented white America. Nokutela had played a fundamentally important role in these achievements; they were truly a team. They would have had considerable cause for satisfaction with their progress as they sailed for Southampton on the *St Louis* on 12 April 1899.[9]

A gigantic scheme in their heads

The American Zulu Mission chose Inanda as the venue for its annual meeting in the first week of August 1900. After one of the business sessions, delegates took off joyously down the dry, dusty track that wound along the ridge towards Durban. The pastor of the Inanda church, the Rev. John Dube, led the way, Nokutela walking alongside him. After about four kilometres, the procession, now swelled with local well-wishers, turned off and gathered at a prominent hilltop from which they could just see the distant Indian Ocean. In a rousing speech, John declared that this was the chosen site for his visionary industrial school, his own Tuskegee. His old schoolmate Gideon Mvakwendlu Sivetye, now pastor of Esidumbeni church, led the prayers. Reynolds Scott, a West Indian builder and Tuskegee graduate who had been inspired to accompany the Dubes home from America, added his support. Entertainment was provided by the choir that Nokutela had been training, and then everyone participated in a grand feast of celebration. Among the invited guests were the local trader and sympathiser George Hodsdon and three American Board veterans, Stephen Pixley (retired pastor of Inanda), Charles Kilbon (to whom his 1896 petition had been directed) and Dube's long-time guide and friend, William Wilcox, back in Natal at Adams. The Dubes' 'gigantic scheme' was about to take off.

An all-African school, free of both mission and state oversight: nothing quite like it had been tried before. Not only did this initiative dispense completely with all the normal protocols of permission and control but it was also begun at a time of intense imperial conflict, a real problem given its dependence on local goodwill and donations. For the South Africa that the Dubes had returned to just over a year previously, in May 1899, was clearly shaping up for war. For some time, Britain had been impatient to extend its reach beyond its two coastal colonies of the Cape and Natal to the South

African Republic in the Transvaal, for political and strategic considerations as well as the allure of gold wealth. Yet all its efforts to outwit the Republic's President Kruger – most spectacularly the botched, freebooting attempt to foment an anti-Kruger uprising in 1895–6, the so-called Jameson Raid – had so far failed. As military action looked increasingly inevitable through 1899, British officials were doing all they could to cast the Boer government as the aggressor.

This tense atmosphere, combined with an economic recession on the goldfields, prompted almost 100,000 African workers to return to their homesteads all over southern Africa and an equal number of Uitlanders (foreigners, mostly British) to make for the coastal cities of Durban, Port Elizabeth and Cape Town. A few missionaries among them were housed on AZM stations at Amanzimtoti and Inanda. By September 1899 British reinforcements were steaming towards South Africa and the Boers were busy plotting a pre-emptive strike to capture the key port of Durban so that the imperial forces would be prevented from docking. White Natalians, nervous at the best of times, became feverish with anxiety as rumours abounded and people stockpiled food. If ever the term 'settler' was misleading, it was here, where whites constantly felt *un*settled by their tiny numbers – barely a tenth of the Colony's population. Up at Inanda Seminary the teachers and refugees sewed a vast American flag, ready to display their neutrality should the Boers reach the coast.

In October, when war was declared, train services out of the Transvaal abruptly ceased, leaving some 8,000 Zulu workers stranded on the mines. The Natal Native Labour Agent in the Transvaal, J.S. Marwick, accompanied them (and probably scores of criminals turned out of the gaols) on a long march to the Natal border. Exhausted and hungry after their two weeks on the road, the workers arrived at a British military encampment inside Natal only to find themselves fleeced of £1 each to board waiting trains to Durban.

With all these events occupying official attention, the Dubes' return had hardly been noticed as they rejoined mission life at Inanda. It is difficult to know what they felt about the war. In the months just before it began, Jan Smuts had penned a virulently anti-British pamphlet, *Century of wrong.* After presenting a long history of the relations between the Afrikaners and British, he concluded that 'We have been spat on by the enemy, slandered, harried and treated with every possible mark of disdain and contempt [and now face] all the forces which underlie the lust of robbery and the spirit of plunder'. It is of interest that this was much the same language that Dube had used in the American press about the predatory British and their villain-imperialist, Rhodes; there are many similar examples in the writings of contemporary pro-Boers. Equally of interest, since he and Dube so often thought alike, W.C. Wilcox expressed a strongly anti-imperialist position in the American press while on a sojourn there, sufficiently publicised to cause tension between the AZM and the Natal authorities. If John did hold similar feelings at the time of his return, he would have been careful to keep these confined to a tight group of close associates. Of course 'anti-imperialist' and 'pro-Boer' were not always the same thing: as he noted to Harriette Colenso a few years later, the Boers 'are today the enemies of our people'.[1]

The Dubes had set to work immediately; apart from other considerations, the American Committee expected to see rapid progress. Both sides clearly understood that the Americans would lend their wholehearted support but also expected the operation to become self-sustaining as soon as possible. In mid-1899 John had called a conference to announce his plans for a school, 'to teach the hand to work, the brain to understand, and the heart to serve'. Another important stage had been reached later in the year, when he was finally appointed to the post that meant so much to him: the pastorate of the Inanda church. The position had remained vacant ever since the destructive contest of 1896 and the Goba party's animosity had persisted. Even though Dube now seemed a popular choice, his opponents started holding separate services in the Inanda day school, believing that it was totally unacceptable for the pastor to have 'tribal affiliations'. Mqhawe had declared him *umfundisi wamaQadi* – pastor to the Qadi – a title probably enjoyed by his father, James, before him. As a result, Klaas Goba, who was still locked in a contest for power with Mqhawe over the Mission Reserve, felt that the new appointment had nothing to commend him whatever. Stephen Pixley, who continued to live on at Inanda, was not altogether sympathetic to his appointment, either. The congregation's loyalties would continue to be divided and efforts on the part of the AZM to heal the division proved futile. 'It is difficult to see how the man can fill the position of principal of a school and at the same time be an efficient pastor,' worried the AZM hierarchy.

Nevertheless, being in charge of such a prestigious church gave Dube a commanding and respectable position from which to pursue his redemptive mission. African convert communities across southern Africa shared the view of John Knox Bokwe, the senior Xhosa churchman, that the ministry was 'the highest and most exalted work a man can do'. The pastor performed the most solemn rites in a Christian's life, of baptism, communion and marriage; and in the AZM at least, it was a position that elevated him to an equal status with white missionaries in church policy matters. Importantly, it also brought the Dubes a much-needed steady income, so that they did not have to draw on funding raised for their school.

In all respects, Inanda seemed preferable to Incwadi as the site for this new venture. Dube could undertake his church duties, he and Nokutela would be back among friends and family whose support they saw as vital, they would be closer to potential white well-wishers and benefactors, and, most importantly, old Chief Mqhawe had offered them £200 to purchase 200 acres of land locally. This base was to give John Dube a sense of rootedness and continuity throughout his life, which was rare for his generation of leaders, most of whom were forced through economic circumstance to make their homes in big towns and cities far from their birthplaces and kin. Apart from his American years as a student, periods of travel on behalf of the school and other organisations, and one interlude during the First World War, Dube lived his entire life in Inanda. This strong connection centred his very existence, enabling him to participate as a notable and respected son in the day-to-day routines of both chiefdom and mission, and shaping his outlook on all the key issues of the day, from urban problems to land ownership. At the same time it gave him the confidence and capacity to pursue his expansive goals. The school at Incwadi was not neglected, however: John Mdima had continued there as superintendent and Dube visited regularly. The inspector of Native Education praised it as 'an excellent school, spacious and well-ventilated building, children clean, well-behaved and attentive, examination results quite satisfactory' in the same year that work was beginning at Inanda.[2]

Following the foundation ceremony, a small group of workers led by Reynolds Scott quarried stone and built housing for teaching staff, accommodation for boarders and a single large room that served as school, dining area and chapel. John and Nokutela concentrated their efforts on local fundraising as well as on recruiting students. From the outset, they faced a certain amount of scepticism towards their educational ambitions. Some African converts found it difficult to conceive of a school not being attached to a religious denomination on a proper mission station, and wanted to know which one it would be, to which Dube testily replied, 'education has nothing to do with church matters ... I should be glad if your questions would relate to education.' Given his unquestioning Christian commitment (once, shocked on hearing an atheist at Speakers' Corner in Hyde Park, he had declared that it was impossible for Africans *not* to believe in God), this might seem surprising – except what he was chafing against was narrow affiliation, not broad principle. Still disbelieving, some accused him of trying to steal people's money when he asked for donations.

In a pamphlet issued in Zulu in July 1901, he explained how the school was being supported from America and called on parents to enrol their sons – but prefaced all this with a lengthy rebuke of those who failed to show support. 'When a white man starts a thing it is expected he will succeed but when a black man starts anything it is expected he will fail … the reason why white people do not respect us is because we are unable to point to anything distinct which we have done for ourselves by our own energy,' he complained. He would look back on these early years with some resentment: 'Who can fully understand the bitter coldness which was experienced when the one who started the school met people who did not bother themselves about his work?' It was burdensome enough being a leading agent of Christian civilisation without the indignity of having to beg for the means to achieve it. Like Wilcox, he expected his hearers to latch on to the value of his work rather more quickly than they were in reality prepared to do. In 1903, for example, Africans donated a total of £48 to his work. This theme of the failure (as he saw it) of his own people to aid such initiatives and to *think* in terms of self-help would become prominent in his later thought and writings.

The hilltop on which the school started to take shape was named Ohlange, deriving from the term *uhlanga*. Signifying the starting point of new growth, and hence the founder of a lineage or 'stem' of a family, *uhlanga* had, under the very trying conditions of colonial rule in Natal, come to connote 'indigenous people' who claimed a right to the land for themselves and their cattle, as opposed to incoming white and Indian settlers who were trying to snatch it away. (Of course, 'indigenous' is not the same as 'original', since hunter-gatherers had been pushed to the margins in an earlier phase of human migration.) As Joe Matthews told the American researcher Gwendolen Carter in 1964, 'It's a very profound name, "where all nations come together", and [Dube] named it that because he wanted all the peoples to come together there and build a new nation.' So the choice of Ohlange for the ground on which the Tuskegee of South Africa would rise was in complete accord with the sense of race pride, Pan-Africanism and autonomy that Dube had begun to articulate so confidently in the United States, and would have resonated too in the Qadi chiefly circle, where there were deep anxieties about land hunger. In time the school itself would come to be known as Ohlange, though it opened on 26 July 1901 as the Zulu Christian Industrial School. This name was carefully chosen to appeal to potential donors and clearly captured something of the Dubes' vision. While 'Zulu' would be instantly recognisable almost everywhere, in one respect it could be misleading: in his advertisements John had to make it quite plain that he wanted to attract African pupils from all over southern Africa and not just Zulu speakers. In a review of the first two years of operation, he was delighted to report that among the 120 boarders were a few from Lesotho, Gazaland, the Transvaal and Swaziland. Though it began with little and resources were always stretched, this was *uhlanga* on a new design: a modern, self-directing and proudly black community.

The first board of trustees was also deliberately all-African (and, according to the strict mores of the time, all-male) and composed of loyal supporters: Dube himself, John Mdima, Madikane Cele, Chief Mqhawe, and Bryant Cele, a Congregational minister and close relative of Madikane's, who was named after one of Daniel Lindley's sons. The teaching staff was also drawn from a select set (and included women, as was quite proper then), consisting originally of the Dubes; John Mdima, who was brought across from Incwadi to act as head when Dube was away; Reynolds Scott and his new wife, educated at Inanda Seminary; Nancy Dhlula, also a Seminary graduate and wife of Coffee Dhlula, a leading local farmer and storekeeper; and Thomas Koza from Pietermaritzburg. Over the next few years, he would recruit more teachers from well-established Inanda families, not least his own (such as his brother Charles and a cousin of Nokutela's, Richard), and when whites were subsequently added to the board of trustees, they tended to be *amaQadi omhlophe*, like George Hodsdon, George Armstrong and Frank Churchill. In every way, then, the 'Qadi-Christian' support base was as crucial to the early success of the venture as American money. Dube himself was most comfortable with this arrangement; he was never given to cultivating wide circles of contacts, or to confiding in more than a handful of close allies. This was a trait that in time would make some supporters suspicious, and attract accusations of indifference and distrust.

Two of the original staff members had been at St Alban's before its closure in 1896, Thomas Koza and Bryant Cele. Another, Skweleti Nyongwana, would join Ohlange in about 1904. A fourth early staffer from Pietermaritzburg was Robert Grendon. He had been born in the late 1860s in South West Africa (Namibia) to an Irish father and Herero mother. He trained as a teacher at the Anglican Church's Zonnebloem College in Cape Town. While this calling provided his bread, it was as a poet and journalist that he became more widely known, and he soon turned to the world of the black press as an outlet for his poetry. He was inspired by the writings of the eighteenth-century mystic Emanuel Swedenborg, whose most famous literary follower was William Blake. Swedenborg was convinced that the people of Africa were, of all earthly beings, the most spiritually receptive and would thus be the first to experience the New Jerusalem: a reborn church on earth, healing all the religious ruptures and convulsions of the past. It was an idea that was eminently compatible with that of African redemption and regeneration, of Ethiopia stretching out her hands to God – and carried the same ambiguous feelings towards those imperialists who had brought progress to Africa, a necessary stimulus to civilisation but with the inevitable accompaniment of abuse of indigenous inhabitants' rights. Grendon had worked in Kimberley and Uitenhage before becoming headmaster at the Edendale Native Training Institution in Pietermaritzburg in 1900. His most important poetic work, 'Paul Kruger's dream' (a monumental 4,750 lines in length), was published in 1902, a year before he joined Ohlange as head of the School Department in late 1903.[3]

The Dubes aimed to cater for both boys and girls, which departed from the established Natal pattern of single-sex institutions. Beyond this rather radical innovation, they shared with all missionaries a conviction that if their pupils lived on site, they could inculcate a different rhythm of life and its virtuous habits right around the clock. Boys had to learn that, in the modern world they were making, girls had roles to fulfil beyond the physically demanding ones of field and domestic labour. Accordingly, boys were required to take on a large number of chores they previously would have shunned, such as gardening, cleaning their living areas and cooking. In this sense, as one American missionary pointed out, boys gave up their liberty to go to school, whereas girls found it there. In Ohlange's first few years, resources stretched only to catering for boy boarders, who paid £5 a year each for their keep, and shared the various household chores.

There were roughly the same number of day scholars as boarders, who were from the start a mix of girls and boys. Whenever the weather permitted, classes were held outdoors to alleviate space problems, but, even so, some always had to be turned away for want of classroom facilities. The Dubes found this very hard and took on some teaching during the holidays, when the regular pupils went home. Both day scholars and boarders paid for their tuition in labour, not uncommonly three or four hours daily. They cleared ground, grew cereals and vegetables, kept chickens, helped with building work, made desks and beds, repaired ploughs, ground corn and maintained the property. In the circumstances, the industrial side of the school's work, overseen by Reynolds Scott until his departure in 1903, revolved around masonry, bricklaying, carpentry and agriculture, for these were the greatest needs. This was how boarding establishments with meagre resources sustained themselves in poorer communities – all the ones the Dubes had been through themselves, the one they had begun at Incwadi, and all those on both sides of the Atlantic they most admired.

It was not just a matter of practical exigency, though. This mode of operation was indispensable to philosophies of self-help at the time, a sort of training for self-determination of subject peoples across faiths, ideologies and continents. Perhaps too much has been made of the 'industrial' content of such institutions, especially the accusation that they were preparing pupils for subservience in a racially defined social order. The criticism overlooks not only the sheer necessity of practical work caused by shortage of funds, but also the role of physical labour in promoting an ascetic, hard-working and virtuous standard of *impucuko*, or civilisation (literally, 'rubbed smooth'), what pupils actually did with their education, and, most of all, what else schools like this had to offer. Not only was Ohlange a challenge to white control on account of not having any, but it also offered to educate pupils beyond Standard 4, then the highest grade in all but four other African (mission-controlled, state-aided) schools in the Colony. Accordingly, book learning at Ohlange was passionately encouraged: each teacher had responsibility for subjects like arithmetic and English, and even Latin was available.

John Dube was a commanding presence at Ohlange, dominating the campus as Booker Washington dominated Tuskegee. His regime was strict and pupils worked extremely hard. The day began early at 6 am in the fields and workshops, and ended with evening lessons. There were sheaves of rules for every aspect of pupils' conduct towards each other, towards teaching staff, towards their families. Sometimes pupils felt they were not getting enough food, just as John had felt at Adams. In consequence, they did from time to time complain, as had happened at Adams. Albert Luthuli, an early pupil, remembered Dube's response: 'Well, boys, times are hard. Would you like me to return your fees and then you can look after yourselves?' All they could do at mealtimes was to keep one eye open during grace to guard their portions. The requirements of Christian duty were never far from mind and periodically, when the head felt that pupils were too slow in embracing Christianity, they were exposed to the zeal of a revivalist movement, in imitation of the event that had led Dube to his faith. These episodes were usually organised by a visiting evangelist, such as the African American preacher the Rev. S.C. Crutcher, who spent lengthy periods at Ohlange in 1902 and again in 1904. Crutcher was aware that they were operating in a generally hostile environment; back home he had written to the *Freeman*, 'other people not of our race are seeking to keep the American Negro away from the natives'.[4]

Nokutela's special gift to Ohlange was a strong music department, offering both vocal and instrumental classes. She was the one, after all, who had completed a formal course in music education in Brooklyn and, with her outstanding singing talents, had won audiences over to their work wherever they travelled in America. Ohlange was to become justly famous for its musical achievements, particularly under Reuben T. Caluza, though what is never recorded is that this reputation was built on a foundation that Nokutela laid down (she probably taught Caluza). Though it was certainly true that John Dube himself possessed a great deal of practical musical experience, particularly in choral arrangement, this was the field in which Nokutela excelled.

Music was vital in another way in the school's early years. It was clear that local fundraising was going to be far more onerous than the Dubes had imagined. In fact it is little recognised just how much of their time was devoted to this work in the first decade of Ohlange's existence. One of their strategies was to form an adult choir, the Inanda Native Singers, under the direction of Alfred Ncamu, who joined the staff sometime in 1903. The choir appeared in and around Durban, as well as touring northern Natal, Zululand, Johannesburg and other parts of the Transvaal. The Dubes frequently travelled with it so that Nokutela could sing. They would have liked to attract white audiences to their performances in the hope of building up a domestic support group similar to the American Committee. Although a handful of whites did turn out to listen and the choir was appreciated wherever it went, donations were disappointingly small. In 1908 the Dubes would found the Ohlange Choir with a similar objective. The repertoire of both choirs included many original songs that they themselves had composed. These were later gathered together in the path-breaking *Amagama abantu awe mishado, imiququmbelo, utando, nawe mikekelo no kudhlala*, which can be translated as 'Songs of the black people, on marriage, dancing, love, and merriment'. Published under both their names, J.L. Dube and N. Dube, the preface to the collection explained that they wished 'to resuscitate the art of poetic creativity and expertise amongst our countrymen' and 'to bring an end to the bad habit that has been spreading in the Black community, of taking the Lord's music and dancing to it because of a dearth of recreational music'.

A number of influences fed into this work. In addition to Zulu folksong and Christian hymnody (so-called *imusic*), the Dubes had clearly been taken by the American minstrel tradition. Originally, in the early nineteenth century, this involved white performers 'blacking' their faces and, in comedy sketches, acrobatics and song (banjos, tambourines and 'rattling bones' being the standard instruments), cruelly caricaturing black people for predominantly white audiences. After the Civil War, while white troupes continued to parody and lampoon blacks, a rising group of African American performers transformed minstrelsy, still indulging in stereotyping but also powerfully recalling the pain of plantation life in what came to be known as 'Negro spirituals', as well as articulating resistance to racial discrimination. (The term 'Jim Crow', by-word for the system of segregationist laws that emerged in the South after the Civil War, derived from an 1820s 'blackface' song.)

The Virginia Jubilee Singers were the first-ever African American minstrel troupe to visit South Africa, under the leadership of Orpheus McAdoo. He had begun his musical career while a student at Hampton; he and Booker Washington had been classmates. After touring abroad with other companies, he formed his own in 1890. Almost immediately they set out for South Africa, where they undertook two extensive tours, the first lasting until 1892 and the other from 1895 to 1897. Most of their audiences were white but they played to enthusiastic black ones too. It is quite possible that the Dubes saw their show in Pietermaritzburg in 1895, although they would already have been familiar with the genre from their extended stay in the United States. From the early days of Ohlange, 'bone playing and cork-burnt faces were standard musical fare'.

Amagama abantu, then, was the first compilation of secular, non-traditional Zulu songs ever to appear. The musical arrangements were all Nokutela's, while John had charge of the words. There were 31 songs in all, mostly light-hearted in tone and on the theme of personal relationships, such as 'A girl that has no boyfriend will marry a mirage' or 'The absurd Mamyoywana' ('She winks her eyes when she sees a man'). A few dealt with longing or suffering ('We're dying of hunger'; 'I sorely miss my home'). Three of the songs (or anthems, as Veit Erlmann has described this particular form) dealt with the theme of African progress. One called for unity:

Let the whole brown community be of one moulding
Like cement
We say to the Sotho, to the Xhosa, to the Shakan
To the Mozambican, by the Zambezi

Another, called 'Amaqabuqabu' ('Innovations'), urged people to 'Abandon your old ways,/O African,/Progress has arrived'. The third in this group was a song to Ohlange, loosely based on 'Nkosi sikelel' iAfrika'. Others have acknowledged the historical importance of this collection, but have attributed all the credit to John, even though it is the first such collection in which an African woman featured so prominently as co-composer.[5]

Dube also put one of his lifelong passions to use in a more adventurous strategy to raise funds: hunting. All the overlords of the Mzinyathi valley had hunted there (though this was not their sole prerogative; any homestead head could organise a chase). Daniel Lindley named it his 'favourite amusement', James Dube had regularly hunted with Mqhawe and various *amaQadi omhlophe*, and John had been taken along as a child. He mostly hunted edible game such as antelope; some fine specimen heads still adorn the walls of the family home at Inanda. His exempted status allowed him to possess a firearm – he acquired a Remington double-barrel shotgun on one of his trips through London – though there would be moments of tension with the authorities over whether he needed a permit to hold it, and over his gunpowder allocation. According to one biographer, Dumi Zondi, now that he had Ohlange to support, he ventured further afield to Swaziland and even Rhodesia to try his hand at securing ivory and big game.

Financial worries were not the only ones in Ohlange's early years. The school had not been open more than a few weeks when, in the course of his rounds, an African police informer dropped by. He reported to his handlers that 'this man is preaching against the Government. He says that the natives here are not properly treated … and that if [they] will submit themselves to his guidance he will show them how to attain freedom.' He added that Dube was a sympathiser of a breakaway church group calling itself the Zulu Congregational Church, under the leadership of one Bafazini Simungu Shibe. On the same tour of duty, he called in at Esidumbeni in the Maphumulo district and discovered that the Rev. Mvakwendlu Sivetye had invited a few local chiefs, among them Swaimana and Meseni, to 'join John Dube's movement', one object of which was to push for the recognition of Dinuzulu as paramount chief of the Zulu. At his next stop, the outstation of Noodsberg, he heard that all the young boys in the day school were being dispatched to Ohlange.

What sedition was being plotted here? All this smacked ominously of conspiracy: an independent school dangerously advocating freedom, embroiling itself in secessionist churches and Zulu royal politics, and attracting entire day-schools of boys from all over the place. Noodsberg had been the site of one of the earliest splits from the AZM, that of Mbiyana Ngidi in the early 1880s, who had taken his congregation into Zululand to form the Uhlanga Church. Zulu-speaking officials with long memories would have been quick to identify Uhlanga Church with Dube's Ohlange.

But the supposed connection to the Zulu Congregational Church concerned another more recent secession, that of Simungu Shibe from the AZM's Table Mountain mission, near Pietermaritzburg, in 1896. This had been the most serious split so far to face the AZM, since Shibe was a well-known and respected graduate of the Theological Seminary at Amanzimtoti and a popular preacher. His departure resulted from a misunderstanding regarding the constitutional relationship between self-supporting churches and the Congregational Union, which had little relationship with the AZM, except that in this case it had taken over some AZM missions near Pietermaritzburg for a decade-long trial period. The Union had asked for Shibe's removal as preacher, as it found him troublesome (he was active in early political organisations like Funamalungelo and clearly assertive on the issue of African rights). Shibe for his part understood 'self-support' to mean that he was no longer 'under', or answerable to, any body other than his own congregation. Most AZM Christians were sympathetic to his argument and so the AZM itself was most concerned when in early 1898 he had formed the Zulu Congregational Church (ZCC) with the Rev. Sunguzwa Nyuswa, another Amanzimtoti graduate, who headed a faction that had split from the AZM in Johannesburg. Soon the ZCC was claiming wide support on many of the oldest AZM mission stations.

These breakaway churches touched a raw nerve among the colonists, as the AZM's Rev. F. Bridgman noted: 'suspicious of an ulterior motive, the Colonist and his Government have not been found wanting in their denunciation.' The 'Ethiopian movement' was believed to be infusing impressionable minds with distrust of and opposition to whites, and was therefore highly dangerous: it was offering the prospect of privilege without responsibility, of freedom without moral purpose. Natal alone among the colonies and states of southern Africa had forbidden entry to the African Methodist Episcopal Church, the leading African American missionary body, active all over the United States and, from the late 1890s, just beginning work in Africa. Moreover, it had long been law in Natal that all mission stations on state land (that is, in the locations) be supervised by a white resident missionary. Now the government was readying itself to extend this requirement to the mission reserves in order to bring Ethiopian tendencies under control. Missionaries for their part did not much like the Ethiopians either, since it was their flocks that were being stolen. Yet the AZM, as the biggest and most powerful of these, was hotly opposed to the extension of this edict, as it would undermine attempts to build a locally autonomous church. Already, when the government first moved to exert some control over the reserves in 1895, the AZM stayed away from meetings in protest. Now another showdown seemed imminent; the atmosphere was very tense.

As if Dube's involvement with independent churches was not alarming enough, there was the matter of Christians forming alliances with chiefs (and thereby undermining magisterial authority) in order to assert the rights of Cetshwayo's heir. Since the bitter civil wars between rival Zulu factions in the 1880s, Dinuzulu had spent a decade in exile on St Helena, returning to northern Natal at the end of 1897 as an ordinary chief with no special claims to leadership of the Zulu (and only after Natal had squeezed the concession that it be permitted to annex Zululand). Now there was the feared agitation – to reassert his claims as king. And Natal was still at war, under the operation of martial law.

Dube (in the report, called 'John Ndube' – he really was still an unknown to the colonial administration) was hastily arrested on 16 November 1901 and taken before criminal investigation officer Clarke in Pietermaritzburg, where he naturally denied all knowledge of the allegations against him. He was able to explain, quite correctly, that the 'intelligence officer' had got the wrong end of the stick altogether regarding Shibe. In fact, Dube had been making strenuous efforts on behalf of the AZM to bring him back into the fold. Dube and Nyuswa, who was more amenable to return, had helped to broker a deal whereby the ZCC would re-enter the mainstream church, but as a concession all African congregations of the AZM, in Natal and on the Rand, would be known as the African Congregational Church. (This was a move that pleased congregations immensely but had the opposite effect on the Natal authorities, who stopped issuing marriage licences to the African Congregational Church's ordained pastors.) A day had been given to the reconciliation at the semi-annual meeting of the AZM at Adams the previous year, although Shibe himself never rejoined the mainstream church. For the moment, Dube's account of his efforts to heal the split rendered the other accusations against him highly questionable, and the only result of the examination was a police recommendation that educated informers be urgently required to watch him, as the serving ones were 'uncivilised, consequently of little use'. It was an indication of the official lack of certainty as to how to deal with articulate, exempted Africans. In this, his first brush with officialdom, Dube emerged the victor.

He was angry, though, about his night in gaol, blaming 'some of our people' for spreading misleading stories about him. He was especially indignant at the apparent need for an armed policeman patrolling outside his cell. Yet he could no longer doubt that he was an object of attention and knew he would have to contend with informers sending a regular stream of reports to Pietermaritzburg. He liked (according to one of these) to tell his pupils the story of David and Goliath. Metaphorically, it carried a powerful message of a subordinated, heathen people conquering the giant of ignorance and emerging as a self-sufficient Christian society. However, it might also be read as a black challenge to white rule. Dube did not choose to clarify his meaning.

The Criminal Investigation Office and the Minister for Native Affairs realised that in order to stop Dube in his tracks they would need the sort of reliable evidence that was beyond an intelligence officer's capacity to provide. Through 1902, they wondered whether it might be a good idea to collect depositions from pupils when they were home on holiday, away from Dube's influence: this might 'induce a wholesome fear in him'. Though it is doubtful that this was ever done, Dube continued to cause sufficient anxiety to be arrested again under martial law in March 1903, and was taken to his first interview with the Permanent Under-Secretary for Native Affairs, Samuel Olaf Samuelson.

Samuelson had held this post since its creation under the terms of Responsible Government in 1893. Africans had been fearful that the settlers' acquisition of direct political power would do them great harm; they nevertheless hoped that they would be shielded by the provision that the Governor could refer any proposed legislation affecting their interests to London for approval. Accordingly, they generally welcomed Samuelson's appointment, believing he would intercede on their behalf. A fluent Zulu speaker, he came from a well-respected Anglican missionary family on the Natal north coast near Stanger; as a teenager, he had been taken to meet Cetshwayo. He liked to think he was continuing a form of paternalistic rule similar to Theophilus Shepstone's and, as Shepstone before him, he did not much welcome the idea of 'detribalised', educated Africans. At the same time he was circumspect in his dealings with them, especially those exempted from Native Law. Whatever he thought of his role, he fell short of expectations, acquiring the name Vumazonke, 'Agree to everything'. He proved powerless to prevent the rush of restrictive legislation aimed at Africans: despite the supposed safeguard of imperial assent, there were more laws of this kind passed between 1893 and 1901 than in the whole half-century before that. Samuelson had lately been invited to sit on the South African Native Affairs Commission, the first attempt by the victorious British after the South African War to lay down a common policy towards Africans, now that the

Transvaal and Orange Free State were under British control.

This was John Dube's first real experience of dealing with the official colonial mind, an extremely difficult mind to know how to deal with. Here was someone purportedly having African interests at heart but deeply suspicious of what he was up to. Dube had expressed his views about such representatives of colonial authority quite forcefully in the American press (fortunately for him, it is most unlikely that Natal officials knew anything about these), and staying true to his stated principles would surely result in the summary closure of his school. He would have to tread very carefully so as not to offend. It was very uncomfortable. For the moment, the way was smoothed by what they held in common rather than what divided them. Samuelson and Dube had many mutual acquaintances on the north coast, most notably Chief Mqhawe: once again, it was very likely that Dube's close association with one of the most senior hereditary chiefs in the Colony helped his cause significantly. As a result, this meeting served to establish a relationship that, though it would be extremely acrimonious at times, did allow Dube some space in which to continue his activities. (In his support a couple of years later, Samuelson appended to an official minute that Dube was 'Principal of a flourishing Native school at Inanda. He is a respected and well educated person; a relation of the Chief Mqawe and well known in the Colony.')[6]

The very next month, those activities broadened considerably. For on 10 April 1903 there appeared the first edition of *Ilanga lase Natal*, 'Sun of Natal', with the subtitle *Ipepa la Bantu*, 'The black people's paper'. Its motto was taken from Romans chapter 13, verse 12: 'The night is nearly over, the day is almost here. So let us put aside the deeds of darkness and put on the armour of light.' *Ilanga*, which had been registered as a newspaper the previous year, was a four-page weekly under John Dube's editorship: to churchman and educationist he now added the 'skin' of journalist. The first few editions were printed at the International Printing Press, owned by a former teacher from Mumbai, Madanjit Vijavaharik, and based at 113 Grey Street, Durban. Then in June, a press arrived from America and a printing shop was thereby added to the industrial division of Ohlange. Reynolds Scott was put in charge and, when he left, Alfred Ncamu took over. Otherwise it was entirely staffed by Ohlange students. The shop took outside orders too; Dube hoped in time it would be the means of 'bringing into existence a new and enduring literature of the famous Zulu nation'.

Ilanga's columns, mostly in Zulu with some Sesotho (edited by Joel Modise) and English content, were filled with current events, social news, round-ups from the mission stations, court and Legislative Council reports, diaries of upcoming church events, debates from the local white press, letters to the editor and articles on Zulu history. There were snippets from the missionary press in America and items from Britain and other parts of the empire. There were advertisements for local businesses and products. Of course there was plenty of publicity for Ohlange: examination results, appointment of new teachers, fixtures of the soccer team, the arrival of new equipment. The first edition carried an inspirational letter from W.C. Wilcox and another shortly after featured Mr Samuelson's views on how Africans should be governed. *Ilanga* also acted as a significant outlet for new poetry. Robert Grendon, writing as 'Vespertilio', composed a special poem for the new paper:

> The truth seek ever to obey,
> Tho' thou to Falsehood for must be;
> At last thou shalt from out the fray
> Emerge, O SUN, triumphantly.

Ilanga pledged to open the eyes of the people to their own best interests, and it took a strong position on what these were. Throughout its pages, but especially in editorials, was an exhortation to an 'improving Christianity': to gain an education, start a business (and advertise it in *Ilanga*: the first few pages of most contemporary papers were wholly devoted to advertisements and Dube clearly wanted to emulate these), buy land, play an active role in social welfare, petition for rights of citizenship – all in a measured and responsible, yet purposeful, manner. As already noted, this was a time when the Natal authorities were tightening their grip on Christianised and exempted Africans, believing them to present a particular risk to white supremacy. The editor accordingly warned his readers that their task would be immensely difficult: white people (*abelungu*) in Natal seemed to prefer hindering and harassing Africans (*abantu*) to helping them with education or jobs. He frequently railed against blatantly discriminatory official practices, such as the refusal to grant marriage licences to African Congregational Church pastors. In this sense *Ilanga*'s audience was clearly educated, devout, and with marked social aspirations. Yet it waded into bigger debates as well, opposing government interference in mission reserves, supporting moves to make migrant workers' long journeys between their homesteads and the mines easier and safer, and later strenuously resisting the importation of Chinese labour to the gold mines. In calling for the defence of the *uhlanga*, the African nation, by opposing injustice and the regrettable defects of colonial rule, it spoke for literate and illiterate alike.

This was not the first paper aimed at an African readership in Natal. Small numbers would have had access to the Eastern Cape papers *Imvo Zabantsundu* and its more recent rival, *Izwi Labantu*. In Natal itself, the Anglicans had founded *Inkanyiso yase Natal* at St Alban's College in Pietermaritzburg in 1889 – it was the paper in which Dube had had his letter published in 1894. Its greatest efforts were directed towards exposing the legal wilderness in which exempted Africans were forced to wander, released from customary obligations but denied full rights as colonial subjects. Beginning as a monthly, it had by 1896 (when it folded) become a weekly publication. It had given way to *Ipepa lo Hlanga*, founded in 1894, also in Pietermaritzburg, which appeared until 1901 and then after a break until early 1904. Unlike *Inkanyiso*, however, *Ipepa lo Hlanga* was independent: it is another instance of that resolute expression of unity and nationhood, *uhlanga*. It was published by the Zulu Printing and Publishing Company under the ownership of Isaac Mkize and James Majozi, both Christian chiefs, and edited by Mark Radebe, a prominent businessman with premises in Commercial Road in the city. All three of these figures had been instrumental in the formation of the Natal Native Congress in 1900 and, in this sense, *Ipepa lo Hlanga* became its mouthpiece.

In the Cape, with its nonracial (though qualified) franchise, African papers were part-financed by white political interests anxious to capture a vote that was significant in some eastern constituencies, especially in a parliament so small that 'the vote of a single member was equivalent to a dozen votes in the British Parliament'. Thus, Cape liberals supported Jabavu's *Imvo*; when the old alignments of Cape politics were shattered by Rhodes's 1895–6 coup attempt in the Transvaal, Jabavu followed those liberals who moved into an alliance with the more conservative Afrikaner Bond against Rhodes and the pro-British Progressives. Rhodes for his part backed the new paper, *Izwi Labantu*. In turn, *Izwi*, whose leading figures were Alan Kirkland Soga and Walter Rubusana, was closely associated with the formation of the South African Native Congress (SANC) two years later in 1898. Despite the high ambition expressed in its name, the SANC was regional in scope, pulling together the vigilance, educational and improvement associations in the Eastern Cape into a greater effort to protect African land and voting rights, and claimed to be more representative than Jabavu's Imbumba movement. This was clearly a time of awakening, of a perception that tighter organisation and a 'printed voice' to go with it were necessary to defend African interests.

George Hulett had presided over the inaugural meeting of the Natal Native Congress, in the Fynney Memorial Hall, Pietermaritzburg, on 1 June 1900. He was a member of one of the most influential families in Natal's 'sugarocracy', a Verulam-based lawyer and sympathiser with those educated Africans who already held individual title to land (and aspired to accumulate more) and greater civic rights. His presence was meant to mollify likely white hostility to this effort to launch an openly political association. The 60 delegates, all Christians, had effusively declared their loyalty to Britain in its war against the Boers and gave elaborate thanks to Queen Victoria, the British Prime Minister, the British High Commissioner and the Commander of the British forces in South Africa. The meeting declared that membership was open to all, exempted or not, that the Congress would bring grievances to the attention of the authorities and that it wished for representation in parliament by four white members directly elected by exempted Africans. Isaac Mkize had been elected first president, Bryant Cele vice-president, Cornelius Matiwane secretary and J.M. Majozi treasurer. A rules committee, consisting of Stephen Mini, Stephen Mlawu, Mark Radebe and Cornelius Matiwane, was also elected.

It has always been assumed that John Dube was present at this meeting and a founder member of Congress. The scant shreds of evidence we have of the event do not mention his name, and there is a strong possibility that he was not much involved in the organisation in its first few years. Apart from being heavily committed at Inanda and possibly reluctant to act in any way that might upset his American Committee or even Booker Washington (whose support he was still anxious to obtain), he seems to have treated it largely as he had the Funamalungelo: Wesleyan Methodist, tuned into a submissive Victorian worldview, and up-country. Although there were exceptions, such as Martin Lutuli from Groutville and Skweleti Nyongwana from the United Free Church of Scotland Mission – who became Congress president in 1904 when he was already working at Ohlange – it was certainly the case that virtually all of the key figures in the early Congress were Methodists and largely based in Pietermaritzburg or old Wesleyan mission settlements such as Edendale and its offshoot, Driefontein; a few came from the Wesleyan station at Verulam. Dube was not disposed to relate easily to such well-established social networks with their own acknowledged leaders and particular local interests. Moreover, such settlements had been established with the express purpose of providing their inhabitants with access to individually owned plots (Cornelius Matiwane had 124 acres at Verulam, for example), something that the American Zulu Mission was extremely reluctant to entertain, so that aspirant landowners from these stations had to find land elsewhere on the open market. This could possibly have been an additional source of resentment. Some who would prove to be long-standing rivals of Dube's were in this up-country camp, notably Saul Msane. This fault line – coast versus midlands – would persist for decades in the regional congress. (There was one delegate from Inanda, Zacharias Goba, another of Klaas's sons and brother of the Cetywayo who had been Dube's rival for the pastorate in 1895. He was probably still in the anti–Dube camp; tensions had continued to persist. There is a small bit of evidence that Zacharias was close to the secretary, Matiwane: he had named his own son Cornelius.)

This is not to say that Dube failed to share the founders' widest aspirations for representation in parliament or more secure access to land, or had suddenly decided that he was not in favour of a broadly based African redemption. It was more a question of orientation. We cannot know for sure but, given his earlier pronouncements and his practical attempts so far to realise his dreams at Inanda, it is likely that he felt uneasy declaring such excessive support for the British and accepting the role of white intermediaries. Mark Radebe welcomed the delegates to the inaugural meeting with the observation that 'The natives must not rely on themselves too much, but endeavour to enlist the sympathies of English gentlemen'; this would have run quite contrary to Dube's ideals at that time. In addition, he was sensitive to his chiefly patrons when it came to calling for the wholesale privatisation of mission reserves: Mqhawe and most of the Qadi still lived on such lands. He nevertheless did articulate a sympathetic position in early editions of *Ilanga*, but it was not long before he was openly critical of the leadership: 'Is Congress a secret society? I understood it watched for all of us in our troubles and was a Congress which could be relied on. Friends, we perish! And yet you remain perfectly silent as if there is nothing descending on us …' Following the Cape examples, he understood the close connection between controlling a newspaper as a more regular and effective means of communicating his point of view than the infrequent meetings of Congress, and pursuing public ambitions.[7]

A close neighbour of his was thinking along the same sort of lines. Down in the valley below, a settlement bearing remarkable similarities to Ohlange was in the process of being established. It was called Phoenix and its founder was Mohandas Karamchand Gandhi. A London-trained barrister, he had come to Natal in 1893 to handle the court case of a client but decided to stay on to agitate against the discriminatory treatment to which he had been subjected – he was famously ejected from a first-class train carriage at Pietermaritzburg – and which the Indian population at large faced daily. Moreover, there were excellent prospects for a Gujarati-speaking lawyer in Durban. He was founding secretary of the Natal Indian Congress in 1894 and set to petitioning at once for recognition of the rights of Indians as full British subjects. He faced deep hostility from whites who were militantly opposed to any 'coolie' rights: the Natal Law Society tried to block his admission to the Natal Bar, and he was physically roughed up when he returned from India with his family in 1897. As a loyal subject of Empire himself, he pledged his support to Britain at the outbreak of the South African War, and helped to organise a volunteer ambulance corps of over a thousand Indian artisans and indentured workers, which served in some of the bloodiest Natal battles until the arrival of the Red Cross. Believing he could do no more in South Africa, he returned to India in 1901 and set up practice.

But a year later he was summoned back, largely to lead the agitation for an end to the harsh discrimination against Indians in the Transvaal, now that the Boers had been defeated and the British were overhauling its legal framework. 'Our position in the Transvaal is and ought to be infinitely stronger than elsewhere,' he wrote: if a solution to Indians' problems could be achieved in the Transvaal, then Natal would surely follow suit. From this time, his struggle to improve Indians' status would dominate his life, and initiate his 'experiments with truth'. In these experiments, he set himself a series of tasks. The first was to uncover the fundamental values of Eastern civilisation; the second, to investigate whether the virtuous elements of modernity, such as individual freedom, might be dissociated from its dark side, primarily the colonial system and racial and religious intolerance; and the third (if the second *were* possible) was to realise in practice a more harmonious union between Eastern and Western belief.

Though based in Johannesburg, Gandhi resumed his involvement in Natal politics and helped to launch a Durban-based paper, *Indian Opinion*, appearing for the first time on 4 June 1903. Edited by Mansukhlal Nazar, a business agent and secretary of the Natal Indian Congress, it was published by the International Printing Press, which was already producing (but about to lose) *Ilanga*. Staffed largely by volunteers, it was run 'for a cause, not for profit' as Nazar was anxious to stress. Gandhi wrote for nearly every edition, including most editorials; apart from the broader 'cause', it was also vital to his own political ambitions. It struggled to stay afloat, though: its predominantly merchant readers were either unable or unwilling to provide adequate support. By late 1904 finances were in such a chaotic state that Gandhi travelled to Durban to take decisive action. The solution to saving

Indian Opinion was to remove it to the countryside, where the entire operation could be self-supporting. Accordingly, he bought a farm out at Inanda, and within a month a shed had been erected for the press. Each settler-worker was granted a plot on which to grow food and was given assistance in the construction of a simple corrugated-iron dwelling, and each would draw the same salary of £3 a month.

There was more than financial stringency at work here. Gandhi explained the purpose of the Phoenix Settlement in a letter to his close friend and associate Henry Polak: 'Phoenix is intended to be a nursery for producing the right men and right Indians.' This was Gandhi's first *ashram*, intended to show that a different mode of life was possible, a collective endeavour based on respect for manual labour, service, self-sacrifice and self-sufficiency to meet the simplest of human needs, and breaking down the restrictive social taboos between caste, class, religion and gender in a way simply not possible in India. These were the ideas that could be infused from West into East. In addition, the small community was made up of both whites and Indians, living and sharing as equals. Phoenix was therefore as ambitious as Ohlange, but in a very different way. And it was not without its agonies: Hindu women would, for example, sterilise knives and forks used by Muslims at meal-times before they themselves would use them, and Gandhi and his wife Kasturbai had a much-publicised quarrel over her refusal to clean out bed-pans.

Many have wondered – it is undeniably tempting to do so – about the connections between Dube at Ohlange and Gandhi at Phoenix. Some have suggested that Ohlange provided a model for Phoenix; others that Gandhi and Dube knew each other and supported each other's ventures. Family members on both sides believe that the two men were friends. The veteran anti-apartheid activist who headed the UN Centre Against Apartheid and became Assistant Secretary-General, Enuga S. Reddy, has done more than most to connect these two figures, writing of the 'friendship and mutual respect' that developed between them. Another notable instance was *Ahimsa-Ubuntu*, the 1996 stage production devised by the eminent sociologist and activist Fatima Meer, in which Dube and Gandhi shared a platform routine. But it is highly probable that this is speculation born of a more recent political era. One can understand the appeal, and even urgent necessity, of locating deep local roots for a nonracial tradition, especially after the destructive African–Indian violence that twice gripped Durban in the apartheid years after 1948.

While there were striking parallels between Dube and Gandhi and their work, and some coming and going between the two centres in the very early

years of the 1900s, there was little that can be elevated to the symbolism
of a common outlook. There were certain practical hurdles: Gandhi by his
own admission was only ever at Phoenix Settlement for brief periods; Dube
was away with Nokutela on a year-long fundraising trip, from early 1904
to early 1905. More importantly, however, political differences made close
association – not so much between individuals as between causes – at best
difficult and at worst impossible. Almost from the first issue of *Ilanga*, Dube
made regular pronouncements about Indians, and allowed others to do the
same. An early item headed 'The Indian invasion' noted that 'we know by
sad experience how beneath our very eyes our children's bread is taken by
these Asiatics: how whatever little earnings we derive from Europeans, go to
swell the purses of these strangers, with whom we seem obliged to trade …'
Another complained, 'we had land, we mortgaged the same, and now what
once was our heritage is enjoyed by Indians.' The sense of rightful occupiers
threatened with displacement was reinforced by another: correspondents
frequently voiced the belief that Indians were harder-working than they,
which is why they feared the consequences for their race.

Gandhi's struggle, projected through *his* newspaper, sought the acquisition
of civil rights for this very same minority; he too was concerned for *his* race.
He believed that Indians were already more advanced than Africans, capable
of higher-order political action to win their rights, and more deserving of
such rights. For this reason, Gandhi was not at all in favour of interaction with
Africans. As he wrote in 1904 of conditions in certain parts of Johannesburg,
'about the mixing of Kaffirs with the Indians, I confess I feel most strongly.
I think it is very unfair to the Indian population and it is an undue tax on
even the proverbial patience of my countrymen.' Unsurprisingly, there were
no African settlers at Phoenix. Yet while he might object to social contact, he
also spoke out against what he saw as the demeaning treatment of Africans.
For example, he accused the Johannesburg municipality of 'persecution' in
its proposal that African cyclists should wear numbered badges to show they
had permits.

Such observations do not diminish the role that either leader played.
Dube and Gandhi, in their own separate ways, were challenging accepted
gender stereotypes, racial and ethnic boundaries and, above all, the
oppressive nature of imperial rule as they interpreted its effects on their
respective constituencies. Gandhi predicated his struggle on a belief that his
constituents, despite huge internal distinctions of class, language, regional
background and religion, were defined by their national origin and the way
in which they had been slotted into southern African society. They were not

'children of the soil', as he put it, and therefore it followed that the struggles of this minority had to be separate. Moreover, as Gandhi's pronouncement on Johannesburg life indicates, assertions of separateness were frequently born out of experiences of interaction. Those who are most dependent on certain kinds of relationships often resent them most, too: Dube's *Ilanga* simply could not have survived without the regular and loyal support of the Haffejees, Randerees, Glowhoosins and Essops who advertised generously in every edition. The story of Indian and African interdependence in South Africa has yet to be properly told.

These two visionaries were not unusually prejudiced for their times; rather, conservative thought jostled with radical aspirations in both of them. Both wished to uphold standards of decency while at the same time challenging the orthodoxy and offensiveness of colonial rule. To complicate matters, these very colonial conditions produced a situation in which claims for greater rights by one subaltern group seemed to imply an equivalent loss of justice for another. Africans laid claim to rights as 'indigenous' inhabitants, while Indians were treated as lately arrived 'aliens': prior occupation implied greater legitimacy. In the early days of their 'gigantic schemes', therefore, material circumstance as well as their own consciousness held their struggles apart. Relations between Ohlange and Phoenix would improve markedly under Gandhi's son Manilal, although it would be some time yet before their respective struggles transcended their founding limitations and merged into a powerful and insistent movement for freedom.

Gandhi and Dube did encounter each other in late August 1905, in circumstances brought about by Marshall Campbell, a leading politician who considered himself an adviser and friend to both – and, as with many such relationships, the strings attached to friendship sometimes threatened to entangle the recipients. Campbell had arrived in Natal as a small child with the rest of his family in 1850 as so-called Byrne Settlers, the first significant wave of British immigrants to the Colony. His father, William, had become a highly successful sugar producer, and was also an enthusiastic preacher, social reformer and temperance advocate. The son continued all these activities. After initial misfortune, bankrupted because of a bad debt for which he had stood surety, he worked his way up through the industry in the 1880s and 1890s by consolidating central milling operations at Mount Edgecombe, in the heart of Inanda. His company, Natal Estates Ltd, was floated in London in 1895 and gradually bought out most of the neighbouring estates in Inanda: Blackburn, Saccharine Hill, Milkwood Kraal, Effingham and Umtata, all of them associated with the earliest history of sugar production in the Colony.

In addition, he had established the first sugar refinery in 1897, close to the harbour.

Such a prominent entrepreneur would have been expected to exercise influence in public affairs. He had been a member of the Natal Legislative Assembly since 1893, and promoted sugar interests on a number of commissions. With S.O. Samuelson, he had recently represented Natal on the South African Native Affairs Commission; it was this experience that had probably engaged his attention to African politics and progress in a more concerted manner. Quite unlike Samuelson, Campbell was a strong assimilationist, pushing for the break-up of the African locations, the introduction of a single legal system for all, and greater resources to be spent on African education and missionary effort. He did not much like the presence of Indian workers in Natal, but he did employ them on his estates and campaigned for their fairer treatment. He was already a *Qadi mhlophe* because of his acquaintance with Chief Mqhawe (later, under Mqhawe's successor, he extended bridging finance to the Qadi for payments on the farm at Incwadi, and may have started doing this during Mqhawe's chiefship).

A supporter of Ohlange, he visited the school regularly and made cash donations. Dube must have felt that he had acquired the beginnings of a wealthy white circle of patronage, exactly of the sort he needed to win Booker Washington's endorsement. Campbell also took it upon himself to advise both Dube and Gandhi on matters of social progress in these formative days of their public lives. He pressed them both to pursue gradual change, in line with his preference for careful control from a leadership which would maintain order. He favoured moderation in all matters in their newspapers. And he urged separation of advancement on racial lines. For the moment, Dube and Gandhi seemed happy enough with Campbell's tutelage; it did not appear to interfere in any way with either's plans. (Dube later noted that it was 'by his gifts and advice that I was able to carry on'.)

In 1905 the illustrious British Association for the Advancement of Science held its 75th annual conference in South Africa, as a symbolic reassertion of belief in the imperial cause following the devastation of the South African War. It was only the third time in its history that the Association had met outside the British Isles (it had established a tradition dating back to 1831 of meeting in provincial centres such as Hull, Bristol, Liverpool and Plymouth) and the first time it had spread deliberations across a country rather than a single town or city. So full was the programme and so lavish the hospitality of the South African hosts, that the Association's president, Professor Sir George Darwin (a son of Charles Darwin), pronounced it 'the biggest picnic on record'. The entire event attracted a huge amount of publicity, with all the main newspapers prominently covering each session. Formal proceedings had got under way in Cape Town on 16 August, with the 380–odd delegates being treated to two days of learned papers in a wide variety of disciplines, from physics and geography to education and anthropology. The conference then adjourned so that delegates could take excursions through the country en route to Johannesburg, where proceedings would resume. Most took a mail boat to Durban, where, on 23 August, Marshall Campbell hosted them at Mount Edgecombe. A guided tour of the sugar mill was followed by a spectacular display of Zulu dancing (courtesy of Chief Mqhawe and the Qadi) and formal lunch, during which visitors were entertained by Nokutela Dube and the Inanda Native Singers: her 'particularly clear soprano' voice attracted frequent applause.

John Dube and Gandhi were both among the guests. It is a measure of Campbell's confidence in Dube that he was called on to address the assembled delegates, the only African to do so through their entire South African visit. It was possibly one of his most distinguished audiences ever. He rose to the occasion admirably, delivering an excellent and entertaining speech, according to the *Natal Mercury* press report. He regretted the lack of understanding between Africans and their colonial rulers and talked of the higher ideals of which Africans were capable: this was why he had founded his school, 'to put brains into the boys' bodies, and to educate them, especially the young boys, to the idea of the nobility of work'. He could not resist noting that if whites supported such initiatives, rather than burdening Africans with all sorts of taxes, there would be no need to import Indian or Chinese workers: Africans were perfectly capable of similar discipline.

It must have occurred to him that this was a sort of Booker Washington moment: in the heart of the sugar belt, his own 'Deep South', he had succeeded in persuading a highly influential and exclusively white audience (except, as far as we can tell, for Gandhi) of the merit of his approach. There were several 'hear hears' and much applause, and a donation of £60 for Ohlange was assembled on the spot. In his vote of thanks to end the proceedings, Professor Darwin himself declared how impressed he had been. Gandhi likewise was impressed and reported Dube's address in *Indian Opinion*, noting that Dube was a leader 'of whom one should know'. These words were almost prophetic: the tax issue to which Dube had alluded would soon engulf him in controversy and propel him onto a much bigger platform of public and political life. In a matter of months, he would be very well known indeed.[8]

Vukani bantu!

Frustrated by the poor response locally to all their fundraising ventures and the solid refusal of the Natal government to offer any sort of a grant to Ohlange, the Dubes returned to the United States in early 1904 to secure a wider network of support. The American Committee by now very much felt that it had its own Tuskegee in South Africa. Two of its members had paid separate visits to the school and both had filed glowing reports. It had already sent close to $10,000 in cash and kind; Ohlange was almost wholly dependent on the cash for operating as well as capital costs, and donations of equipment, such as an incubator, grist mill and engine, had helped to expand the industrial plant. The Dubes' most pressing need now was for more dormitory accommodation for both boys and girls: round-the-clock tuition was, they felt, the only effective way to inculcate proper ideas and habits in a growing number of pupils.

John Dube must have agonised over the necessity of leaving his two most precious projects, both still in their infancy, in the hands of others. He fell back on his most trusted lieutenant, John Mdima, who was given overall charge of both Ohlange and *Ilanga*. Apart from continuing as head of the academic division of the school, Robert Grendon was given (or just took – it is unclear which) extensive responsibility for the English content of the paper. Dube did contribute material of his own from abroad, but much editorial and other copy was Grendon's. That explains how, over the following year, several articles would appear that 'ran counter to everything for which Dube and his college professedly stood': criticisms of industrial education, for example, and even of William Wilcox, as well as all sorts of declarations of Swedenborgian belief. Grendon was not an easy character, sooner or later falling out with virtually everyone with whom he worked; the moment the Dubes returned in May 1905, he would be dismissed. The experience would do nothing to reduce John's intense dislike of delegating responsibility outside a very tight circle.

By way of compensation, the trip itself was largely successful. After an emotional farewell concert, the Dubes had sailed for Southampton in mid-February. They could not have spent long on their journey north to Liverpool – their contacts were not well developed in England – to join the *Campania*, a regular on the transatlantic route for the Cunard line. They arrived in New York on 19 March and over the following 15 months John spoke and Nokutela sang, just as they had done in 1898–9, in the hope of keeping Ohlange afloat. First, they spent some time in Brooklyn, meeting up with old and new friends and members of the Committee. S. Parkes Cadman, who had lately become pastor of the Central Congregational Church, Brooklyn, was now chair. Cadman had been born in England in 1864 and spent his teens as a coal miner. After graduating from theological college in London, he settled in America and was active in New York's Methodist churches before moving across the bridge to Brooklyn and Congregationalism in 1901. A passionate believer in ecumenism, in later decades he would help to found the Federated Council of Churches in America and become internationally known as a pioneer of radio evangelism. He would also be a prominent religious leader of the American eugenics movement; there was a close fit between liberalism and paternalism in the early twentieth century.

Under Cadman's direction, the American Committee reached a new level of organisation and effectiveness. Not only did it support Ohlange's teachers and campus development, but it also asked supporters to sponsor individual pupils at $30 each, and paid the costs of other Dube relatives and associates to attend college, including Qandeyana Cele, John Mdima and Lindley Seme. Qandeyana, like his brother Mabhelubhelu, attended Slater Industrial School and Hampton; he later married a white American, Julia Smith, before returning to take over his father's mission at Amatata. Lindley graduated with a science doctorate in New York and returned to Inanda, where he led an almost hermit-like existence for the rest of his life.

A.T. Pierson and his son Delavan were also still active on the Committee, and still providing numerous progressive causes with an outlet in *Missionary Review of the World*. In its pages, military intervention as a means to resolve conflict (in South Africa, the Philippines and Europe) was brought into question, there were campaigns for justice for Native and African Americans, condemnations of anti-Semitism, graphic exposés of the extensive abuse of African rubber workers in King Leopold's Congo, and expressions of support for a spirit of independence in African churches in South Africa.

It had already published three articles on Ohlange, two by Wilcox and one by Dube. Dube published another piece in its pages on this trip, comparing and contrasting the experiences of African Americans and black Africans. He noted that the main difference was that while nearly all African Americans grew up under Christian influence, in Africa Christianity had touched only a few places. There were similarities in their experiences, though. Black communities on both sides of the Atlantic faced many obstacles to progress, some of their own making and some caused by whites who wished to hold back any advancement, and there was a sad lack of unity in the face of such challenges. He argued that salvation would come through industrial education and concluded hopefully that 'attempts to keep the black man down will not win ultimately'. It was a position completely consistent with all of his previous published views: criticism of whites' exercise of power, devotion to education and Christianity as the path to progress, and a call to unity.

Another very dedicated member of the American Committee at this time was Sidney Dix Strong, pastor of the Pilgrim Church in Chicago and secretary of the American Board of Commissioners for Foreign Missions. Himself a graduate of Oberlin, he had encountered Dube there many years before, and was now a trustee of the university. In 1903 he led a delegation to South Africa to investigate the progress of the Board's work. During their eight-week tour of the country, he and his associates were warmly received at Inanda. Though not on their official itinerary, they called at Ohlange, where their visit caused much excitement and was celebrated in *Ilanga*. Dube also arranged a special visit to Mqhawe's homestead, where they were similarly treated to a rapturous welcome. Strong's wife had died on the return voyage to Chicago and he wanted to throw himself into a cause to take his mind off his deep loss. That cause was Ohlange, which is how the Dubes came to spend a considerable amount of their time in the Chicago area.[1]

As the Midwest's dominant city, Chicago was a brash, bustling, even chaotic concentration of two million people. From small beginnings as a trading post on the Chicago River where it emptied into Lake Michigan, it had grown as a centre of farm implement manufacture and food processing and packaging. In 1871, the year of Dube's birth, the city suffered a devastating fire and was virtually rebuilt in the years following; it would become known as the home of the skyscraper. Transport was a key theme in the city's history, both in terms of what it produced (Pullman carriages were made here) and of how it expanded. Its growth had been driven largely by a bewildering number of competing transport companies – streetcars, elevated railways and intercity express services, each with its own track, stops and fares. There were so many tracks, in fact, that the central business district became known as 'The Loop'. One visitor in 1900 felt that 'the sky is made of iron, and perpetually growls a rolling thunder. Below are wagons of every size and kind, whose approach cannot be heard in the midst of the noise.'

On the city's outskirts, by contrast, were leafy, select villages like Oak Park, where many of the Midwest's leading philanthropists lived and worshipped. In such places, alcohol was prohibited, churches abounded and 'going out shopping' was unheard of: greengrocers, bakers, ironmongers and the rest delivered everything. Sidney Strong introduced the Dubes to two potential donors, Douglas and Emaroy June Smith. Mrs Smith's father, Frank Thomas June, had been one of the charter members of Oak Park's First Baptist Church. His financial success had been built on manufacturing, first school furniture and then sewing machines. Douglas Smith was also a native of Oak Park and well-to-do entrepreneur (he would in later years make a large fortune as president of the Pepsodent Corporation, the leading toothpaste manufacturer in the United States, but would lose a good chunk of it again on speculative investments). The Smiths had established a fund for foreign mission work; as admirers of Booker Washington, they also supported a number of educational charities for the Chicago poor. They had much in common, then, with those 'self-made', politically conservative and devoutly puritan entrepreneurs on the American Committee who saw it as their duty to foster the same ethos among those whom they considered less developed. The Smiths were sufficiently impressed by the Dubes to agree to fund a dormitory; they would remain important benefactors for many years.

While in Chicago, John and Nokutela may also have visited Hull House, which, like their own Ohlange, was a path-breaking social reform initiative. By far the best-known 'settlement house' in the country, Hull House had been established 15 years earlier by two remarkable women, Jane Addams and Ellen Gates Starr. It embodied the concept of bringing wealthy middle class and urban poor closer together. Residents lived on cooperative lines and volunteers offered cultural and educational opportunities in an effort to alleviate poverty. Hull House had already expanded to cover nearly a whole block of the city, with living quarters, a theatre, nursery, library, day schools, art studios and meeting and club facilities. Thousands participated in its programmes each week.

At some point, the Dubes met up with John's brother Charles and Adelaide Tantsi and may have been present at Charles's graduation in 1904, when his degree was finally conferred on him by Wilberforce's president, Joshua

Jones. He had made a real mark on campus life, as a band master, treasurer of the Sodaban Literary Society and first lieutenant of the Arnett Guards. He had also become very involved with the AME Church, largely through his association with Adelaide, to whom he was now engaged. Perhaps Nokutela and John spoke and sang at Wilberforce, then the foursome visited Hampton. On their travels, they inspired more interest among African Americans, not so much in terms of donations as from those wishing to volunteer to work at Ohlange. However, when, back in Brooklyn in late 1904, John wrote to the Natal authorities asking whether such volunteers would be permitted entry, the response was not encouraging. They feared 'that American Negroes would teach our people racial ill-feeling', he explained somewhat bitterly in a letter to Washington.

There were many speaking and singing engagements on the East Coast towards the end of their stay. At the West Side YMCA in New York, John told his audience of the great benefits that Christianity had brought to African women: 'indeed,' he added, 'I may say it has made men of them.' Reacting to the ripple of puzzled amusement this caused, he explained that English was not his mother tongue and challenged his audience to follow him in Zulu, of which he then gave a demonstration. But this linguistic slip was also an expression, unintended perhaps, of what he considered to be the proper virtues of manliness: an ethos of self-control, hard work, wholesome morality and intellectual discipline, all of which typified his ideal of progress. While women too should aspire to such qualities – hence Dube's remark – these were better played out in support and nurturing roles, as helpmates to their menfolk and mothers of their children.

There was a clear gender division here, with women and men being assigned different roles in the 'civilising mission'. Moreover, the 'ethic of manly action' was strongly conveyed in pursuits from which women were expressly excluded, such as hunting as a leisure activity – one of Dube's loves, as has already been noted. Yet he did not perceive this differentiation as entailing any sense of subordination; in fact, he called it 'mischievous' to consider women intellectually inferior to men. Moreover, the division of roles was somewhat more complex than men expansively occupying public, and women confined to private, domains. Firstly, manliness as ideology denied, or at least suppressed, the sorts of emotions shared by both men *and* women, such as sexual desire. These remained resolutely unspoken. Secondly, it was clear that some women would have to take public, leadership roles to further the cause of progress: Nokutela herself was a case in point. Few African women of her generation had appeared on so many platforms, before so many audiences. Yet, significantly, she took none of the formal positions, or credit for success, that he did; society (and Dube himself) would not accept that. The notion of 'equals' had distinct limitations.

There were also meetings in Boston, the city where John Dube had first tasted American life, at Ruggles Street Baptist Church and then at Tremont Temple. He placed himself in a proud tradition by speaking at Tremont. Over four decades earlier, in December 1860, the great Frederick Douglass and co-abolitionist William Lloyd Garrison had presided over a commemoration there to mark the first anniversary of the execution of John Brown. Brown had raided a federal armoury at Harpers Ferry in Virginia in October 1859, in the hope of obtaining the weaponry to help foment a slave revolt and to free the country, as he saw it, of a 'disastrous way of life'. His attempt failed and he was arrested, tried for treason and hanged in December 1859. It was one of the events that helped to precipitate Civil War. Several Bostonians opposed to the abolitionist cause had disrupted the 1860 Tremont meeting and evicted the participants from the hall, an event captured in a wood engraving by the popular contemporary artist Winslow Homer.

On this trip, the Dubes would certainly have been exposed to the debates sparked by the publication the previous year of W.E.B. Du Bois's *The souls of black folk* (not least because Pierson had already given him a platform in *Missionary Review*). Back in 1895, Du Bois had welcomed Booker Washington's Atlanta speech. Since then, Washington's word had remained dominant on matters to do with the advancement of African Americans; his autobiography, *Up from slavery*, had been published in 1901 and had confirmed his pre-eminent position. But over this period since 1895, Du Bois had embarked on an academic career (he was the first African American PhD graduate from Harvard and in his first post, at Wilberforce, he taught an early group of black South African students) and had given the complex and related issues of leadership, industrial education and racial equality further thought. This collection of his writings examined the separate, subjugated, sorrowful world of African Americans 'within the Veil', as he called it. In one of the essays he used an aphorism that would become his most famous: 'the problem of the twentieth century is the problem of race'.

He also expressed the most overt criticism yet of Washington's social and educational philosophy. Du Bois did not entirely dismiss industrial education or even separate development for African Americans. But he questioned the subservience, gradualism and lack of political engagement that these implied in a Washingtonian scheme of things, and called for a new, more assertive activism in pressing for equal rights and full participation in all walks of life and all types of education. This argument was very close to the one that J.E. Bruce had articulated several years earlier, although Bruce himself tended to think Du Bois too intellectual and elitist. (Bruce by this time had turned his attention to the institutional violence of Southern segregation and the lawless tyranny of lynching, in his book *The blood red record*.) Washington's critics were also growing weary of what Moses calls the 'ironic juxtaposition' of his behaviour towards white and black: dictatorial in the face of any criticism from black quarters and irritatingly servile towards whites.

The Dubes probably followed media coverage of Du Bois's preparations for what would shortly become the Niagara movement. This was the forerunner of the National Association for the Advancement of Colored People, the organisation that over subsequent decades would spearhead the civil rights movement in America. On an international level, Du Bois was also closely identified with the Pan-African movement, in which Dube would later show some interest, although Du Bois's name would be more closely associated with a South African contemporary, Sol Plaatje. A few years later, Dube would give very favourable coverage to *The souls of black folk* in *Ilanga*, but for the moment he did not declare himself too openly. He was still immensely keen to secure Washington's approval for his work in South Africa, believing that this would enhance his own status and facilitate fundraising at home. Yet Washington remained annoyingly reticent, so that when the Dubes returned to Natal in March 1905 they still had no official endorsement from Tuskegee.[2]

There was a very uneasy atmosphere awaiting them back home. The 1899–1902 war had caused an economic boom with its high demand for labour and produce and, as a result, many African households saw their incomes increase. War is not the most dependable stimulus to economic growth, however, and as soon as it ended, recession set in. Jobs were suddenly scarce, wage levels dropped and demand for agricultural goods slumped. The Natal government found itself with mounting public debt and a growing budget deficit, and its response to all this had merely made matters worse for Africans. The Colony's whites, somewhat augmented in number with increased immigration, had moved to consolidate their interests; agriculture in particular emerged as a strong voice. Now encouraged by all sorts of new incentive schemes, farmers began to evict scores of tenants so as to put their land to more productive use. The effect was to intensify land hunger and social distress in most African locations, to which the Minister for Native Affairs, George Leuchars (himself a midlands farmer), seemed impervious. A correspondent in *Ilanga* referred to him as 'a good for nothing Whiteman ... harsh, cruel and remorseless'.

The mission reserves were also targeted. The government had decided that these lands, transferred by deed of trust to missionary bodies decades earlier, were not being used for the purpose intended. Far from creating an amenable pool of Christianised workers acculturated to labour market demand, there was no proper control of inhabitants: some did not pay rent at all, others paid a nominal sum to the mission, white missionaries had withdrawn from various stations and chiefs held sway in many areas. That African pastors were a common sight, especially on American Zulu Mission reserves, was taken as a sign not of success but of weakness. So in 1903, in the face of stiff missionary opposition, control of the reserves had reverted fully to the Natal Native Trust, the body responsible for all African locations in the Colony. The confusion of 'dual authority' shared between magistrates and missionaries would be a thing of the past. At the same time, a punishing new £3 annual rent had been imposed on every hut and house on these reserves; some of it, the government said, would be handed back to the missionary societies for their work.

Since Mqhawe's own homestead and most of his chiefdom were on mission reserve land (it had long spilt over into the adjoining Ndwedwe location too), the new rent was particularly onerous for the Qadi. Mqhawe sent his principal *induna*, Nkisimana, along with his senior councillor, Madikane Cele, to the local magistrate with a blunt message for the Secretary for Native Affairs: neither he nor his people would be paying the £3. And since the government wished to kill him, he would prefer to be transported, hanged or shot. Mqhawe was also in arrears with the supply of men for *isibhalo*, forced labour, despite the magistrate's observation that there were 'large numbers of young men in his tribe who loaf about'. He was also the only chief in the Colony who indicated that he would not assist with the first full census in 1904 (though he did in the end comply with its requirements). These signals of his deep resentment at the mission reserve tax earned public admiration from Harriette Colenso, who thought the old chief was 'doing his duty to the community'.

The American Board asserted that the rent was 'excessive' and a violation of the original purpose of the reserves: many Christians on the mission reserve, like their traditionalist counterparts, were in great difficulty. Scores of widows applied for exemption, some households were forced to sell all their small stock to pay, and many landed in the magistrate's court as debtors. Dube had initially promoted the idea that African pastors should be given assistance from the rent but later, on his return from America and seeing for himself the effects on both his own congregants and traditionalists, he changed his mind, angrily noting, 'What I have seen at Inanda is worse than anything I have seen in Natal. People who could not pay the rent at a given time were taken to court and fined £2.10.0, and if they did not find the money they were compelled to be put in prison, and after they came out they would still have to pay the £3.' He wholeheartedly supported Wilcox, who was implacably opposed to the American Zulu Mission taking any of the tainted money.

The mission reserve rent could not be enforced on those smaller parcels of land inside the reserves, the glebes, which were owned outright by the mission churches. So the way to deal with residents here was to make them feel increasingly hemmed in and deprived of customary rights. The Mission Reserve Supervisor visited the Inanda glebe at the beginning of 1905 and, in a highly confrontational style, warned members of some of the oldest, most respected Christian families – such as the Mdimas, Semes, Mfekas, Gumedes, Gobas and John's mother, Elizabeth – that if their cattle and goats wandered onto the mission reserve, these would be impounded, and that they no longer had any rights to collect firewood in the surrounding bush.

Clearly there was a concerted effort not only to squeeze Africans for more revenue but also to clip the wings of the African middle classes. The rent was introduced at the same time as the painful destruction of those churches on reserve lands that were not under the direct control of white missionaries, including an outstation of the Inanda church under the ordained pastor Jwili Gumede. Naked greed was plainly also a motive: an upbeat government report on Inanda noted that 'the land could easily be used for growing crops of all kinds ... the reserve is very valuable being so close to market', as if no crops were being grown there already.

Now, not many months after the Dubes' return, there was talk of yet another tax: a 'head tax', or poll tax, payable by all the Colony's unmarried adult males, unless already paying hut tax or under indenture. It would therefore include whites, free Indians, Africans living in 'upright' houses and traditionalists who did not yet head their own homesteads (but who had long been expected to contribute towards the annual hut tax). Homestead heads warned that the tax would cause great trouble among their younger men, who were already showing signs of disrespect. Through 1905 there were a number of exceptional weather events – a devastating hail storm, strong gales, heavy snow, followed by a particularly hot summer – all taken as signs of trouble to come. Unsettling rumours spread easily in this oppressive climate; in some areas, homesteads began slaughtering white-coloured fowls and animals. Madikane Cele registered the mood when he told James Stuart in May that 'there is a restlessness in the hearts of all the people. What is now clear is that we shall be done harm, we shall die, we shall be done harm by the government.' Marshall Campbell and even S.O. Samuelson thought the poll tax a step too far, unless the hut tax were to be repealed and *isibhalo* ended. Gandhi, on the other hand, felt that 'a little judicious extra taxation would do no harm' in curbing Africans' idleness and forcing them into more regular work.

The Poll Tax Act, No. 38 of 1905, was passed in August. Knowing the deep disquiet it was causing, it is little wonder that Dube chose to raise this matter in his address to the delegates from the British Association for the Advancement of Science. Campbell himself took a delegation to the Minister for Native Affairs and Dube sought an interview with S.O. Samuelson; he was especially anxious that the over-eighteens attending Ohlange should be exempted from paying. While the Under-Secretary for Native Affairs received him 'cordially', he gave absolutely no ground. Magistrates were required to explain the tax carefully to Africans and advised to stress that it was not racially specific. *Ilanga* reported the scenes in Durban when Stuart, now in his capacity as the city's criminal magistrate, held his meeting. The overwhelming response from the audience of young men was that the government should 'build a large prison to extend from Durban to the Tugela and put us all in it' because they would not pay. *Ilanga* was critical of such an attitude – the paper and its editor were deeply committed to the rule of law – but found just as much fault with the tax itself and with a system that smacked of compulsion, since no proper discussion of the merits and demerits of the law had been allowed. This last issue was more than a procedural matter, for it brought into question the dehumanising attitude of colonial officials. It was, in fact, one of the bitterest grievances voiced by many chiefs: that they had not been permitted any opportunity to deliberate on and reply to the government on the subject of this new tax; they were now treated like nobodies.[3]

Although the poll tax was enforceable only from May 1906, collections were set to begin in January, so that the public purse would contain at least some cash before the end of the 1905 financial year. Mqhawe instructed the Qadi not to pay. By early February, the Ndwedwe magistrate reported that exactly £1 had been collected from them, and the same each for a number of other chiefdoms in his area – and this only because, by his own admission, a few men were 'compelled to pay the tax owing to their being refused outward passes' to work on the mines. Clearly there was a form of passive resistance under way; magistrates across the Colony were similarly faced with sullen nonpayment. Then, on 8 February, on a farm called Trewirgie near Richmond in the Impendhle division south of Pietermaritzburg, the first scuffle and deaths occurred in the series of violent confrontations and retributions that would come to be known as the Zulu or Bhambatha Rebellion, or *Impi yamakhanda*, 'War of the heads', against the poll tax. A police expedition bungled the arrest of a group of men accused of threatening a magistrate the previous day; in the ensuing confusion, two white policemen were killed. The Governor declared martial law the following day as the panicked authorities sent troops to Trewirgie, where they destroyed homesteads, confiscated cattle, arrested many men and summarily shot two of them in public. As the force moved southwards in a wide arc towards Ixopo and the coast at Mthwalume, snuffing out any signs of resistance to the tax, there were reports that men on the Qadi farm at Incwadi, also in Impendhle, were plotting 'concerted action' with chiefs in several divisions.

Dube now had an extremely important role to play in Inanda. First, through the pages of *Ilanga*, he gave a clear message to Christians, though strongly laced with sarcasm:

> here is a splendid opportunity for you despised 'Mission Kaffirs' to prove that your education is a blessing in the Country and not a curse as anti-mission Colonists would make people believe. Pay up your poll tax first, and explain to the people why the Government found it necessary to impose this tax. The Government has not taken the pains to explain to the Chiefs and headmen all about this measure, probably because they were not aware how widespread the opposition to it was.

Then he joined with his brother Africa, now a senior Qadi *induna*, Madikane Cele and others to exert influence in the chiefdom. The poll tax was abhorrent, not least because it was yet another burden payable to a state in which Africans had no representation. Now that it was law, however, it had to be paid. Mqhawe was still chief, but he was old and frail, and his heir Mandlakayise, more combative than his father, had become prominent in the ruling circle. On the same day that martial law was declared, George Armstrong sent his carriage up to Ekumanazeni to fetch Mqhawe for a meeting at his home to resolve the Qadi position. Armstrong was the *Qadi mhlophe* who had known Mqhawe longest and had by this time joined Campbell as a member of the Legislative Assembly. Both Henry Winter, the Minister for Native Affairs, and Samuelson, his Under-Secretary, travelled down from Pietermaritzburg: it was simply unthinkable for a chief of Mqhawe's stature to be disobeying the law. Many senior Qadi attended this meeting, including Mandlakayise, Madikane Cele and Nkisimana. Dube himself was probably among them and in all likelihood helped to arrange the meeting, for this was a critical moment not only in the life of the chiefdom but for Dube's own future: Ohlange and *Ilanga* depended on Mqhawe changing his mind. A large body of followers accompanied their chief, carrying sticks that they refused to put down, and wearing hats that they refused to take off.

Mqhawe himself was ill and in great pain, and Nkisimana did most of the talking on his behalf. He claimed that the chief had not definitely instructed his people not to pay, but he did stress that the magistrate had not explained the tax properly to them. He also recounted the many grievances with which they had to contend, such as the reserve rent, hut and dog taxes, and that the young men, from whom most of the money came for all these payments, said they had no more for a new tax. Winter asked Mqhawe why he had not come personally to his department with these complaints. The chief replied that in order to do so, he would first have been required to make a written request before the local magistrate. Winter denied this was the procedure, but Samuelson had to point out to him that Mqhawe was correct: it was now virtually impossible to approach the Minister's office directly. Both Winter and Samuelson judged that the Qadi were fully informed about the poll tax but nevertheless had to agree to a further meeting with Nkisimana, Mandlakayise and the principal Qadi *izinduna* from Impendhle, Lower Tugela and Maphumulo divisions: Mqhawe was so deeply aggrieved that he would not readily give in. It was only after this second meeting that he was persuaded to drop his resistance, and messages to this effect were conveyed to all sections of the Qadi.

Yet rebellion was spreading elsewhere. In early March, while operations to the south of Durban were still under way, open conflict erupted in several areas bordering the Thukela River, first among Chief Gobizembe's Ntuli people and then among Chief Bhambatha's Zondi. Bhambatha fled across the river to consult with Dinuzulu, regarded by the colonial authorities merely as one among many chiefs, but by many Africans in Natal and Zululand as a princely figurehead, the son of the last Zulu king, a rallying point for resistance against the poll tax. Leaving his family at Dinuzulu's homestead, Bhambatha returned to the Greytown area. After an engagement with a contingent of armed police, he and his rebel force retreated back across the Thukela to the dense bush of Nkandla and Qudeni where, through April and May, they dug in. George Leuchars was in charge of operations in this region and set about a massive onslaught against those chiefdoms thought to be sympathetic to the rebels – shelling homesteads, burning crops, rounding up suspects and confiscating cattle. Among the loyal African participants assisting him was 'A' Squadron of the Natal Native Horse, composed of men from Edendale.

Dube did not take at all kindly to the Edendale levies' participation. It was one thing to pay the tax in order to stay within the law, but quite another to come out against those who were, however foolishly, openly resisting: they did, after all, have deep and real grievances. He thought it better (as apparently did Dinuzulu) not to show any more compliance with colonial authority than was absolutely necessary. As a result, Dube felt more distanced than ever from the 'Edendale element' and thus the Natal Native Congress. This explains the otherwise breathtaking timing of a letter he wrote to Samuelson at the end of March. He desired help, he said, in the formation of 'a Native Congress on a larger scale and under different conditions than the one we have had … it will not be merely a kolwa matter, but we propose to take in all the chiefs and leading men in Natal and Zululand.'

Samuelson consulted the recommendation of the South African Native Affairs Commission, which he had after all helped to produce, that such political associations ought to be encouraged ('public expression being far better than discontented silence'). Probably finding the reminder unpalatable, he referred the matter to the Minister for Native Affairs. The idea of *any* sort of political association, especially one in which Dube was involved and which united chiefs and Christians, was odious to Winter. He issued a quick reply to Dube that this was emphatically not a good idea at the present time, that Africans were not yet qualified to be entrusted with such a level of representation, and that *Ilanga* would have to adopt a far more respectful tone towards the government and 'white race' in general, before any such assistance was forthcoming. Dube's approach did at least show that he felt ready to mount a rival organisation: this was his bid for power, yet he had sought support in quarters where he was least likely to find it. He continued to be critical of whites – in an article on 27 April, for example, he upbraided colonists for depriving Africans of access to land and education. And he did not drop the idea of somehow bringing Christians and chiefs together. Some months later, he requested from Samuelson a list of all the chiefs in Natal and Zululand; Samuelson sent him the relevant sections from the latest Blue Book.

Dube's frustration at the lack of firm leadership from Africans themselves showed in an editorial he wrote for *Ilanga* the very next week, on 4 May. Entitled *Vukani bantu!* – 'Wake up, people!' – it complained of Africans' apparent indifference to their plight. Whereas Indian and coloured people raised money to take their grievances to the British government, Africans did nothing similar. He therefore called on them to collect funds so that they too could send a delegation to highlight matters such as the suffering caused by onerous taxes and rents. Perhaps he thought that such a delegation, though less effective than an organisation, might be more achievable. Officialdom was, however, as offended as it had been at Dube's suggestion of a new congress. The insinuation that Africans ought to go above the heads of the Natal government to seek redress must have rankled; many beyond Natal's borders were questioning its trigger-happy handling of the rebellion. This time he was called before the Governor, Sir Henry McCallum, ironically of course the representative in Natal of the British government, the very body that Dube felt might ease Africans' suffering.

In addition to McCallum, Charles Smythe, the Prime Minister, and S.O. Samuelson were in attendance at the interview on 17 May. While Dube may have been in trouble, few Africans could claim to have this sort of attention from, and access to, the most senior political figures of the day. The Governor explained that it was not one article, but rather an accumulation of articles, that was the problem. Since the start of the rebellion, he had failed to find '*one single loyal sentiment,* or anything to support the Government in the difficult task before it' in *Ilanga*, and that the Zulu content was far worse than the English in this respect. Dube was very measured in his response, indicating that he had no idea that the paper had created such a negative impression. He did add, though, that 'a certain change in my own mind, largely due to what I regard as injustice, perhaps may in large measure have influenced some of my articles unintentionally'. When probed on what this injustice was, Dube replied that it was the indiscriminate confiscation of cattle from those who had not been guilty of rebellion. The Governor claimed that according to 'Bantu custom', rebellion was a collective rather than individual transgression and that all members of a chiefdom should therefore bear the punishment. Dube retorted, 'I expected the English Government to deal more justly with the natives than the Bantu custom would have done,' to which McCallum could only reply that any other method would have been impossible to implement.

Dube was pressed again on why he did not do more to help restore peace to the Colony and gave a very frank account of the sleepless nights he had spent 'trying to think how I could influence my own people not to rebel against the Government but to take the proper course for their rights', and to find ways of bringing Africans' viewpoints to the attention of the legislators. The Governor told him that this amounted to an acknowledgement that he had made a mistake, since this was no time to be discussing legislation. Whites would, when conditions returned to normal, know best how to make laws, 'and I presume you acknowledge we are the ruling race,' he added. The only way he could come out of the discussion in firm control was to pull racial rank and adopt a condescending and slightly threatening tone, for he could not match Dube's sense of argument and reason. Despite the rather intimidating line-up ranged against him at his interview, Dube had not given way at all on the main accusations against him. He was, however, required to print an article in the next edition of *Ilanga*, to make clear that he was loyal and to urge others to behave likewise.

When his apology appeared, he repeated his belief that people should obey the law, said he had not intended any offence, and managed moreover to accuse those who translated his Zulu articles into English of putting the wrong slant on his words (in this matter, he was later backed by an independent expert). He defended his right to express African grievances, 'but I can realise at a time like this we should all refrain from discussing them'. He ended on an equivocal note: 'the attitude of the Government towards us, although by no means perfect, is infinitely better than under our old kings.' This careful construction appeared in English in *Ilanga* on 25 May under the heading 'The Governor rebukes Dube', the wording of which would merely have intensified his readers' sympathy for him. Moreover, the Zulu version, headed 'The Governor and Mafukuzela', omitted one key paragraph containing the most obviously apologetic statements.

There was more official correspondence about this; the Governor was quite determined to demonstrate who was in charge. In what was clearly a case of censorship in a context where, equally clearly, he did not want to shut down *Ilanga* for fear of making a martyr of Dube, McCallum required him to print a new Zulu version, omitting reference to the way in which his work was translated (because it reflected poorly on government functionaries) and withdrawing statements that amounted to a defence of his actions rather than an apology for them. He was also ordered to 'give his readers the information' that the Edendale members of the Natal Native Horse were doing what all loyal Africans should do, fighting for the 'Great White King'. While some African papers elsewhere in the country were critical of Dube's apologetic stance, all this certainly helped to boost *Ilanga*'s circulation in Natal, Zululand and on the Reef.

Between Dube's first printed apology and the required corrections, Bhambatha Zondi and his followers had been ruthlessly flushed out of Mome Gorge in the Nkandla, Bhambatha himself had been killed and decapitated (though some believed he had escaped), hundreds of others lay dead, and McCallum had declared the rebellion at an end. But the Governor was too hasty. Violent conflict erupted again in Maphumulo, one of those divisions bordering the Thukela, as military retributions relating to earlier phases of the rebellion caused growing desperation among Meseni's Qwabe and Ndlovu's Nodunga chiefdoms. In the third week of June, Ndlovu's men attacked a store on the main road through the area, killing one white trader and injuring another. One soldier among the small detachment of troops that arrived to drive off the rebels was also killed. This incident prompted a much larger-scale mobilisation of troops and firepower, from Durban and Pietermaritzburg as well as the Transvaal. Rebels began massing, too, across the Thukela, but they were armed with less effective assegais and sticks.

A relentless onslaught followed against Ndlovu, Meseni and their allies, in which the Qadi *induna* in Maphumulo, Situlumana, and 400 of his men took part. Mqhawe had apparently instructed them to show their loyalty, though some younger men did join the rebels. After a week, Meseni and Ndlovu came out of hiding to give themselves up. 'Mopping up' continued for weeks, laying waste to many northern areas of the Colony; thousands were killed and left homeless. The missionary A.T. Bryant wrote of the 'miles and miles of country, [throughout which] one finds no remaining signs of life save the batches of deserted females and children, huddling together in solitude and bereavement …'. Gandhi, who had assembled a small ambulance corps, was shocked by what he saw in Maphumulo: 'this was no war, but a man-hunt,' he wrote. Most of the wounds to which his corps attended were the result of vicious flogging by troops. His reflections in the field led to him taking the final vow of celibacy, *brahmacharya*, that would underpin much of his commitment to passive resistance for the remainder of his life.

Nor was this the end of the violence. Three of those who had been implicated and injured in the very first incident of the rebellion in Richmond had recovered sufficiently by September to stand trial. Despite protestations from London, they were found guilty and condemned to hang. Many had had enough of this kind of retribution and there were calls from colonists and Africans alike for clemency. Dube added his voice with a poem in *Ilanga* called 'Shwele baba' ('Forgive us, father'). Part praise poem, part prayer, it was addressed to the Governor, asking him to 'display mercy, you of the house of power'. But it was all in vain; McCallum took off for a hunting expedition and the Richmond three were executed.[4]

Mqhawe's intervention in the conflict was his last real exercise of leadership of the Qadi. During the night of 17 November 1906, in his mid-seventies, he passed away at his homestead at Mzinyathi. Madikane Cele, his *insila* of old, Mandlakayise, Nkisimana and Dube himself were with him when he died. In the morning, George Armstrong, Stephen Pixley and teachers from Ohlange and Inanda Seminary were among the first to arrive. Together, these mourners represented the remarkable network of contacts that Mqhawe had created in the long years of his rule. He had virtually rebuilt the chiefdom from the earliest days of the Colony's existence, and to the end remained one of its most senior and respected hereditary chiefs. He had allowed schools and churches among his people, sent his heir abroad to be educated and even bought land, all to introduce progress as a gradual and beneficial process, without losing the habits and customs passed on to him by his forebears. This was why Dube so admired him: Mqhawe's leadership provided exactly the template Dube thought was necessary in order to make the most effective transition from traditionalism to modernity. Madikane, momentarily relinquishing his pastoral duties at his Amatata Mission, took charge of arranging the burial and *ihlambo*, or ritual cleansing, ceremonies at Mqhawe's homestead (although Samuelson expressly forbade the carrying of assegais and the killing of game, normally an integral part of purification). For the funeral itself, attended by hundreds of Qadi, Armstrong provided an elaborate coffin. Dube was among the main speakers, recalling Mqhawe's good deeds, his ability to command respect, his obedience to government.

Obedience to government: this was uppermost in his mind. The consequences of disobedience were devastating, but even obedience was damaging enough. His attitude to those Africans from Edendale and, to a lesser extent, other Wesleyan missions seems to have softened as a result of the fact that there was active Qadi participation in putting down the last wave of rebellion. Further, one of his oldest associates, Mvakwendlu Sivetye, whose Esidumbeni Mission was in the heart of Maphumulo, had also been helpful to the authorities in this final phase, allowing his mission to be used as a temporary military base. Only a minority of mission residents sided with Sivetye, the very one who had called Meseni and other local chiefs together some years previously to discuss a movement to recognise Dinuzulu as paramount chief. The entire episode had been traumatic for such leading Christians and their communities: loyalties had been torn apart by the cause and course of the violence, expressed not least in the pages of *Ilanga*. It was clearly not possible to adhere to a position of minimal compliance as Dube had hoped. The colonial state insisted on more overt signs of allegiance, even if these were extracted under duress. In such circumstances, he seems to have decided that this was no time for weakening the progressive ranks, for he was cooperating with the Natal Native Congress again in the following years, even though the old fault lines remained and would crack open again.

Yet there remained that defiant, independent streak. In the wake of the rebellion, the Governor set up a Native Affairs Commission, composed largely of Natal colonists of a paternalistic leaning, to investigate the causes of the rebellion and to make recommendations for the future governance of the Colony's African population. The Natal Native Congress chose its own representatives to put the Congress case, but Dube was not among them. Instead, he appeared before the commissioners with other African witnesses from Inanda on 5 April 1907. It was his first experience of such a commission; he could not fail to have noticed that while white witnesses were heard singly, African ones, whether traditionalists or Christians, were heard in groups. He made it very clear that he was speaking on his own account. Unlike his peers and despite the fact that he had an impressive command of English, he chose to give his evidence in Zulu.

In his lengthy testimony, he raised a number of specific complaints: the legal limbo into which exempted Africans were pushed, the difficulties of acquiring private land, the lack of government support for industrial education, the mission reserve rent, the obstacles to mission work in the locations, the need for a cautious phasing out of polygamy and *lobolo*. Asked about Ethiopianism, which many whites thought underlay the rebellion, Dube claimed, somewhat disingenuously, not to know much about it and distanced himself from it (mentioning Booth as one who had tried to preach it) by pointing out that the vast majority of African Christians had been on the side of the government.

But there was one dominant theme running through much of his evidence: the very survival of African people, he felt, was at stake. He dwelt at length on the problem ('evil', he called it) of white men, especially policemen in outlying stations, 'using their authority to carry out their lustful desires' in seducing young African women, and criticised a system in which complaints against such practices often resulted in punishment of the plaintiff in the magistrates' courts. He noted that the government treated Indian and coloured people 'in a far more considerate manner' than it did Africans and came back to that old sore point: Indians had 'usurped' the position of Africans, and if they continued to be brought into Natal, 'aboriginal natives would go to the wall'. He felt that Africans ought to be employed on the sugar and tea estates, and suggested that there should be an apprenticeship system for young African men for this purpose. He was clear that the root cause of all these troubles was the attitude of whites. Some whites 'would sooner beat their native servants than their dogs', and those whites who did try to be fair were ostracised by their fellows. Moreover, whites, who were supposed to be enlightened, refused to appoint educated Africans to clerical positions in public offices, preferring 'raw natives' or Indians. Such practices, he said, 'aroused feelings of hatred in the native'.

These were strong words, more discordant in tone than those of other African witnesses. Yet anxiety followed assertiveness: when the commission's *Minutes of Evidence*, along with its *Report*, were published a few months later, he began to worry about the effects of what he had said. Once again he felt that the English translation was poor, but in a rather anxious letter to Booker Washington he noted reassuringly that

> you may regard me as a political agitator … but I am sure if you knew me, you would know that I am not in the habit of speaking as I did upon that occasion. Things had gone so bad, that I as one of the leaders of the people felt it my duty to speak the whole truth. You will be interested to know that I am better respected by the authorities for that reason; for they had come to a point in their rule of the natives when they wanted to know how the natives felt.

He reiterated the point that 'They want our ignorant people to stay in their heathen condition so that they can only use them as beasts of burden. Those who aspire to something higher are not wanted.' (He made a similar observation in an article for *Missionary Review of the World* at this time: 'Ever since responsible government was granted to Natal, there has been an absence of proper consideration for the natives.')

He was pleased, however, to report to Washington that the Minister for Native Affairs had offered to investigate hiring an agricultural instructor for Ohlange. This was part of a slightly more conciliatory approach to African administration, as recommended by the Native Affairs Commission. Another indication of this was the appointment of a new Governor, Sir Matthew Nathan, in September 1907. Nathan had already served terms in Sierra Leone, Gold Coast and Hong Kong, but his experience helped little in Natal. His criticism of practices such as excessive labour control, as well as his mild attempts at reform, did not go down well with most colonists; he would not last long. Probably through the offices of Marshall Campbell, Nathan agreed to open the new June Building in November 1907. In imperial terms, this was a great honour for the Dubes and all who had worked so hard to develop the school, and helped to establish Ohlange as a 'must see' place for visiting dignitaries. F.R. Moor, who had succeeded Smythe as Prime Minister, even donated an ox for the feast. The Ohlange choir sang a special song in Nathan's honour, 'We welcome you our Supreme Chief/For your feet you have placed here'. Yet Dube could not resist a reminder that it had been American assistance that had enabled the new classrooms and dormitory to be built in the first place, and in a gesture bound to recall Britain's defeat in the American War of Independence, he had the band play 'Yankee Doodle' as the Governor's party arrived.

One notable feature of his statements to the commission had been their concentration on the day-to-day, lived experiences of African people. Yet at the same time, he was putting forward a more messianic, and narrowly ethnic, approach to the way in which salvation would be delivered. Another of his articles had appeared in the *Missionary Review of the World* in May 1907. In it, he wrote,

> Prior to the advent of the white man the Zulus were the dominant race south of the great Zambezi. Today they are intellectually superior to many of the tribes of South Africa, but apart from being specially gifted they have been providentially watched over as their geographical position forces upon them an association with the white man and his civilisation more intimate than that of any other native people in South Africa ... As the Zulus were conquerors and leaders of the native tribes of South Africa in physical warfare, has not God ordained that they shall conquer the same tribes by peaceful methods and lead them to industrial, intellectual and spiritual advancement?

This is strongly redolent of his earlier observations about the providence of slavery, that even though the slaves' suffering had been intense, their civilisation had been more thoroughgoing. While he and Nokutela had been happy to stress their Zulu affiliations in their earlier fundraising efforts across America, and he had long connected himself to the royal line, his elaboration of a special role for the Zulu people as a whole in the deliverance of all Africans took all this to a new level. Was it just another angle in his pitch for funds, or was there something more significant to it? In an obvious sense, of course, there is no conflict in these statements and writings, since in practice virtually all the people whom he included in his 'aboriginal native' category were Zulu speakers. Zulu and *uhlanga* were one and the same. In another sense, however, this preordained role for the Zulu does seem to run counter to his more broadly based commitment to redemption and race pride, to opening Ohlange to all Africans, and to his own observation that it was a welcome sign of progress that 'tribal antagonisms are dying down'.

For the few writers who have attempted to understand these apparent contradictions, they are manifestations of early nation-building efforts on the part of Zulu-speaking intellectuals. Especially for those based in the 'melting pot' of the Witwatersrand, an appeal to cultural symbolism represented a bid for control of the process. Back in the region itself, something similar was occurring for slightly different reasons. Christian communities, battered by hostile colonial legislation and shocked by the government's response to the rebellion, were seeking new political allies: 'in one direction lay the possibility of a nationalist alliance with similar groups in other regions of South Africa. In another, lay the possibility of an ethnic alliance with Zulu royalists north of the Thukela.' Dube was prepared to consider both possibilities, although perhaps there were more than two such ways forward. His aspiration to bring Christian and traditionalist leaders together, as voiced in his letter to Samuelson (and in ways he was already highly skilled at effecting), did not necessarily rest on an ethnically exclusive approach. In fact, the more broadly based nationalist politics of a later phase incorporated this very type of alliance. At this stage, then, Dube was keeping a number of options open. Whether these were sharply contradictory, or could coexist in an ambiguous assemblage, remained to be seen.

He did form much stronger bonds with Dinuzulu at this time. Those biographers who were closest to Dube – Nxaba, Dhlomo and Zondi – all point out that he and Dinuzulu belonged to the same age-set, the Mbokodwebomvu ('Grinding stone red with blood'; also called inHlansi, 'The spark'). Though such age-sets, or *amabutho*, had been stripped of their military significance in 1879, Dinuzulu had enrolled a few new ones, 'the names to be assumed by all such Zulu youths as appeared to fit the age'. He had probably formed the Mbokodwebomvu just prior to his departure for St Helena in the late 1880s, when Dube was at school at Adams or possibly in America. As noted of this time, Dube was already identifying himself as a member of the Zulu line and did choose to reproduce an imposing image of Dinuzulu's father, Cetshwayo, in his first publication, *A talk upon my native land*. It could be, therefore, that membership of the same age-set helped to strengthen his sense of connection even then, but it probably grew in significance in these later, post-rebellion years when such relations were again in need of repair after another destructive military conflict.

Dube's connections with Dinuzulu seem to have fitted into a wider set between the Qadi and the uSuthu leadership. Each hint in surviving sources about these associations might seem slight on its own, but together they suggest close and ongoing contact, particularly since Dinuzulu's return from exile in 1898. In that year, Situlumana reported from Maphumulo that he had received word that Dinuzulu wished to appoint Mqhawe as his *induna* over the whole of Natal. The most senior Qadi *induna*, Nkisimana, confirmed that during Mqhawe's time there had been much coming and going between the Qadi and uSuthu. This proposal of a special role for Mqhawe had apparently divided opinion in the Qadi ruling group; it had been the 'dressed people' – Christians – associated with the Qadi, together with some senior *izinduna*, who were most in favour. In any event, no decision had been reached and the matter faded away without further discussion or resolution. This could well complement Mvakwendlu Sivetye's attempts to garner support for Dinuzulu in the early 1900s. He and Dube after all were 'dressed people' and, though Sivetye was not a Qadi, his closeness to Dube may very well suggest that the two had some common purpose.

Then, soon after Ohlange opened, there were reports that Dinuzulu had sent at least one pupil, Makaza Dhlamini, to attend. The news that Mqhawe had assisted Dube to set up a school in which the government played no role whatever would have spread rapidly among chiefs and been a great talking point, so it is hardly surprising that the uSuthu might have been eager for information on this striking development. If there was indeed any truth in the report, it would have afforded another opportunity for continuous contact between Ohlange and Nongoma. A few years later, in September 1905, Dube and Dinuzulu had both been invited to the Zulu Orthography Conference in Durban by the convener, William Wilcox. Skweleti Nyongwana and Harriette Colenso were also among the delegates. Given the increasingly tense atmosphere at the time, it is hard to imagine that discussions between them were confined to orthography. Finally, in the first days of the rebellion, Dube linked 'Dinuzulu, Mqhawe and Mafukuzela' [i.e. himself] as being falsely credited with possessing magical powers and accused of fomenting rebellion.

Apart from his public declaration of an association with the prince, this news item points to the widely held suspicion, especially on the part of whites, that Dinuzulu had been behind the poll tax resistance. He was also believed to have been responsible for a rash of assassinations of loyal chiefs afterwards, in reality committed by embittered rebels who were wandering the hills, unable to return to their homesteads for fear of arrest. Dube used his paper tirelessly to refute such allegations and to proclaim Dinuzulu's innocence. Accordingly, he welcomed the news that Dinuzulu would visit the Governor in Pietermaritzburg in May 1907, in an attempt to prove his loyalty (albeit reluctantly: he was deeply embittered by the actions of the Natal authorities towards him). Dube was in the capital to meet the delegation, which was accompanied by Sir Charles Saunders, the Commissioner for Native Affairs in Zululand. Dube held extensive talks with both Mankulumana, Dinuzulu's principal *induna*, and the prince himself. The fact that he felt at liberty to describe personal details for his readers – such as Dinuzulu's expensive attire, his stoutness and buffalo-like neck – indicates the intimacy between them. After the formal meeting, Dinuzulu and his considerable entourage (which now included Harriette and Agnes Colenso, who continued to be the most indefatigable supporters of the Zulu royal house in its struggle against decimation) proceeded to Durban. Dube was once more on hand to record every detail for *Ilanga*'s readers, including the response of ordinary Africans when word leaked out that Dinuzulu was in town – large crowds gathered, shouting '*Bayede!*', the royal salute, in the hope of catching a glimpse of him out shopping, but he was whisked away so as to avoid any public disturbance.

Despite Dube's certainty that Dinuzulu had succeeded in clearing his name, this was not to be the end of the matter. Later in 1907, Siyekiwe, Bhambatha's wife, and Mangathi kaGodide, one of his most senior commanders, both gave sworn statements before magistrates to the effect that Dinuzulu had encouraged Bhambatha to fight and was still hiding some of the rebels. Still determined on a showdown with Dinuzulu, the colonial government turned this evidence, flimsy though it was, into a pretext for the declaration of martial law in Zululand in early December. Dinuzulu's arrest was obviously imminent; there was fresh nervousness that there would be more destructive violence. As Natal troops moved northwards once more, intense rumours circulated in Inanda that they were coming for Dube and Mandlakayise. As Dube wrote in reply to Marshall Campbell's anxious request for clarity, local people could not understand why soldiers were coming to a peaceful place 'when the Boers are in open rebellion in the Free State and the Transvaal'. However, he also offered the confident reassurance that 'so long as I have influence in this district nothing of a serious nature, other than idle rumours, will ever take place'.

At the same time, he wrote a letter to Dinuzulu. Addressed to 'Wena kaCetshwayo, Mbokodwe ebomvu!' ('You, son of Cetshwayo, of the Mbokodwebomvu regiment!'), it warned the prince against listening to those who advised him to resist arrest, for they wished to destroy him. Instead he advised, 'Come out openly and give yourself to Sir Charles Saunders ... the scoundrels that are among the whites will stir up dust with you always, lying, until it really will appear to be the truth that you have something to hide. Work with the Government, nothing bad will happen to you.' Harriette Colenso

The many sources of influence in the Qadi ruling group: a composite image showing (from left) James Dube, Chief Mqhawe and his servant/adviser, the Rev. Madikane Cele. (Campbell Collections, University of KwaZulu-Natal)

The Inanda church, where James Dube was ordained and John Dube served as pastor in the early 1900s. (Campbell Collections, University of KwaZulu-Natal)

An illustrious tradition: the illustrations in John Dube's first publication, A talk upon my native land: *a youthful photograph of the author and line drawings of James Dube and King Cetshwayo.*

Nokutela Dube in the late 1890s. *(Cherif Keita)*

William Cullen Wilcox, John Dube's mentor. *(Cherif Keita)*

Charles and Adelaide Dube and their children Sadie and Frederick.

John Mdima, dedicated helper to the Dubes. *(Campbell Collections, University of KwaZulu-Natal)*

One of Nokutela Dube's early needlework classes at Ohlange; she is standing on the right.

An early shoemaking class at Ohlange. John Dube is on the far right.

The Boys' Building at Ohlange, built with American donations and opened in 1907 by the Governor of Natal, Sir Matthew Nathan.

The Girls' Building at Ohlange, built with American donations and opened by the Governor-General of South Africa, Viscount Buxton, in 1917.

The 1914 Congress delegation to Britain: (from left) Thomas Mapikela, Walter Rubusana, John Dube, Saul Msane and Solomon Plaatje. (Historical Papers, William Cullen Library, University of the Witwatersrand)

Solomon kaDinuzulu on his 1927 visit to Inanda Seminary, pictured with the principal, Margaret Walbridge. (Campbell Collections, University of KwaZulu-Natal)

John and Angelina Dube with their children in the mid-1930s: (from left) Nomagugu, Joan Lulu, James Sipho and Douglas Sobantu. (Campbell Collections, University of KwaZulu-Natal)

John Dube receives his Honorary PhD at Inanda, 1937. William Campbell is addressing the crowd. (Campbell Collections, University of KwaZulu-Natal)

From left, the Rev. Posselt Gumede, pastor of Inanda, Chief Albert Luthuli and John Dube in the late 1930s. (Mwelela Cele)

John Dube's grave at Ohlange. (Heather Hughes)

made a similar appeal to Dinuzulu; when troops arrived at Nongoma, he surrendered without question.

There were a number of preliminary trials to be heard before Dinuzulu's got under way in Greytown in November 1908. He was charged with 23 counts of treason. It was largely due to the efforts of the Colenso sisters, especially once again Harriette, that he was given a fair hearing, with an impartial judge from outside Natal, strong defence counsel in the form of the Cambridge-trained barrister and ex-Prime Minister of the Cape, W.P. Schreiner, and plenty of witnesses. Dube drew much closer to the Colensos over the matter of funding the defence – the two sisters never really recovered financially, and it was onerous enough for him, given his responsibilities towards keeping Ohlange going. He informed Harriette that he had 'privately started' a movement in Durban among the town's African population to collect money. There was, of course, extensive trial coverage in *Ilanga*. In the end, Dinuzulu was cleared of all but three rather minor offences: harbouring rebels, allowing Bhambatha and his family to stay with him, and not reporting their visit. He was sentenced to a fine and four years' imprisonment. This was not as harsh as it might have been but was still a great deal more severe than the 'nothing will happen to you' that Dube had clearly anticipated.[5]

In addition to the considerable support he lent to Dinuzulu, Dube was simultaneously pursuing more broadly based alliances both in Natal and across other regions of South Africa. He and Wilcox launched a Zulu Industrial Improvement Company in 1908. A cross between Joseph Booth's African Christian Union of a decade earlier and Booker Washington's National Negro Business League, founded in 1900, its aim was the acquisition of land and the provision of industrial training. It hoped to support struggling African farmers, traders, artisans and the like who were trying to defend themselves 'against the exposure of total hire', by offering them a secure base from which to launch themselves as entrepreneurs. This was one of a number of such self-help schemes appearing at this time and later, too – the Natal Native Congress had started one the year before, called Isivivane. Their motives were understandable – if anything, the appeal of a livelihood independent of white employers grew stronger as whites tightened their grip on power – but they were hopelessly undercapitalised. The task of raising large sums for land purchase defeated nearly every attempt; Dube's and Wilcox's goal was a massive £50,000, to be secured through share subscriptions. Thus, while their venture was announced with great fanfare in *Ilanga*, and Wilcox worked with his characteristic enthusiasm to find backers, it failed to garner the necessary support. It showed promise for a time, then faltered and finally had to be wound up in the 1920s.

Another of Dube's cross-country initiatives at this time was the attempt to revive a Native Press Association. Across the four South African colonies, independent African papers shared a generally precarious existence. Hampered by small circulation, lack of equipment and inadequate staff, they were also denied access to the increasingly organised British imperial system of gathering and distributing news. They compensated by exchanging copies and quoting each other. In 1903 Sol Plaatje, editor of *Koranta ea Becoana*, had initiated an attempt to launch a proper press agency. Willan speculates that he may have been inspired by J.E. Bruce; Plaatje, like Dube, had been in touch with him. Alan Soga, editor of *Izwi Labantu*, was chosen to lead the Association and Plaatje became its secretary. Most other editors joined, but there was one exception: the senior newspaperman of his day, John Tengo Jabavu, still presiding over *Imvo Zabantsundu*. The same lack of resources that had led to the formation of the Association also crippled its operations and it folded after a year.

Yet the need to try to improve conditions for the independent African press persisted. In 1908 Dube was active in trying to resuscitate the Association, to present, as he explained, 'a united front by [ex]change of articles on important questions affecting our people'. Soga was supportive, as were F.Z.S. Peregrino, the Ghanaian-born editor of the *South African Spectator* in Cape Town, and the editor of Mafeteng-based *Naledi ea Lesotho*, who had put out a very specific call for press unity. Jabavu, however, remained hostile, much to Dube's annoyance. Not only did this prevent unity but, worse, Jabavu 'favours the Boer Party in politics and we native people have been badly treated by the Boers'. More to the point was that Plaatje's *Koranta*, Soga's *Izwi* and Peregrino's *Spectator* were all facing severe financial difficulties. Dube made a trip to the Cape on this matter, probably (as always) combined with seeking funds for Ohlange, but nothing came of his efforts on behalf of a press agency.

A growing commitment to broader issues and interests was bound to result in some disengagement from local ones. The first casualty was his pastorate of the Inanda church. He had offered to give this up in 1907, but his congregation had invested so much in his incumbency and was reluctant to see him go. A year later, however, 'having given nominal service until his salary has dwindled to a nominal amount', Dube bowed to pressure from his peers and resigned. Local disappointment was such that it took almost four years to appoint his successor, the candidate who had been waiting in the wings all that time, the Rev. Cetywayo Goba. Dube's resignation signified a parting of the ways with the American Zulu Mission in more ways than one, for he was becoming increasingly vociferous about white missionaries' lack of support for African advancement: despite his claims to defend their achievements, *Ilanga* had called for a walk-out from the African Congregational Church in 1907.

He was growing apart from the Qadi ruling circle, too. Mandlakayise had been appointed Qadi chief in an acting capacity only, which annoyed him intensely and reinforced a tendency to adopt a far more insular approach to Qadi interests than his father had done. To compound matters, Dube had begun to purchase land in the vicinity of the school, something he seems to have resisted in Mqhawe's lifetime, out of deference to the old chief. Mandlakayise objected fiercely, summoning Dube to explain why he had 'gone behind his back' to buy land. The effect of such tensions was that Dube seems to have been relegated to a lesser role in the chiefdom's affairs.

Closer to his immediate interests, there were now able, willing and trusted individuals to shoulder more of the day-to-day Inanda operations. His brother Charles and fiancée Adelaide Tantsi, who had returned from America with John and Nokutela, had married in Johannesburg late in 1905 before taking up teaching posts at Ohlange. Adelaide had given birth to their first child, Tokozile Sadie, in 1907, while Charles had risen rapidly to the headship of the school. (Dube continued all this time, and for many years after, to be styled 'Principal', while Charles was called 'Headmaster'.) This meant that John Mdima was slightly displaced but continued in a senior position at Ohlange and to lend valuable support to the Dubes. (Among the very first photos to be published in *Ilanga* a few years later were those of Charles Dube and his family, and John Mdima.) Skweleti Nyongwana, who had been working on the paper almost since its inception, now took increasing charge of editorial matters. He had for some months been in the employ of Ralph Tatham, an attorney with socialist sympathies who was anxious to expand his business among Africans. Nyongwana and Dube had entered into a disastrous agreement with Tatham in early 1907, whereby Tatham would purchase half the plant and assets of *Ilanga* for £300. In return the two of them would help him with his business affairs – including, apparently, introducing him to Dinuzulu. Nyongwana signed a new contract with Tatham, but Dube got cold feet over the *Ilanga* deal, upon which Tatham dismissed Nyongwana. It all ended in court in July 1907, with Nyongwana suing Tatham for moneys owing and damages incurred as a result of his failure to honour their contract. The proceedings revealed that Tatham was in fact in acute financial difficulty. Dube gave evidence for the plaintiff, who was awarded some back pay. The judge commented that he thought Tatham's contract 'distinctly harsh and one-sided'.[6]

Dube remained fiercely committed to both Ohlange and *Ilanga* as living symbols of what Africans could achieve by and for themselves. Yet precisely because he had earned a reputation as an outspoken editor and successful educationist, there was a growing expectation that he could not continue to hide at Inanda, that he would have to be drawn into wider, more explicitly political involvements. The dilemma for him was that some of Ohlange's most valued supporters were determined that he should resist such attractions. There would be some difficult decisions ahead.

Playing with fire

The Bhambatha Rebellion had pushed John Dube to prominence in more ways than one. He had spoken out against the unjustness of so many aspects of the episode – the poll tax, the lack of consultation, the refusal to heed Africans' warnings about their distress, the vicious behaviour of troops, and picking on Dinuzulu as the ostensible cause rather than reflecting on deficiencies in policy. He had also, in the face of all the destructive bitterness, called for greater unity of African voices in Natal and beyond: this was the only way that they could defend their interests in anything like an effective manner. There was a certain urgency to this. The time was one not only of political adjustment in Natal in the wake of the rebellion, but of dramatic constitutional development across the four colonies of South Africa, as Britain urged them towards closer union. It looked as if Africans would be completely omitted from both of these processes, objects rather than agents of change. His attempts to revive the Native Press Association need to be seen in this light.

Dube's first act of leadership of an overtly political campaign was against Natal's Native Administration Bills in the middle of 1908. Three bills had been published in the *Government Gazette* on 21 April, all concerned with the administration of African affairs, and all ostensibly based on the recommendations of the Native Affairs Commission. Dube must have been heartened by some of these recommendations when they had appeared the previous year, since they had formed key points of his evidence: police outstations should be withdrawn, educated Africans should be employed in clerical positions in the public service, and government should stop the physical dismantling of churches not under the control of a white missionary. Others would have accorded with his own opinions, too, such as that chiefs should be more adequately informed of intended legislation affecting them and that arbitrary arrests, handcuffing and flogging should cease. In general, the commissioners wished to see a more efficient and considerate form of administration for Natal Africans. The draft legislation, however, fell far short of expectations. The first bill allowed for four extra white members in the legislature, who would represent African interests. The second, and key, bill provided for the employment of four new Native Commissioners to oversee the work of magistrates. They would have similar powers to the Supreme Chief and would therefore in effect be above the law. These officers, together with a new permanent Secretary for Native Affairs and four nominated individuals, all white of course, would sit on a new Native Council with legislative powers, subject to parliamentary veto. The third bill concerned closer control of African settlement in locations. This was the government's answer to a more efficient system, virtually none of it based on the commission's recommendations. Even S.O. Samuelson was disappointed, and resigned as Under-Secretary.

Within days of publication of the bills, the Natal Native Congress organised a meeting in Pietermaritzburg to frame its response. Its leaders sought an interview with the Minister for Native Affairs to express their deep misgivings, but he counselled them to take more time to consider. So Congress organised meetings across Natal, to which both traditionalists and Christians were invited. The outcome of all these was a large gathering in Pietermaritzburg in early June, attended by some 200 delegates. In two days of deliberations, they unanimously rejected the intended legislation, and with the help of a lawyer produced a carefully worded petition giving their reasons and suggesting their own solutions. Instead of white voters electing other whites to represent them on legislative bodies, they wished 'to ask for the extension of the Franchise to the Native Races of this Colony'. They felt that the second bill 'may prove detrimental to the interests of the Native people' and that the third was entirely unnecessary: the locations should be left alone. Instead, they asked that freehold title deeds be given to all those living on mission reserves. There were nine signatories to the petition, several of whom were old Congress stalwarts, such as Mark Radebe, Stephen Mini and Skweleti Nyongwana. At least one, Christian Lutayi, was an illiterate chief. The chairman and secretary respectively of the petitioners were S.E. Kumalo and John Dube. Congress had apparently also consulted Harriette Colenso as to the petition's contents. It was handed to F.R. Moor, in his capacity as both Prime Minister and Minister for Native Affairs, on 10 June.

Congress had also elected a 15-member committee to watch the progress of the bills and to take necessary action. Under their auspices, several further meetings were organised, to report back and raise the money for the lawyer's fee and travel expenses. At one of these, a speaker voiced the anxiety of many, that if the new system of administration was brought in, 'Natives will become like meat cooked in a pot which, after a time, falls to pieces, bones and all – it, so to speak, rots there.' A new association, Iliso Lesizwe Esimnyama (Eye of the black nation), emerged in the inland districts of Natal to coordinate the responses of Christians and traditionalists; largely based in Edendale, Ndaleni and Driefontein, its membership overlapped extensively with Congress. The Congress chair himself, S.E. Kumalo, was a representative of this constituency.

The petitioners then sought a meeting with Sir Matthew Nathan to express their profound objections. Their lawyer, Robert Harrison, had advised them that they were quite entitled to do this, but the Minister for Native Affairs took extreme exception that they had not approached him first. The Minister agreed to meet them on 2 September, by which time the first bill had been dropped and the second had been reworked and was well on its way to becoming the Native Administration Act. He did agree to forward their petition to the Governor – which in effect meant it would be sent on to the Colonial Office in London – but could not hide his annoyance that there were a 'good many chiefs' among the delegates who ought to have remembered that they were government servants and should therefore have obtained permission from their magistrates before approaching him. He thereby chose to reopen an old sore point, rather than in any way to deal with the substance of their objections or suggested remedies.

It is important to remember that while we now think of this kind of petitioning as a polite and largely ineffectual method of politics, this was certainly not the case at the time. White rulers in Natal found the idea of African subjects questioning their legislative programme and administrative arrangements deeply distasteful. Even more objectionable to them was the practice of Africans approaching the Governor or appealing to the British parliament. While there was a gap here for Congress to exploit, between the settler administration which passed legislation and the British government that supposedly protected African interests, Africans knew it was not very wide, for in truth no level of government in this imperial hierarchy deemed it appropriate for Africans to inform their white betters as to how they should be governed. There was another gap, even if as narrow. While chiefs could be reminded that they were 'servants of state', there was nothing to stop exempted Africans from engaging in such activities, however unwelcome to government. The authorities tended to be wary of punitive action against such exempted Africans, lest it be discovered to be 'unconstitutional' and cause more fuss than was necessary.

Bullying and threats might work, though. F.R. Moor got hold of Dube after this meeting and warned him that he was 'playing with fire'. Petitioning, then, *was* of a very different and more serious order to the authorities than running campaigns through the press, whether for African unity or asserting Dinuzulu's innocence. Even before he got back to Inanda, Dube wrote a letter to the Prime Minister, characteristically offering not an apology but an explanation for his actions:

> My main desire is to bring about such a relationship between Europeans and Natives of Natal as to ensure the peace of the country and the progress and welfare of both races. I believe that you are animated by the same desire but fear that you have misunderstood my criticism of the Native Bills. I have not criticised these Bills because of any desire to oppose the Govt or to create friction between the Natives and the Authorities, but in the hope that I might prove to you and the very large number of members of Parliament who support you, that in bringing forward these Bills which you honestly believe will benefit the Natives you are really calling into existence measures which, I think, will cause discontent and probably further trouble with a section of the Native population …

He ended his letter with some Zulu expressions clearly intended to reassure and indicate his goodwill: *Ungangifulateli 'Pambana noMkandlu'. Yini inceku yako etobekileyo.* (Don't turn your back on me. "[I don't want to] be at odds with the government." Your humble servant.) Later the same day, he wrote to Moor again. He had had a 'fatherly talk' from Marshall Campbell, he explained, who urged him to stay out of politics because it would harm Ohlange and his educational work. He also told Moor that Campbell had discussed with him rumours that Africans in various places were collecting money to send him to England, but he denied any involvement in such a plan. Samuelson, who saw these letters, did beg to point out that *Ilanga* had editorialised on 10 July, 'Well, what are we to do? Let us collect money in all the country and send delegates across to the King, and let us spread out before him all our troubles, there is no people which should die without the knowledge of their Chief.' To this Dube replied, 'I had not the slightest desire to go myself.'

Campbell's arm-twisting was at least accompanied by promises of reward. Thus, Dube was able to report in late October that Colonel Stanford, a prominent Cape liberal, had visited Ohlange, and then within another few days, 'We have had a very enjoyable visit from the Hon. J.X. Merriman and Dr [Meiring] Beck … Mr Merriman gave us £3 for the school and Dr Beck £1. We are thankful to you for getting them to visit.' Merriman, Prime Minister of the Cape, and Beck, another of the Cape delegates along with Stanford, were in Durban for the National Convention to decide the form that closer union of the South African colonies would take. While they hardly donated great sums, Merriman's endorsement was highly prestigious. Coming as it did in the wake of several other leading public figures, his visit confirmed Ohlange's place on the map of 'must see' establishments of the day. Moreover, the pressure seemed to work: Dube was conspicuously *not* among those who reassembled in the same month to draft a further petition against the Native Administration Act, in the hope that the King would withhold consent, since it was 'opposed to the spirit of good and just Government and constitute[s] an infringement of the rights and liberties of your Petitioners and the whole Native population of this Colony'.

It is not altogether clear what 'staying out of politics' was supposed to mean to Dube. What seems most to have rankled Campbell and Moor was that the Natal Native Congress was able to assemble large, supportive crowds and to work across the insider–outsider divide, both of which achievements profoundly destabilised whites' sense of order and control. (As one official was later to put it, 'This policy of combination … is the reverse of the policy of the Natal Government. It has always been recognised that our safety... was due to their lack of combination.') Dube continued to make political interventions through the pages of *Ilanga*, much of it in keeping with the line taken in the petition; as far as the government was concerned, this was not very satisfactory, either, but was the lesser of two evils. With some regularity, the matter of closing down *Ilanga* was raised. It is both a tribute to Dube's negotiating skills and an indication of his stature in the eyes of the leading politicians of the day that he was able to keep it open for publication.[1]

And it was through *Ilanga* that he led a campaign to raise awareness about the dire consequences for Africans of moves to closer union. In a series of articles through September and October 1908, on 'Natives and closer union', he noted that the four colonies seemed to be hurtling towards an agreement. The Transvaal had been granted self-government at the end of 1906, just four years after the South African War had ended, and the Orange River Colony followed months later. And no sooner were all four colonies on an equal constitutional footing than the so-called Selborne Memorandum began to circulate in July 1907. Named after the British High Commissioner, it floated the real possibility of union, and urged that colonists themselves should take the idea forward. One result was that the Customs Conference scheduled for May 1908 was used as a forum for discussing possible political arrangements. Out of this meeting had come the plan for a National Convention somewhat later in 1908.

Dube was alarmed that African interests had been so completely neglected in all of this. What mattered most was an understanding between 'Boer and Briton', rather than one between black and white, as a way of protecting Britain's long-term imperial interests in the subcontinent. Africans had been bitterly disappointed at Britain's decision to leave the franchise issue to the white electorates of the northern colonies when they won self-government, which of course meant an entrenchment of the status quo. Dube foresaw that unless there was some mechanism for extending the Cape's colour-blind franchise in any union settlement, the result would be 'black British subjects, who, for an indefinite period, if not forever, must be debarred from all representation and held down as mere aliens in the land of their birth and ancient origin'.

Dube was involved in a failed attempt to assemble a 'Vigilance Committee' from across the four colonies to lobby the National Convention when it convened in Durban. Whatever other practical difficulties stood in the way, his most immediate was his undertaking to Campbell. *Ilanga* did reproduce in full the petition that the Natal Native Congress had intended to submit to the Convention, but it was never tabled. Its central point was that 'any scheme for the Closer Union of the Colonies under the British Crown should include a provision that representation should be accorded fairly to all sections of the community without distinctions of colour'. In the event, the National Convention agreed that whatever franchise regulations obtained in each colony should be carried forward when they became provinces of the Union. However, only whites would be eligible to stand as members of the new national parliament.

Africans were generally deeply disappointed at the outcome of the Convention. While many may have exhibited complacency before, believing that their interests would somehow be taken care of by liberal delegates or by Britain, they reacted more forcefully once the draft South Africa Act was published. This was the catalyst for the organisation of a national gathering in May 1909. The Native Congress of the Orange River Colony took the lead in the initiative; even J.T. Jabavu, usually at odds with his fellows over strategy and tactics, lent his support, at least initially. John Dube was chosen to represent Natal, along with Simeon Kambule, member of Edendale's foremost family and prosperous landowner, now resident at Driefontein. Here again, as in its action against the Natal legislation, Congress was attempting to present a balance between 'coastal' and 'up-country' interests. Dube had known Kambule since at least 1904, when he had called on him and his wife, Esther, during his first visit to Driefontein.

Waaihoek was Bloemfontein's 'model location', laid out in the 1890s with wide straight roads lined with plots of some 15 square metres, taps at street corners and night soil removal. Residents rented stands from the municipality and built their own homes. The unusual thing about Waaihoek was that men and women lived there in roughly equal numbers, suggesting a settled family life. One observer described the neat houses built of large, sun-baked bricks, lace curtains at the windows and solid furnishings within. It was therefore a most respectable venue for the delegates who assembled for the proceedings of the South African Native Convention. Even though there were less than 40 of them, this was an important moment, 'a major step towards the formation of a permanent national African political organisation'. Not only were there representatives from African congresses in all the southern African colonies and protectorates, but also from the African Political Organisation, representing coloured South Africans and based in the Western Cape under its founder and redoubtable leader, Dr A. Abdurahman. Although Dube was very much against racial mixing, he was generally well disposed to the African Political Organisation and did look with great sympathy on the constitutional plight of coloured people at this time. (There was also one enormously influential coloured person in his background, still revered in his family, Nancy Damon.)

In a forceful speech on 26 March, and drawing on the transatlantic influences that had shaped his political outlook, Dube noted a clear parallel between Africans' dissatisfaction with the draft Union legislation and that of British colonists in America: 'the cry was "No Representation, No Taxation" … their cause was that all civilised men should be voters and not be debarred.' Abdurahman's address focused on the extraordinary insensitivity of the terminology in the draft legislation to describe those who would be eligible to stand for parliament: those 'of European descent'. (And although Alan Soga considered himself African, rather than coloured, everyone knew that his mother was a Scotswoman.) The overwhelming message from the deliberations was support for union, but rejection of Africans' and coloureds' exclusion: more African and coloured voters in the Cape stood to be disenfranchised than the total number of eligible white voters in Natal. After close deliberation of each clause of the draft South Africa Act and the formulation of responses to them, the Convention laid plans to remain in existence and elected a committee for this purpose. The veteran Cape leader Walter Benson Rubusana was elected president, John Dube was chosen as his vice-president, Alan Soga as secretary and the Rev. Joel Goronyane, prominent Thaba Nchu landowner and Bloemfontein businessman, as treasurer. Among other committee members were Thomas Mapikela, Chief Silas Molema and Dube's Natal colleague Simeon Kambule.

So Dube was now office-bearer of a national political organisation, his name closely linked to a talented group of other national figures. The remarkable Walter Rubusana had been active in the Eastern Cape since the emergence of the very first African political organisations there in the 1880s. He and his close associates had worked diligently to consolidate a number of scattered regional associations into the South African Native Congress (SANC), whose aspirations for unity chimed with Dube's own. Its stance was opposed to that of John Tengo Jabavu's, who, through his paper *Imvo*, was more involved in Cape electoral politics than in establishing African organisations. Dube already had a well-established relationship with Alan Soga, editor of the SANC's paper, *Izwi Labantu*, and Rubusana was chair of the board of directors of the Eagle Printing Press, which published it. Like Dube, Rubusana was an ordained Congregational minister and dedicated educationist, responsible for establishing a number of African schools in the Eastern Cape. He was also able with facility to straddle the 'insider–outsider' divide. An adviser to the Thembu Paramount Chief Dalindyebo, whom he had accompanied to the coronation of Edward VII in 1904, he was determined that Christianity and the oral traditions of the Xhosa people should coexist. He had recently published *Zemk' iinkomo Magwalandini* ('Defend your heritage'), a compilation of Xhosa oral poetry, praises and Christian history. Some 16 years his junior, Dube impressed Rubusana greatly. The new vice-president and Kambule travelled home via Johannesburg, where they addressed a packed meeting of Zulu mine clerks and workers in Doornfontein, organised by the Reef branch of the Natal Native Congress.

Predictably, there was trouble about his role when he arrived back in Inanda. Campbell, who was now chairing the Ohlange board of trustees, would have known of Dube's activities – they were reported in all the papers – and, though sympathetic to the Convention's resolutions, continued to apply pressure on him to disengage himself from politics. Just three months after his election, then, we find him writing to Campbell that 'I wish to assure you that I have found by sad experience that politics work against the interests of the work to which I have devoted my life, that of educating my people. I have decided to leave politics severely alone.' More rewards followed: Campbell promised to pay for a new roof for one of the school buildings at Ohlange, and contributed £400 towards interest arrears and reduction of the bond on the Qadi farm. Dube mentioned in the same letter that he had decided to take another fundraising trip abroad, this time to England, and asked Campbell to write him a reference. Campbell conferred with Nathan, who was winding up his duties in Natal, having fallen out with the Colonial Office; he would shortly become Secretary of the British Post Office. The two men agreed that Dube might well be using the cover of fundraising for political purposes – why else *England*? Nathan pointed out that 'as he could scarcely be stopped going it is as well that he should consider himself beholden and therefore to some extent responsible to you'.

There was indeed a very good reason for Dube's trip. Since the Bloemfontein meeting, the four colonies had all ratified the South Africa Act; the next step was the assent of the British parliament. The South African Native Convention and various other African and coloured organisations had decided that a delegation, to be led by W.P. Schreiner, should travel to London to petition parliament not to pass the Act with the colour bar clauses in it. Schreiner, together with Theo, his brother and fellow Cape MP, led a small, vocal group of political figures determined to do all they could to defend, and even extend, the Cape's franchise policy. He had resigned his nomination to the National Convention because he was leading the defence at Dinuzulu's trial, so the delegation to London presented him with an opportunity to campaign abroad, as he had been doing at home, against what he saw as a 'blot' on the draft Union constitution.

Dube must have agreed to be part of the delegation – the enthusiastic audience at his Doornfontein meeting had expressly begun collecting money for this purpose. Rubusana was certainly under that impression, which is why he sent Dube a telegram on 14 June, saying: 'Deputation England of which you are part starts twenty third. Wire money collected to East London.' It had only been four days since his most recent promise to Campbell; all he could do was to send an immediate reply saying, 'Cannot go as Deputation. My educational work debars me taking active part in politics.' He then sent both telegrams to Samuelson (who, like Nathan, was about to leave office): 'I wish you to assure the Minister for Native Affairs for me that my trip to England is absolutely to raise funds for my school and that I have decided to leave politics alone … If I may go at the same time as they it will be merely for company and if I take any part in politics in England in any shape or form, the authorities will know it,' clearly suggesting he faced accusations of duplicity.

What had happened? On his departure at the Cape Town docks, this question was put to Rubusana, who reluctantly disclosed that 'I understand pressure has been brought to bear on him, I should say indirectly, by the Natal Government, not to go … if he had gone there was just a possibility of the grant being taken away from him.' In truth the 'grant' still only stretched to the support of one agricultural instructor; however, it was such a tight operation that every small amount mattered, symbolically if nothing else. To be quite sure that Dube would stick to his word, Campbell had also tied his hands in the letter of recommendation he produced: 'Mr Dube is devoting the whole of his time to educational purposes, he has promised that in no way will he meddle with politics in future. His one object in life is to help his own race to a higher standard of life.'

Before his own departure, Dube asked Campbell to look over the draft of a pamphlet, *The Zulu's appeal for light and England's duty*, which he had produced to help with his fundraising. It began,

> Among the greatest heroes of mankind and the best of England's sons I rank the great and good Lord Nelson. Not because he fought great battles and won great victories; not because he gained for England the dominion of the sea … but because he gave her the best advice man ever gave, when, high from the top-mast of his *Victory*, to every Briton in every time, he sent forth the watchword, 'England expects that every man shall do his duty'.

It was replete with photographs and accounts of 'barbarian, heathen life' in beehive huts and of how Ohlange could transform it into something productive and progressive. Although noting that 'it was hard to be despoiled of one's native land, and to see it crushed under a foreign yoke', this was merely a prelude to celebrating the benefits of British colonial rule. Returning to the theme of the opening lines, its author, 'a mere Black man', pleaded with his readers to do their duty – 'help me to bear the burden – the White man's burden' – to support Ohlange's work. It ended with a series of testimonials from white churchmen and a brief personal background that highlighted his struggles to become educated and enlightened. He made liberal use of stylised contrivances that were already becoming archaic: 'methinks'; 'forsooth'; 'I fain would think'.

It was, all in all, a calculated attempt to ingratiate, as he made clear in his covering letter to Campbell: 'You will see that I have appealed on a broad Imperial basis and gave a vivid picture of the ignorance of my people which will appeal to the good people [in England].' Yet it did not quite overcome its self-imposed contradictions. If Empire was such a blessing, what was he doing declaring his independence from its educational provision, and if Africans were destined to be such lowly creatures, why was he trying to rise above his station? He did not seem comfortable about the prospect of appealing to English audiences; this was not a milieu with which he was familiar and in any case he would rather have been taking the trip for a different purpose. This sense of awkwardness is the most pronounced feature of his pamphlet. Campbell provided the money to finance its publication in England. Whether it struck the intended chord or not is unclear.[2]

Dube's preparations for departure included appointing his now most trusted supporter, brother Charles, as acting principal of Ohlange as well as editor of *Ilanga*, though in practice the almost equally trusted Skweleti Nyongwana took editorial responsibility on the paper. Accompanied as always on such missions by Nokutela, he then left Cape Town on 7 July, a respectable distance behind the various members of Schreiner's delegation, which included Rubusana, Mapikela, Jabavu, Abdurahman and Daniel Dwanya. In London, two others were recruited to help: Pixley kaIsaka Seme, who was now at Oxford, having completed his studies at Columbia, and Alfred Mangena. Though he had been born near Ladysmith, Mangena had grown up in the Eastern Cape and, after an apprenticeship as a gold assayer in Johannesburg, completed his formal education in Cape Town. Disqualified by age to enter the civil service examination, he decided to travel to London in 1902 to become a lawyer. During the Rebellion in 1906, he won admiration from many black South Africans for his attempts to challenge through the British courts the legality of McCallum's declaration of martial law and the trial of the Richmond accused. Seme himself had produced a glowing pen portrait of Mangena for *Ilanga* the previous year, shortly after he had been called to the Bar at Lincoln's Inn.

The Anti-Slavery and Aborigines' Protection Society was assisting both the delegation in its work and Dube in his. This was the first time that he had come into contact with the Society; it would play rather a large role in his public life in future years. The Aborigines' Protection Society had been established in the 1830s 'to oppose the exploitation of indigenous peoples in British colonies' and had just merged with the Anti-Slavery Society, which had generally focused its efforts in territories outside the empire. The former's small support base was largely Nonconformist but also contained a few free-thinking libertarians, whose main activity was to bring cases of suspected abuse to the attention of the Colonial Office. Importantly, it also facilitated high-level metropolitan contact for those of all races in the empire who campaigned for fairer treatment of indigenous people. It did, however, also tend to dictate the terms upon which 'darker-skinned' subjects – there was an undeniable whiff of superiority in its attitude – would engage with British sympathisers.

The Society's joint secretary, Travers Buxton, introduced the Dubes to a number of influential church leaders. Among them were Wardlaw Thompson, secretary of the Colonial Missionary Society; D. Burford Hooke, Thompson's predecessor and editor of its mouthpiece, *Evangelical British Missionary*; Frederick B. Meyer, one of the most influential evangelical preachers of his day, the leading Nonconformist figure in the Keswick Movement (founded in 1875 to promote social and spiritual purity in the face of moral decline, and in which Arthur Tappan Pierson was also heavily involved) and president of the World's Sunday School Convention; and Robert F. Horton, lately president of the National Free Church Council and minister in charge of the Lyndhurst Road Congregational Church in Hampstead. They all lent their names to the Dubes' fundraising activities.

But before they embarked on any such activities, Dube did all he could to assist Schreiner's delegation, while careful not to be seen to be playing an active campaigning part. He was present, for example, at a breakfast for the delegation and influential British sympathisers, hosted by the Aborigines' Protection Society, at the Westminster Palace Hotel on 27 July. Schreiner, Abdurahman, Jabavu and Rubusana all spoke, as did the radical parliamentarian Sir Charles Dilke. Probably deeply frustrating to him, he was not among those who had been introduced to the Colonial Secretary the week earlier, or attended the parliamentary sessions in late July and August, which saw the South Africa Act through its final stages. Members of the delegation drew as much attention as they could to the iniquity of the legislation, focusing their campaign on the immediate issue of the 'direct forfeiture of the constitutional rights' of African and coloured voters, who would immediately be debarred from standing for the Union parliament. Despite their best efforts, they were drowned out by the official delegation – including Merriman, Botha, Smuts and Moor – who not only attracted more attention from the press and public, but also did their best to discredit Schreiner's mission ('one of the most unkind things ever done to the natives', according to Merriman).

Schreiner held Dube in high regard; he had probably come to know him during Dinuzulu's trial and must have sympathised with his plight in London, caught between his political and educational commitments. The following year, he would write to his friend Sydney Buxton (later Governor-

General of South Africa) that he 'is one of the real leaders of Native thought'. It was probably he, then, who introduced the Dubes to London contacts of his who might assist them. One of these was Jane Cobden Unwin, suffragist daughter of the radical statesman Richard Cobden, and wife of T. Fisher Unwin. Unwin was his sister Olive's publisher, who agreed also to publish Dube's pamphlet. This association-by-print must have pleased Dube immensely. Olive Schreiner was by far the most influential South African writer, social theorist and political activist at the time; she too had strongly condemned the racial exclusions in the Union legislation and, months earlier, 'this noble champion' had been featured in *Ilanga*. Another of the Schreiner circle was Percy Molteno, Cape-born politician and son of John Molteno, the first Prime Minister of the Cape. He was now a Liberal MP in the House of Commons. Both Jane Unwin and Percy Molteno lent their names to the Dubes' fundraising activities.

But it was Molteno's older sister, Betty, who was to become more important to the future of Ohlange. She had been an educationist herself, the principal of the Collegiate School for Girls in Port Elizabeth from the 1880s. Both Molteno and her life-long partner, Alice Greene, who joined the staff of the Collegiate School in 1887, had left their posts because of their pro-Boer sympathies in the South African War. They were close friends of Olive Schreiner, part therefore of a small set who not only voiced strong criticisms of British imperialism, but supported votes for men *and* women of all races and were socialist-leaning in their thought. Some years later, Betty Molteno explained that 'after the Boer War I saw that Boer and Briton would have to unite, but would they try to do it at the cost of their dark brothers? Broken-hearted I went to England. For eight long years I remained away from Africa – in body – never in soul and spirit.'

There was yet another delegation in London, too. Since 1906, Gandhi had been involved in a major campaign in the Transvaal against harsh new registration laws for 'Asiatics' (traders and businesspeople of Indian and Chinese origin), requiring them to re-register by submitting to the deeply degrading measure of giving all 10 fingerprints as a form of identification. It was the first time *satyagraha* was being tried as practical politics, involving the principle of passive resistance and its key techniques of 'ethical training of key *satyagrahis*, the use of print media, the use of powerful symbols (the burning of registration cards), honesty in negotiating with one's adversaries, the penitential approach to prison-going'. Both Indian and Chinese supporters had come forward to participate. In a partially successful attempt to persuade the British government to disallow the legislation, Gandhi had visited London in 1906. However, the Transvaal had introduced the same law again in 1907. As resisters started filling the gaols – Gandhi did a stint himself – he had reached a compromise with Smuts, the Transvaal Colonial Secretary: if 'Asiatics' registered voluntarily, the offending Act would be repealed.

However, there was so much confusion surrounding the terms of this deal that it had collapsed. So too had the passive resistance campaign, and Gandhi was now back in London (Olive Schreiner had scandalised the crowd at the Cape Town docks by warmly shaking his hand on his departure), hoping to use the attention generated by the passing of the South Africa Act to highlight the many grievances of Indians in South Africa. Although his small delegation achieved little on the official front, it did help to spur a passive resistance support group into action, whose main roles were to collect signatures for a petition and donations for the wives and families of those resisters who were serving goal sentences.

Betty Molteno met Gandhi in London, and it was probably as a result of this encounter that she became a benefactor of Phoenix Settlement ('Your sweet Phoenix is a poem – a dream of loveliness,' she would later write to him). She and Alice Greene also began to support Ohlange at roughly this time, again most likely as a result of meeting the Dubes in London. In a couple of years, they would be described as Ohlange's 'principal supporters'; Molteno would even purchase a small cottage there. Though not entirely corresponding to the sort of society she envisioned, Phoenix and Ohlange must nevertheless have seemed to her by far the most progressive self-help initiatives at the time. Possibly through her influence, or possibly more directly, one 'Mrs Dube' was listed among the supporters of the passive resisters in early 1910, having collected eight signatures and 6s 6d for the fund. It is highly likely that this was Nokutela; if so, it is one of the very few records we have of her independent political views. It is tempting to think that the admiration that Dube himself expressed for the passive resisters in Natal a few years later might partly have come about through similar influences.

Between September 1909, when Schreiner's delegation returned home, and February 1910, the Dubes concentrated on raising money in England for their school. They were particularly anxious, they said, for 'more land for the purposes of agriculture, more farm implements and tools, more workshops, a boarding house and especially an endowment fund'. As always, John spoke and Nokutela sang, in various churches and halls in London and other cities, including Sheffield and Nottingham – wherever they had been invited, through the offices of their sponsors. There were occasional lighter moments, with visits to attractions such as the British Museum, the London Zoo and the Lord Mayor's Parade.

Then on 12 February, they departed for New York on the *Umbria*, arriving at Ellis Island 10 days later. Once again, they made Brooklyn their base in order to meet up with their American Committee. It was still in existence, with figures like Louis Stoiber and Francis Sutton providing a strong thread of continuity, though it had lost some of its momentum. One possible reason is that ventures like Ohlange would have been expected to be self-financing by then. Another is that some committee members had apparently lost faith in Dube: the industrial side of the school had not made the sort of progress they had expected, and there may have been some disquiet about his political intentions. Whatever the reasons, there was need to look further afield for support. And he clearly needed it, in view of the possible withdrawal of the admittedly meagre funds trickling in from domestic sources.

It is unclear exactly where the Dubes travelled on this extended American visit. John's reports on his travels for *Ilanga* dwindled and, when he did write, it was to refer to the very great difficulties they were experiencing in their work – though he also noted they were meeting with some success – rather than to report on sights and events. They did meet Lindley Seme, studying medicine in Canada, and a daughter of an old associate studying at Hampton – it is likely therefore that they visited Hampton, though whether they ventured into Canada is uncertain. There was one notable success, something he had been working to achieve for a decade: Dube met Booker Washington in New York in March, was able to convince him of his commitment to keep Ohlange going on Tuskegee principles, and finally received Washington's endorsement for his educational work. He also made visits to New Hampshire and Massachusetts. From Northfield, he sent back news of the principal of Mount Hermon, where Pixley Seme had schooled. Olivia Phelps-Stokes, whom he had encountered on his very first American sojourn and who had heard him speak in the company of William Wilcox, also lived in Northfield. His visit there was possibly connected to the fact that her zealously religious family, committed to educational work in America and Africa, was about to launch its philanthropic foundation, called the Phelps-Stokes Fund.

He was in Washington DC in May for the World's Sixth Sunday School Convention, probably through the offices of Frederick Meyer, his English sponsor who was then the Convention's president. There were strong overtones of the 'Zulu's appeal for light and England's duty' in his address to this gathering. Of the 1879 Anglo–Zulu War, he noted, 'It was very hard for the Zulus, who were free and independent, to come under a foreign yoke, but when we look back, we see the providence of God in it all, because into all that territory of ours missionaries have brought the wonderful story ...' More memorably, Dube was caught up in a minor revolt over the exclusion of black delegates from the official Convention parade. At a protest meeting in a local church, his friend Louis Stoiber, together with several visiting English delegates, denounced this decision of the local organising committee as 'worse than un–Christian'. The 'climax' of the protest was reached, according to the media report, when Dube told the congregation that 'he had broken bread with his British friends in London and New York restaurants, but had met with a consistent refusal to be served in Washington'.[3]

Dube was still out of the country when the Union of South Africa came into being on 31 May 1910. The mood was largely one of subdued resignation among those who had fought so hard for their inclusion in the new dispensation. There were one or two small concessions to African sentiments, however. The new Prime Minister, Louis Botha, chose that day to announce the early release from custody of Dinuzulu, who would be settled on a farm purchased for him in the Transvaal, with his pension restored. Botha and the prince had had a long association. During the civil war in Zululand in the early 1880s, the desperate uSuthu, weakened following Cetshwayo's death, had turned to a group of Boers living along the Transvaal–Zululand border, of whom Botha was one, for assistance. Calling themselves 'Dinuzulu's Volunteers', the Boers had ensured the defeat of rivals to Dinuzulu's succession, in return for access to a vast stretch of land in the north which the Boers named their New Republic. This land claim had proved controversial to the uSuthu, who had not intended to alienate quite as much of the kingdom to the Boers, and to Britain, concerned at Boer attempts to secure access to the sea. Britain had eventually pegged back their entitlement and declared the remainder of Zululand a British Colony. It had been in the face of ongoing resistance from the uSuthu that Dinuzulu, still a teenager, had been found guilty of treason and exiled to St Helena. Botha felt that Dinuzulu had not been given a fair trial in the aftermath of the Bhambatha Rebellion. His gesture was therefore a mild swipe at the Natal authorities as much as an attempt at recompense. Dube sent a delighted message from America, and would have endorsed *Ilanga*'s comment that 'We believe the Premier [Botha] is conscious of his responsibility to God ... it makes us feel that we can trust him ... It also gives us a sense of freedom that might even be put in the scales or even against the Non-possession of the franchise.'

Although there was a tacit agreement that African affairs should be above party politics, Botha nevertheless made some senior government appointments calculated to mollify African opinion (but by the same token provided grist to the mill of more extreme segregationists in the cabinet, like J.B.M. Hertzog). Henry Burton, a Cape MP who had staunchly defended his Colony's franchise arrangements, became Minister for Native Affairs. On his first tour of duty later in 1910, this new 'Chief', as *Ilanga* called him, visited Ohlange, where he told students, 'You need not be afraid that we shall oppress you; we shall do what we can to improve your conditions.' It was yet another visit arranged by Marshall Campbell, himself rather proud of all that Ohlange had achieved. He had been nominated to serve in the new Senate by the outgoing Natal administration. Joining him there, and cause for widespread satisfaction among politically conscious Africans, was W.P. Schreiner, who had been appointed one of the four senators with special responsibility for African interests across the Union. Another of these four was F.R. Moor, whose appointment met with a far more muted response. In any event, Dube was extremely well connected in the new government.

Another kind of government seat caused some jubilation among Africans. Walter Rubusana was the victorious candidate for Tembuland in the new Cape Provincial Council elections, the first and only African ever to hold such office. *Ilanga* was ecstatic at his win – there were long stories and a poem in his honour, and he received a hero's welcome when, soon after his election, he visited Durban and preached in the Beatrice Street Congregational Church. (He would lose his seat five years later, when Tengo Jabavu stood against him, thus splitting the African vote.)

True to their commitment to keep functioning, members of the South African Native Convention gathered again in Bloemfontein for a second conference in March 1910. Many of its leaders had devoted a great deal of time and effort to consolidating the organisation over the past year, although the Natal Native Congress was in some disarray at this time and had not participated as fully as other regional associations. It had, moreover, been unable to send representatives to this second conference, for reasons beyond its control: in a last punitive measure before Union, the Natal government required all Africans attending meetings of a political nature to obtain prior permission from the Secretary for Native Affairs. Rubusana had been re-elected president and Dube vice-president. Though he was still abroad, Dube must have indicated to his Convention colleagues that he believed his educational and political roles to be quite compatible, despite the difficulties attending this decision; his re-election was thus a symbolic gesture of some importance.

Then in May 1911 the Convention met for its third annual conference, this time in Johannesburg. By now, there were ominous political signals emanating from the Union parliament that must have affected the tone of proceedings. Colour bars were being introduced into jobs on the mines and the defence force and into church attendance in the Transvaal and Orange Free State. More worryingly, on the land there were moves to curtail the buying activities of African land syndicates and to impose heavy taxes on 'squatters' (semi-independent sharecroppers) on white farms: indications of a quickening process of dispossession and destruction that was 'the lot again and again of blacks in South Africa'. Since surviving reports of the 1911 proceedings are patchy at best, it is not clear exactly who was elected to office. Yet again, Dube does not seem to have been present; the Natal representatives were Skweleti Nyongwana, who would certainly have acted wholly in Dube's interest, and Cleopas Kunene, editor of *Ipepa lo Hlanga* in the early 1900s and now active in the Johannesburg branch of the Natal Native Congress (which at this stage tended to ally itself with Dube and his faction in internal Congress disputes), who became secretary. Neither was Rubusana there, having departed for London in the previous month in the company of Chief Dalindyebo, to attend the Universal Races Congress. He was, however, elected president for a third term. It is possible that the same happened in Dube's case.

The choice of Johannesburg for the venue was of great significance, and revolved around the fact that Pixley kaIsaka Seme was now back from his studies in America and Britain. Not only had he acquired legal training (having completed his degree at Oxford, spent time in the Netherlands studying Roman-Dutch Law and been called to the bar of Middle Temple in June 1910), but also an American accent, the skills of typing and stenography, a driving licence, a taste for fine clothing and an impatience to push forward with the 'regeneration of Africa'. Such had been the title of his medal-winning speech at Columbia in 1906, which opened with the declaration that 'I set my pride in my race over against hostile opinion'. This young orator went on to argue that genius was a quality that could arise among individuals of any race, and Africa possessed a great many geniuses, stretching back to the grandeur of ancient Egypt. In more recent times, Africans' suffering and bondage had not diminished their ability to produce 'sons, who ... are marching to the future's golden door bearing the records of deeds of valor done'. Indeed, he noted, Africa had produced leaders in almost every field imaginable, from astronomy to theology, and from military generals to presidents and emperors. Returning to his initial theme, he claimed that Africans as a race possessed a remarkable 'recuperative power', one indication of which was the number of its most talented sons and daughters who had gone abroad to study, then returned 'like arrows, to drive darkness from the land'. It is safe to presume that he counted himself amongst this talented leadership, and now he had come home, to drive darkness from the land. Though he had spent a few weeks in late 1910 being fêted at home in Inanda – 'his success sends a thrill of happiness through thousands of his people', hymned an *Ilanga* report – he soon set up office in Johannesburg, employed a young clerk, H. Selby Msimang, and was admitted as an attorney of the Supreme Court in January 1911.

The legal profession suited the mercurial and self-confident Seme perfectly. If the man of the cloth had symbolised the apex of respectability in the first wave of modernity that swept the quiet mission stations scattered across the South African countryside, then the man of the law – for both were exclusively masculine – played a similar role in the next wave, emerging as this did from the ferment of urban life. All the professions were fundamental to the shaping of African middle-class consciousness, excluded as its members were from the circles controlling finance, manufacture and mining, and with no prospect of gaining entry either through social mixing or intermarriage. But for a combination of reasons, the legal profession was almost revered. 'Justice and fair play' held out the promise not only of more equitable political representation, but also the securing of basic rights such as access to land and defence against harsh treatment by those who might be tempted to abuse their power. Further, this was a profession that permitted its members an independent platform to challenge any number of discriminatory practices through the courts. For decades, Africans had taken to hiring white lawyers to represent them; now, as the first fully qualified African lawyers returned from courses of study unavailable at home and set themselves up in practice, there was a definite expectation that they would achieve great things on behalf of all Africans. Moreover, because of the prestige they enjoyed, they were always regarded as potential political leaders: this would be the case all the way through the twentieth century. (Gandhi himself also exemplified this connection.) And being independent, they did not face the red tape of officialdom or the anger of white patrons when it came to such involvement.

In the early years of Union, such expectations were tempered only by the tiny number of qualified African attorneys and advocates. Apart from Seme, there were but Alfred Mangena, Richard Msimang and George Montsioa. Mangena had returned a few months before Seme; he could thus claim the accolade of being the very first qualified African advocate in South Africa.

He opened his practice in Pretoria, with a branch in Johannesburg, in the middle of 1910. A few years later, the two of them would go into partnership. Richard Msimang, from Edendale, had been among Dube's very first pupils at Ohlange, and had completed his education in Somerset in England. He returned to South Africa later in 1910, to set up as an attorney in Johannesburg. Remarkably, therefore, George Montsioa was the only one of this early group *not* from Natal. He had grown up in Mafeking and had been called to the bar at Lincoln's Inn. He had first been based in the northern Transvaal but, like the others, had gravitated to Johannesburg to practise.

By 1910 this City of Gold had become the 'industrial hub of sub-Saharan Africa'. In just 25 years, it had been transformed from a rough mining camp to an outwardly respectable town, centred on a bustling business district whose tarred streets were lined with a bewildering mix of architectural styles, but all suggesting solidity and purpose. Its quarter of a million inhabitants made up a truly cosmopolitan assemblage, from every corner of southern Africa and every continent on the planet. A decade earlier, Olive Schreiner had summed it up as 'a great, fiendish, hell of a city which for glitter and gold, and wickedness, carriages and palaces and brothels and gambling halls, beat creation'. Electric trams were now rendering carriages obsolete, but the rest could still have belonged to a description in 1910.

Most of the working population was male, African, and housed in bleak, single-sex mine compounds. The 100,000 indentured Chinese workers who had been imported after the South African War to plug a chronic labour shortage in the mining industry were all in the process of being shipped back to China (something for which the South African Native Convention had expressed its gratitude: its stance was that all labour needs should be met from the indigenous population). In all the respectable, white suburbs was secreted an army of domestic servants, still also overwhelmingly male and African. The rest of the labouring poor, roughly a quarter of them women, lived in racially and ethnically mixed slum yards (these were the conditions about which Gandhi had earlier complained), large urban spaces tucked behind high walls and down alleyways, with corrugated-iron shacks built around the perimeter and shared facilities, such as a single tap, in the middle: 'all day long, even in the rain, there was a long queue of children and women waiting with their buckets.' The yards stretched from Malay Location on the western fringes of the city centre to Doornfontein in the east, close to the mine dumps, which covered everything in a thick film of yellow powder every time the wind blew. Some seven kilometres further out to the west, a mixed area of freehold plots called Sophiatown had begun to attract owners and tenants since the early 1900s; this was where most middle-class Africans gathered. Even further out, Klipspruit had been established as the first urban 'location' for Africans; built on a disused sewerage works, it was a deeply unpopular place to live.

Africans' movement was governed by a confusing system of municipal passes and permits, some issued to seek work, some issued monthly, some for single occasions and some to cover curfew restrictions at night, as well as a kind of 'exemption pass', meaning the bearer was not subject to these constraints. It was all part of a web of control and labour allocation, accompanied by regular police harassment to seek out and punish offenders. Into this world, 'where life really was experienced as a maelstrom', simultaneously creative and destructive, Seme inserted himself, anxious to make his mark. This was the place that would shape future forms of political organisation and contests over the distribution of power; this would be the crucible of the New African.[4]

Hard on the heels of the 1911 annual meeting of the South African Native Convention in May, there followed committee meetings of the same, on 17 June and 7 August, in Seme's chambers on the corner of Rissik and Marshall streets. He was urging its leadership to put it onto a more secure footing with a stronger voice, catering not only for the educated classes but also for chiefs (and hence their followers). There had always, in fact, been a sprinkling of chiefly participation in most of the old colony-based Congresses, and some Convention leaders, as we have seen, had close dealings with leading chiefs. Thus, while they had never been expressly appealed to before, it was neither a radical nor contentious development to involve chiefs in this way. Nevertheless, perhaps an urban, cosmopolitan outlook helped nudge the inside and the outside people closer together in this nationalist vision.

The August meeting did receive encouragement from some chiefs, and considered a draft constitution drawn up by Seme that reflected this broader conception of unity. He shortly afterwards issued a prospectus calling for a national organisation, a Congress, whose aim would be to set aside differences of language, region and ethnic affiliation, in order 'to talk and think loudly on our home problems and the solution of them'. It would, he said, come into being at a meeting of delegates from across southern Africa in December. This proved to be rather too ambitious; the meeting was delayed by a month. It was over Seme's name, then, that the 'warning' or clarion call, *inhlabamkhosi*, went out to chiefs and the African middle classes to assemble at Bloemfontein on Monday, 8 January 1912.

Between 60 and 100 'chiefs and gentlemen' responded, and duly met in Waaihoek, Bloemfontein, for four days of formal proceedings. They represented virtually every African political association and large polity in the country, from the Cape Peninsula to the far northern Transvaal, from the protectorates to major towns and cities. The one exception, as always, was Tengo Jabavu and his latest incarnation, the South African Native Races Congress, which he had formed on his return from the Universal Races Congress in London. This weakened representation from the Eastern Cape, although Walter Rubusana, an enthusiastic supporter, was there.

Seme delivered a keynote address in which he made a direct connection between Africans' exclusion from decision-making in South Africa and the need for them, in consequence, to find more effective ways to defend and promote their interests, both political and economic. Like Dube (and many others) before him, he used the language of racial awakening to inspire and unite: 'Ethiopia shall stretch forth her hands unto God.' At the end of his speech, he moved that the conference establish the South African Native National Congress. Several delegates, including many chiefs, rose to support the motion, which was carried unanimously amid jubilant cheering. The meeting agreed that the purpose of Congress was to promote unity and cooperation between African people and the Union government, to promote Africans' social, economic and political development, and to incorporate chiefs more fully into the political affairs of the nation. A committee was then appointed to draw up a constitution.

Then came the all-important business of electing office-bearers. A special committee had been tasked with putting forward nominations for the presidency; its suggestions were John Dube, Edward Tsewu and Sefako Makgatho. Tsewu, a minister who had headed the Iliso Lomzi, one of a number of political associations that had come together to form the Transvaal Native Association in 1910, was relatively unknown. Makgatho was more prominent. Educated in Britain, he had been based in Pretoria for a number of years and had helped to found the Transvaal African Teachers' Association and African National Political Union. The latter had also merged into the Transvaal Native Association, of which he had become president. Of the three, then, Dube was easily the best-known nationally, with almost matchless experience. He was elected by a large majority.

He was not there, however, to witness this moment of history, nor to receive the congratulations of the house. He claimed to have been unavoidably detained at home by 'pressing educational and editorial calls'. His brother Charles, who had probably never attended a political meeting in his life –

his milieu was teachers' federations, social clubs and business associations in Durban – deputised for him. This had been arranged beforehand with Seme, on a visit that John had undertaken to Johannesburg, ostensibly to raise funds for Ohlange. It is almost certain that the two had discussed his candidature for the position of president on this occasion. Seme, wishing to 'be content to keep the substance and forswear the show', would not have left something as important as the first figurehead to chance. However, right up until the moment of election to his most influential office, it appears that John Dube was afraid of losing vital support for Ohlange. In what had become a pattern, he may have hoped that election *in absentia* would be treated in certain quarters as greatness thrust upon him, rather than actively sought, and therefore an enhancement of his stature rather than a detraction from his educational obligations.

There was every reason to elect Dube as first president. The only other serious contender, Walter Rubusana, had declined to stand. Apart from his other commitments and despite his best efforts, African politics in the Cape had split in three, with Alan Soga's alienation (he had become embittered at being omitted from the Schreiner delegation) adding to the long-standing rift between these two and Jabavu. Such factionalism could not be allowed to weigh down the new organisation. Dube was held in high regard for keeping *Ilanga* going under very difficult circumstances; two of its sister papers, *Koranta ea Becoana* and *Izwi Labantu*, had folded in the years immediately preceding. He was also admired for fundraising tirelessly to keep Ohlange open, for this was an institution of which they were all immensely proud. Everyone knew how difficult it was to achieve *anything* in the febrile climate of Natal, and many would have sympathised with his dilemma in dealing with those white politician 'friends' who pressured him to choose between roles. Given the strong desire to bring chiefs into Congress, his well-known closeness to Dinuzulu would have been another important factor: ever since the prince's trial, there had been a story about him almost every week in *Ilanga*. There was also Dube's special link to a man widely regarded as an inspiration, Booker Washington. The assembled delegates clearly considered that what he stood for politically was in step with the values of their new Congress, and his commanding oratorical performance would be necessary to articulate these in fitting style. It should also not be forgotten that although this was an exclusively male gathering, Nokutela's talents were well known and respected in these circles: her tireless fundraising for Ohlange, significant contribution to music education and public speaking in the cause of African progress. The Dubes' songbook had just been published, and she had recently taken a leading role in the 75th anniversary celebrations of the American Zulu Mission. She thus provided a most admirable role-model of African womanhood. Finally, Seme, as Congress catalyst, owed Dube an enormous debt for the support he had received through his education abroad, especially in America.

The remaining executive positions were filled by nominations from the floor. Dube's new executive consisted of Seme as treasurer, Solomon Plaatje as general secretary, George Montsioa as recording secretary, and Thomas Mapikela as speaker. There were seven vice-presidents, including Sefako Makgatho, Simeon Kambule and Alfred Mangena. In recognition of the role he had played in preparing the ground for the formation of Congress, Rubusana was made an honorary president. A number of chiefs, including Dinuzulu, were appointed to an 'Upper House' of Congress; their role was to advise the Congress 'Commons'. The Rev. Mqoboli of the Wesleyan Church became chaplain, with Henry Ngcayiya, president of the Ethiopian Church, as assistant chaplain. The rest of the conference was spent deliberating on papers on a variety of topics of close interest to the members, from obstacles to land ownership and the meaning of segregation to the problems deriving from liquor and the state of family life. There were also resolutions to be drafted, approved and published; Rubusana was put in charge of a committee to see to this. The conference closed in upbeat mood, with the chair exhorting the delegates to return home to spread the word that they were 'now trees of one and the same forest'.

Dube issued an acceptance letter at the beginning of February, thanking his colleagues for their confidence, 'all unexpected and undeserved'. He described the inauguration of Congress as the 'renaissance of the race': although it could claim ancient rights to the continent, yet as citizens of a new world it was 'young and inexperienced'. He foresaw many difficulties in reaching the goals of Congress and counselled that its watchwords should be '*festina lente* – hasten slowly' – to be 'up and doing', but to do so cautiously, 'making progress prudently'. He referred directly to the conflict that had dominated his public life for the past few years:

> Throughout ten long tiring years and up to the present moment I have sacrificed all my time, all my strength, and all my means upon this altar of my people's supremest need – the need of an enlightenment, of knowledge, of understanding, of refinements of manners and refinement of mind. And if for the nonce I am ready to respond to my compatriots' call to serve them in the more urgent, and withal more perilous sphere of political activity, I shall on

that account by no means lessen my educational and editorial efforts on their behalf. On the contrary, I cherish a hope that my more honoured position in the Native Commonwealth, and my wider contact with the Native world, may rather tend to make those efforts still more extensive and effective.

He said he was choosing Booker Washington as his 'patron saint' as the most famous living example of what his race could achieve and one who had similarly toiled for its educational progress. But he went further, noting that 'political emancipation and rights' were even greater needs. Finally, he declared his deep respect for the country's rulers and his faith in the righteousness of Congress's cause. As he pointed out, 'Whatever political rights the British citizen now enjoys, he has won only at the cost of centuries of constant struggle; and surely he will not think ill of us if we now humbly follow in his footsteps.'[5]

This letter was widely published in the press and as a single document for circulation (appearing as far afield as in *Tuskegee Student*), and eagerly read by many, not least white government officials and patrons. His emphasis on the need within Congress to proceed with care and to restrain fervour and ambition; on the lawfulness of its demands; on its loyalty to government; and his earnest claim to the fundamental compatibility of his roles – it may well have been composed largely with this sort of audience in mind. For all this, the sincerity of its sentiments should not be doubted, although it has to be added that these were set at odds in a way now deeply ingrained in his public persona, reaching far beyond his recent contests with Campbell. The old race pride is there, as is his determination to assert his independence – but not to the dangerous extent of rupturing the bonds that tied him to the respectable world of sympathetic missionaries, settlers, colonial officials and benefactors.

Dube had never wanted to be 'the lizard that looked on while the family ate', as the Zulu saying put it, and was not going to become that lizard now. There was something else, too: while his words accorded a central guiding role to Booker Washington, his very act of assuming the presidency accorded more with a guiding role for the likes of J.E. Bruce. There was still a great deal of 'creative conflict' in him, likely to affect the manner in which he would discharge his presidential duties.

Our gate post

Once Dube had accepted the presidency, he threw himself into the position with considerable energy. He inspired enormous enthusiasm for the new organisation and led a concerted national campaign against government policy. In both these ventures, he oversaw Congress's first real attempts to connect with ordinary Africans in towns, on farms and in the reserves. His responsibilities would take him all over South Africa as well as abroad again. He would, as president, achieve the greatest prominence of his career – but also plummet to the lowest point in his life.

Within weeks he was in Cape Town, heading the first Congress delegation to the Minister for Native Affairs. The occasion had been organised by Solomon Plaatje, the new secretary, who, like Dube, was well connected in the new government. He was known to Botha, Schreiner and Merriman, able to talk to them 'as one politician to another'. He was rather closer to Henry Burton, who had practised as an advocate in Kimberley, where Plaatje had been based in the 1890s. Burton had won a celebrated test case on behalf of an African client, which resulted in an improvement in the day-to-day conditions of Kimberley's African community. Plaatje, Mapikela, Makgatho and Tsewu had arrived ahead of Dube and had already met with the executive of the African Political Organisation, pledging that the two organisations would meet at least once a year to discuss joint interests and actions.

When Dube joined them, the delegation met Burton and Edward Dower, his Secretary for Native Affairs, to discuss a wide range of matters that the constituent regional Congresses had wished to be put forward. These included passes for African women, the so-called black peril scares and the Squatters' Bill then before parliament. The Orange Free State stood alone in the Union at that time in enmeshing African and coloured women in its web of pass laws; elsewhere, provincial authorities (and colonial ones before them) had considered there to be too few women in urban areas to warrant their inclusion. Thus, women, like men, had to obtain and pay for permits to seek work, rent a plot, entertain visitors, organise social events, and prove they were in employment or were self-employed. Both women and men were thus subject to frequent searches, assault and abuse at the hands of the police and deeply resented these intrusions.

The 'black peril' issue was one that periodically reared its head, particularly in urban areas such as Johannesburg. House servants were still predominantly African and male, and the nature of their work meant admission to employers' intimate domestic spaces at times when women were at home and men out at work. Though actual incidents of assault in such conditions were rare, these were exaggerated in the press and fuelled a kind of social panic among whites, especially at times of heightened political uncertainty. A secondary form of 'black peril' also developed, concerning relationships between black male and white female servants, which were considered to upset the proper social hierarchy. African men found guilty of such liaisons were far more severely punished than white women were. These scares, which entirely neglected the problems of white men sexually assaulting black women, deeply offended respectable Africans. The Congress representatives asked Burton to set up a commission to look into the matter, something which did subsequently happen, and for which Congress was later able to claim some credit. Finally, the Squatters' Bill was a piece of legislation that had been introduced for debate the year before; it would have limited the number of Africans permitted to reside on white-owned farms. The delegation argued that it would result in a great deal of homelessness and requested that it be dropped. (This, too, subsequently occurred, though its lapse was more likely the result of objections from white landlords dependent on tenants' income, than of Congress representations.)

Burton and Dower received them courteously and assured them that their grievances would receive consideration. Dube won a small but significant freedom from Burton, to hold meetings wherever he liked, without having to obtain permission each time beforehand (as long as he informed the local magistrate), in order to tell Africans about the formation of Congress and to report on the Cape Town meetings. Congress deputies also met the Minister of Railways and Harbours, J.W. Sauer, to discuss the indignities that African passengers encountered on the rail network. A white man was then on trial in Pretoria, for example, charged with assaulting Sefako Makgatho on board a Transvaal train. Before he left, Dube stopped by to greet Senator Schreiner as well as Merriman, who had declined a position in Botha's cabinet, choosing instead the role of elder statesman and MP for Victoria West. Merriman's diary entry of the encounter not only gives no hint of a recollection that the two men had met before, at Ohlange, but also reveals a certain tendency to stereotype: 'John Dube called, a typical Zulu with powerful cruel face. Very moderate and civilised, spoke extraordinarily good English.'

Dube travelled home via Kimberley, Bloemfontein and Johannesburg to report on the Cape Town mission before addressing a Durban audience in early April in the Union Theatre in Victoria Street. All these meetings attracted large, enthusiastic crowds who, animated by their president's forceful performance, punctuated proceedings with deafening cheers. In the Union Theatre, for example, 100 Congress delegates attended a morning report-back, and over 2,000 – now including women as well as men – squeezed into the same venue for evening entertainment, including performances from several choirs, among them Ohlange's under the baton of Charles Dube, the presentation of a formal address to John Dube, and yet another presidential report. Dube made it clear that they had been given a sympathetic hearing and had every confidence that their requests would be granted. The mission had, therefore, been a great success.

Buoyed by this promising beginning, over 600 members attended a meeting in Pietermaritzburg just days later to bury the old Natal Native Congress, hopelessly divided, and to form a new, united one as the regional affiliate of the national Congress. In fresh elections, Stephen Mini was elected to the chair, Christian Lutayi as his deputy, Cornelius Gumede as secretary and the Rev. S. Msimang as treasurer. Then 'the President of all South Africa' spoke, and suggested that a 10-person committee be chosen to represent Natal directly on the national body. Among its members were Stephen Mini, Skweleti Nyongwana and Dirk Zibisi. While the Natal branch executive was heavily up-country in its composition, the new committee was self-consciously more representative of the region as a whole.

Despite these attempts to balance various factions and interests, the new-found unity was also short-lived. Notable by his absence was Martin Lutuli. Dube, never one for taking challenges to his leadership lightly, had reprimanded him for 'usurping the rights' of the chairman by holding an unconstitutional meeting and sending resolutions to the Chief Native Commissioner. Dube and Lutuli went back a long way, having worked together in church affairs since the early 1890s – Lutuli signed Dube's very first petition in 1896 and assisted him in bringing Nyuswa's Zulu Congregational Church back into the American Zulu Mission. Even so, procedural disagreements have a habit of reflecting principled ones. In retaliation, Lutuli refused to allow Congress speakers whom he associated with the 'Dube faction' to address meetings in Groutville. This particular rift would widen over time.

Zibisi was an enthusiastic new recruit to Congress. A well-to-do farmer from Mphaphala, near Eshowe, and often referred to as 'Jani Dube's *induna*' – to most ordinary people, John Dube was 'Jani Dube' – he was instrumental in carrying Dube's message into Zululand, where he told several meetings that the president had been chosen 'to be our gate post (*impundu*) to stand between us and the Government. He is working for the emancipation of us black people from the bonds by which we are at present bound.' Others like Zibisi fanned out over Natal and Zululand on Dube's behalf. The pattern of attendance that had emerged in previous years, of 'combination', a mix of inside and outside people gathering together to listen to Congress speakers, now repeated itself; there were always some chiefs turning out in person, too. For example, Paulus Ngwenya (also styled an *induna* of Dube's) addressed a gathering at the homestead of one Mazihila, near Mooi River, in April. He told the assembly that the wages earned by labour tenants were too low to meet homestead obligations; that relatives of mineworkers killed underground should receive compensation; that the dog tax was too onerous; that there was no justice in the courts for African defendants because the European interpreters did not do their jobs properly; and that white men who seduced African girls seemed always to escape punishment.

A meeting in Pietermaritzburg attracted mostly *togt* (day contract) and ricksha workers and evictees from white farms, who clamoured to tell Dube of their many sufferings. And at Mthwalume on the south coast, nine chiefs were among the large crowd who turned out to hear Dube. He reported that the Squatters' Bill, which would have meant mass evictions, had lately been dropped. This caused considerable excitement: some of those present were waving eviction notices and took Dube's announcement to mean that they were no longer under threat. Whether Dube drew a sharp enough distinction between their fate and that of the Squatters' Bill is not known, but he collected up the notices and offered to refer their plight to government. In the meantime, other labour tenants in the vicinity stopped paying their rent altogether.

Dube had intended to make his way to Cape Town immediately after this meeting – among other matters, he had been summoned to give evidence before a Select Committee on Native Affairs – and asked for the loan of a horse to hurry him back to Durban. This is when he had his celebrated fall, which laid him up at home for a few weeks.

> Our leader is wounded,
> Our hearts are all bleeding;
> For us he was riding
> Swift to his goal.
> Fast flew his horse,
> But his thoughts flew still faster,
> Prayers for his people
> Poured through his soul …

Predictably, this flurry of meetings caused extreme anxiety among officials. One admitted that there was already a general feeling among Natal Africans that they were not being justly treated by the government. Dube's speeches not only accentuated the anxiety, but 'this policy of combination which [he] is permitted to advocate' threatened whites' safety. Before long, letters streamed back and forth, accusing him of making 'too liberal a use' of Burton's generosity and of 'unsettling the native mind'. He vigorously denied these charges, accusing informers of misrepresenting him: 'My meetings are held solely in the interests of the Native Congress. Natives have of course brought matters to my notice but I have never … used [these] for the purpose of fomenting agitation. My loyalty to the Crown is well known.' Nor did magistrates like him collecting money, which he (and his fellow speakers) did on each occasion, to help the work of Congress, but they realised they were powerless to stop this practice.[1]

Dube was sufficiently recovered from his injuries by July to make the journey to Cape Town and may well have met with Schreiner concerning the grievances voiced at his meetings. He was also the main speaker at a Missionary Exhibition in the City Hall. Even the press report of his speech managed to convey the force of his performance. Commencing with the disarming observation that perhaps he should have had a label like all the other 'native crafts' being exhibited, he recounted his efforts to lift African boys and girls to a higher plane of being at Ohlange. Yet he was bitter about the disabilities that continually undermined this work – the discriminatory laws, the social prejudice – and gave these as his primary reason for becoming Congress president. Since 'a just government derives its rightful powers from the consent of the governed', it was time to campaign for representation, for 'our liberties and rights as taxed and governed bodies are not safe without it … we are going to come before the government, not with assegais in martial array, but peacefully as loyal subjects, and pray to be heard as to these of our grievances'. He concluded:

Ladies and gentlemen, I stand here tonight to plead the cause of a humble, of a helpless people, much despised perhaps by you but very dear to me. From the furthermost corners of this great sub-continent, thousands of black faces are turned to me this day, and are turned to you, hopeful and expectant; while on their behalf I deliver to you, the governing races in the land, their prayer for some amelioration of their lot. They beseech you in the name of Christ, to stay at length the harsh hand of class oppression and colour prejudice, and to remove from them the manacles of class legislation that hold them down. I plead for the brothers and sisters of my race. I plead for my native land. Nor will you, born children of freedom, wonder why ...

Throughout his presidency, Dube talked about Ohlange whenever he could. This was especially the case before audiences in which there might be one or two potential donors, but the reason went far deeper. Ohlange was, quite simply, his proudest achievement, not only because of the immense amounts of time and labour that he and Nokutela had spent on it, under very trying conditions, but also because it remained central to his ideas of independent social progress. That is why he insisted on keeping the titles 'Principal of Ohlange' and 'Proprietor of *Ilanga*'. Though he was now quite separated from the routine of the paper's production, he took care to ensure that its editorial policy was consistent with his own views and that it remained closely integrated into the life of the school. Nor was he involved in Ohlange's day-to-day operations – he was happy to delegate this role to Charles – but continued to act as the school's policy-maker, ambassador and fundraiser-in-chief. It had by this time added commercial courses to its academic and industrial ones, could name no less than two South African senators among its trustees (Campbell and Churchill), and preparations were under way to build the long-planned girls' dormitory. This would bring the value of the plant to an impressive £10,000, 'of which the government had given not a penny', he noted defiantly. What a contrast to the attitude of Merriman, who paid another visit later in 1912: 'We all went to John Dube's in afternoon – he has 185 pupils, pathetic in its strivings ...'

Also towards the end of 1912, Ohlange welcomed its most prestigious visitor yet: Gopal Krishna Gokhale, the best-known Indian nationalist leader of his generation. Born in 1866 in the ancient cultural centre of Maharashtra to a high-caste *khot* (rent collector) family, he had been fortunate to obtain good schooling, which launched his career in both education and politics. He rose to the position of college principal, and in 1905 was elected secretary of the Indian National Congress. He also served on the Imperial Legislative

Council and undertook two trips to London to campaign for Indian rights. Gandhi revered him as a mentor and had long wanted him to visit South Africa, not only to witness the problems of South African Indians at first hand – the punishing £3 tax payable by every non-indentured adult male, the lack of educational facilities, the limited job opportunities, the discrimination against traders – but also to use his influence abroad to obtain some relief for them. On Gokhale's month-long visit, Gandhi accompanied him everywhere and so in all likelihood finally saw Ohlange for himself. Marshall Campbell also received Gokhale at Mount Edgecombe. In spite of his disappointment in these two protégés, who had both failed to stay out of politics, Campbell continued to offer support of various kinds to Dube and Gandhi. In addition to his time on the Ohlange board, he funded prizes and necessary repairs at the school and, in November 1912, allowed a mass rally of 10,000 Indian workers on his estate, which Gokhale addressed.

All through the year, Dube travelled up and down Natal, explaining to people why Congress had been formed. Then in November came a high point: he crossed the Thukela, where only his *'izinduna'* had spoken before, to convene a meeting on behalf of Congress at the courthouse in Eshowe, the administrative centre of Zululand. A number of prominent chiefs attended, not least among them a member of the royal house, Mtonga Zulu, son of Mpande. As the district commissioner drily commented, 'well-known supporters of the uSuthu cause, who are not in the habit of attending at the promulgation of Government laws or notices, or at the visit of any of the Ministers or high officials, were noticed amongst those assembled.' The 300-strong crowd was made up mostly of outside people, with a sprinkling of Christians. A few white missionaries and officials were also present. One of these was Carl Faye, from the Department of Native Affairs, who attentively recorded Dube's speech in shorthand – the proceedings were entirely in Zulu – and then, with Dube's help, translated it into English for later publication in his compendium, *Zulu references for interpreters and students*.

Dube began by noting how much it meant to him to be in Zululand, 'our "England"'. There followed all the familiar tropes of his progressive nationalist appeal. Rivalries between chiefdoms within Zululand, and between the Zulu people and other polities like the Sotho, Swazi and Thonga, had been profoundly damaging. The lack of unity had allowed the government to pass laws 'against our feelings' and had distracted people from looking after their land: 'whilst we have been busily occupied in this way, people like Indians have come into our land and lorded it over us, as though we, who belong to the country, were mere non-entities.' He explained the system of parliamentary representation that Congress was urging for Africans and why the current arrangement of seeking redress through magistrates was wholly inadequate. To achieve anything at all, he stressed, they would have to be united and not feel afraid. Their cause would also require knowledge – by which, of course, he meant education. Therefore, he urged his listeners to stand together and to acquire knowledge and ingenuity, as the white people had so successfully done. Like the accomplished apostle that he was, Dube asked those who accepted his message to raise their hands. Some doubted the practicality of his message: as one chiefly representative put it, 'Can a rat speak to a fish?' – a reference to Africans, who were land-lovers, and whites, who had come from across the sea. Yet to Dube's immense satisfaction, Mtonga Zulu was so enthused that he raised both arms, which prompted another listener to comment, '[that] made me feel like putting up both my legs'. There was much laughter and applause, and shouts of 'It is the voice of the people!'

In the course of his speech, Dube also noted disquieting signs that the government was considering depriving them of even more of their land, 'the land of our birth, our only land, our home; we have nowhere else to go'. Halfway through 1912, there had been serious rifts in Botha's cabinet, resulting in departures and a reshuffle. Burton had been moved to Railways and Harbours and, to the dismay of many liberal parliamentarians as well as Congress, Hertzog became Minister for Native Affairs. Almost at once he began pressing for a more coherent policy towards Africans based on segregationist principles. There had of course been countless social practices, from slavery at the Cape in its earliest colonial days to the isolation of African and Chinese workers in mining compounds on the Reef in the twentieth century, whereby white rulers had allocated different spaces and statuses to different groups on the basis of their supposed race. But outside the frameworks of legality and custom, there existed as many instances of intermingling, exceptions to the rule and opportunities for those with a few resources to exploit loopholes: 'the planting of van Riebeeck's hedge gave segregation a symbolic antiquity, but that hedge had hardly been an effective barrier'. Only in the years immediately after Union did the terms 'segregation' and 'separation' begin to refer to a political ideology that would regulate relationships between races more rigidly. There was little consensus, however, as to how they would be applied or indeed what they would mean. As Richard Solomon wrote to W.P. Schreiner from the High Commissioner's office in London, 'I am anxious to see what Hertzog means by segregation. I don't like the word' – and Schreiner agreed.

Dube had specifically quizzed Burton at their May encounter on whether he supported segregation. 'No,' replied Burton, 'not in the sense you use the word, of entire separation of the two races, but in the sense of separation of areas in which the two races can own and acquire land – yes.' Later in the year, around the time of his Zululand visit, he made his own views clear. As he understood it – and intimated to Burton – segregation implied a complete separation of black from white, which in his view was not only completely impractical but highly undesirable. It was the state of the country before white people even arrived, and there was no going back. Separate land allocation was simply unworkable because it could not be achieved fairly: 'were Zululand still open, had you not already carved out all the prime parts there worth having, I for one should be delighted to betake myself into a second Basutoland established there.' Instead, in the absence of available land, a civilised society required increasing integration, not separation: 'the greater the distance between the white man and the black, the greater the loss to each.' Moreover, if there were to be total separation, whites would have to do all the menial jobs in their portion and would surely refuse to work for the 'wretched wages' that Africans received. A far more sensible approach would be for employers to educate Africans to be useful – not 'be so obstinate and short-sighted as to cut your own throats'. And for their part, 'no single native would be prepared to move, unless compelled by force ... But to prostitute your power to so immoral a proceeding would indeed be a sad object-lesson to us, a shameful reflection on a people professing to be guided by the spirit and teachings of Christ.' Whenever he discussed the matter, his meaning was very clear: separation was undesirable. But if this was what the future held, only an equitable division of land would work; and Africans would never have their due share unless they had parliamentary representation to insist upon it.

It did not take long for Hertzog's militancy on other issues – particularly his outspoken support for the principle of 'South Africa first', which questioned loyalty to the British Crown and therefore South Africa's dominion status – to cause an even more serious cabinet crisis, resulting this time in his departure from Botha's ministry altogether, without having introduced any segregationist legislation at all. But that was not the end of the matter. Growing tensions in the white body politic, between Hertzog's nationalist supporters in the Free State and the more moderate supporters of conciliation, were destabilising the government barely three years into its existence. One way of easing the situation was to offer a sop to the nationalists. As if to underline the common understanding among white politicians that

African affairs really were above party politics, it was Hertzog's replacement, the old Cape liberal Sauer, who introduced the Natives Land Bill in early 1913. Its contents made quite clear that the intention was not complete racial separation or the dismantling of an already integrated economy. Rather, it was a mechanism that would enable the state to replace a free market in land with the legal principle of 'possessory segregation': areas where Africans could live and buy land and from which whites would be excluded, and vice versa.

The bill appeared late in the session and was rushed through parliament, leaving little opportunity for public consultation or debate. Introduced in the House of Assembly on 24 April, it was gazetted on 5 May, was the subject of nine days of debate in late May and early June, passed its third reading in the Assembly on 11 June, passed through Senate on 15 June after two days of debate, received the Governor-General's assent on 16 June and became law on 19 June. Though it was contested at every stage, its opponents were in the minority. The new Act contained a 'Schedule of Native Areas', which included all the locations and reserves that had been demarcated in colonial times, as well as those tiny pockets of freehold African land dotted across the provinces. Together, these constituted some seven per cent of the country's total land area; as Schreiner pointed out in the Senate, 'it assign[ed] to 17/24ths of the population a fraction of the country to live in'. Inside this fraction, Africans could occupy, lease and buy land; outside it, they could not. *Indian Opinion* called it an 'act of confiscation'. The Act did acknowledge that seven per cent was unworkable, so it also made provision for the appointment of a commission, to be chaired by Justice William Beaumont, to suggest enlargements. This would turn out to be a useful shield against criticism – 'wait to see what the Commission recommends' – rather than any sort of equitable solution to the allocation of land.

Beyond the broad principle of possessory segregation, the legislation did not really lay down any uniform pattern. There were different conditions and clauses, and delays in enforcement, in each province. For example, so-called squatting – the practice whereby Africans leased farmland from white owners, paying their rent mostly in produce – was outlawed in the Orange Free State, by now the centre of South Africa's commercial maize production: labour service was required there, not an improving peasantry. The property restrictions were invalidated in the Cape because they interfered with qualifications for franchise rights; and elsewhere, exceptions could be made. In the Transvaal, the limit on the number of African workers on any farm was lifted; and in that province and Natal, Africans officially registered as resident on white farms and paying taxes at the time of promulgation were legally permitted to remain, unless of course the landlord wished to remove them for other reasons. Despite these variations, the foundations of 'one of the most extreme forms of racial discrimination in the twentieth-century world', devised for the economic advantage of the small white minority but at the expense of everyone else, were laid in the matter of a few months.[2]

Congress members gathered for their first annual conference in Johannesburg in March, feeling quite put upon. This was mostly to do with the impending legislation but also partly to do with the treatment recently meted out to their *Mongameli* (leader). The previous month, Dube had been making his way to a meeting in Bloemfontein in connection with plans to launch an Inter-State Native College, a scheme begun in the early 1900s and whose principal supporters were Jabavu and the missionaries at Lovedale. At Van Reenen's Pass (the Transvaal–Orange Free State border), the police detained him for not being in possession of an outward pass, which caused 'telegrams to fly all over, from the Cape, Pietermaritzburg and Bloemfontein' before he was able to proceed. However, the delay meant that he missed the meeting altogether, and the hoped-for representation from every province was not realised. There was real resentment in Congress that Dube had been slighted in this way.

In response to the draft legislation, Congress appointed a deputation to present its objections to government. There were many landowners and aspirant landowners among its members who felt as though their opportunities for purchase were being cut off. Yet Congress leaders were as concerned at the prospect of agricultural tenants, whether prospering or struggling, being turned off private farms and forced into already overcrowded reserves, where there was no land at all to support them. Indeed, Dube had recently addressed a well-attended meeting in Ixopo, at which his audience complained of the hardship of those facing eviction from white land and the lack of dipping tanks for their use. He had urged his hearers to 'make me your greyhound and place me at your head to lead you and represent your grievances to Government'. He himself was to head the deputation, which also included Rubusana, Msane and Mangena.

By the time they arrived in Cape Town in May (there was always a delay because of the need, on every such occasion, to raise the necessary fares from supporters), the bill had begun its progress through parliament and they were outraged by its contents. They met with Sauer on four occasions. He himself admitted it was a 'bad law' but insisted it would offer some protection to Africans and they should wait for the final recommendations of the Land Commission. When Merriman met with them, he described their reaction to the draft legislation as 'very violent'. He too counselled 'caution and moderation' and believed he had succeeded. Dube, he thought, 'may be a valuable agent if properly handled, or a very great source of danger if allowed to feel no-one sympathizes'. In truth, the delegation must have felt collectively that 'no-one sympathized'. This was not only the biggest challenge that Congress had thus far had to face, but it also seemed to constitute virtually the only organised opposition to the measure. Jabavu, for example, had supported it. Congress leaders were therefore not going to stand by without a contest.

In July, Dube chaired an expectant meeting in Johannesburg to report on the Cape Town visit and to decide the next steps Congress would take. Rubusana gave the approximately 200 delegates a full account of all their discussions with ministers. After much deliberation, it was decided that the proper course would be to exhaust all constitutional means at home to get the Act annulled, failing which a delegation would travel to London to put their case to the British public, parliament and the King, who had a year to disallow the legislation. Plaatje had already written to Lord Gladstone, the Governor-General, asking him to withhold his assent; he, however, was not inclined to intervene. Dube now contacted him again: would he meet with Congress to hear its views? Again Congress received a negative response. Its leaders probably possessed sufficient acumen, as well as experience of broken British promises, to know that this 'constitutional' course had little chance of getting the legislation repealed. It could, however, mobilise opinion, generate publicity and attract support in pursuit of their ultimate goal of parliamentary representation. It was the only acceptable means they had.

There were more confrontational ways of making demands known, although their outcome was no more certain. Some weeks earlier, a dispute had arisen over the working hours of skilled white miners, mostly of British extraction and with a history of militant trade unionism, at the New Kleinfontein mine on the East Rand. Underground conditions were generally poor: there was constant pressure to speed up production, which meant supervising more drills per shift; being paid per shift rather than per hour, men could be left waiting in holding areas for hours; and always the threat of phthisis hung in the air, along with the dust. African miners were as susceptible, of course, but there was almost no attempt at this time to unionise them. Moreover, African mineworkers' interests tended to be seen as conflicting with those of their white supervisors: they were pinned back by the job colour bar, while white miners were always wary of being undercut by cheaper labour. As Dube had trenchantly written some years earlier, 'white miners oppose any reforming of native people, on the ground that the native may one day oust them from skilled labour, and that Christianizing them is a stepping-stone to this.'

Before long, the dispute had become a stoppage, then a localised strike, then escalated into a Reef-wide white workers' general strike. Tensions between the strikers and bosses spilled over into serious skirmishes and much bloodshed before Botha and Smuts felt compelled to intervene personally. The negotiated settlement reinstated the status quo ante. In the aftermath, some African miners refused to go underground until their working conditions had improved, but they were driven back to work by the police; in terms of the 1911 Native Labour Regulation Act, strikes by African workers were technically illegal. All this was happening while Congress was considering its tactics. Some Transvaal delegates thought it was time to call a strike in support of their own demands, but they were overruled. In fact, Dube, Plaatje and other Congress leaders specifically distanced themselves from such action. If they were to have any hope of winning constitutional rights, they could not be seen to be engaging in such behaviour.

At the time another extra-parliamentary challenge to state authority was unfolding. In the wake of Gandhi's earlier *satyagraha* campaign and the halting of all indentured immigration, the Union government had been planning to regularise Indians' position in South Africa. After several stalled attempts, the Immigration Act was enacted just two days before the Natives Land Act. It brought no real relief from hardship or discrimination: the hated £3 tax, which reduced most time-expired indentured workers to a life back under indenture, remained in force, despite Smuts's word to Gokhale that it would be repealed. The rest of the Immigration Act was a litany of restrictions on immigration, on movement between provinces, on trade and on land acquisition. Gandhi's response was to prepare for a fresh wave of *satyagraha*. In late 1913, large groups of resisters crossed from Natal into the Transvaal, courting arrest. Many, including Gandhi himself, were sentenced to prison terms with hard labour. Support spread to the northern Natal coalfields, where Indian miners struck, and to the coastal sugar belt. Some 15,000 workers, including those from Mount Edgecombe, left their estates (but not before cutting all the cane) and gathered in towns like Verulam and Stanger; some made their way to Phoenix. The campaign ended only when Smuts finally agreed to repeal the £3 tax and to relax constraints on Indian wives entering South Africa, measures contained in the 1914 Indian Relief Act. Other restrictive measures still applied, however. Shortly afterwards,

Gandhi returned permanently to India.

It was at Phoenix station at the height of *satyagraha* that Dube witnessed one attempt to force estate workers to end their action. About 500 of them gathered on open ground nearby and were surrounded by estate managers as well as white and African policemen. When they refused to move, the police first used whips, then sticks and rifle butts. They then attacked women in the group. The strikers, true *satyagrahis*, continued to sit motionless. Mounted police were then brought in and galloped through the crowd, causing extensive injuries. This still did not remove them, so one of their leaders was hauled before them and tortured in full view of all. This did elicit some movement from the crowd, at which the white policemen opened fire, causing death and further injuries.

Some months later, Dube told a visiting priest from India that he had been horrified: 'after being an eye witness to the struggle, instead of taking the Indian workers as uncivilised and treating them disdainfully, I have acquired a sense of respect for all the Indians.' Yet he gave a telling explanation as to why he did not consider *satyagraha* a feasible strategy for Congress. Indians, he felt,

> could display extraordinary endurance. If our Natives come in their place, nobody can control their violent nature. For their safety they would certainly retaliate. The white men of this place require only this much. If any brother of mine kills a white man after being excited, it would precipitate a great disaster upon us. Thousands of brothers of mine would be put to death in no time and we would be totally ruined. We do not possess so much prowess also to wage a *satyagraha* struggle. Only the strength of the Indians can endure it.

This account helps to explain why Dube, and perhaps other leaders, ruled out anything similar: passive resistance, as Gandhi's campaigns of 1907–10 and 1913–14 demonstrated, would require mass participation of a highly disciplined kind, and they considered that the masses were not ready. Their chosen strategy did, nevertheless, carry risks. For one thing, there were enormous expectations from the crowds they addressed that Congress could relieve their hardship. For another, it would require them to collect enough money to get a delegation to London and back. With the exception of Queen Labotsibeni of the Swazi, who had put up £3,000 to establish the Congress paper, *Abantu-Batho*, this was not an organisation possessing wealthy backers or ready campaign funds. Those several Congress supporters who were comfortably off generally had many calls on their resources and, though they always gave something, could not be expected to carry the full burden of expenses. Saul Msane was appointed chief fundraiser, to be assisted by a special committee.

The other important task was to gather evidence of the hardship that the Land Act was causing. Dube would tour Natal, and he and Msane would cover the Transvaal; probably the youngest delegate present at the launch of Congress, H. Selby Msimang, would accompany Dube around Sekhukhuneland. Plaatje would focus on the Free State. It was in this province that he did indeed witness the 'great rural spasm' that the Act precipitated, as evicted families wandered the dust roads, sleeping in the open and desperately trying to keep cattle alive and to save their children from illness: this was the middle of the highveld winter. Plaatje later graphically captured their plight in his book *Native life in South Africa*. Many drifted across into the south-western Transvaal, where there were still undercapitalised white farmers willing to accept tenants.

In Natal, Dube gathered a long list of cases of hardship for the consideration of the Chief Native Commissioner. The problem was, he observed, that since the introduction of the Squatters' Bill during the 1912 session of parliament, 'eviction by farmers has been much increased … [N]ow the Natives' Land Bill has become law, [natives] are prevented from entering into agreements with landowners as rent-paying tenants, and only under servile conditions, with the result that in many cases they become wandering and helpless vagrants.' But here, as elsewhere, officials disputed the scale of the problem, temporised or evaded responsibility. Plaatje and Dube, together with Makgatho, encountered a similar attitude in F.S. Malan, newly appointed Minister for Native Affairs following Sauer's death, when they visited him to report what they had witnessed in country areas and to inform him of their intention to take a deputation abroad. He too refused to deal with the implications of the Act and focused instead on dissuading them from the idea of a delegation. All this merely deepened Congress leaders' resolve: if they could not overturn the Act, they could at least mount a vigorous protest against its consequences. That the delegation should proceed was growing into a cause in itself. Yet there were sympathisers cautioning Congress not to put all its newly gathered eggs in one basket. Harriette Colenso told Dube that Congress was more important than the Land Act: 'Before, the Abantu were dumb, now they have found their voice and John Dube has largely helped in finding it.'

Preparations for their campaign were interrupted in October by the news that the exiled Dinuzulu had passed away at his Middelburg farm at the age of 45. As soon as he learned that the prince was ill, Dube made his way to Middelburg but arrived too late. He did have talks with Mankulumana, the prince's most senior adviser. Dinuzulu had not named an heir, and this was an obvious point of discussion. As he was widely regarded as their link to the Zulu royal house, thousands of Zulu workers in Durban turned out at the Racecourse and the Point to hear Dube's reports of Dinuzulu's death. Meanwhile, in order to forestall any official objections, Dinuzulu's body was rapidly removed by train to Vryheid, then onward by wagon to Nobamba for burial.

Before the funeral could proceed, the matter of the succession had to be resolved. There was division in royal circles over whether it should pass to David Nyawana or Solomon Nkayishana. Mankulumana's and Dinuzulu's personal attendants declared their support for David. Seme, who had taken charge of Dinuzulu's medical treatment and financial affairs, and Harriette Colenso were both consulted. Along with several of the most senior royals, their verdict was that Solomon was the rightful candidate, and he was duly presented as such. Both Dube and Seme played a prominent part in the funeral ceremony, attended by some 7,000 mourners. Dube was probably somewhat put out by Seme's interposition in the succession issue. When, weeks later, Harriette Colenso made known her plans to introduce Solomon to Botha, Dube reproved her for her haste. While he cited etiquette as the reason – the proper mourning observance was a year, which she readily conceded – it may well be that he had sided with Mankulumana in favouring David.[3]

Through the remainder of 1913 and early 1914 there was an edgier tone to Congress meetings. Officials were increasingly resentful that such meetings were allowed at all, and Dube played on this. For example, Charles Dube took the Ohlange choir to the Pietermaritzburg YMCA Hall for a musical evening devoted to collecting funds. Harriette and Agnes Colenso were in the audience. Much of the singing was about Dube, praised as 'the bull that rescues', and Dinuzulu's, Bhambatha's and Mankulumana's names were heard in the words to other songs. Dube got up and announced that he would not address the meeting because there were informers (*izincekwana*) in the hall – they wanted to try to catch him but he was not in the mood to accommodate them. What was striking about meetings at this stage was the apparent willingness of ordinary people to donate to the cause of the London mission.

There was also growing anger at the government's refusal to address their grievances while at the same time deprecating their plan of action. Officials had been going round the country trying to dissuade Africans from having anything to do with it. On behalf of Congress, Dube addressed a petition to Botha in February on this very matter. He reiterated that they would prefer to settle the land question at home but that they were being ignored. He recounted the consequences of the Land Act: enforced servitude; ever-higher rents; the hardship of those made homeless; and the duplicity of officials, who explained the Act differently to whites (the Act favoured their interests) and blacks (the Act was meant to protect them). One clause of the petition read,

> We make no protest against the principle of separation so far as it can be fairly and practically carried out. But we do not see how it is possible for this law to effect any greater separation between the races than obtains now. It is evident that the aim of this law is to compel service by taking away the means of independence and self-improvement. This compulsory service at reduced wages and high rents will not be separation, but an intermingling of the most injurious character of both races.

It is of interest that he used the term 'separation', implying something quite different from the land arrangements embodied in the Land Act, to which he and other leaders were opposed 'root and branch', as he put it. There was, at this time, much talk among Africans about the desirability of complete separation of the 'black house' from the 'white house', especially in Natal and Zululand. Stephen Mini was such an advocate, and it was heard from several quarters at Dinuzulu's funeral, not least in Dube's speech. There had even been a collection for land purchases for the 'black house', and many of the self-help and improvement schemes being started up were probably motivated by such an intention. Whether this was wistful longing for a haven from persecution or a realistic political programme, it was a position that came increasingly to be identified with Dube.

Botha deputed Dower to reply to the Congress petition and he did so at great length, refuting every point Dube had made and accusing him of misunderstanding the Act. He concluded that the legislative provision for Africans, consequent upon the recommendations of the Land Commission, would be generous, and would even form the basis of administration of these areas by Africans themselves. Neither Dube nor any other Congress leader had ever raised the prospect of separate political institutions: this was not the sort of representation they were after. There was nothing else now to be done except to petition parliament in Cape Town one last time and then, failing a response, proceed with the delegation to London.

Dube had already approached the Anti-Slavery and Aborigines' Protection Society for assistance with its work. He must have been somewhat surprised by the response, that assistance would not be possible. The Society believed that the Act did actually hold out the prospect of protecting African land rights and was certain the Land Commission would add substantially to the scheduled areas. It was therefore not disposed to take any action likely to undermine the Botha government's efforts. Moreover, Harris and Buxton, the joint secretaries of the Society, were aware that virtually all white politicians sympathetic to African interests had counselled against this delegation, as there was scant chance of success. Their dilemma was that Congress could not be prevented from this course of action and, without some skilful management from an organisation like the Society, might cause unnecessary difficulty. This was the reasoning that led, after further correspondence, to a revision of its position: the Society would, after all, help with arrangements in London.

The second annual conference of Congress in late February 1914 was meant to have taken place in Nancefield in Johannesburg but was banned, ostensibly because of prolonged tension from the miners' strike, and hastily moved to Kimberley. It was dominated by preparations for the trip to Britain. The Bishop of Kimberley and Kuruman made a late attempt to stop them, urging them to have faith in Dower. W.P. Schreiner tried likewise to persuade them of the futility of the undertaking. In the middle of proceedings, Dower himself suddenly telegrammed through that he would attend: this was taken as a sign that there might yet be concessions. Despite entertaining the delegates to dinner and exhorting them to look to the beneficial aspects of the Act – namely, the measures for territorial separation, which he believed Dube supported – his visit 'was entirely barren of results', as Plaatje put it. Dube's view was that the Act was 'class legislation, pure and simple'. The only acceptable separation would require a line being drawn from Port Elizabeth to the Zambezi, with whites on one side and Africans on the other. Africans would never have this sort of fairness until they had representation. Then the members of the deputation were chosen: by formal vote, John Dube would be accompanied by Sol Plaatje, Sefako Makgatho, Saul Msane, Thomas Mapikela and W.Z. Fenyang. (Fenyang withdrew in favour of Rubusana, and Makgatho did not get to Cape Town in time.) Elka Cele, treasurer of the fundraising committee and a long-time Qadi associate of Dube as well as being related to him by marriage, proudly announced that £1,353 had been raised to support the delegates on their trip. Spirits were high. At a large reception in the City Hall, delegates watched films, listened to music and danced, and Dube was presented with an illuminated address crafted by the sisters of St Joseph's Convent, Mafeking.

In the middle of preparations for his departure, Dube was invited to call on Henry Rider Haggard, the celebrated author of *King Solomon's Mines* and other dashing imperial tales. Haggard's first visit to Natal and Zululand, the setting for these novels, had been as an aide to Henry Bulwer, Governor of Natal, in the 1870s. Two officials he then befriended, Theophilus Shepstone and James Stuart, had awakened his fascination with Zulu culture and history. Now he was on tour as a member of the Dominions Royal Commission, a body set up to investigate how best South Africa, Canada and New Zealand could play their imperial part. In the intervening years, he had developed a keen interest in land reform. He had campaigned for the return of peasant farming in England, investigated the Salvation Army land colonies in America and involved himself in rural development in his native Norfolk. With land issues uppermost in Dube's mind, they had much to talk about.

Dube detailed all his objections to the Land Act before discussing broader social problems. He believed that racial attitudes were hardening: whites had been 'tightening the screw' and in response Africans felt they should 'go away and live in their own country'. Since power lay in the hands of whites, it was their responsibility to bring about better understanding. One way of demonstrating this would be to spend a greater proportion of the taxes raised from Africans on their education: a national education system was the greatest need. Haggard, who had been taking notes, read these back to Dube, who agreed they were an accurate reflection of their conversation. Haggard's verdict was that Dube 'impressed me most favourably while the case which he advanced seems to me one hard to answer'.

A year after they had first lodged their objections to the Land Act, members of the Congress delegation gathered in Cape Town. They wished to submit a final petition to parliament requesting that the most harmful clauses of the Act be suspended until the Land Commission had made its recommendations and to plead for some measures to alleviate hardship. But they discovered a snag: they had only until 19 June to ask the King to disallow the Act, and it would have taken longer than that to have their petition discussed in the House of Assembly. So they could not, in fact, take *all* the constitutional steps that would have made their case watertight. Instead, they had talks with various politicians, including Merriman and even Botha himself and the Governor-General. All of them expressed the same familiar reprise: not to go ahead with the London mission.

Dube suddenly seemed to cave in to all this pressure. A faint trace of an earlier pattern was discernible in the uncomfortable letter he wrote to Merriman, claiming that his part in Congress 'was thrust upon me by my native people' and that he proposed 'to return from England and devote my life to the prosecution of my work at Ohlange and I am sure … you will appreciate the delicate position in which I have been placed'. After conferring with Botha, who felt that Dube was in the 'horns of a dilemma' and that the 'manly course for him to take' would be to back down, Merriman called him in for a private chat. He warned Dube that he would return 'with a sense of failure'. In reply Dube focused on the injustices of the Land Act and reminded Merriman that Congress's requests for relief had fallen on deaf ears. In an apparent attempt to blame others for his predicament, he accused certain 'hot heads' (probably meaning Plaatje) of insisting on proceeding. In a calculated appeal to Dube's ethnic vanity, Merriman replied, 'I am surprised at a Zulu being led by people like that, you ought to lead your people in the right way.' In truth, even before the close of the Kimberley conference, Dube had secretly confided to Dower that he wanted to abandon the idea of the delegation. But his status as president would have suffered irreparably had he insisted on overriding the wishes of either his executive or the delegation members, so he had continued with arrangements. Now Merriman and Botha were needling him for exactly this reason.[4]

The only small relief was the support given the delegation by the South African Society, a body formed just a month earlier 'to promote the welfare of the Native and Coloured races'. Its leading light was Colonel Walter Stanford. W.P. Schreiner, Betty Molteno, Alice Greene, Maurice Evans (an authority on 'race relations' from Natal) and the Morija-based missionary Edouard Jacottet were also involved. It hosted a public meeting for them in the City Hall library on the eve of their departure. The audience was 'small but appreciative'. It was nevertheless a dejected John Dube who sailed with Rubusana on 15 May; the others departed the following day. There was not much to lift his spirits in London, either. They arrived to find themselves tightly controlled by John Harris of the Anti-Slavery and Aborigines' Protection Society. He instructed them not to speak to the press or address public meetings before an attempt had been made to secure an audience with the Secretary of State for the Colonies, Lord Harcourt. Harris sent Harcourt a letter of explanation. It took a week to receive the response that he would not make a decision until he had seen a written statement of the points that Congress wished to raise. Dube and Rubusana had in readiness drawn up such a document. It contained a crisp statement of their objections to the

Land Act – that Africans were deprived of the right to purchase land, as well as to lease white-owned land; that workers had to obtain permits to leave farms, which amounted to a form of slavery; that it confined Africans to too little land; that there had been spirited protest at every stage through parliament. For all these reasons, they requested that the King disallow it.

But this document was never submitted to Harcourt. Instead, Harris set up a Society sub-committee to draft the letter that *was* sent off in the deputation's name. It did note the 'deep and widespread regret amongst the natives of South Africa' caused by the realisation that the King would not disallow an Act that had already 'rendered landless and homeless a large number of His Majesty's native subjects'. It then made two limited requests: to suspend the most harmful clauses of the Act until the Land Commission had announced its findings, and to examine documented cases of hardship with a view to remedying these. It concluded by expressing confidence in the same point that Dower had made in reply to Dube's petition, namely that the land settlement for Africans would ultimately satisfy their needs. That being the case, they commended it as the basis for 'a native policy of the Imperial and South African Governments'. The delegates had come to London to register their emphatic protest at the Land Act – and here they were, cornered into lending it support. Although Dower had dispatched an official to shadow the delegation and limit its effectiveness, his services were hardly required.

Their disconsolate wait through an oppressive June heat wave was relieved by various receptions organised by well-wishers, among them Jane Cobden Unwin, Sophie Colenso (sister-in-law to Harriette and Agnes), the prominent social and suffragist campaigner Georgiana Solomon (who was also a close friend of Betty Molteno and Alice Greene) and the Liberal MP Sir Albert Spicer. Finally, Harcourt replied that he would meet them. There was, however, a charade-like quality to the way things went after that. Harcourt exhibited a complete lack of interest (though they did try to rescue themselves: Harris afterwards regretted that they 'did not in their interview confine themselves to the points urged in their letter to him') and a meeting with MPs and Peers in the Committee Rooms at the House of Commons achieved little.

Harris continued to manage their every move, tetchily upbraiding Dube for not having consulted him before arranging an interview with the *Methodist Recorder* and for not reporting his movements regularly enough. He did set up interviews for them with some of the big dailies, like the *Manchester Guardian*, *Daily Chronicle*, *Morning Post* and *Daily News*, but not before the

Society had issued a statement to the South African press, through Reuters, that the delegation had made a mistake in coming to London. This made Dube very angry. His patience worn thin from weeks of intensive minding and stretching their budget to cover delays, he sent a strongly worded, even petulant, letter to Buxton: 'This has had a disheartening effect on the Natives and has placed a weapon with which to hammer us in the hands of our enemies out there' – and asked that the statement be withdrawn. Curiously, though signed by him, this letter was not in his hand.

Although the deputation received a column's worth of coverage in most of the papers they spoke to, by now media attention was focused on the death and funeral arrangements of the veteran Liberal Unionist politician Joseph Chamberlain. The evidently patronising tone of Harris's reaction to the press reports, that 'by your statesmanlike conduct you have captured the Press of England', could not have convinced anyone, least of all the two seasoned editors among them. Harcourt's Under-Secretary sent a note of rebuke that they had not gone to the South African parliament for redress (a point Harcourt himself would repeat in August in the Commons), and shortly after that, in mid-July, Dube sailed for South Africa alone, on SS *Kenilworth Castle*, leaving Rubusana in charge in London.

There certainly did not seem to be anything to be gained by prolonging their visit. Though the remaining members continued to address public meetings, the Anti-Slavery and Aborigines' Protection Society was anxious for them to return home. In any case, the country was by now caught up in events far larger than their land rights. Everyone was watching nervously as the assassination of an unpopular Habsburg archduke in the Balkans triggered the unravelling of decades-old treaties and *ententes* across Europe, and generals stirred armies – in Austria-Hungary, then Germany, then Russia and France – into full mobilisation. This struggle for the mastery of Europe turned into a world war when the Liberal government in Britain voted in early August to join the conflict with France and Russia, committing not just its own resources but also those of its colonies and dominions to a war effort.

Rubusana and the others were perplexed and upset that Dube had abandoned them with insufficient funds. Before his departure, Plaatje noted, Dube 'shared our last few pounds with us on the ground, he said, that he was not going home but going to tour the country on our behalf … he left while we were using our passage money pending the results of his efforts.' But then he cabled them to say he was unable to collect money for them and they should come home. They were therefore forced into asking for assistance from Harris, with whom they would all rather have had nothing more to do. One of the Society's committee members extended them a loan of £65, guaranteed by the Wesleyan Missionary and the London Missionary societies. In return, they had to agree to leave as soon as possible, not to ask anyone else for support, to have their fares as well as board and lodging paid directly by the guarantors, so that the money could not be used for anything else, and to undertake to repay the loan if Congress failed to do so. Plaatje refused to be bound by such conditions, preferring to make his own way in Britain while he completed his book. Rubusana raised money from a friend. They squabbled among themselves until Rubusana, Mapikela and Msane sailed home separately, and so the deputation 'ended in smoke', as Plaatje put it. (Congress would finally honour this debt, but it took two years to do so.)

Dube did have another pretext for his abrupt departure. Harris had taken him aside in London to inform him discreetly of a most important campaign that his Society was about to launch: to contest the legitimacy of the British South Africa Company's claims to unalienated land in Southern Rhodesia. It was the Society's view that Africans living on this land should be involved in the resolution of this issue, and Dube's delegation had agreed to speak temporarily on their behalf until such time as contact could be made with their representatives. Dube, it will be remembered, had voiced strong criticism of the Company's land-grabbing activities in the 1890s, so he must have looked forward to the assignment Harris had in mind for him with some relish, to sound out African leaders in Southern Rhodesia, prior to Harris himself making a visit. From Madeira he wrote to Harris that he was hurrying home 'in connection with the Rhodesian business' and on arrival in Cape Town he hinted darkly to a journalist that he was engaged on urgent business the exact nature of which he could not fully divulge.

It sounded all very cloak-and-dagger and was also somewhat confused. In September, Harris wished to make quite clear that Dube 'is not going on any mission with instructions from England'. Yet later in the year, he was again anxiously writing to Dube in strictest confidence about 'the reception which prominent natives may give us in Rhodesia … it would be exceedingly unfortunate if for any reason they are led to suspect our motives. Have you any connections in Salisbury or Bulawayo to whom you could write privately and confidentially telling them who and what we are?' Dube subsequently tried, but was refused permission, to travel into Southern Rhodesia. Though Harris *was* allowed in on condition that he terminated all contact with Dube's Congress, he failed to find African leaders to work with. It was left to the Society to brief lawyers in London to represent African interests when the case finally came up before the Privy Council in 1919; its decision was that unalienated land belonged to the British Crown.

Whatever else he was up to, Dube made his way straight from the ship to a Congress meeting in Bloemfontein, anxious no doubt to explain his solitary arrival back in the country. While it was in session, official news came of the outbreak of war. Immediately, delegates voted unanimously to suspend all public criticism of and campaigns against the government on account of the hostilities, and pledged loyalty to the South African and imperial governments and the Crown. Dube went on to address gatherings in Kroonstad, Johannesburg and Durban. Some were well attended, others not; all were rather deflated. While he cited the war as the reason for the deputation's lack of success, this was hardly the whole story. For him at least, it was more like deliverance from a burden he was only too relieved to offload. For their part, listeners were keener to have reassurance that their land and cattle would be safe than to contemplate a failed appeal to the King or help stranded delegation members to get home. In mid-1914 Hertzog had finally broken with Botha and launched his National Party, which soon became a rallying point for opposition to Britain's war effort and particularly South Africa's invasion of German South West Africa. By November, some 12,000 Afrikaners had joined an uprising to topple Botha's government; over 300 combatants were killed before it was put down. Dube had been trying to explain to African audiences how far away the fighting was – 'a man walking to the place would die of old age before he reached there' – but with armed rebels and government troops roaming the countryside and seizing Africans' stock and horses, it seemed very much closer.[5]

Dube did not return to devote himself to Ohlange in the way he had claimed to Merriman he would like to do. For many months – at least since the delegation set off – he had been weighed down by a personal matter that caused him much anxiety. In November, the news broke, as it was bound to do, that a female student at Ohlange had recently borne him a child. Dube apparently admitted parental responsibility immediately. Betty Molteno and Alice Greene were the ones to discover the misdeed: deeply distressed, they conveyed the news to John Harris as he arrived in Johannesburg. He pounced on it as vindication of his dislike of Dube and as reason to distance the Society from him. But then the baby died and a local committee hurriedly set up to investigate cleared him of any wrongdoing. A strong 'code of privacy' meant that in the public domain, at least, the matter seemed to blow over, although he lost valuable support and whispers escaped into respectable circles. In *The history of Rasselas* (the one work Samuel Johnson set in Africa), the poet-sage

Imlac tells Prince Rasselas to beware teachers of morality: 'they discourse like angels, but they live like men.' Why *had* this 'teacher of morality' behaved quite so recklessly?

This man, so confident of his destiny to lead, so sure of the righteousness of his mission and so capable of articulating his views, had, in truth, been obsessed for two decades by a sense of utter personal failure on one deeply significant matter: he and Nokutela had been unable to produce children. The importance of fathering children was shared by outside and inside people alike. On one side it completed a rite of passage to manhood, while on the other it fulfilled the ostensible reason for Christian marriage. On both sides it ensured continuity of the family line, of special moment in leading and chiefly families. So the expectations that John and Nokutela would perpetuate the Dube house were enormous and their inability to do so nothing short of calamitous. Underneath all the public achievement, then, was this terrible sense of inadequacy: the 'father of the nation' could not call himself a father in his own home. We have an idea, too, of how Nokutela felt: in that schoolgirl essay of hers, she had noted solemnly, almost like a portent: 'If a person had no children, he troubled very much.' Even at that young age, she clearly knew about the social expectation of parenthood. There is no way of knowing whether she already suspected she could not bear children, but it is doubtful that she could have foreseen quite how painful the consequences would be. She and her husband's commitment to the education of future generations is all the more poignant in the light of their own sadness.

On their return to Inanda in 1899, they had taken in two young girls, probably relatives of Nokutela's, to live with them. While this allowed a semblance of family life, Dube was seemingly prepared to stake his respectability – indeed, his entire redemption project – on finding out whether he could, in fact, father children. As early as 1902, a rumour surfaced that he had made a local girl pregnant. If there was any truth in it, he would have realised that it was Nokutela who was infertile; under these circumstances, it would seem that Charles and Adelaide's eldest son, Frederick, was groomed as a sort of successor to the Dube legacy. The 1914 incident brought Nokutela very great hardship. It was not only that she was reminded publicly of her inability to exercise her wifely responsibilities to so prominent a leader. In clearing Dube of any misdemeanour, the committee of investigation was in effect declaring its sympathy for his predicament – and she probably would have known the girl concerned. After all they had achieved together, she and John became estranged, and she withdrew from Ohlange to a lonely existence on a farm near Wakkerstroom in the Transvaal.

With their joint vision (this was *her* redemption project, too) and home life shattered, Dube found it impossible to continue as normal at Ohlange and spent the remaining years of his presidency based largely in Johannesburg. Evidently expecting to be there a long time, he bought a property in Sophiatown, whose uniform 46-square-metre plots were now home to about a thousand people, took an office in downtown Johannesburg on the corner of Simmonds and Market streets, and applied for his old Natal exemption from Native Law to be recognised nationwide. Congress business through these years was awkwardly suspended between defence of African interests and its own self-imposed avoidance of protest activity. The 'smoke' of the deputation débâcle also lingered, impeding its work. While Seme was irritable enough with Dube over the whole affair, Msane never forgave him; R.V. Selope Thema, a young Lovedale-trained clerk in Richard Msimang's legal practice who had taken Plaatje's place as general secretary, was soon identifying two camps of 'ites' in Congress, Msaneites and Dubeites. The former used the pages of *Abantu-Batho*, and the latter *Ilanga*, to trade insults. Personal contests compounded deeper troubles. Little was achieved by way of consolidating the organisation, of integrating the regional branches, of agreeing a constitution – this was completed only in 1919 – or of bringing the financial affairs of Congress under proper control. To be sure, these were difficult tasks under even favourable conditions: South Africa's geography, communications network and distances would present formidable challenges to any organisation with national aspirations all through the twentieth century. There were plenty of reasons, then, why these war years were not Congress's proudest or most productive.

Dube not only used his office for Congress activities. More important was his pecuniary occupation at the time, as a director of the Native Farmers' Association of Africa Ltd, a company that Seme had established in the eastern Transvaal. While in some respects resembling other self-help initiatives to encourage ownership, agricultural capitalisation and improvement, the Association functioned more like a land agency. H. Selby Msimang was the Association's representative on the spot. It purchased a number of farms around Wakkerstroom (hence Nokutela's settling there), including Daggakraal, Driefontein and Vlakplaats. While the plan was to subdivide and sell or lease lots, it was not long before the enterprise was in difficulties. In 1912 it had sold 2,500 morgen to one Chief Moloi for £34,000, repayable over 12 years. By 1916 Moloi was seriously in arrears and the sale was cancelled. Though Dube denied wrongdoing, the Association was accused of inadequately compensating him.

Another deal also went awry. Seme had been in negotiations to buy Mooifontein, a large farm in the Middelburg district, from its white owner. Confident that his application for special permission to purchase would succeed (since this was subsequent to the passage of the Land Act), he had begun reorganising production on the farm. In an attempt to attract those with some capital, he raised the rent for a 10-morgen plot to over £60; this meant several sitting tenants had been forced off. Seme's application failed, however, and in mid-1916 all the tenants were given notice to quit. These episodes seem to have seriously undermined the credibility of the Farmers' Association, though it continued selling land until well into the 1920s. There was also carping conflict with other similar initiatives, such as Msane's Natal-based Native Centralisation Scheme, as recrimination leaked into the gap between promises of economic self-sufficiency and capacity to furnish the necessary material resources.

Dube frequently shuttled to Inanda in an attempt to keep some semblance of authority at Ohlange. In early 1915, he appointed a new editor to *Ilanga*, still produced on the campus with the help of pupils' labour. Ngazana Luthuli replaced Skweleti Nyongwana, whose growing business interests drew him away to the Ematsheni, the main African market in Victoria Street, Durban. Luthuli, a cousin of Martin Lutuli, had long been known to Dube. He had taught for many years at Adams, where he had taken a special interest in orthographical matters, had led the school choir and had composed hymns for the AZM's hymnal. He had interrupted teaching for a time to act as interpreter for the British Consul in Swaziland. He became extensively involved in the life of Ohlange and its choir, and would serve the paper as 'the embodiment of loyalty' to Dube until 1943, when R.R.R. Dhlomo would replace him. Charles, now permitted to style himself 'Acting Principal', took over the main responsibility for fundraising and oversaw the long-cherished goal of opening a girls' section. Music continued to dominate Ohlange's cultural and social life: a talented ex-pupil, Reuben Caluza, had just joined the staff and was already taking composition and performance to new heights. In addition, moves were afoot to turn it into a proper 'high school'. Without the charismatic leadership of John and Nokutela, however, the Ohlange vision began to crumble. In 1916, the school accepted its first white teachers, Dr Humphrey and Mr Peast. There were some complaints about this from African supporters, but it seems as if the government had agreed to pay their salaries. There was no other way to survive, explained Dube.

He was also keen to maintain a presence in Natal regional politics. He did his best to drum up support for a war recruitment effort among Africans for non-combatant service in German South West Africa and German East Africa. He organised several meetings for this purpose, but it was notable that in areas down the Natal south coast where just a few years earlier he had commanded enthusiastic audiences, he was now heckled when he asked for volunteers. The English had taken their land, they shouted, so did not deserve support. There was such an acute labour shortage for the war effort and so few volunteers coming forward that magistrates had to apply coercion. Rumours thrived on the evident restlessness and resistance, too. Several of these hinged on an imminent German invasion to liberate Africans and one, which Dube had to refute firmly, had him and Bhambatha on hand to assist when the force landed in St Lucia.

No more successful were Dube's efforts to inspire men to join the Native Labour Contingent, bound for service in France. The government even recognised Solomon as Chief of the uSuthu, the title his father had been stripped of, as a means of encouraging support, but this ploy failed too. Congress had generally been disapproving of the conditions under which the Contingent was to be housed at the front, in compounds similar to those on the mines: this was the only way, the government thought, of preventing African troops acquiring ideas about equality and racial mixing. In spite of its misgivings, Congress responded positively to all the government's requests for support during the war. Once again, this was the logical outcome of a chosen strategy of proving responsibility as prospective citizens.[6]

Dube also returned to Natal to give evidence to the Natives Land Commission. In his excessively lengthy introductory remarks at this sitting, Justice Beaumont seemed determined to forestall any protest from him, telling him that part of the purpose of touring the country was to dispel some of the 'wild ideas' that Africans had about the Land Act, that in trying to reach a settlement its work would trespass on the rights of whites as well as blacks, and that he was of the view that the locations were 'by no means overcrowded'. Colonel Stanford jumped in to say that they all knew Dube's views on the Act and that really what they wanted from him was to look at a map and make suggestions as to where land could be purchased for African use. Dube had come prepared. Already the Inanda Land Syndicate, of which he and Charles were members, owned some 1,400 acres of the old Boer farm Groeneberg, close to Ohlange, and he also individually owned a considerable block of Piezang River not far away (this was the land he had purchased in 1906, just after Mqhawe's death). He and Qandeyana Cele (one of those whom he had, years before, helped to America) were easily the largest African landowners in the vicinity; while they seem to have had tenants on most of their holdings, they also grew sugar. He was anxious to make further acquisitions and had brought with him letters from Dalmeny Estates, the Inanda Wattle Company and Natal Estates, all offering to sell land. He therefore suggested that the commissioners declare this 'scheduled native land'.

Having dispatched his personal business, he complained at length about the effects of the Land Act, taking issue with virtually every point in Beaumont's long preamble, particularly that Natal Africans already had sufficient land. Once again he claimed that if a single large territory – the whole of Zululand, say – were to be given to Africans, he would not object, 'but I know very well that that cannot be carried out under present European civilisation in South Africa'. Try as they might, the commissioners could not get Dube to agree that the Act was intended to protect Africans: they would be penned in like pigs, he said, and what about population increase? That point applied to white people, too, observed Beaumont. 'I would rather expand in 132 million morgen than expand in 10 million morgen,' retorted John Dube.

Congress leaders were critical of (but probably not surprised at) the Land Commission's report, published in September 1916, in that it 'fail[ed] to carry out the alleged principle of territorial separation of the races on an equitable basis'. It removed none of the disabilities in the 1913 legislation, and the only additional land recommended for African use had been 'studiously selected on the barren, marshy and malarial districts', especially in the northern provinces. Beaumont did submit a minority report to the effect that Natal and Zululand should be exempted from the Land Act, but that was never seriously considered.

Nyongwana continued to be a fiercely loyal ally of Dube's in the Natal Native Congress. While Dube was away in London, there had been a meeting in the government buildings in Pietermaritzburg; the Chief Native Commissioner himself had been asked to say a few words before its business began. A terrible row had followed, between veterans Martin Lutuli (acting as chair in the absence of Stephen Mini), Isaac Mkize, Mark Radebe and J.T. Gumede, on the one side, and Nyongwana and fellow Dube supporters, on the other, over the Land Act. Lutuli and his allies wanted to accept its provisions and felt the deputation was a distraction. Nyongwana raged that the meeting should never have been held in a government building as 'it is the Government that is killing us' and that they should not have white men addressing them: 'we don't want the white people. They are responsible for our present position … we are willing to be imprisoned.' In fact, he fulminated, the meeting should never have been called at all: Dube would not recognise it, Mini would not recognise it. In this way Lutuli and Dube grew more implacably opposed to each other, while Gumede's resentment led him to lay a complaint against Dube for defamation of character and to resign from the Natal Congress. Ranks did close again in the face of external threats. By the following year, the Natal Congress was expressing its unanimous confidence in 'the celebrated President of the S.A.N.N. Congress' in the face of accusations appearing in *Abantu-Batho*.

To some extent, these tensions were indicative of the growing dominance of the Durban branch within the provincial Congress, as old landed interests gave way to more aggressively urban-based ones. Despite the distance he frequently had to travel, which meant he was 'sometimes behind, like a dog's tail', as he put it, Dube was very much involved in Durban branch and public (a distinction almost impossible to draw) activities. When Marshall Campbell was awarded a knighthood in August 1916, it was Dube who led the Africans' celebrations in Durban, though not without some rancour. Indian well-wishers had been first to organise their event, and secured the Town Hall – 'an extraordinarily fine building', Haggard had called it – for a lavish celebration. Dube's application for use of the same venue was rejected on the grounds that Africans were not clean enough. Therefore, the African gathering had to be held in the open near the Racecourse. In his speech before Campbell's arrival, Dube told the 800-strong crowd, 'It is you people who helped to build the Town Hall, every bit of it. You carried the bricks and the stones, and mixed the cement. We are the people of the land, we were born here, and yet we have been refused, whereas the Indians were not.' He also began a campaign against Durban's restrictive by-laws and urged Congress supporters to become involved in a new advisory committee that had just been established by the Council.

In the middle of all this, Nokutela Dube died, on 26 January 1917. Days before, she had suddenly taken ill with a kidney infection. A neighbour telephoned Dube and he arranged for medical help as well as transport to get her through to Johannesburg. But it had been too late to save her and she passed away in the Sophiatown house. It was a large funeral, attended by most of the Congress executive, including Msane and Mangena and their wives and Seme, and a good number of the Natal Congress as well, including Cleopas Kunene and Skweleti Nyongwana. Other prominent figures such as Daniel Letanka, editor of *Abantu-Batho*, and Ray Phillips of the American Board came to pay their respects. Many old friends travelled from Natal. Dube and his aged mother, Elizabeth, along with several of Nokutela's relatives, led the mourners. There was a sea of floral tributes, the centrepiece of which was an elaborate glass-domed arrangement from Seme. Nokutela's musical talents and contributions to the founding of Ohlange were specially remembered in the service. She was buried in Brixton cemetery, in grave number CK9763. In the depersonalising system then in use for African burials, the 'CK' stood for 'Christian Kaffir'. And then, as Doris Lessing noted simply in her autobiography, 'Women often get dropped from memory, and then history.'

Just three weeks later, Dube was rousing Congress to renewed action in response to yet another piece of threatening government legislation. On the back of the Beaumont Commission's findings, the government introduced the Native Affairs Administration Bill into parliament. Dube called an extraordinary meeting of Congress for 16 February to consider a response. In his address – Dube at his most powerful – he declared the moratorium on political agitation at an end, even though the war was still raging and would not be over until November 1918: 'We hold ourselves in conscience bound once more to raise our voice as loudly and seriously as ever, against this menace to our welfare and an unjustifiable encroachment on our rights.' The new bill, he continued, was a natural progression from 'that deplorable mistake, "Act 27 of 1913", and it manifests the same detestable spirit'. It was in reality a more extreme version of the Land Act and could only have become draft legislation as a result of one very basic problem: the complete absence of Africans from government. As taxpayers, they had a right to 'some small voice, some small share' in decision-making. After debate, Congress passed a resolution requesting that the bill be postponed for a year and the Land Act be repealed forthwith.

Despite voicing sentiments with which everyone could agree, this performance was not enough to secure Dube's tenure as president. Nokutela's passing had been a reminder of the long shadow still cast by his transgression, and that merely seemed to darken the other long shadow, the unseemly end to the deputation abroad. Perhaps tempers were frayed, too, with the lack of momentum in Congress. At the next executive committee meeting in early June, Selope Thema read out a letter from Travers Buxton of the Anti-Slavery and Aborigines' Protection Society. The Society had for some while been doing its utmost to discredit Plaatje's uncompromising criticism of the Land Act now that his book *Native life in South Africa* had been published, and in the letter urged Congress to unite behind Botha's land policy: the government's intentions were honourable and there was still hope that more land would be found for African occupation. As a way of persuading them that it would be but a small step to take, Buxton reminded them of the formulation that had appeared in Congress's response to the Beaumont Commission report and, before that, in Dube's 1914 petition to Botha: that they made no protest against the principle of separation if carried out fairly.

While this had never been contentious before, Seme and Msane seized the moment to extract Dube's resignation, ostensibly as a means of clarifying Congress's stance on the land question. Selope Thema (who, having gone with Dube's general position, also felt he should resign, only to be told he was not the target) wrote back to Buxton that the bill before parliament 'we are given to understand … is the final settlement of the land question and if so it only means that we shall be contented with 18,000,000 morgens of which almost a half is unsuitable for human habitation, stock-breeding and agricultural purposes ... A parliament of white people only cannot settle this question: nor can we accept any such proposal made by such parliament.' Congress, then, would not bow to the Society's pressure. In any case, the bill was soon withdrawn, and the Land Act would continue to form the basis of land apportionment until the 1930s.

Everyone accepted that separation would never happen in a way that would be acceptable to Africans unless they had direct parliamentary representation and that, in any case, separation was undesirable. Yet this was possibly too obscure a line of reasoning out of which to fashion a direct political message. There were, however, other reasons why Dube had become a liability. The uncomfortable matter of the deputation must also have been reopened at the meeting. Not long afterwards, an item headed 'Icala La Pesheya' ('Mistake overseas') appeared in *Ilanga* over Dube's name, with a request for financial contributions to make good the losses that Congress had incurred three years earlier. A special meeting to elect new office-bearers was called for late June 1917, and thus did Dube's presidency come to an end.[7]

A person's worst enemy

Dube returned to Inanda to take up residence again and ostensibly to rest after Nokutela's funeral. But there was to be no rest: he was too immersed in local politics and pitched into a confrontation with municipal officials almost immediately. What was really incensing Africans in Durban, workers as well as the middle classes, was the introduction of new by-laws which, in Dube's view, were oppressively harsh. For years, Durban had exercised a peculiarly Natalian system of control: it arrogated to itself the monopoly of *utshwala* (sorghum beer) sales through its beerhalls, and the proceeds paid for the costs of administering the city's African population, still largely migrant. In fact the system depended on the cheapness of single 'temporary' workers; they were often called *izimpohlo*, 'bachelors'. It could thus be said that African men, in their leisure time, were paying for their own subjugation. While the beerhalls were undoubtedly popular, many also patronised the illegal shebeens beyond the city limits, on which women brewers depended for their income. Dube and many of his associates were highly critical of both the legitimate and the illegal drinking arrangements, being strong temperance supporters.

In the war years and after, Durban's African population grew rapidly, an indication of which can be seen in the numbers of Africans in employment: a total of some 21,000 in 1915–16 rose to around 29,000 by 1920, of a city population of just over 94,000. This was partly due to economic expansion connected to import substitution and the servicing of wartime shipping, partly because of deepening impoverishment in rural areas as the Land Act bit harder. Among those migrating townwards were greater numbers of women, who were making inroads into at least one male-dominated employment sector, domestic service. In a rare insight into how effectively black women were pressing their claims to urban space, the beach superintendent complained bitterly to the town clerk that African and Indian nursemaids were appropriating beach shelters for their use, to the extent that 'Europeans are compelled to sit on the grass or hire a camp chair'.

Since his appointment as manager of Durban's Native Affairs Department in 1916, J.S. Marwick had embarked on a concerted attempt to tighten controls on a variety of such liberties. Several of these naturally targeted African women, requiring them to carry passes, undergo invasive medical examinations and stay in municipal compounds when visiting husbands from out of town. Others concerned stricter conditions for workers' registration, new curfew restrictions and anti-typhus measures involving the 'dipping' of African men – this was how they described it, treated as though they were cattle. Although women and men were to some extent differentially affected by these regulations, they all emphasised Africans' inferior status in the social order and severely proscribed their freedom of movement and ability to make ends meet in town.

In protest, the Durban branch of Congress planned a meeting for an early February Saturday in the hall of the new Depot Road Location, a reluctant development to accommodate a small number of African families. Being a municipal facility, they had to apply for permission to use it and Marwick granted it on condition that proceedings were conducted properly, speakers should not express any contempt for government or city council, no seditious language was to be used and it all had to be over by 6 o'clock. It was the first time that Congress had been subjected to such restrictions. The branch chair, France Xulu, went to Marwick's office in the morning – the chief of police and the chairman of the Native Affairs Committee were in attendance too – to register Congress's displeasure. Marwick's response was to ban the meeting forthwith. It was too late to get word out, and those who arrived for it were roughly dispersed by the police and drifted across to the Ematsheni, where Marwick's actions 'flashed like lightning to the knowledge of everybody'. An angry Dube declared that Marwick should forfeit the name Muhle ('Good one', earned for accompanying Zulu workers home during the South African War) and instead ought to be called Mubi ('Bad one'). One Phika Zulu, a grandson of Mpande and Marwick's 'Chief Induna', heard it all and reported to his boss, but it was hard to challenge anything that had been said in a speech. However, Dube repeated the allegation a few days later in *Ilanga*:

Mr Marwick is ruling in such a manner as to cause the good understanding and sympathy between the Natives and Europeans to vanish away, thus causing mistrust and hatred to increase between them. He came with the idea that 'I know the Kaffir', he must be handled harshly and drastically in order that he may bow down to the white man and say 'Chief, Father' (meaning Lord and Master). In fact Mr Mubi (as that is the name they have now given to him) does not know the Natives, if he holds any such opinion of them.

Marwick seized his moment. 'It is desirable that I institute proceedings against Dube forthwith – not only to put an immediate stop to his becoming the focus of a false agitation against me – but to vindicate my authority,' he wrote to the town clerk, who gave his wholehearted support. Dube, the focus of Marwick's determined action precisely because of his pre-eminent position in local politics, was thus charged with defamation of character. He hired Alfred Mangena, now in partnership with Seme, to act for him. When the case came to court in September, his defence revolved largely around inaccurate translation of the original Zulu story into English. No less an authority than A.T. Bryant was engaged as his language expert, but the judge ruled that disputes over translation were 'so slight as to be practically immaterial'. He found in favour of Marwick; Dube was fined with costs, leaving him with a bill of over £900.

This outcome considerably enhanced his status and he immediately launched a public appeal to raise the amount. Sympathisers soon donated nearly half of it, with lists being published every week in *Ilanga* of who had given what. Before, when he held out the collection plate, it had been for an organisation or institution; this was the first time he had publicly asked for financial support in a personal contest. It was a particularly 'chiefly' thing to do, expecting supporters to help him out in time of need; after all, it had been on their behalf that he had spoken. They responded accordingly, thereby acknowledging his right to their assistance. Agitation against the by-laws went on, Dube in the lead. Early the following year, he again ventured rather close to the danger of legal proceedings when, in a speech in the Victoria Street cinema, he lashed out at medical examinations and passes for African women. These practices should be halted at their source, Dube declared: when a snake reared its head, should it not be killed before the poison was discharged from its fangs? When his remarks were reported in the *Natal Advertiser*, he quickly dispatched a letter to the editor refuting them and *Ilanga* too denied everything he was alleged to have said: another defamation case was clearly to be strenuously avoided. (Emboldened by his previous victory, Marwick did initiate the process to secure city council backing for a further one.) Dube meanwhile continued on his fundraising travels – it was hard to know whether he was collecting money for Ohlange, the costs of the trial, or both – and continued, too, to protest very volubly against passes for women, the focus of agitation in virtually every centre across the country at that time.

He also delivered another impassioned attack on mission reserve rents and the 1913 Land Act, especially the reduction of tenants to near-slavery, in evidence to the Natives Land Committee. There was a personal edge to his anger at the restrictions of the Act: his mentor, fellow contrarian and partner in the Zulu Industrial Improvement Company, William Wilcox, had been forced to wind up his work in South Africa. He had established two settlements, Tembalihle and Cornfields, on land near Estcourt that he had acquired through the company. However, the residents were facing hardship themselves and were no longer able to support him as well as to meet the mortgage repayments, and he had departed for America, saddened and penniless: 'to my great grief I do not see how I can stay'. This marked the definite end of the company, whose assets were still being liquidated in 1922 by R.N. Drummond, an Estcourt-based solicitor who was also the town's first mayor.[1]

In South Africa's urban centres, notably Cape Town and Johannesburg, the First World War had not only given impetus to industrial expansion but also to worker militancy, as prices outstripped wages, rents rose sharply and land hunger tipped ever-larger numbers into towns. (The appointment of Dube's successor to the Congress presidency, Sefako Makgatho, was in part a reflection of this new mood.) These conditions, coupled with 'the extra-contractual element' – all those repressive practices such as passes, curfews and medical examinations to which Dube was opposed – led to a wave of strikes, boycotts and stoppages across South Africa, culminating in a strike of over 70,000 African miners in 1920. These years also saw the first serious attempts to channel worker action into effective organisation. Some were small-scale and halting, such as the short-lived Industrial Workers of Africa in Johannesburg, although one was to sweep across the country through the 1920s: the Industrial and Commercial Workers' Union, founded in the Cape Town docks in 1919 by Bennett Ncwana and a charismatic Malawian, Clements Kadalie. In Durban, young male migrants had been hard hit by the increasing difficulties of amassing *lobolo* in order to marry, and older ones suffered because they were unable to remit wages to families. The dockworkers, municipal workers and ricksha pullers all came out on strike in this period. Perhaps it was in the nature of their part-proletarianisation that Dube's patriarchal moderation (becoming known as a *hamba kahle*, or 'go carefully', approach) continued to hold some appeal to them.

Marshall Campbell had introduced the ricksha to Durban in the early 1890s. It had quickly become integral to the town's transport system, as ricksha pullers, or *abawini*, took residents on shopping and other outings, delivered heavy parcels for the post office, carried passengers' luggage to and from the station and, from about 1905, provided a spectacle for tourists along the beachfront. By 1918 there were some 1,500 carriages on the streets. Although the work was physically punishing, pullers enjoyed a certain degree of autonomy: they hired their vehicles for a fee and thereafter worked on a freelance basis, and were exempt from the curfew. Pulling was popular for the further reason that accommodation (though often not very salubrious) was provided by the hire companies.

The largest of these, Durban Rickshas Ltd, announced in April 1918 that it was raising its weekly charge from 10s to 12s. Some 80 pullers promptly signed off, returned their uniforms, lamps and bells that the company issued as part of the hire agreement, and made their way to the Racecourse to join virtually every other puller in Durban for a mass meeting. Dube had already been approached to lead the pullers' action and was waiting to address their gathering. He had initially been reluctant to represent them, because they had no association with whose leaders he could negotiate. However, when it became clear that the strike would be unanimously supported, he had agreed to step in. While sympathetic to their cause, he was firmly opposed to militant confrontation and union organisation: the path from nonconformism to socialism may have been short for some, but for a respectable leader like Dube was the wrong one altogether, especially with the example of the Russian Revolution still reverberating everywhere. Instead, he advised the pullers to take their grievances to Marwick. The opportunity to reduce the tension in his own relationship with the Native Affairs manager must surely also have crossed his mind. The pullers, led by Dube, duly processed in orderly fashion to the Town Hall.

Inside, officials frantically summoned the management of Durban Rickshas Ltd. A widespread and lengthy strike was too much for Durban's white population to contemplate, and after discussion the company agreed to revert to the 10s rate. The mayor himself emerged to address the pullers. He rebuked them for downing their rickshas before announcing the outcome of the talks. The pullers hailed Dube as their hero. He in turn thanked the mayor and reminded the workers that they had taken the correct course of action by heeding his advice. Following this apparent success, he held a number of workers' meetings later in 1918 to protest against low wages and rising prices but also to dissuade them (unsuccessfully) from strike action. He put his name to a petition to government, municipality and employers, calling for better wages which would take age into account; behind his name he added the comment, 'For the native workers'. He addressed further meetings in Pietermaritzburg and the midlands to highlight the problems of the poorly paid. He would never lose this common touch. Right up to the late 1930s, workers were still prepared to elect him as their representative to intervene with the city council.

The war had also led to a certain political expectancy. Some 860 Africans had lost their lives in the conflict, including over 600 who drowned when their troopship, the *Mendi*, was rammed in fog in the English Channel in 1916; surely their sacrifice had not been in vain. Messages directly to Congress – for example, a British Secretary of State had told Plaatje that his government would do all it could to help Africans to regain their freedom when the fighting was over – as well as in the international media led many in the colonies and dominions to suppose that their aspirations would be taken care of in the post-war settlement. Had not a key figure in the peace process, President Woodrow Wilson of the United States, pledged that there would be 'just democracy throughout the world'? Such an anticipation of hope was mirrored in the black press across South Africa.

Congress therefore decided that it would be appropriate to send a second delegation to Britain to press Africans' claims in its post-war imperial policy, and then on to Versailles for the peace conference. As head of the Natal section, Dube was still on the executive (into the early 1920s, he was also chair of the finance sub-committee and Natal representative on Congress's Mendi Memorial Club) and found himself at odds with everyone else over this plan. Unsurprisingly, he argued that nothing would be gained by it, but his protestations were brushed aside as pique and personal sensitivity. In Natal itself, Stephen Mini and the Pietermaritzburg-based Josiah T. Gumede, who was a prospective delegate, were in favour. There had been a certain amount of disagreement between Dube and Gumede for some time, though they did sometimes agree, too: friction should not always be treated as an impassable barrier. Nevertheless, the coastal and up-country tendencies once more became pronounced; and various fault lines would beset Congress business through the remainder of Dube's life. Although the delegation went ahead, consisting of Plaatje (as leader), Gumede, Selope Thema, Levi Mvabaza and Henry Ngcayiya, Dube's predictions proved accurate: it failed in its objectives, and this would be the last time Congress ever turned to Britain for assistance. Plaatje produced his masterpiece, *Mhudi*, partly as a reflection on this failure; it is an evocative parable of the kind of society he wanted South Africa to be.[2]

Foremost on his mind through all this – far more important than rising worker militancy or what would unfold at Versailles – was one very large imponderable: how he was to keep Ohlange going. As the campus had developed, so it required ever greater quantities of funding to operate. Despite the fact that a magnificent new girls' dormitory had finally been opened by the Governor-General, the school announced it was unable to accept female students owing to financial constraints. Moreover, a teachers' course and high school course (to prepare boys for Fort Hare) had been added to the curriculum, which in turn meant additions to the staff. Ohlange, in short, had become an educational institution offering the widest possible choices to its students, from shoemaking, printing and farming to music, teaching and university entrance, just as Dube had always desired.

During his Congress presidency, however, Ohlange's finances had become 'entangled'. Each year the debt mounted, as fees (£4 per term in 1920) failed to cover costs. The American Committee had largely wound down its work – it had outlived its intentions by many years already, although Louis Stoiber, Parkes Cadman and a missionary with extensive South African experience, J. Dexter Taylor, were still active until the late 1920s – and he had lost his most prominent local patron on Marshall Campbell's death in 1917. Campbell had always come to his rescue 'when the budget failed to balance'. There seemed no prospect of attracting other local white support on terms with which he was comfortable. The choir toured, numerous other music groups since established at the school did their bit and the past pupils' association sent what it could, but these sums were simply not enough to cover costs. Beginning in late 1919, he issued a fretful call through *Ilanga*, which appeared regularly over the following months: 'It is 19 years now since Ohlange School was established. I have seen good and bad times but now need help with a problem: the pupils are going hungry, the buildings are becoming dilapidated. Please help, parents, sisters and brothers of those who are at school here at Ohlange. I appeal to you, my people.'

It had been his dream and expectation from the very beginning that 'his people' would fund Ohlange. Until this happened, he had been prepared, with Nokutela, to forgo time for leisure, take lengthy trips abroad (he had never much enjoyed the actual travelling involved) and speak endlessly to possible donors, but he had reached a point where he no longer felt able to do any of this. If his activities and pronouncements to this point suggested that he had barely missed a step after the setback of losing the Congress leadership, the realisation that he might have to admit defeat – surrender control of Ohlange or even close it down – caused him to stumble and lose his footing, and not without considerable bitterness.

The 1920 Native Affairs Act, 'the highpoint of liberal segregation', as it has been called, was a reincarnation of the aborted 1917 Bill that Dube had called 'intolerable'. Ushered through the legislative process by Jan Smuts, who became Prime Minister on Botha's death the year before, the Act accepted that there would be no further land added to the 1913 dispensation and instead offered a limited form of representation on local councils in African areas, greater consultation with chiefs, a permanent Native Affairs Commission and periodic conferences with African leaders. When the draft legislation was published for comment, Dube positively welcomed it as 'the best attempt yet made to meet the requirements of the bulk of the Native people ... I support the bill with my whole heart. This is what we have always been wanting the government to do. We have no voice ... in the administration of our interests, and these councils will meet the general need.' He even toured Natal and Zululand promoting the new Act. His position was in line with that of the national Congress at the time. Nevertheless, his apparent about-turn was an indication of his acceptance that he might have to work within the system rather than outside it if Ohlange was to survive.

He may have hoped that his last-ditch appeal for support would be more sympathetically heard than previously. This moment of reckoning for Ohlange coincided with a renewed upsurge of the same intellectual ferment, of race pride and determined self-help, which had inspired its beginnings. Just two years before, in New York, there had been an immediate and overwhelming response to the formation of the Universal Negro Improvement Association (UNIA). Its leader, the Jamaican-born Marcus Garvey, had arrived in America to learn about Tuskegee so that he could replicate the model back home. But he learned more of African Americans' suffering and frustration than Tuskegee could ever teach him, and launched his message of self-made success at a time of feverish market speculation: hundreds of thousands signed up across America, the Caribbean and West Africa. UNIA's constitution declared its aims to be 'to establish a Universal Confraternity among the race; to promote the spirit of pride and love; to reclaim the fallen; to administer to and assist the needy; to assist in civilizing the backward tribes of Africa'. Garvey's injunction 'Look up, you mighty race!' was backed by the announcement in 1919 of the formation of the Black Star Line Steamship Company. This would be a transatlantic venture in which Africans would direct operations and reap dividends, unlike the earlier trade in which they had been the shackled, dehumanised victims. He also declared himself 'Provisional President of Africa'.

Garvey's message soon reached South Africa, via newspapers, leaflets, and individuals returning from visits to the States (including Adelaide Dube's father, James Tantsi, a prominent AME churchman; the AME itself was at pains to distance itself from Garvey). Landless peasants, tenants threatened with eviction, clerks struggling to pay mortgages on a toehold in the countryside, underpaid migrants: there was no lack of an enthusiastic audience. Kadalie and Ncwana declared themselves disciples with the launch of their *Black Man* magazine in Cape Town, though Kadalie was soon to break his links; while adherents such as James Thaele and Wellington Butelezi spread the idea of 'black government by black men for black men'. Garveyism may also have infused the millennialism of the Israelites, an independent sect led by the prophet Enoch Mgijima. They had dug themselves into their holy village of Ntabelanga near Bulhoek in the Eastern Cape after the Passover gathering in 1920, their resolve strengthened by rumours of the imminent arrival of African Americans to help them. The result was a violent confrontation with the police in May 1921, resulting in nearly 200 deaths; it became known in the black press as the Bulhoek massacre.

Among those introducing Garveyism to Durban were a West Indian, Ernest Wallace, and an African American known only as Moses. In October 1920, Dube's Natal Native Congress hosted Moses, who spoke at length to a gathering of over a thousand about UNIA's intentions to free Africa of foreign domination with its fleet, flag and guns. Afterwards, Dube questioned Moses closely. He had been a student of African Americans' political and economic achievements for decades, knew about Liberia and probably had a greater sense of perspective on the Black Star Line than most of the audience – it possessed only one vessel so far, and though an immense achievement and fêted wherever it called, it was already experiencing acute financial difficulties and had lately been taken out of service – all subjects on which Moses touched. Just months later, Dube presided over a meeting in Dundee, at which Selope Thema and his Transvaal colleague C.S. Mabaso called on the audience to prepare for an African American invasion that would help them to repossess Zululand. Though not in the natural constituency to be swept away by its ornamentalism and grandiose claims, Dube would have understood the connection between Garvey's vision and the earlier Ethiopianism that had fired his own. He may also have known that his old correspondent John Edward Bruce was now one of Garvey's most prominent supporters as contributing editor to UNIA's journal, *Negro*

World (and possibly even that Garvey had bestowed the title 'Duke of the Nile' upon him). Those in the Natal Congress more receptive to this radical brand of Pan-Africanism included Petros Lamula, Josiah Gumede and his Pietermaritzburg-based associate A.P. Maduna.

At precisely this time messengers peddling a rather different solution to Africa's ills arrived in South Africa. The Phelps-Stokes Fund had established a commission to investigate education systems in colonial Africa and to recommend possible models for the future. Among its members were the Fund's director, Thomas Jesse Jones (who also held a post at Hampton Institute); James Emmanuel Kwegyir Aggrey, a Ghanaian educationist who was at that time completing a PhD at Columbia; and a member of the Union Native Affairs Commission, Charles T. Loram. Loram had lately served as inspector of Native Education in Natal, and like Aggrey, had been a doctoral student at Columbia. His thesis had been published some years earlier as *The education of the South African Native* and, was the leading statement of liberal segregationist thinking on the subject. It argued that 'the education given at present cannot but have the effect of causing the Native to despise manual labour and to incline to the clerical occupations ... the work which the Natives will be required to do will be, for the most part, industrial and agricultural'. Given that his fundamental assumption was that whites knew best what Africans needed, it is hardly surprising that his study contained no mention of Ohlange.

The make-up of the commission itself was meant to be a shining example of interracial cooperation; indeed, Aggrey's most famous aphorism likened his favoured approach to a piano: 'You can play a tune of sorts of the white keys, and you can play a tune of sorts on the black keys, but for harmony you must use both the black and white.' He deeply admired Tuskegee and was also a correspondent of John Edward Bruce – he addressed him as 'Daddie' – all of which serves to underline the point that while there were distinct positions in 'race thinking', there were also several countervailing overlaps. Aggrey's stature in the eyes of most of his African audiences was immense: he was described as 'one of the greatest luminaries that have lightened the horizons of Africa, and who ... has taught the world the distinctive qualities and attributes of the African race'. On the South African leg of their journey around the continent in early 1921, he spoke unflaggingly at 120 meetings, urging listeners to shun Garveyism and to work with those well-meaning, liberal whites who had recently mooted the idea of formal cooperation through the so-called Joint Councils. 'They who preach "Africa for the Africans" are mad,' he proclaimed; 'if you stood alone you would soon be in deep darkness again. That which we have, and what we are, we owe to the Missionaries.'

Aggrey visited Ohlange and Inanda Seminary, where he was given an enthusiastic welcome. His address in Durban was, however, less favourably received – it was 'tantamount to a vote of no confidence', recorded *Ilanga* – by an audience too weary of the machinations of Natal settler paternalism to entertain the idea of mutual aid and goodwill, and in any case fired up by the excitement of Garveyism. Aggrey's public statements did nevertheless accord closely with many of Dube's: the need to harmonise interests between races; the need to move forward cautiously; the need to assert the dignity of African peoples. Yet what Dube had learned by hard experience was that whites seemed willing to cooperate only when cooperation was all on their terms. Behind the scenes, he had been making tentative approaches to Loram for assistance in bailing out Ohlange. The chief inspector's response had been to suggest that the Native Education Department take Ohlange over, which is not quite what Dube had in mind. One imagines that he was not as enamoured with Natal's provision of African education as the Phelps-Stokes commissioners had been. In their report, published the following year, they would praise it highly: 'The system is undoubtedly the most effective organisation which the Education Commission observed anywhere in Africa. With adequate financial support and some improvements now in process, the Natal system of Native schools should become the ideal for all other systems in Africa.' At least one rising educationist at the time, Albert Luthuli, felt that Loram's policy was 'cutting off their air supply', an observation with which *Ilanga* and probably Dube himself agreed. Charles Dube, president of the Natal Native Teachers' Union, could in one speech both flatter Loram's promotion of manual work, on the grounds that Afrikaners and African Americans alike persuaded their youth to 'till the soil', and underline its narrowness by pointing to the 'marvellous advances' of West Africans, who had their own magistrates, judges and councillors.[3]

Not long after the commission's visit, Dube received an invitation to attend the Pan-African Congress in August 1921. This was the initiative of W.E.B. Du Bois, who had denounced the Garveyists as a 'horde of scoundrels and bubble-blowers, ready to conquer Africa, join the Russian revolution, and vote in the Kingdom of God tomorrow'. Du Bois had maintained a commitment to a more refined Pan-Africanism through his National Association for the Advancement of Colored People (NAACP) since its formation in 1909. After the war, he had been dispatched to France with Robert Moton, Washington's successor at Tuskegee, to keep a watching brief on African interests at Versailles and to investigate complaints of maltreatment by African American servicemen. He used the opportunity to hold an impromptu Pan-African Congress; few organisations had been able to send delegates and it was poorly attended. The next, and hopefully more representative, Congress was planned for two years later. There were to be sessions in London, Brussels and Paris, the first catering mainly for delegates from British colonies and the second and third for those from French ones. Du Bois himself had an unashamed preference for francophone imperialism. Plaatje, the obvious choice as Congress representative as he had made an effort to get to the 1919 event, was touring the States and unavailable. He did have a paper read out at the Paris session, however, by Du Bois himself.

In his current predicament, Dube was drawn back to ideas of race pride and equality – waves of Pan-Africanist sentiment often reflected a deep sense of pessimism about Africans' survival in the world – not of the confrontational style of Garvey but of the more measured style of Du Bois. He still carried enough weight in the national Congress movement to secure nomination as its representative to the London gathering, and had clearly indicated his intention to seek assistance for Ohlange as well, as the following poem by one of his supporters indicates:

He went! He went!
From his native land
Seas he crossed
And into committees ...

People and your houses
Young men, young women
Check your pockets and donate
So Dube can get well ...

He had company on this trip: on 2 August 1920, he had married Angelina Sophia Khumalo in Evaton, south of Johannesburg, where she had been teaching. She grew up at Roosboom, part of the Driefontein complex of African-owned farms near Ladysmith. In the 1970s, when it was already imperilled as an apartheid 'black spot', elderly Roosboom residents could point to an old tree under which Dube himself had called Congress meetings. Angelina told Jordan Ngubane that her grandparents had been slaves to the Boers and had escaped at the time of the Great Trek in the 1830s. Her parents, the Rev. Benjamin Khumalo and his wife, were members of the AME Church, which they must have encountered outside Natal, as in colonial times it had been prohibited from operating there.

After schooling locally at St Hilda's, an Anglican girls' school established in Roosboom in 1902, Angelina had gone to teach in Evaton, drawn to the Wilberforce Institute. Despite Ohlange's advertisements to the contrary, it was not the only independent school, free of white control and modelled on Tuskegee, to have been established in South Africa. Ohlange and Wilberforce Institute were even connected through close personal friendship, for this Institute had been founded in 1903 by Charlotte Manye Maxeke and her husband, Marshall Maxeke, classmates of Charles and Adelaide Dube from their Wilberforce University days. Charlotte Maxeke had, since 1912, been the leading female voice in the national Congress (although women could not yet become full members) and an outspoken critic of pass laws; she had recently formed the Bantu Women's League, which in time would become the women's wing of Congress.

The Maxekes had founded their school at Ramokgopa's Kop in the northern Transvaal for 'all blacks seeking greater knowledge in this land'. With the help of Johannesburg congregations of the AME Church, they had acquired three plots in the newly surveyed township of Evaton, south of Johannesburg, in 1907. The school relocated there the following year as the Wilberforce Institute. Despite support from the AME, it had been worse affected by financial crises, staff shortages and lack of equipment than Ohlange, yet by the 1920s could boast primary, secondary and teacher training departments and an informal training programme for ministers. The two institutions may even have exchanged teachers, which would explain the presence at Ohlange in 1915 of David Opperman, a member of the remarkable Opperman family of Evaton, who dedicated their lives to the support of Wilberforce. Angelina's brother Orpheus was also teaching at Wilberforce at this time.

Family tradition has it that John Dube had been keen on Angelina's aunt Sophia, who lived in Sophiatown and ran a special hostel for visiting chiefs and other dignitaries to the mines, but she told him she was a confirmed spinster and her niece would make a better wife. Angelina already had family connections in Inanda, her cousin Ivy having married one of Klaas Goba's sons; another relative, Donga Khumalo, lived at Amatata and was a friend of the Dubes. At the time of her marriage, she was 21 years old; Dube was by then 49. Despite the age difference, it was to be a very happy marriage and Angelina would bear him the children for whom he longed. There were six altogether, four of them surviving to adulthood: Nomagugu (born 1922),

Douglas Sobantu (born 1924), Joan Lulu (born 1931) and James Sipho (born 1933). Mzimandla, the first-born, died in infancy in June 1921 and Laura, born in 1927, died before her second birthday.

So it was that John and Angelina Dube – several of the male delegates were accompanied by their wives, and he indicated in a letter that she had been invited too – were present at the opening of the London session of the Pan-African Congress on 28 August 1921, in the imposing Central Hall, Westminster, close to the Houses of Parliament and Westminster Abbey. Du Bois opened proceedings with an account of attempts to table Africans' aspirations at the Versailles Peace Conference and in the US Senate. Thereafter, discussions focused largely on West African problems, reflecting the geographic concentration of delegates: the way in which colonial officials treated the raising of legitimate grievances as disloyalty, the need for greater educational provision and economic opportunity. There was obvious resonance with the situation in South Africa and no doubt elsewhere across empire. The two days of deliberations ended with a 'Declaration to the World', drafted by Du Bois, which observed first that 'England, with all her Pax Britannica ... has nevertheless systematically fostered ignorance among the Natives, has enslaved them, and is still enslaving them, has usually declined even to try to train black and brown men in real self-government'. It then outlined an eight-point programme, committing the 'Negro intelligentsia' to campaign for recognition based on achievement rather than skin colour; access to education; the granting of local self-government to suppressed peoples; freedom of religion; 'tolerance of all forms of society'; international collaboration in pursuit of justice, freedom and peace; return of people of African descent to their native lands; and the establishment of institutions under the auspices of the League of Nations to safeguard African interests. So radical was this document considered to be that the subsequent sessions refused to endorse it.

As the Pan-African Congress continued on its stately progress across Europe, it is possible that the Dubes also travelled on the continent. They were back in London by early October, when Dube steeled himself for the painful task of approaching the only person in the only organisation he imagined might yet be able to save Ohlange on more favourable terms than Loram had offered: John Harris of the Anti-Slavery and Aborigines' Protection Society. In his letter of approach, he noted that since its foundation, Ohlange had 'sent out hundreds of educated men some who have become ministers of religion, teachers in public schools, carpenters, shoemakers, printers, generally leaders among our people'. While awaiting

Harris's response, Dube spent several weeks in London acting as principal informant for the linguist Clement Doke, who was researching the phonetics of Zulu. He and Angelina then set off on a fundraising tour that took them as far as Lancashire. For this purpose, he put another pamphlet together. Although the title, *The Zulu's appeal for light*, bore strong similarity to the original 1909 version, this one was shorn of the florid appeals to patriotic duty, taking a more businesslike 'facts and figures' approach to school life and including a number of testimonials to demonstrate his trustworthiness. Harris (who had had no direct dealings with Dube since the débâcle of 1914) meanwhile consulted various contacts. Notable among them were Lord Buxton, who had just vacated office as Governor-General, and Howard Pim, a Johannesburg-based Quaker accountant who chaired the city's Joint Council. Pim, never having heard of the principal of Ohlange, had in turn to call on some of *his* contacts (he would, on first meeting Dube, describe him as 'strong-willed and a great egoist'). Discussions were further delayed when the Dubes decided to set off home on account of Angelina's health: their first baby had died the previous year, and she was again pregnant.

They returned on SS *Kenilworth Castle*, which must have brought back some painful memories for Dube. On their arrival in Durban in late April 1923, Dube was fêted as a hero: one of the firms that had long advertised in *Ilanga*, E.A. Tyeb & Co., otherwise known as Ngobamakhosi, laid on a sumptuous banquet for the Dubes at the Luncheon Rooms in Queen Street. The 30-odd guests included several Indian well-wishers as well as Josiah Gumede; Petros Lamula, Norwegian Mission pastor and member of the Durban branch of Congress; Violet Sibusisiwe Makhanya, Inanda Seminary graduate, teacher and founder of the Bantu Purity League; and a number of close Inanda associates: William Bhulose, owner of a number of trading stores and landowner there; Jonas Mfeka, another Inanda landowner who had been an early teacher at Incwadi and, more recently, composer of Marshall Campbell's *izibongo*, or praises; Bertha Mkhize, Inanda Seminary graduate, Durban seamstress and the Dubes' close neighbour; Reuben Caluza, head of music at Ohlange; and Charles and Adelaide Dube. An associate of the Tyebs known only as Rooknodeen acted as master of ceremonies and drove the Dubes home the following day.

In June, John Dube received Harris's proposal for a rescue package for Ohlange. Teachers' salaries would be taken over by the Department of Native Education, subject to a number of conditions. First, that a governing council be established, to be chaired by Charles Wheelwright, the Chief Native Commissioner of Natal, and consisting of three African members (of whom he would be permitted to be one) and three whites, including the Rev. A.E. Le Roy, head of the American Zulu Mission ('one of the few Europeans able to get on well with Dube'). Second, that day-to-day management fall to an executive committee consisting of Le Roy, Dube and the Chief Native Commissioner. Third, Ohlange become incorporated, with Dube and *Ilanga* both required to move off the campus; in return, he would be given assistance to build a new house on his farm nearby. Finally, the principal be white and employ as many other white teachers as 'he may desire'; Charles Dube would be able to stay on as vice-principal.

It was also suggested that 'reference councils' (similar to the old American Committee) be formed in Britain and America. Whereas the American Committee had let Dube and his trustees spend funds as they saw fit, Harris, Pim and company saw an opportunity to intervene decisively. As Harris noted to Buxton, 'I have always found the African particularly weak in handling money matters.' (His observation needs to be set against the statement issued three years later by the London 'reference committee' under the chairmanship of Buxton. Noting that the value of the Ohlange property was in the region of £10,000, 'it says much for the work of the Founder, Mr John Dube, that there is no mortgage of any kind on [it]'.) Dube was shocked at the proposal. 'If it did not emanate from so benevolent a source one would mistake it for the spirit of the top dog,' he noted carefully but resentfully. He pleaded for a compromise that would 'not altogether disintegrate the only institution in this country which we may look upon with pride and call our own'. Once again, negotiations stalled.

A week after he lost the presidency of Congress back in 1917, an editorial had appeared in *Ilanga* headed 'Isita somuntu umuntu', a well-known idiom literally translated as 'a person is his own enemy' but figuratively intended to mean 'we people are our own enemy'. Its theme was that Africans were fond of blaming whites for their ills, but the unpalatable truth was that the enemies were within the black house: the one who had been chosen to lead in Bloemfontein had been 'hit' by his very own people. It was an idea that Dube now developed into a publication titled *Isita somuntu nguye uqobo lwakhe* (A person is his own real enemy). It was issued in late 1922. So popular was it that he was to enlarge it for re-issue in 1928.

Reflecting on its author's own record, *Isita* begins by noting how easy it is to blame whites for stealing land, imposing taxes, paying exploitative wages and restricting freedom through passes and curfews. But this is not the 'truth' of the situation: instead, Africans have to examine themselves. There is a copious account of all the things that are wrong with their attitude. Africans refuse to unite in the cause of emancipation, will not hold down regular employment, lack an entrepreneurial spirit, shun the talented craftspeople and artisans among them, misuse funds in all their organisations from churches to football clubs, are impatient to get rich, are envious of others' achievements and get easily indebted by asking for advances on wages. Women neglect their children and rabble-rousing townspeople have only themselves to blame for the curfew. Moreover, there are many whites who are friends of Africans, both in South Africa and abroad, and many whites have died in the cause of African freedom. The Africans who have achieved most are those who have been prepared to learn from whites: 'let us enrol ourselves in the school of struggling' instead of fearing the label 'good boys', Dube implores. 'Who is one's enemy? It is one's real self,' is repeated throughout, like an incantation. Other solutions he lists are to acquire formal education, work regularly for whites and start small businesses. Yet it is not entirely clear – Dube was a master of complex literary convention – who exactly the enemy is. Although he calls it an exercise in 'introspection', *Isita* can be read as an embittered attack on those who had failed to support him, as a last, desperate call to 'his people' to avert this disaster, or as lacerating self-criticism for having to concede to white interference.

As it turned out, Wheelwright strengthened Dube's position on the future of Ohlange considerably. The idea of its having survived for so long as the only institution of its kind struck a chord with the Chief Native Commissioner, for it fitted well with a felt need to locate sources of legitimacy for educational development 'along their own lines'. Accordingly, he used his influence to ensure that Ohlange would continue to be managed predominantly by Africans. In the deed of trust finalised in 1924, a six-member board of trustees was appointed, in which final authority for all school matters was vested and whose membership revealed Dube's continuing preference to rely as far as possible on those most closely related to him: John Mdima, his brother Charles, himself, Wheelwright, Pim and a local businessman, Thomas Griggs. It also stipulated that the principal should be African. Charles Dube did not remain on the staff; he took this opportunity to branch out into business, opening the Dube Hotel in Durban and a 'native chemist', and operating one of the earliest African-owned bus companies in the city.

Ilanga relocated to offices in Durban and under Dube's continuing proprietorship was put on a proper commercial footing; it may be around this time that A.C. Maseko became his secretary. Dube's family vacated the house that he had lived in since 1901, and moved into a newly built one close to the school property, on the edge of a ridge with commanding views all the way to the sea. A reference committee was set up in London, with the old and much-reduced American Committee serving a similar purpose in that country; their role was to raise the funds to cover maintenance of, and repairs and extensions to, the fabric. The London Committee was a most august one – including Lord Buxton, Viscount Gladstone, Sir Thomas Fowell Buxton, Sir Thomas Inskip (the Solicitor-General) and the Bishop of St Albans – which met regularly at the House of Lords and managed to raise funds even from such bodies as the Rhodes Trust. Dube was not to have a particularly easy relationship with it. Nevertheless, Ohlange was able to continue advertising itself as 'The Great Bantu National Institute because it is managed and run solely by Natives who are devoted to the great work of uplifting the Native races of South Africa'.[4]

Because of the help that Pim provided, Dube signed up to the Durban Joint Council, but his engagement with its activities was desultory, as was the history of the Durban branch itself until the late 1920s. Its first meeting had been held in April 1922, having been convened by a body calling itself the Native Affairs Reform Association, the same body that had hosted Aggrey and Jones. One of its leading lights was William Bhulose. Although he was also an active member of the Durban branch of Congress, it would appear that Congress had wished to avoid direct association with the Joint Council. (The Reform Association also subsidised the Abantu Social Club, an elitist institution 'where country members visiting town can rest and obtain their meals and see the latest papers', located in the Star Buildings on Umgeni Road; interestingly, Dube was not listed as a member.) There was a scrupulous attempt to ensure equal representation of whites and Africans on the Durban Joint Council, but in practice equality was extremely difficult. While whites were elected on the basis of organisational representation – for example, the Natal Teachers' Association, the National Society of Journalists and the YMCA – African members continued to sit on the Council in their individual capacities and so only ever represented themselves.

In reality, Dube had other priorities. On his return from London, he presented several verbal reports on the Pan-African Congress. He told his listeners that 'important progress in the cause of freedom for the black races' had been made, and that if they trusted him, 'further progress will soon be attained'. He also intimated that he would very much like to discuss with Solomon kaDinuzulu some of the intentions and aspirations voiced in London. White encroachment on his physical and metaphysical space at Ohlange had discomposed him enough for him to look for other refuges in which his race pride might be expressed. The difficulty was that such refuges were ever more difficult to locate in the tighter confines of segregationist legislation and social engineering. He had always been on cordial terms with Solomon, whose autonomous legitimacy (even though underwritten by government policy) was undoubtedly attractive. He may also have been exploring ways in which the provisions of the 1920 Act might be exploited in pursuit of solving the problems of black oppression. His overtures to Solomon seem, however, to have been a reaction to similar approaches undertaken by several others jostling for position and influence.

One spokesman for educated Africans' interests in Zululand itself was Samuel Simelane, a Dutch Reformed pastor who had schooled at Amanzimtoti and had built a church close to Solomon's court at Mahashini. In early 1921 he and Mnyaiza, another of Mpande's grandsons and Solomon's closest adviser, had discussed the implementation of the Native Affairs Act in the territory with Wheelwright. They also discussed Simelane's scheme for an agricultural cooperative, a response both to landlessness and to the lack of purchasing power to alleviate it, and for this he and Mnyaiza had established a Zulu National Fund (on the Reef called the Imali yo Umpini). Later in 1921, Josiah Gumede visited Solomon to report on his tour abroad as a member of the Congress deputation as well as to discuss plans for *his* cooperative society. It had been launched on 16 December 1921, while Dube was still away; its name, Inkatha – a sacred grass coil containing *insila,* the body-dirt of the king, which represented the essence and unity of the Zulu – clearly indicated Gumede's hope of securing royal patronage. However, as had been the fate of so many similar previous undertakings, it failed to attract subscribers; months later, it was absorbed into yet another (and no more successful) self-help scheme, Ukuzaka kwaBantu, run by his close associate Petros Lamula, which Lamula based on the ideals he had set out in a book of the same name. Simelane took over the name Inkatha for his organisation.

Renewed interest in Solomon must in turn be seen against a backdrop of quickening ethnic awareness among educated Zulu speakers both on the Reef and in the region itself. A Zulu Institute had been founded in Johannesburg in 1917, becoming the Zulu National Association two years later. What resurfaced in such efforts were the old fears of the *uhlanga* under threat and of the middle classes under siege; indeed, one can see this motif in Dube's *Isita*, as well as in Lamula's work. It is significant that *Abantu abamnyama lapha bavela ngakhona*, Magema Fuze's history of the Zulu written soon after the turn of the century (making it the first-ever written in Zulu), was finally published at this time – and paid tribute to Dube in the prologue. Such consciousness was not necessarily perceived to be at odds with the inclusive programme of the national Congress; its constitution appeared to allow for the play of both, as a 'Pan-African Association', which also accommodated a role for chiefly politics, as long as this did not become cause for inter-ethnic rivalry and strife.

Solomon's association with leaders such as Dube and Seme went back to the start of his reign. Seme had married his sister Phikisile Harriette and continued to provide legal services. He would have kept abreast of Congress matters through such personal contacts, but it was only in 1921 that he had chosen openly to send a representative to one of the provincial meetings in Pietermaritzburg. It had discussed the range of hardships facing African landowners and tenants on white farms and the great land shortages of chiefs and their people in the reserves, and had called for the repeal of the 1913 Act, the pass laws and the Masters and Servants Act. It had also welcomed the growing sense of unity between traditionalist and educated leaders. While Solomon's interests may have intersected with those of Congress, his priorities were different: being preoccupied with a campaign for recognition as Zulu king, he was anxious not to alienate either the government or his traditional constituency. Because he was direly in need of finances, migrant workers in particular were important to him, as they were most able to pay tribute. Huge swathes of the old kingdom had been alienated for white farming. Solomon himself had previously been a tenant on a white farm, and even the graves of the Zulu kings were now located on privately owned land. It was clearly important to return some of this to collective custodianship.

Further, as chief of the uSuthu, he saw one of his main tasks as healing the deep division between the uSuthu, the Buthelezi and the Mandlakazi. Accordingly, he held two *ukubuthwa* ceremonies to enrol new age-sets and carefully arranged a number of marriage alliances. He also made efforts to cast himself as a forward-looking leader and to invent suitable new kingly traditions. These included construction of a 'modern' residence at Mahashini and purchase of an urban one in Sophiatown, acquisition of a large American car, confirmation in the Anglican Church, support for the education of chiefs' sons and incorporation of symbols of Zulu monarchical authority into formal Western dress. Reluctant to engage in any activity that did not have official permission, he was nevertheless interested in exploring Congress support as a means of enhancing his status.

The first item on the agenda of the Natal Congress annual meeting in Estcourt in April concerned preparations for the establishment of a formal relationship between the royal house and Congress. Whatever was decided – evidence suggests that a contest ensued over who precisely had rights of access to Solomon – it was overshadowed by the outcome of the elections for office-bearers. Dube and other long-serving members such as William Bhulose and Stephen Mini were displaced by the 'Garveyite' element led by Gumede, who was elected president, Maduna and Lamula. While this came as a shock, and clearly indicated a major shift in the outlook of Congress's ordinary members, it is important not to over-emphasise the divisions. As a result of his involvement in the 1919 deputation (*Ilanga* warmly commended his efforts abroad) Gumede had become a regular Natal representative in national meetings and deputations of Congress. This in itself had cast him in more of a prominent leadership role – and he would use his regional position to become national Congress president three years later.

According to his biographer, Gumede had remained an Aggrey adherent until at least 1923, when he was involved in Congress debates about two new pieces of segregationist legislation, the Natives Urban Areas Act and, in Natal, the Natives' Education Bill. Frustrations over his stalled cooperative and his continuing economic insecurity combined with these experiences to push him in a more radical direction. Yet in many ways his aspirations were similar to those of the more solidly middle-class members of Congress who had been in control of the organisation for so long. He had recently purchased two cars from money collected from Congress members on the ground that Congress should provide his transport – this had caused some trouble in the Pietermaritzburg branch – and was as keen on self-help and to explore relations with Solomon as most other members of the Natal executive. (He and Dube also shared the uncomfortable experience of owing money to the Anti-Slavery and Aborigines' Protection Society after deputations abroad; at the time of the 1924 meeting, Gumede had not yet repaid his.)

There had been rumblings of dissatisfaction with Dube's leadership for a year or more. At the annual conference in 1923, he had been accused of 'doing nothing about the worsening native situation' and ought to be replaced, a call that had come from some chiefs as well as urban members – largely, it has to be said, from Pietermaritzburg. He had enough supporters to contest the accusation successfully, but perhaps his downfall was not such a surprise after all. Leaving Natal matters for the moment to the new leadership, Dube moved to secure his position in Nongoma – it is unlikely that Solomon or the government would have countenanced a role for Gumede, and in any case Dube was able to draw on an unrivalled set of royal connections. Simelane's Inkatha had its first formal meeting at Mahashini in October. Before an audience of 500, the existing members – Simelane, Mankulumana and Mnyaiza – were confirmed as office-bearers, while Dube and Bhulose shared the chair. Another Zululand-based member of Congress, the Rev. Timothy Mathe, also joined the executive. The only part that Solomon played was to attend a closed meeting beforehand to discuss the matters that would come before the house in the public proceedings. These were that Africans should have the vote (a matter that was not discussed further), the establishment of a national church at Mahashini and the role of local councils under the 1920 Act. The church proposal was delegated to a sub-committee, although nothing came of its work, while a resolution was passed that the 1920 Act not be implemented in Zululand, on the ground that it would interfere with Solomon's rule.

Dube's support for the Act was of course well known, so it is ironic that he now had to turn about from his about-turn. The resolution was a compromise in order to ensure a working relationship with Solomon, and there was to be no escape from 'working within the system', since Solomon was a paid government functionary. Nevertheless, a Zululand Congress had effectively been established, in which the interests of the middle classes predominated over those of traditionalists (even though in this setting, *they* were described as the 'outside people'); very few chiefs had been invited to attend. This was to be Dube's political base while he sought to re-establish his leadership south of the Thukela. Up to this point, the only challenge to his position had come from within the Natal Congress. This would soon change, making his prospects far more uncertain.[5]

The Elephant of Inanda

For a brief moment in the summer of 1930/1, Durban seemed the most likely venue in South Africa for the inauguration of the Communist Party's 'Native Republic'. The party had succeeded in rallying African workers to support a mass pass-burning campaign, culminating on Dingane's Day, 16 December. On that morning, a huge crowd gathered at Cartwright's Flats on the edge of the city centre; encouraged by the local organiser, Johannes Nkosi, thousands handed over their passes for burning. Either this would lead to victorious freedom of movement in Durban or it would lead to mass arrests, fines and imprisonments. Later in the day, as the assembled crowd began to march behind a large red banner, the police charged. Nkosi tried to calm the situation but the police felled him and three others; his body was severely mutilated and his skull fractured. Despite widespread police harassment in the days that followed (though no one was ever arrested for the four murders), workers continued to march in defiance and burn their passes. Watching them from a distance, from the relative safety of his Chevrolet, was John Dube. It seemed as if this is what had become of him: politically sidelined, reduced to the status of a gentleman onlooker. Or so thought Eddie Roux, a communist activist who was, at Dube's invitation, then teaching at Ohlange. More than this: in Roux's view, Dube had 'sold out', thrown in his lot with the forces of reaction. Was this indeed the point he had reached?

Six years earlier, at around the same time as the founding of Inkatha and his loss of the provincial Congress leadership, he had begun to participate in the Governor-General's Native Conference, an annual event launched in 1922 in terms of the Native Affairs Act. Although it was hardly the representative forum most would have wanted, many Congress leaders responded positively to this body in an attempt to 'establish a modus vivendi with Government', among them R.V. Selope Thema, Selby Msimang,

Sefako Makgatho, Sol Plaatje, Charlotte Maxeke and William Washington Ndhlovu, Dube's colleague in Inkatha (whom he had known as Dinuzulu's secretary-in-exile in the Transvaal). Dube's pronouncements on matters long of importance to him – land and segregation, taxation, the treatment of Africans in court – suggested his position had not changed and neither had he toned down the language he used. He noted, for example, that 'the Natives did not see how they could be segregated and yet be given sufficient land for development ... If the Europeans threw the Natives far away and told them to develop along their own lines the former would be evading and shirking their responsibilities.'

Dube severely criticised the effects of the Natives Urban Areas Act, passed the year before: 'Natives were being driven away from the towns, discharged from jobs in which thousands had sacrificed their lives in the interests of the white people.' He also had bitter words for the new government, which had come to power in the wake of Smuts's ruthless suppression of the white miners' strike of 1922. A coalition of Hertzog's Afrikaner nationalists and Colonel Creswell's Labour Party, it wasted little time in tightening industrial colour bar legislation and elevating the condition of 'poor whites', both in towns and in the countryside. As a result, Dube observed, Africans 'were greatly disappointed to see Crown land being cut up for poor white settlement when the whites already had so much land at their disposal'.

The following year, he aimed his verbal arrows at chiefs: 'the people wanted to progress', he claimed, 'but some chiefs were not worthy to rule progressive people. How could they be led by ignorant people? Some of the chiefs were born fools.' A new Native Administration Bill was also under discussion, which 'actively embraced a strategy of retribalisation' and would permit government of Africans by proclamation, which, under these circumstances, Dube believed to be a retrograde step. He also felt that the few land rights Africans had in the locations were at risk. 'How could the Natives progress if they were liable to eviction? Their very title was threatened. At any time a whole tribe might be shifted so a man contented himself with a wattle hut: there was no inducement to build decent houses.' Finally, he announced that there had been further land alienation in Natal, a point that Hertzog had to concede.

Dube was sharply aware of the obvious problem with this forum: 'this Government Conference is looked on with suspicion by a majority of Natives ... all its members have been appointed by the Government and have been looked upon by the Natives as puppets of the Government and not real representatives of Bantu interests.' He had discovered very quickly that there were few pressure points from within, and this was what disabled them. He attended no more; in any event, the conferences came to a halt in 1927. After the passage of the Native Administration Act of that year, there was to be no significant new legislation concerning African people for some time, so the government saw no need to convene further conferences. It may also have feared that they might be used to channel protest against three new bills that Hertzog introduced in 1926 (but would not become law for another decade).

Dube had continued to be active in Inkatha. A great moment of opportunity occurred in 1925, when the Prince of Wales visited South Africa. Solomon saw an opportunity to turn the atmosphere of pomp, celebration and rapturous welcome into an occasion to bolster his own kingly ambitions. The 60,000 Zulu men who assembled on the Eshowe golf course on 6 June did so as a nation; it was the first mass assembly permitted since the 1879 conquest. Dube was on the platform to watch Solomon's arrival in an enormous blue open-topped car. Leopard skins, symbolic of Zulu royalty, were draped over the seats. His military-style uniform was also trimmed with leopard skin and his epaulettes carried brass insignia displaying another royal symbol, an elephant. The response from the gathering was an immense roar of 'Bayede!', the royal salute. When Edward arrived, also resplendent in ceremonial dress, Solomon led another round of 'Bayede!'

The morning was taken up with the formalities of gift-giving. Edward presented senior Zulu chiefs with silver-topped ceremonial sticks, and Solomon with a gold one. As a suitable token of reciprocity, Solomon had financed a hunting expedition to procure the elephant tusks that he now presented to Edward, 'not only from himself but from the whole Zulu nation'. Edward then received Solomon, accompanied by a small retinue including Mnyaiza and John Dube, on the luxurious White Train which was carrying him around the country. The afternoon was given over to a display of dancing. Magnificently dressed in monkey-skins and feathered headdresses, the dancers 'surged forward and rolled back, like breakers of the sea. Advancing and receding, they were frightening and yet thrilling,' recalled one who witnessed it as a child. It was surely the most dazzling spectacle of the entire royal visit. Through the performance, Solomon engaged Edward in conversation, as if they were two equals exchanging pleasantries.

In fact, throughout the day's proceeding, there was 'a sort of running ambiguity as to whether it was Edward, Prince of Wales, or Solomon, King of the Zulus, who was actually the drawcard'. Solomon, still not formally king, nevertheless bade farewell to Edward having secured unofficial recognition, greatly helped by the rumour that the Prince had conferred this title on him on the train. Dube was thus intimately complicit in the promotion of Solomon's growing influence. (He had earlier had his own moment of prominence, too: he recalled that it had been 'a great moment in my life when I was called upon to extend publicly to the Prince of Wales a welcome from the Natives of Natal'.)

The annual Inkatha meeting in October that year clearly reflected the successes of Eshowe. Solomon issued the invitations himself rather than remaining behind closed doors, and many more chiefs or their representatives attended. A matter of great concern to them all was the recent Union-wide imposition of a £1 poll tax, plus a 10s local tax to set up councils. The meeting accepted the necessity of these, even though it continued to be opposed to the setting up of local councils in Zululand. Of particular relevance to chiefs was a discussion about the education of their sons. A Zulu National Training Institution specifically for this purpose had been established in Solomon's ward in 1920. Though the principal, Leonard Oscroft, was an Anglican minister (and adviser to Solomon) and the Anglican Church played a central part in the realisation of the scheme, it was government-financed and -controlled. Dube had been especially enthusiastic about the venture and the resolution passed at the 1925 meeting, that chiefly sons' education should be compulsory, carried his strong imprint, reinforcing his recent pronouncements at the government conference.[1]

At this point, Dube absented himself from his local political engagements for another extended trip abroad, his seventh (which also turned out to be his last), to attend a missionary gathering and to raise funds for Ohlange. It was a momentous time to be in Europe. The World War and revolution in Russia had between them ushered in a period of profound instability, an 'age of anxiety' to some, the 'roaring twenties' to others, depending on whether one treated the break with the old order as lamentable or liberating. The enormous task of economic reconstruction had given rise to a new, polarised politics on the streets, as rising inflation led to mass union activity – Dube arrived in London in the aftermath of a 10-day general strike – and a backlash from right-wing parties; Mussolini was already in power in Italy. Belgium, which had been the scene of the most intense fighting of the war on battle fields such as Flanders and Ypres, was still coming to terms with the loss of life, destruction of property and psychology of occupation, as recriminations and counter-recriminations concerning collaboration with or resistance to occupying forces continued.

It was perhaps for reasons to do with a general 'healing' process that Le Zoute in Belgium was selected as the venue for an international conference on 'The Christian Mission in Africa' in September 1926. This had grown out of the Phelps-Stokes Commission's work. Following its 1921 report, the commission had produced another in 1924 and both had concentrated the minds of many missionaries and colonial officials on the requirements of trusteeship in Africa. Out of a planning meeting near London came two initiatives, the establishment of the International Institute of African Languages and Cultures and the 1926 conference, convened by the International Missionary Council. The Le Zoute gathering attracted over 200 delegates, mostly representatives of missionary bodies and governments: Lugard, lately Governor of Nigeria, was there, as were Louis Franc, former Belgian Secretary of State for Colonies, and General de Meulemeester, ex-Governor of the Congo. Dube was accompanied by the Rev. Z.R. Mahabane, then president of the African National Congress (ANC). They were joined in Belgium by D.D.T. Jabavu, Tengo Jabavu's son and a professor at Fort Hare, and Max Yergan, an African American who arrived in South Africa in 1922 (after considerable problems with immigration authorities, finally settled by Aggrey's intervention) to build a YMCA movement.

On their way through London, Dube gave a hard-hitting interview to the *Christian Science Monitor* on the Pact government's 'civilised labour' policy. A Wage Board had recently been set up to determine wages in industries where there was no collective bargaining mechanism. In effect, it upgraded the wages of unskilled white workers and paid no attention at all to jobs occupied by black workers. It was thus 'the most powerful yet most subtle colour bar' in operation. Hard on its heels came the Mines and Works Amendment Act, or 'Colour Bar Act', which Hertzog steamrolled through the legislative process because of opposition in the Senate. It reserved certificates of competency for all skilled work to white and coloured workers (although the mechanisms already in force to restrict coloureds' entry to trades meant that this was hardly meaningful for them). Dube was particularly exercised by the Act. As 'the last in a series of bad laws, [it] is almost more than we can bear. The Native Land Act has caused a great deal of suffering, and we see little hope of being able to escape becoming serfs ... the outlook is very gloomy, for we cannot look forward to anything appreciably better, even from another government.' Even leaders of the Joint Council dissociated themselves from this more aggressive segregation policy.

Because he was not representing any organisation, Dube had been invited to Le Zoute as a consultative member. He made a large impression on proceedings, as several subsequent reports testify. 'I shall cherish longest the memory of what took place on Saturday morning [the fifth day of proceedings],' recorded Edwin Smith, author of the official conference report. 'When the time came for devotions a stout Zulu – John Dube – stepped forward and announced the hymn: "Jesus shall reign where'er the sun." In response to his invitation several members offered prayer. There was silence, and presently it was broken by the voice of John Dube praying in Zulu. Few persons understood the language; those who did speak of the beauty of that prayer. Everybody entered into the spirit of it.' J.H. Oldham, one of the main architects of the conference, singled out the 'distinguished representatives of the Negroes of America and the peoples of Africa ... Dr John Hope, Mr John Dube and Mr Mahabane'. Hope was a close friend of Du Bois, an active member of the NAACP, and had accompanied black troops to France as a YMCA organiser. In the aftermath of a wave of post-war lynchings in the South, he had organised and led the Commission on Interracial Cooperation. (Three years later, Dube would be among those, with the likes of Pim and Selope Thema, to join the inaugural executive of the Inter-Racial Council of South Africa, modelled on Hope's body. It would later become the South African Institute of Race Relations.) Since 1898, Hope had been Professor of Classics at Atlanta Baptist College, which had become Morehouse College. Dube would have sought out Hope at Le Zoute; apart from other matters of common interest, one of his tasks in America was to enrol his nephew Frederick at Morehouse.

The proceedings at the conference trod an uneasy path between the sensitivities of colonial administrators and white settlers and the aspirations of African Christians. In the end, the conference passed a number of 'emphatic' resolutions, among them the importance of guaranteeing to African people the security of land tenure, a complete rejection of the use of forced labour for private enterprise and the need to investigate the impact of migrant labour on family life. Dube felt reinvigorated. 'We are passing through a perplexing period in South Africa. What with colour bars and restrictions of one sort or other, the white people are sitting upon us very tightly. But Le Zoute has given me fresh courage.'

From Belgium, he travelled back to London to make arrangements to meet his reference committee – lords and bishops required a great deal of notice – and then on 26 October, on the *Majestic*, to America. Ohlange desperately needed repairs and improvements, in addition to which a new trades building was planned: this was surely the influence of Wheelwright and others keen to hold Dube to his commitment to industrial education. He had not been for 15 years in the country that had exerted so powerful and formative an influence on him and he covered much ground on this trip, from East to West coasts and from the Deep South to the industrial North. In New York, he met Parkes Cadman and Louis Stoiber and then set off for the Southern states, speaking about Ohlange and examining developments in African American schools.

Among these was the historic Penn School on St Helena Island, one of a string of islands off the Georgia and South Carolina coasts. The school had been founded in 1862 for freed Gullah slaves who had worked in the rice plantations that were so much a feature of this region, and whose language and culture retained elements closely connected to Sierra Leonean Krio. It was a so-called Jeanes school, after the philanthropist Anna Jeanes, who had established a foundation to upgrade the skills of African American teachers in the South, and to train them in implementing systems of vocational and industrial education. It was an approach particularly favoured by the Phelp-Stokes Commission. 'I have received inspiration,' he wrote in the Penn School guestbook. After settling Frederick into Morehouse, he travelled north in January 1927 to call on his old friends Douglas and Emaroy Smith. They were now living in Winnetka, an exclusive, planned village on the outskirts of Chicago that was aesthetically pleasing, well lit and an exemplar of road safety. The idea of a trades building appealed to them greatly, and Mrs Smith pledged $3,500 (about £700) on condition that it would cost $7,000 and the other half of the sum be raised first.

It was in Chicago, however, that Dube became seriously ill. It is probable that his diabetes was first diagnosed here. Although insulin had been discovered as a treatment, the condition was still generally treated by dietary means. Dube felt he could not sustain the rigours of the special diet doctors prescribed for him while constantly on the move and therefore decided to return home sooner than intended. There was one leg of the journey that he was determined to complete, however: the 2,800-kilometre train ride to Glendale in California, for a reunion with William Wilcox and his wife, Ida Belle. Though it had city status, Glendale was in reality a pleasant suburb of Los Angeles where the Wilcoxes were living in retirement. Indefatigable in his support of Dube, Wilcox wrote on this occasion one of his last articles, which he called 'John L. Dube, the Booker T. Washington of South Africa', to assist him in his fundraising. (He died less than a year after Dube's visit.) Dube was with the Wilcoxes for several weeks, before returning to New York and sailing for England in early April.

He arrived in London on the Easter weekend, thinking he would be able to meet with some of his supporters to secure the other half of the funds required for the trades building, before departing a few days later for Cape

Town. Dube had warned Harris that his plans had changed due to illness, but Harris had been unsympathetic – 'I imagine like most Africans, he is dying one day and exuberant the next,' he sniffed to Buxton. Harris therefore pulled him up sharply: no one would be in town for Easter; Dube had failed to give notice of his date of arrival; he had arranged a number of meetings which Dube would now be unable to address. As Dube proffered apologies and set sail, Harris wrote a blistering letter to Pim in Johannesburg: 'We are very annoyed with Mr. Dube ... A Committee which includes Lord Buxton and the Solicitor-General should not have been treated in this manner.' He added that Dube had 'gone a long way towards prejudicing their doing anything further for the Ohlange Institute'. Although Pim jumped to Dube's defence, confirming that he was indeed ill, the London Committee failed to recollect its sense of balance and wound up its work the following year.

Despite this setback, Dube did eventually raise all the money required for the new building: the London Committee had already collected some £300, which it handed over, and the remainder came from sympathisers in South Africa and America. He still had a loyal band of fundraisers in Inanda, Angelina Dube and Bertha Mkhize among them. Both were involved in an organisation called Daughters of Africa, founded to inspire African women to combine race pride with Christian belief and to support them in their special role as educators of the next generation. Angelina became its president. They visited many mission settlements in Natal, organising branches of Daughters as well as explaining the significance of Ohlange and asking for financial assistance, so that women could finally be educated there.[2]

Dube returned to a rather changed situation in Durban. At the invitation of the radicalised local branch of Congress, Kadalie's Industrial and Commercial Workers' Union had established a branch in the city in 1925. A.P. Maduna was the first secretary but for various reasons was soon replaced by Alison George Wessels Champion. Champion's father, George, had been a founding member of the Inanda church and had gone to live near Stanger in the 1860s as helper to one of Lindley's daughters and her farmer husband. His son A.W.G. Champion had been born there in 1893 and had been baptised by Wilcox. Like Dube, the younger George attended Adams, where his teachers included Ngazana Luthuli and Gideon Mvakwendlu Sivetye. Also like Dube, he had been a 'difficult' pupil, not taking kindly to discipline and therefore being frequently punished. While Dube's formal schooling had ended in conversion, however, Champion's had ended in expulsion. He drifted to Johannesburg and worked briefly as a policeman before becoming a mine clerk. His natural organising ability soon enabled him to progress, and it was as president of the Transvaal Native Mine Clerks' Association that Kadalie had met him and persuaded him to take over the Durban ICU office. He was in his early thirties when he arrived in the city; he had the advantage of an exemption certificate.

Relations between the two men began politely enough but soon soured when it became clear that Champion not only had gathered around him those whom Dube considered trouble-makers, but would also pursue a rather more adversarial approach to winning support. Champion was (again, like Dube) a most accomplished orator but also tapped into popular culture in a way Dube would or could not. In his efforts to 'represent, rather than organise' workers – this was not a trade union in the conventional sense – Champion embarked on a highly successful campaign of litigation against the hated by-laws, such that 'dipping', the curfew and the character reference workers had to get on their passes when leaving an employer, were all declared unlawful. This strategy proved so popular that by 1927 an estimated 26,000 workers and urban dwellers had taken out ICU red cards, of a total African population of around 40,000, and the Durban branch of Congress had more or less thrown in its lot with the union.

In the Natal countryside, the ICU was also catching a new wave of rural distress. Bucking international trends of falling agricultural prices, an upsurge in demand for wool and wattle from the mid-1920s had caused a change in patterns of land use, and labour tenants faced eviction in many areas. The difficulty was that they had nowhere to go, since the locations were already seriously congested. When the ICU arrived, promising to restore land to them, its message was enthusiastically embraced: in the Umvoti district, storm centre of the Bhambatha Rebellion, 'the roads every Sunday were crowded with blacks streaming to [ICU] gatherings' through 1927. Farmers and magistrates in a number of districts reported rising levels of restlessness among African workers.

This was in stark contrast to Dube's own engagement with agrarian issues. As one of the very few Africans 'who had money in that time and needed labourers to work for him', he had 380 acres under sugar cane at Inanda, a large holding for an African grower but of course minuscule by comparison with the neighbouring white estates. (The poor state of the roads was a great drawback, however: his brother Charles had sold his 45 acres, which had also been under cane, for this very reason.) While Dube's lands were secure, he was anxious to do what he could to assist those longstanding residents on the Inanda Mission Reserve, where no titles had ever been issued to the original Christian community. They were now calling for title to their holdings as the only defence against newcomers, those being evicted from white farms. They felt that the official Mission Reserve Committee, dominated by Chief Mandlakayise's *indunas*, was making decisions inimical to their interests by allocating new gardens that encroached on the holdings they had long held by custom. Their leader was the Rev. Posselt Gumede, pastor of Dube's old church, an accomplished composer of hymns and father of Innes B. Gumede, a young doctor who was to become Dube's personal physician. Dube did all he could to intercede on their behalf with the Chief Native Commissioner in Pietermaritzburg.

As a prominent local farmer, Dube had been closely involved in launching the Inanda Agricultural Show in 1925, the first in the province to cater for African producers. Based on the Fort Hare and Lovedale shows, it was intended to 'create the desire to produce good work always ... [to] stimulate a strong desire for competition ... [and] enable the farmers to show their goods to the public', in the words of 'Amicus Homini Gentis' (H.I.E. Dhlomo). Its main impetus came from Margaret Walbridge, the principal of Inanda Seminary and keen Loram supporter. She had hired Henry Ngwenya, the son of an ex-pupil, as farm manager to strengthen the school's agricultural department and conduct extension work in the surrounding area. Together with the agricultural instructor at Ohlange, E. Gule, they set out to promote the interests of 'this progressive community' at a time when its integrity was under severe pressure.

The first show had been a great success. Some 434 entries were submitted in eight classes, ranging from livestock and garden produce to home industries; many local dignitaries attended, including Chief Mandlakayise, and two busloads of people drove out from Durban. Dube acted as master of ceremonies, overseeing the judging in the morning, a sporting competition in the afternoon and a film in the evening on 'Life at Tuskegee Institute', loaned for the occasion by Sol Plaatje. Walbridge was pleased to report that 'As a direct result of the show, three Natives have purchased the better plow ... on exhibition at the show and one Native has purchased a harrow, also on exhibition at the show.' By the time the show came around in 1927 and Dube was back from his trip, its benefits as a detraction from countryside militancy had won the attention of the *Weekend Advertiser*, which proclaimed that 'it must take its place with the events of outstanding importance this year in Natal'. Dube, now the show's president, delivered a double-edged speech in which he warned that 'unless the Native made good use of his land, the white man will have to come and claim it, as being left idle' and the Chief Native Commissioner, who opened proceedings, exhorted the crowd to heed these words. The Inanda Show rapidly became a model for several others, from Umbumbulu in the south to Nqutu in the north. They would last until the mid-1930s, when they collapsed under the strains of economic depression, the spread of malaria and East Coast fever and lack of official support: by then they had outlived their usefulness, as far as the government was concerned.

A month after the 1927 show, Dube locked horns with Champion, using close and influential allies in his cause. He had introduced Solomon to Inanda Seminary and the show preparations in June (Walbridge noted afterwards that Dube and Solomon were 'the foremost men of the Zulu nation and it is an honour to have them come in this friendly way') and now prevailed upon him to denounce the ICU in an *Ilanga* article that Dube could well have written for him. Solomon admonished its leaders for not having reported to him and urged chiefs to quash the movement among their people. Dube added his own commentary: 'The leaders are irresponsible, they do not understand the relation of capital to labour ... Are any of the leaders engaged in business employing a number of people for farming and paying 8 shillings a day for their workers? How about that for men of Groutville, Amanzimtoti and Ifafa! Are they prepared to pay their employee that wage? How long can they raise cane at a profit if they pay such wages?' (According to one of his old workers, Dube paid £2 a month plus board and lodging – higher than the rate on white farms but far lower than the ICU's demand.) Later in the month, Dube and Solomon and several prominent chiefs reinforced this message at a mass meeting on the Mount Edgecombe estate, now under the control of Marshall Campbell's son William. This prompted one ICU organiser to declare that Dube, 'the Elephant of Inanda', had been bought off by the 'Marshall Campbell clique', which in turn was working hand in glove with the government.

Dube ordered that Champion receive no positive coverage in *Ilanga*. In retaliation, Champion branded him a 'Judas Iscariot', attempted to launch a paper of his own, *Udibi lwaseAfrika*, and produced a pamphlet putting his side of the story. Lamula and Gumede in the 'official' Natal African Congress – it had changed its name in 1926 in line with the national body becoming the African National Congress in 1923 – supported Champion. Dube and his old Natal Native Congress supporters, including France Xulu, closed ranks. The trouble with Dube's NNC was that it tended to be a law unto itself: 'its meetings were spasmodic and its officers were not subject to regular elections'. The coastal and inland branches were never supposed to have constituted themselves so distinctly from the provincial body, so that the national Congress had to tread an uneasy path of recognising the Natal African Congress while keeping communication open with the Natal Native Congress.

Dube became consumed with his effort of seeing off the ICU, and was even prepared to enlist old adversaries. In early 1928, amid signs that Solomon was parleying with the enemy (he had met Kadalie in Estcourt), Dube wrote in the strictest of confidence to J.S. Marwick, now an MP representing Natal landed interests. The letter was in connection with a motion that had been put down for discussion in the House of Assembly, that Africans should enjoy the same trade union rights as other workers. He began by noting that while he agreed with the ideals of the ICU, 'the upliftment of the Bantu races and the protection of the workers', he felt its methods were wrong, it was causing strife between black and white and was misleading people with 'dangerous propaganda, their absurd promises, their international socialistic inclinations and communism'. All this was 'contrary to the spirit and traditions of the Bantu race' and, as a leader, he could not let this go unchallenged. He then set out his own position:

> We have got to maintain, in my opinion, the sense of paternal and tribal responsibility ... with all its obligations of courage, honour, truth, loyalty and obedience for all we are worth ...
>
> Don't think for one minute that I am not progressive. I am as anxious as any man can be for the development of my people, but on right lines. My aim is to acquire the White man's civilisation with all its benefits without sacrificing the honourable traditions of my own race.
>
> Mr. Marwick, I want you to realise that I am a Muntu of the Bantus. If there is anything I am in earnest about it is the advancement and upliftment of my own people ... I will fight this for all I am worth, and the I.C.U. with their pernicious propaganda I have no time for ...

There are signs in the letter that Dube was distressed – repetition of sentences, uncharacteristic word errors ('empathise' instead of 'emphasise'), and a slightly pointless, rambling style – and it was not at all clear what he wanted from Marwick. This is a puzzle, since he was aware that he was taking an enormous risk in writing at all: 'I rely on you not to do or say anything that will prejudice my ideas and my position in regard to the Bantu people.' The explanation may lie in another letter he wrote just four days later, to J.D. Rheinallt Jones, a leading and outspoken figure in the Joint Councils, whose wife, Edith, was supportive of Ohlange's fundraising efforts; it is highly ironic that just when he had handed over control of the school, his anti–ICU stance was attracting local donations as never before. This was an apology for having missed a talk by Mrs Jones, on account of a very unfortunate accident. While out hunting, Dube had mistaken his servant for a buck and had shot him; the servant was critically ill in hospital. It is highly likely that he had written the letter to Marwick in the immediate aftermath of this incident. His judgement had failed him in more ways than one.

The ICU had in reality already passed its high point. A vicious campaign of repression by local police and white vigilantes, coupled with drought-induced crop failure, all but extinguished its presence in the countryside. Although the Durban branch remained the most powerful in the country, augmented by a Women's Auxiliary under Bertha Mkhize, the by-laws had been reworked, dipping and the curfew were back in force, and there was no more money to fight a new round of legal battles against them. The union's self-help business schemes – so similar to countless others that had been launched over the decades in a desperate bid to avoid wage labour – had foundered and there were questions about Champion's handling of the union's finances. With his threatened removal from office, he formed his breakaway ICU yaseNatal in May.

Inkatha was facing its own difficulties, yet it remained Dube's principal organisational vehicle in this contest. Power struggles in the leadership were causing division (for example, following Mankulumana's death in 1926, Solomon had moved to appoint Chief Mathole of the Buthelezi in his stead) and perceived government hostility to the organisation was turning some chiefs away. As a means of overcoming internal strains and external threats, its constitution was redrafted to strengthen the role of the elected committee and confine Solomon's to that of protective patron; it also articulated more clearly the need to 'keep alive the nation's fine traditions'. The annual meeting in July 1928 was the biggest yet, although Solomon himself did not attend. Frustrated and disappointed in his bid for recognition, and increasingly indebted, he had become heavily dependent on alcohol and was indisposed. The new constitution was ratified after some discussion and a new committee was elected, which included William Bhulose as chairman and Dube as an executive member. It was in this capacity that he welcomed Hertzog to a mass meeting of Solomon and his followers at Nongoma soon after, to hear more about the intended 'Native Bills'.[3]

The ICU yaseNatal's final burst of popular protest in Durban centred on townspeople's rights to consume food and (alcoholic) drink of their choice. In March 1929, the city council made application to construct a new beerhall at Sydenham, one of those areas of informal settlement just beyond the municipal boundaries where many women depended on brewing for their livelihood. This was the point: if a beerhall was to be constructed, any other kind of brewing in the vicinity would be deemed illegal. People approached Champion to resist this development; he wrote to the council and union protest marches began on weekends through May. A boycott of the existing beerhalls began too, enforced by union pickets. In a separate development, the manager of one of the dockworkers' barracks at the Point suddenly forbade the manufacture of *mahewu*, a fomented porridge. When the inmates protested, their leader was stripped of his worker's badge, thus precipitating calls for strike action and support for the beerhall boycott. Though Champion was not at all keen on this more militant display of solidarity, he nevertheless harnessed it to his campaign. J.T. Gumede, the ANC national president, added his voice of support on a flying visit.

Towards the middle of June, the campaign turned violent. Boycotters stoned the Point beerhall and some tried to stop Africans patronising white and Indian eateries as well as the beerhalls. Police dispersed crowds of protesters, and in the gathering mêlée Champion called on his supporters not to march through the streets. But events had slipped out of his grasp: a large crowd of white vigilantes, incensed at the ICU yaseNatal's exuberant disorder in the city centre, besieged and stoned its Workers Club. As the news spread and crowds of Africans arrived on the scene to assist those trapped inside, there was mayhem: two whites and six Africans were killed and many were injured. Yet the sacking of the club and a stepping-up of police harassment – even the first-recorded use of tear gas – did not reduce support for the boycott. As one commentator has put it, 'people could be roughed up for their tax receipts, prosecuted for drinking illegal liquor, chased out of Durban for not having a pass, but they could not be forced into the beerhalls.' Revenue slumped from a projected £52,000 to just over £5,000 in the year from June 1929 to June 1930. The scores of arrests, trials and imprisonments severely impaired the union's organisational ability, although the leadership remained largely intact.

As the boycott dragged on, Dube (who had had at least one of his Congress meetings disrupted by beer boycotters, or possibly members of an *amalaita* gang, largely made up of off-duty male domestic servants) secured an interview with the Minister for Native Affairs, E.G. Jansen, probably through Marwick. Accompanied by France Xulu and G.G. Nxaba, to whom he was related by marriage and who would write one of his earliest biographies, he told Jansen that Africans needed some sort of say in the city council to quell urban unrest and added the suggestion that Solomon ought to be recognised as king to shore up the rural order. He also led a deputation to the Native Administration Committee of the Durban City Council. He laid the trouble squarely at the door of the council and local employers, as the minutes of the encounter record: 'in the minds of many Natives, they considered that they were being treated "worse than a white man's horse", and received very little consideration. [Dube] further referred to the wages received by Natives which in his opinion were insufficient to maintain their families.' A new Native Advisory Board, recommended by the commission set up to investigate the beerhall riots, began its sittings in early 1930.

The tail-end of this phase of Dube's contest with the ICU yaseNatal was conducted on his own terrain: Inkatha. In an effort to bolster flagging support, Champion called a gathering of chiefs in Durban in mid-1930; with 6,000 people turning out, it counted as quite a success. But this was Champion's undoing. As Solomon (whose judgements were by now erratic in any case) appeared to embrace this new initiative, and Inkatha appeared unable to restrain him, powerful figures in government acted to secure Champion's banishment from Durban. Into the vacuum thus created stepped the Communist Party. It tried to keep the beerhall boycott going, but also turned its attention to an anti-pass campaign that would culminate in a mass pass burning at the end of the year. The tide had turned in several ways, though. Firstly, these years marked the onset of a deep global recession and workers began facing wage cuts and job losses, which put a brake on militant action. Further, Dube and his regional colleagues had not been the only Congressmen alarmed at the radical turn in their organisation. Led by Seme, they had determined to unseat J.T. Gumede as president at the annual meeting in 1930. So by the time Dube sat in his car watching the pass burnings, he was back on the national executive of Congress with the education portfolio, under Seme as president. Far from being sidelined, it seemed as if he had made a comeback, yet what sort of comeback remained to be seen.

Dube's differences with Champion were real. What Champion held up to the older disciplinarian was the unpredictable, uncontrollable, combustible aspects of modernity that Dube found almost unbearable to contemplate. He did try to keep his eye on what was fundamentally at issue. In an important paper delivered to a missionary conference at the time, Dube reminded his audience that the 'determination to make South Africa predominantly a land for one race only ... has led to many unjust laws'. He commended the ICU at some length for 'serving a useful purpose in bringing to light certain very serious conditions of Native farm labour in this country', but regretted its leaders' 'violent and abusive language', which alienated those who were otherwise in some sympathy with its goals. He continued this theme some months later, at a conference convened by the Joint Councils (which he conspicuously attended in his personal capacity, rather than as a Joint Council member): 'the interests of the Natives have fallen into the hands of agitators, and I, for one, cannot find the Native very much to blame for this ... the formation of I.C.U. branches has been the inevitable result of the Government's inept handling of the situation.'

Yet their enmity tended to obscure their commonly held dispositions and aspirations. Champion proved as willing to plead with authorities, seek chiefly support and discourage strike activity as Dube; neither of them had much sympathy for communism. Champion joined the Joint Council but was excluded as his ICU became more confrontational. After the lifting of his banning order in 1933, the two men participated in the same committees and boards (such as the Durban Native Advisory Board) and promoted similar schemes and ventures (such as the sale of plots in Clermont township and the formation of business leagues). They took their quarrels into all of these, and their respective organisations continued to haggle over membership and seats. Where they could not both be accommodated, they were involved in rival organisations, as in the establishment of the Bantu Social Centre in town (sponsored by the Joint Council and the Rotary Club) and the Bantu Social Centre in Inanda, Champion's alternative. Champion's militia broke up Congress meetings, while 'an almost secret caucus of Congress members in Dube's best books met at Adams, where a new Congress constitution, debarring leaders of other political organisations from Congress membership, was adopted'. Through the 1930s, their differences would cause severe tension even on the Congress national executive.

Champion had bought a house at Inanda, between Ohlange and the Seminary. As if to try to blend him into his notable neighbour's surroundings, his entry in Skota's *Who's who* did its best to make him respectable: 'to see him on his farm gives a different impression than one gathers in his office and on public platforms'. But harmony between them was simply never going to be possible. After his banning order was lifted Champion returned in October 1933 to a boisterous welcome at the ICU Club, with plans for an ambitious new cooperative venture. It is surely no coincidence that at precisely this time Dube, having become highly excitable when confronted with any challenge to his authority, found himself in the extraordinary position of being charged with incitement to public violence.

In the late morning of 18 November, a coloured man called Joe Smith was making a drunken nuisance of himself in the Victoria Street market. A constable tried to arrest him, Smith resisted and a scuffle ensued as a curious crowd gathered to watch. Eventually the constable wrestled Smith into a ricksha, at which point Dube emerged from the crowd, shouting wildly in Zulu, 'Shaya maphoyisa!' ('Strike the police!') As the crowd became threatening, the constable transferred Smith to a nearby lorry and headed for the police station. At his trial the following January, Dube was found not guilty – but only on a technicality. He should, noted the magistrate, have been charged with incitement to assault a police officer in the course of his duty.[4]

11

The black ox has nowhere to feed

What the ICU's populism had drawn out in Dube was a growing preoccupation with social order and orderliness, both in town and countryside: how to control urban crowds, how to encourage progress in the locations, above all how to harmonise what he called 'old and new social codes'. He had once been thought of as the agent of destabilisation; now he considered others to be threatening the same thing. He seemed to feel and behave as if he had lost control not only of his school but also of the process of a managed passage to modernity with it. On the one side, he complained that Africans in town were out of control and that criminality was on the rise. On the other side, as chiefs came to rely more on their government salaries and less on the will of their people, so the impulses for an enlightened approach to transition from the old order seemed to have weakened. Chief Mqhawe, his one great role model, was long gone and few others had come forward to continue the remarkable experiment he had begun. Solomon, in truth, was no help.

He was not of course the only respectable public figure grappling with such anxieties, and they were not altogether new (and would long continue as a preoccupation). The very establishment of Joint Councils represented an attempt to maintain (or create) urban middle-class order, as did the promotion of 'serious leisure' through the Bantu Social Centres in Johannesburg and Durban. Sibusisiwe Makhanya had established her Bantu Purity League (with Dube an active member) to promote the moral rectitude of young women and Angelina Dube would be involved in setting up an Association of Bantu Parents with similar aims. The Catholic African Union, established in 1928 by Father Bernard Huss and others, was an attempt to offer workers a more conformist social programme in direct competition with the ICU.

There was another dimension to this issue of orderly transition. While Dube frequently referred to the 'darkness of tribalism' – no more so than when addressing missionary audiences – he never imagined that modernisation implied cultural death. As the case of the Qadi under Mqhawe had shown, schools and churches certainly introduced new ideas and ways of life, but people did not cease to be *African*; much of what they carried forward was grounded in their old culture. Conversely, he deemed that very many Western customs were quite unsuitable for adoption by Africans. This was the very essence of the 'New African' of whom he was a foremost living embodiment, from his everyday habits to his race pride, his public achievements and his extraordinary network of contacts. *Ukuziphatha kahle* (Good manners), a work he published in 1928, explored these themes more fully.

Ukuziphatha, Dube pointed out, was aimed at young people and those who taught them, so that 'a nation of people who originated from that which was built up by our ancestors' will continue. The first part was laid out in two columns, appropriately illustrated, so that 'traditional' and 'civilised' practice in a number of settings could be compared and contrasted: cleanliness; housing; kissing; dress; character; engagement; weddings; and death and mourning. In the section on cleanliness, for example, 'Each and everyone should have his own plate, fork and knife', which contrasts with the old habit 'of eating together, drinking from the same clay pot [which] was good, but now there are so many germs that this habit is no longer safe'. However, he continued, 'I do not think we should adopt the western custom of eating at table with our children … it is advisable for children to use their own smaller table, the mother or elder sister helping them to use forks, knives and spoons correctly.'

Much of the work was taken up with the proper supervision of children: in olden times, 'right through the day, it was known where each boy was, and what he was doing'. As far as girls were concerned, 'traditionally, there was nothing more important among maidens than respecting their virginity … [This] should be used as the foundation for the civilisation of our nation.' The second section consisted of lists of 'helpful tips' on correct behaviour, covering everything from table manners and etiquette when visiting or receiving guests to instilling respect in the young and the correct formalities of letter-writing. He made it clear that the principal means of integrating the best of the old with the best of the new was education.

The Pact government ushered in a strident segregationist discourse whose justification was the barbarism of Africans. There was a great deal of equally insistent effort among the African intelligentsia through the 1920s to demonstrate progress, respectability and capacity for civilisation. Selope Thema wrote of Africans' qualities 'which are indispensable to human progress and happiness ... the Christian religion has not come to Africa to abrogate Bantu traditions and customs, but to give them their completion.' *Ukuziphatha* can also be read as Dube's contribution to this effort.

There was a further reason, too, for the timing of its appearance. He was now the father of a young family, and this work might well shed some homely light on his approach to parenting. His various commitments took him away a great deal – one Christmas, his daughter Lulu recalled, he arrived home so distracted by his various commitments that he had forgotten to buy presents, and the children had to wait for these until New Year, when the shops reopened. The heavier responsibility of child care thus fell to Angelina. Lulu was not yet born when *Ukuziphatha* was published, though she remembered how both her parents 'taught us to behave, to be simple, to have manners ... we had to have manners.' Jordan Ngubane, a young journalist who began his career on *Ilanga* and who visited frequently, recalled that 'an atmosphere of reverent awe pervaded the air about his home when he was in'. These memories are suggestive of the strictly patriarchal regime laid out in the manual. Thus, girls should 'consider other people. Being self-centred is a bad habit. You must always be neatly dressed and wear clean clothes. It is a disgrace for a girl to keep on biting her nails, playing with her hair, putting a pencil in her mouth.' As for boys, 'there is nothing more exciting than hearing people say, "He is a little gentleman" ... you must remember to greet your parents and other members of the family every morning, and wish them good day. When going to bed, wish them good night. Bid them goodbye when you go to school ... if you meet a female whom you know, take off your hat.'

Ukuziphatha belongs to that genre that became known as conduct of life literature, after Ralph Waldo Emerson's volume of the same name, with its central question, 'How shall I live?' Such works explored the relationship between fate and character, interior self and public persona. African American writers took up the issue in specific ways, attempting to identify those aspects of character that would contribute to individual self-help as well as collective success in an ill-disposed environment. The conduct of life idea featured strongly in the works of thinkers as widely divergent as Booker Washington and Marcus Garvey. While it had been a theme in Dube's earlier work, this was his more sustained attempt to lay down a series of guidelines that might yield results in South African conditions, where alignment of old and new was an added concern.

This was also the subject of his paper to the 1928 General Missionary Conference and featured centrally in the first-ever Zulu novel, Dube's *Insila kaShaka*, published just two years later in 1930. It was his only major venture into fiction, although in many ways he had long been immersed in creative literature. In oral mode he had composed speeches, sermons and songs; in written mode he was one of the most accomplished practitioners of a formal, literary Zulu. He read widely, and had encouraged many writers of short stories, poetry and drama by publishing their work in *Ilanga*. Among them was William Plomer, whose very first poems were published in the paper under the pseudonym P.Q.R. At the time of working on *Insila*, Dube was also involved with F.L. Ntuli on a Zulu translation of Rider Haggard's *Nada the Lily*; published as *Umbuso kaShaka*, Dube wrote the preface.

Insila was translated posthumously into English by his friend J.D. Boxwell as *Jeqe, the Body-servant of King Shaka*, which Boxwell dedicated to Angelina Dube. It is a historical romance that tells the story of young Jeqe, whose bravery in battle brings him to the attention of the king. As a reward, he is appointed Shaka's body-servant. But Shaka has become a tyrannical ruler and Jeqe is required to show his worth and prove his loyalty by carrying out a number of cruel tasks. He resists the impulse to flee and even foils a murder plot. But when Dingane and his accomplices kill Shaka, Jeqe runs away and becomes a wanderer, living on his wits and facing further tests of endurance. He succumbs to fever and survives only because he is discovered by a kindly woman who nurses him to health before sending him on his way into Tongaland. Here he falls in love with a beautiful girl called Zaki; she, however, has been promised to another. She returns Jeqe's love and agrees to marry him, but her previous suitor, on hearing of these developments, swears to kill him.

There is a fight in which Jeqe is critically wounded, but he is discovered by some visiting herbalists, who remove him to an island and heal him. He lives among them for a long while, learning the art of medicine. He is finally reunited with Zaki, who has waited patiently for him, and they settle in Swaziland where Jeqe uses his skills to positive effect and he and Zaki raise a family. Years pass, and then Dingane sends to the Swazi king for a doctor. Jeqe returns to his homeland in disguise, to be reunited with his parents, who tell him that life under Dingane is intolerable. He arranges for them to travel to Swaziland before waiting on Dingane. The king discovers who Jeqe really is, but not before he is safely back in Swaziland; the Swazi king Sobhuza vows to protect him, which leads to war between the Zulu and the Swazi, in which Jeqe's sons display great bravery and which the Swazi win.

This storyline is interspersed with much ethnographic and historical detail (which can be seen as yet another way to present accepted etiquette) and contains several well-known praises, songs, fairytales and myths. Though these might at times seem like long diversions, they are part of the didactic purpose of a textbook, which Dube probably intended and which indeed it very soon became. More fundamentally, and entirely in keeping with Dube's views on these matters, what *Insila* presents is 'traditional society ... recast as a rational order in which the modernised subject feels at home'. It is also deeply nostalgic, for a time long gone when his benign forebears had ruled the Qadi – one scene is set in the Thukela valley where they were once settled – and for his own time in another place: Dube was a great friend of King Sobhuza's, and the family regularly spent holidays in Swaziland; it was where he taught his sons to hunt. He felt a freedom there that had disappeared from his surroundings at home.[1]

Insila presents an image of African society in which people can live peaceable and fulfilling lives under wise and capable rulers. Yet Dube soon became involved with the author of a novel that projected an altogether more ominous outlook. George Heaton Nicholls had been born in sight of the industrial furnaces and factory chimneys of Rotherham in Yorkshire in 1876 and had joined the army to escape an unhappy home life. He guarded a group of Boer prisoners of war in Ceylon in 1902 and accompanied them back to South Africa, where he left the army. He joined the British South Africa Company as a district administrator but while on leave was retrenched, so he found his way to Australia, where he worked on ranches and sugar estates before returning to civil administrative work in Papua New Guinea. He then married a South African and they settled to sugar farming in the Mfolozi region of Zululand in 1912.

Here he had written his novel, *Bayete!*, the theme of which concerned everything that might pose a threat to his new-found sense of security and stability. Foremost among these was 'Ethiopianism' – though in white settler discourse, this carried none of the positive connotations of redemption and deliverance that it did in African usage. Rather, it was politics disguised as religion, a dangerous conspiracy to overthrow white rule and chase whites into the sea. Nelson, the protagonist of the novel, is a chief's heir but spurns this future for an American education. He returns to Africa to lead an anti-white uprising; too late, after fighting between black and white has begun, he sees the futility of what he has done: 'the eternal problem of Africa ... could not be settled by blood – but by understanding ... Of what value to remove the yoke of white superiority if he killed the very spirit of civilisation which had redeemed his race from Chaka?' The events at Bulhoek and the white miners' strike finally prompted him to seek a publisher and the book came out in 1923. By this time, Heaton Nicholls had entered parliament as the MP for Zululand.

Not long after, Hertzog signalled his intention to sort out a common 'Native policy' for South Africa. He introduced four bills for discussion in 1926 and appointed a Select Committee to gather evidence and to prepare these bills for the legislative process. One dealt with coloured representation and the other three concerned Africans: the Natives' Representation in Parliament Bill, the Natives' Land Bill and the Natives' Council Bill. The first proposed abolishing the Cape franchise, the second to act on the recommendations of the Beaumont Commission and find more land for the locations, and the third to set up a national council to accommodate the requirements of African representation. There followed a long process of Select Committee deliberations, revisions and a general election that suspended all sittings. In 1930, the Select Committee turned into a Joint Committee of both Houses, with an agreement to work entirely behind closed doors so that party politics were kept out.

Heaton Nicholls had been a member of the committee since its establishment. His determination to secure 'permanent European dominance' was probably no more ardent than most other segregationists in government, but he had a keener sense than most of the importance of co-opting African support. His idea was to promote what he called 'communalism', by maintaining and developing the locations to secure 'the civilised advance of the Zulu nation *en masse*, as a separate entity. That included the gradual recognition of an elite as it emerged ... Zulus, when sufficiently civilised, could become citizens of the European state; but meanwhile, until they were civilised, they marched with the mass of their fellow tribesmen.' He was quite explicit that communalism would keep communism out. In line with his approach, he proposed that parliamentary representation for Africans should be in the Senate, by African senators; that there should be a halt to further African additions to the Cape roll (to end representation in the House of Assembly, in other words); and the locations and reserves should be doubled in size, with the land being acquired by means of a proper land bank. In this way, 'tribal life' could be properly reconstituted. The next step was to win African opinion over, which had to be done with the utmost circumspection given the confidentiality of deliberations. Heaton Nicholls already knew Dube well, since both of them had been trying for some time to secure Solomon's recognition as king and both detested the ICU. Dube was enlisted to travel the country to meet all the most influential leaders, and to sound them out on the proposals.

Dube called on some of his oldest contacts and associates – W.W. Ndhlovu and Chief Gilbert Majozi (also active in Inkatha) in Natal; R.V. Selope Thema and H. Selby Msimang in the Transvaal; and Thomas Mapikela in the Orange Free State. They were hardly representative. Seme had been making overtures to Champion, and Dube had thus fallen out with him and resigned his education portfolio, so it might have been difficult talking to anyone who feared becoming embroiled in their dispute. Though it might be supposed that these stalwarts could be depended upon for support, they would not endorse the proposals as they stood. They liked the idea of a land bank and direct representation in Senate, but otherwise had some amendments of their own, and these were all they were willing to put their names to. They drew up a document stating that all the African reserves should be large and compact, like the Transkei; each one should have a council with legislative powers; any African should be entitled to live in any reserve; and trading rights and the civil service in each should be fully opened to Africans. Importantly, they demanded that the new areas be surveyed *before* any legislation was passed. Dube signed the document too. They had lost much ground, literally and figuratively, but they were still prepared to try to push back the borders of the little that was left.

Dube then travelled to the Cape and spoke to all those 'worth seeing', assuring Heaton Nicholls that 'all of the Transkei is with us in this matter'. He evidently did not visit the Ciskei but had been told that men such as Meshach Pelem (long a Congress supporter) and D.D.T. Jabavu, a vociferous anti-segregationist, might be willing to compromise. But his intelligence was wrong and Jabavu was most angry at the proposal regarding the Cape franchise. He had formed the Cape Native Voters' Association to defend it and there was no way he would agree to any compromise. That is as far as the proposals got. Heaton Nicholls had had to make his own compromises in the Select Committee in the meantime, which rendered them even less attractive. It was to be some years yet before these bills were tabled in parliament. After the formation of the United Party in 1934, the Cabinet took over the drafting process and they were only released, finally, in 1935. Nevertheless, it can hardly be claimed, as Heaton Nicholls does in his autobiography, that his efforts 'met with the full approval of a number of the leading natives at that time'.

The points that Dube and his colleagues had made about the draft legislation were incorporated and extended in his testimony to the Native Economic Commission. In many ways, this stands as his last major statement on matters that had engaged him through his public life. He had prepared a written submission on which he was closely questioned at great length in the hearings. Uppermost in his mind and, he said, in the minds of all African people was the land issue. They needed far more of it, particularly those who could not afford to buy. The land ought to be purchased for them and handed over; all the African areas ought to be properly surveyed and divided into building plots, grazing grounds and gardens. People could pay a nominal rent for their plots. 'There are only one million of you and there are about six millions of us; and one million of you have three fourths of the land, and six millions of us have one fourth of the land. That is not fair ... In asking [for more land] I do not think we are asking for charity; we have contributed to the development of South Africa with our labour – we have done our share in that respect, and in the matter of taxation, both direct and indirect.'

He vigorously fought off the commissioners' views that Africans did not know how to use their land properly, that any more would just be wasted, that Africans multiplied too fast, that they had too many cattle: 'the black ox has nowhere to feed, and the white ox has all the pasture ... I am sorry if I cannot make that clear to you.' He denied that 'tribal life' was a stagnant form of existence; in any case, it was closely tied to the allocation of land and that was one of its advantages. He wanted to see enlightened chiefs and councillors opening the way to progress. Industrial and academic training were inseparable: 'a carpenter must know arithmetic in order to make his own specifications' although there could be no progress until Africans' education was properly financed. He highlighted the plight of African farmworkers who, he felt, were 'almost in a state of serfdom'. Labour tenancy arrangements had led to widespread indebtedness; 'the Native is given only a part of his legitimate wage and the rest go[es] towards maintaining the European standard of supremacy.'

He had as much to say on city life as on rural issues. 'It seems to us Natives that ... we are just so many horses that have to be stabled after they have been working – just as though we are not human beings ... the [Natives] Urban Areas Act restricts our freedom of movement and our activities.' He thought hostels depressed wages and that workers should be allowed to bring their families to town, where decent housing should be provided. He wanted to see all industrial colour bars removed and favoured trade unions for African workers because 'I have thought a great deal that Natives are exploited by their employers and they should organise themselves in self-defence'. A special grievance was the colour bar preventing employment of African court interpreters, which led to widespread miscarriage of justice. He also thought Africans were far too heavily taxed and that proper representation was an urgent necessity. African representatives in the Senate would be 'something' but 'the chief place where we would feel we had adequate representation would be ... in the House of Assembly'.

He felt that Africans' health was declining due to malnutrition, insanitary living conditions, and the negative effects of 'contact with other races'. He had referred in his written statement to the consequence of declining fertility rates and suggested to the commissioners that this was a serious interference with patriarchal control: 'old men look askance at the non-childbearing woman'. Overall, he was gloomy about the future, unless 'Natives can have a degree of freedom in exercising intelligence in their own areas' – that is, developing industries, markets and roads throughout the locations, so that men would not have to go so far to work. Similarly, Africans should have full trading rights in towns and women should be encouraged to start businesses: 'we want to compete with other people, whether they be white, yellow or black; we want a place in the sun.'

From his vantage point at 'the apex of subordination', Dube had delivered a sharp criticism of white supremacy and had offered an alternative social model of equal opportunity, social redistribution, meaningful political representation, just exercise of authority and orderly progress by example. It was a tempered rather than aggressive nationalist vision that demonstrated marked continuities with his earliest views. What he did not say in his evidence, however, was how he thought his ideals might be realised, and this was where their weakness was revealed. He had done his best to give them practical substance, though he had faced insurmountable obstacles of various kinds and had not yet found a more effective organisational vehicle.[2]

The 'communalism' that Heaton Nicholls wished to promote, and Dube to modernise, was under very great stress in Zululand. Soon after returning from his secret mission, Dube attended a meeting at Mahashini to discuss Inkatha's parlous finances. There was mounting evidence of fraudulent and extortionist practices in collecting funds – 'tribute' – and Solomon, who had had always enjoyed open access to these, was hopelessly indebted and increasingly incapacitated. What complicated any resolution was the rift between Dube and Seme over the latter's attempts to draw Champion into the fold. To his extreme annoyance, Dube had battened down his Natal Native Congress hatches again, instead of cooperating with this careful attempt to reconstitute the provincial ANC. Against this backdrop, Dube feared that Seme would use the scandal of Inkatha's finances to discredit him and so did all he could to suppress any information on the matter. There was another scandal brewing, too. Inkatha had launched a Shaka Memorial Fund to construct a stone monument to the founder of the kingdom. *Ilanga* had called for contributions and funds flowed in from everywhere. By the time the unveiling ceremony came, it was discovered the stonemason was still owed over £3,000 and the funds had simply disappeared. Dube's response to all this was to tender his resignation from an unravelling Inkatha and Memorial Committee to Solomon, in person.

He did not, however, abandon contact with the royal circle; far from it. When Solomon died in March 1933, he had apparently not named an heir and the sons were all still young. Solomon's brother Arthur Edward Mshiyeni was installed as regent; to the relief of Natal officials and doubtless to those older Congressmen who had been temperance supporters all their lives, he was altogether different from Solomon. Lovedale-educated, he was 'abstemious, particular about his appearance and polished in manner', enthused the Chief Native Commissioner, Harry Lugg. He was also more cooperative with authority. Dube quickly established a rapport with him and, in his address at the purification ceremony marking the end of mourning for Solomon, asserted once more that 'we want the head of the Zulu nation to be a Paramount Chief who is so recognised by the Government'. Mshiyeni was to be Dube's close ally in the last political campaigns he undertook.

Hertzog finally laid his two 'Native' bills before parliament in 1935. The Representation of Natives Bill provided for the indirect election of four white senators to represent African interests, including those African voters on the Cape common roll, to which there would be no new additions. It also provided for the creation of a Natives Representative Council, a new body that would consist of the Secretary for Native Affairs, six Chief Native Commissioners, and 16 African representatives, four nominated and 12 indirectly elected. It would be purely advisory. The Native Trust and Land Bill would belatedly implement the Beaumont Commission's proposals, roughly doubling the size of the reserves. Parliament would acquire the land on Africans' behalf.

The government called regional conferences for discussion of the draft legislation in September. For the Natal event, Lugg made every effort to invite a wide range of chiefs and middle-class figures who represented 'respectable' opinion in the region. There were about 120 delegates in attendance, three-quarters of them chiefs. Two of the most senior men in the kingdom, Bokwe Zulu and Mathole Buthelezi, were present. Apart from Dube, Congress supporters included William Bhulose, Abner Mtimkulu (who arrived from the Cape in the early 1930s and quickly rose to be Dube's deputy in the NNC), A.W. Dhlamini (president of the Natal Bantu Teachers' Union),

Z.K. Matthews (cousin of Sol Plaatje and first graduate of Fort Hare, who headed Adams for a time and had just returned from postgraduate studies at the London School of Economics) and Selby Ngcobo (a young teacher at Adams). This was one of the first official meetings attended by the 'chief-designate' of Groutville, Albert Luthuli.

The first morning was taken up with speeches by Douglas Smit, the Secretary for Native Affairs, and other government officials, all urging support for the legislation. The delegates were then left in the charge of Dube and Mshiyeni. It soon became clear that there was a great deal of opposition to the bills: 'the intelligentsia were raising all manner of questions, relevant and irrelevant ... as the talk continued the Regent became visibly impatient, while Dube seemed distressed.' Discussion got so heated that proceedings had to be stopped to eject certain of the participants who had begun to heckle and were 'upsetting' the conference. The atmosphere was strained until the evening adjournment.

By the following day, some chiefs had given up and gone home and Dube had absented himself. Mshiyeni did not wish the discussion to continue. Carl Faye, Lugg's official interpreter, took the opportunity of drawing up what he thought had been the opinion of the conference for the official record. Smit and Lugg were called into the hall to hear the results. After the formalities of expressing thanks, Mshiyeni announced that they thought they could accept some of the proposals in principle but, beyond that, wished for copies of the legislation and more time to debate it.

It is no wonder that Dube had seemed 'distressed'. Z.K. Matthews, Selby Ngcobo and Albert Luthuli were among a younger generation of Congress leaders far more sensitive to the popular opposition to Hertzog's bills than the old guard. While they respected Dube, they were alarmed at the soft approach he seemed to be taking. Just before the conference, they asked Dube's attorney, Denis Shepstone, to arrange a meeting so that they could explain their reservations. When Dube arrived, 'he didn't ask us what we had come to do, he just gave us a terrific harangue about how we were trying to take his leadership away from him, and that he had worked for this leadership from his young days, and that now he was an old man, and that the young men were coming along'. The effect was to drive Dube closer to Mshiyeni; it was the symbolic moment of the passing of his influence in Congress.

The regent was not present, however, at the follow-up meeting in October, having been admitted to hospital. Dube, who was clearly unwell himself, took the chair alone. Fewer delegates attended this time: 40 chiefs, among them Bokwe and Mnyaiza, and some 15 educated leaders. Luthuli, Ngcobo and Matthews were all there again, representing the Bantu Teachers' Union. After hours of discussion and a special trip to consult with Mshiyeni, a series of resolutions was issued. The bills were too weighty to be passed into law without being properly discussed at a full 'Council of Abantu', as envisaged in the Representation of Natives Bill. Therefore the legislative process should be deferred until this council had met. However, representation as laid down in the bill was wholly inadequate for all the people of the region and therefore should be 'appreciably increased'. Finally, there should be a conference of chiefs convened annually to consider all matters affecting Africans. This was Natal's response. Even the chiefs had been less than enthused by Hertzog's legislative plans.

Opposition across the country was mounting, although Congress under Seme's ineffectual leadership seemed unable to rise to the challenge of coordinating it – a mere 43 delegates had attended the 1933 conference. Momentum came instead from D.D.T. Jabavu and a young Johannesburg doctor, A.B. Xuma, who moved to assemble the most representative gathering possible in Bloemfontein on Dingane's Day in December 1935. Some 400 delegates attended the All-African Convention, half of them from the Cape. Natal sent the smallest delegation of 30 members, among them John Dube, Abner Mtimkulu, William Ndhlovu, Walter Kumalo, A.W.G. Champion, Stephen Mini, Z.K. Matthews, Selby Ngcobo and, in a new departure, Mrs W. Sebeta (voting rights for women were debated in this forum). Dube reported the decisions of Natal and hoped that the assembly 'would not be productive of inflammatory oratory, and that the best brains would be used in drafting its resolutions'.

The resolutions drafted by the 'best brains' were many and all carried the same message of rejection. Predictably, there was implacable opposition to any tampering with the Cape franchise system, a subject that took up much of the convention's deliberations. Dube regretted this fact in his reflections on the event, feeling that 'the interests of the great mass of Bantu people and their urgent need for more land' had been overlooked. There was an echo here of his old dilemma, caught between two constituencies: he had been leaned on very heavily by Heaton Nicholls and the Minister for Native Affairs himself to oppose the resolutions emanating from the Cape.

As Dube's influence in Congress circles waned, so his stature in white liberal ones grew. His stand against the ICU prompted a closer look at this leader who had caused so much trouble to officialdom in the past. He was drawn more fully into the Joint Council, invited to address meetings of the Rotary Club and wrote the 1934 Christmas editorial for the *Natal*

Mercury, the first African to do so. He used the occasion to urge more assistance for African farmers. The following year he was among six Natal Africans selected as recipients of King George V's Silver Jubilee Medal; in his letter of recommendation, Lugg called him 'the [American Zulu] Mission's outstanding product'. Among others chosen were Stephen Mini and Mshiyeni. Also in 1935, William Campbell had Dube and Mshiyeni on hand at Mount Edgecombe to receive the delegates of the Empire Press Union. The press union had been founded in 1909 as a forum for English-language papers across the British empire and dominions, and at its regular conferences discussed such matters as press cable rates, newsprint rationing and the impact of broadcasting. Its president in the mid-1930s was Major John Jacob Astor, member of the Anglo-American Astor dynasty and proprietor of *The Times*.

As a senior newspaperman himself (though one who had never enjoyed the benefits of a press union), it was entirely fitting that Dube should address this gathering. His talk was 'frank and outspoken', and a deliberate counterpoint to the Zulu dancers who provided the entertainment. He regretted that delegates had not visited mission stations to talk to educated Africans who were trying to uplift their fellow beings, and to witness the value of education. 'The large majority of Europeans in South Africa are opposed to the education of the Native as they think it is spoiling him ... the Native should be allowed to enter the skilled trades and then he will be fully qualified to assist the European in the development of the Union.' At the same time, he said, 'I do not think we should ever forsake the traditions of our race.' He told them that he was the grandson of Cetshwayo, 'one of the greatest and strongest of all Zulu chiefs'. Perhaps he had never forgotten the noble inheritance he had set out as his own in his first publication, *A talk on my native land*, over 40 years earlier.

Edgar Brookes, ex-professor of political science at the University of Pretoria who had recently become principal of Adams and president of the Institute of Race Relations, was deeply impressed by all that Dube had achieved. In 1936, he put a proposal to the Honorary Degrees Committee of the University of South Africa (Unisa), then the award-granting body for a number of South African university colleges. It was that Dube should be awarded an honorary PhD. After a brief survey of his many achievements, Brookes's proposal pointed out that 'He occupies a unique place in Natal public life, among Europeans as well as Bantu, is highly and generally respected, and stands for moderation, racial co-operation and sane constructive policies, while a firm champion of the rights of his people'. He wished, he said, to 'honour a man who has been a genuine South African patriot, a true servant of his country, and a pioneer under great difficulties in several important fields'. There was one other candidate to consider that year, the Rev. Andries Dreyer, key historian and ideologue of the Nederduitse Gereformeerde Kerk and author of such works as *The Cape Church and the Great Trek* and *The struggle against liberalism.*

The vote was unanimous in favour of both. When the proposals came before the full University Council, Dube's candidature won by 17 votes to 6. It was the first time that an African had been accorded this honour in South Africa. Dube was in the Bantu Social Centre when the news was brought to him and he and his friends were 'astonished and overjoyed'. Congratulations flowed into *Ilanga* and several receptions were held in his honour. Unisa's rector, F.D. Hugo, had suggested that Dube receive his award at the next graduation ceremony at Fort Hare. Dube was too ill to attend, however, and a special ceremony was held at Ohlange. Hugo and Campbell were the main speakers.[3]

There is a fitting symmetry to this high point of recognition and the work that Dube published in the same year. For some decades, another of his neighbours in Inanda had been the remarkable prophet Isaiah Shembe. He had founded his church, the AmaNazaretha, in Durban but in about 1916 had acquired 50 acres of land in the valley below Ohlange and invited his followers to settle there with him. It was called Ekuphakameni, 'Elevated place'. Shembe, who seems to have been introduced to Christianity by an independent church, was himself illiterate; his achievement was to build not only a church on the basis of biblical interpretation but also 'a new Zulu society on the broad basis of the old, and give this new society roots and values'. It was, in other words, a regeneration of Africa. God had given Shembe a covenant 'to lead the people from white bondage'. There was place for ancestors as well as the communion of saints; *ukuhlobonga* (external sexual intercourse) and alcohol were forbidden but polygamy was allowed. Intricate ritual practices – concerning prayer, pilgrimage, dress and dance – as well as a strict social code enforcing chastity and respect – shaped worshippers' lives. Shembe built his reputation as a healer as well as a diviner and Ekuphakameni steadily became the centre of one of the largest and most complex of the independent churches in South Africa.

Dube was fascinated by Shembe. Here was an alternate version of redemption based not on book learning but on visions and voices, achieving a degree of respectability yet functioning entirely outside the parameters of respectable society. (Shembe faced enormous hostility from missionary circles and officialdom in the early years of his church, but this had largely dissipated by the late 1920s.) Whereas Dube had faced a relentless struggle to fund his redemptive project, Shembe's much poorer followers happily brought him cash gifts with which he purchased ever more land for them to settle on. Dube's last major work was a biography of Isaiah Shembe. The prophet had recently died (Dube had been one of the main speakers at the funeral, and had helped to sort out the will) and a group of church members approached him to produce the book, supplying him with all the information they could.

The biographical element of *uShembe* focuses on the prophet's early life, involving episodes in which he is visited by presences and experiences dream sequences, up to the point where he is baptised and begins to preach. It is one of the most detailed accounts of this period and remains the most important source of information on the making of the prophet. The remainder of the work takes the form of a compendium of information and explanation about Shembe and the church. A short section contains a series of 'tests' as to whether Shembe is a false prophet or not; Dube's verdict is not altogether clear. He presents a number of testimonies of those who had been cured through Shembe's powers of healing and reproduces a selection of hymns and prayers, as well as an explanation of doctrine (baptism, circumcision and marriage), ritual (such as the pilgrimage to Nhlangakazi, site of Shembe's covenant with God) and a list of instructions and prohibitions. Shembe is given his own voice to issue advice; it is almost in the form of a sermon. There is a rather unflattering, even envious, account of Shembe's schemes for collecting money: leading people to believe they would be cursed if they failed to donate, and demanding money before worshippers were permitted to take part in the dancing, for example. At the very end of the work, Dube includes accounts of some of those who had been close to Shembe, including Mlangeni, his longest-standing adherent, and Solomon, who married one of Shembe's daughters, Zondi.

Shembe had by the 1920s become something of a local celebrity and gave his life story to several other enquirers, among them the Assistant Chief Native Commissioner, the Ndwedwe magistrate, Native Affairs interpreter Carl Faye and a *Natal Mercury* journalist. That he was approached to produce the work suggests that Dube had privileged access to information. That the AmaNazaretha chose him for the task suggests their skilfulness in securing legitimacy among the most socially respectable, especially at a time of uncertainty when Johannes Galilee Shembe was succeeding to his father's position. One commentator has noted something else significant: *uShembe* is 'visionary, full of the voices of the powerless who have found their lives illuminated ... and desired this to be set down in print because print and writing were seen as a medium of the powerful'.

Dube was probably happier, however, in more refined circles. One of these was the Zulu Society, founded in 1936, whose object was 'to take care of and preserve the heritage of our language ... and to commend what is becoming in our heritage of traditions, laws, usages and customs'. It was an initiative of the Natal Bantu Teachers' Union and warmly welcomed by Lugg, himself a collector of Zulu history and custom, who ensured that it received an annual grant of £250. Mshiyeni was appointed its patron and Dube one of its advisers, as were Sibusisiwe Makhanya and Phika Zulu, the municipal 'induna' who had reported Dube to Marwick so many years before. Despite its grant and the appointment of six sub-committees, it was never able to produce a membership list and the executive continued in office indefinitely. It became an 'almost arcane cultural nationalist organisation without any constituency beyond its office holders'. It is interesting to note, though, that Dube still kept open a more expansive sense of cultural nationalism. In the late 1930s he inaugurated a day at Ohlange to commemorate founding national figures: it was called Shaka and Moshoeshoe Day.

The Natives Representative Council (NRC), unveiled in 1937, hardly had a larger constituency in Natal. Even the long-time *Ilanga* columnist and retired school teacher Josiah Mapumulo thought it 'a fraud, a deception, and empty meaningless show'. Dube and Ndhlovu campaigned in Zululand, hoping to secure the chiefs' vote. At a meeting in Eshowe, to which they were accompanied by Mshiyeni, Dube told them, 'We are grateful for what has been conceded in the way of Parliamentary representation for us. It is the thin end of the wedge, or expressed in Zulu, is like a beast grazing on the edge of good grazing and hoping eventually to get into it.' Dube and Ndhlovu were duly elected, while Arthur Sililo, a member of Dube's Congress faction, took the only urban seat. Lugg nominated Mshiyeni. (Every one of them was a member of the Zulu Society.) Champion, who had also stood, was kept firmly out, though he would gain a seat in the 1942 elections. The ANC decided to support candidates in the elections and among the other newly elected councillors were Jabavu, Selope Thema and Mapikela.

When the NRC convened for its inaugural sitting, Dube's fellow African councillors nominated him chairman of their caucus; he became a 'Leader of the House', of sorts. The visiting African American scholar Ralph Bunche observed this opening of the NRC in Pretoria in December 1937. Smuts, deputising for Hertzog, opened proceedings. This was followed by several other official speeches, after which Dube was invited to say a few words. He thanked the previous speakers and suggested there be a photograph taken of all the council members. He in turn was thanked by Smuts – and so on. Bunche thought the entire performance a charade, an impression reinforced by the seating arrangements for the opening ceremony: the white members (among whom were Heaton Nicholls and Loram) were on the platform and the 16 'Native Councillors' looked up at them from the hall below. The first formal sitting was no better, even though everyone was now around a table, on the same level. It was impossible to have free and fair discussion, because 'the chairman of the meeting is head of [the] department which must, of necessity, be under fire'. Rheinallt Jones explained Dube's limp attitude as a sign of advanced age.

Dube was more interested in using his influence as a councillor behind the scenes than in the forum itself. He had already been agitating on the matter of Mshiyeni's recognition and stepped up his campaign after 1937. He wrote to and met the Chief Native Commissioner in Pietermaritzburg, as well the Minister for Native Affairs. Lugg was supportive all through, but it was not until 1939 that Mshiyeni finally had the title 'Acting Paramount Chief' conferred upon him. In the congratulatory letter that Seme wrote to *Ilanga* on the occasion of the 'restoration', he acknowledged the role that Mshiyeni's 'Chief Councillor', John Dube, had played. It was clear, however, that the title would not pass automatically to the heir. At the time of Solomon's death, Mshiyeni and other senior royals had named the oldest son, Victor Phikokwaziwayo, as heir. However, this had not been a unanimous choice and the matter had been left open. Dube did what he could to promote Victor, since this was Mshiyeni's choice, but in 1940 Mshiyeni suggested the candidature of another son, Thandayiphi. He was to be no more successful. In 1935 R.R.R. Dhlomo had named Cyprian as successor in his textbook *Izihali zaNamuhla*. Cyprian's mother, Christina Sibiya, later came forward with a letter allegedly written by Solomon, which also named Cyprian. Having been nominated by the 'written word', he succeeded to the headship of the uSuthu in the mid-1940s.

When Z.R. Mahabane took over the presidency from Seme in 1937, Dube rejoined the ANC executive as leader of Natal. In an effort to heal Natal rifts, Mahabane had given Champion the lands and locations portfolio, to which Dube took extreme exception. When Dube refused to recognise Champion's position, Champion threatened to take him to court. The secretary-general, James Calata, dissuaded Champion from this course of action and wrote a frustrated letter to him, asking that he 'make every effort to convince Dr

Dube and the Natal Congress of the necessity of linking up our forces and closing our ranks'.

Yet when the occasion demanded, these two old foes could at least bury their hatchets. While Calata was doing his pleading, Dube attended a rally of over 1,000 workers at the Bantu Social Centre that had been convened by Champion's ICU yaseNatal. In his speech, he declared that there was no other country where workers were so badly paid, and that they were not benefiting now that the economy was expanding again after the depression. Dube proposed a motion to lay the workers' general complaint before government officials and employers' bodies. The complaint was this: 'that in spite of the admitted general prosperity of the country the Native had not been affected and is still receiving the same wages as during the depression. We desire ... a minimum wage to be fixed throughout the country.' The workers elected Champion and Dube to lead a deputation to the relevant bodies. Neither Dube nor Champion favoured strike action as a means of achieving workers' demands. Whatever their own personal contests, they did nevertheless provide a forum for the expression of grievances and helped to popularise the minimum wage demand of 5s a day.

The ANC's 1939 annual conference was held in Durban for the first time in a determined effort to reduce tension; Dube, as provincial president, agreed to share the platform with Champion. One outcome was that 'Natal actually came in and Dr Dube also came in'. The conference passed a number of significant resolutions, indicative of its determination to re-engage with events after years of stupor. It accepted the principle of the Non-European United Front, a left-wing organisation that had been formed earlier in the year by Yusuf Dadoo and others, with primary bases in Johannesburg and Cape Town. It supported recognition of African workers in terms of the Industrial Conciliation Act, and agreed that it would not encourage Africans to support the war effort until 'full democratic and citizenship rights' had been granted to them. Apparently the most memorable event of the conference was the arrival of Mshiyeni, upon which Dube 'jumped up and performed a Zulu dance of excitement'; it caused quite a furore. In his presidential capacity in 1943, Xuma invited Dube to become honorary life president, a gesture as much to acknowledge his long years of service as to keep the truce in Natal.

There was no such thing as retirement for Dube. Though his health was rapidly declining, he tried to go on fulfilling his various public commitments as normal – the same dogged determination that had always driven him never let up. He won a second term on the NRC in 1942 (he had to be carried in and out of the last meeting he attended) and was invited to sit on Xuma's

Atlantic Charter Committee (which would result in the document *Africans'
claims*) but was too ill to attend the sessions. He brought a number of younger
men onto the Natal Congress executive as his way of showing displeasure
with the idea of a separate Youth League – perhaps, too, a last attempt to
control the process of generational transition in the face of a noticeably more
radical rhetoric. In October 1943 he suffered a stroke, which confined him
to his Inanda home. Anxiety at his sudden disappearance from public life
manifested itself in lengthy and voluminous debate through the pages of
Ilanga as to who might succeed him, as Champion and Mtimkulu shaped up
to contest the provincial Congress leadership. He and Angelina at last made a
will. He was too ill to sign it and was reduced to making the mark of a cross,
as the illiterate chiefs had always done. He lingered until 11 February 1946,
passing in the early morning. It was his 75th birthday.

His funeral was held two days later, in the Industrial Hall at Ohlange.
People turned out in their hundreds, leading figures as well as ordinary
admirers. Two old AZM colleagues, the Rev. N.M. Nduli and the Rev.
R.M. Ngcobo, officiated. The testimonies were many and effusive. Herbert
Dhlomo, one of the leading playwrights and poets of his time (and brother of
the new *Ilanga* editor, R.R.R. Dhlomo), composed a valediction:

> Oh weep! Mafukuzela great is dead!
> The giant who pained through laborious years
> To woo for Africa the place that's hers.
> Weep not! For a golden circlet crowns his head!
> Weep not for him. He lives! He speaks, is free! ...

Last to speak was Charles Dube, his only surviving brother, who traced
their lives since boyhood. Then John Langalibalele Dube was buried on the
side of a hill above the school, so that he could keep watch over Ohlange
for ever.[4]

Where there was once a pool

The tributes paid to John Dube at his funeral and memorial service, as well as in the several lengthy obituaries that appeared in the press, were effusive in their praise of this figure who had dominated African political life in South Africa for nearly half a century. Yet it was to be more than a decade before Mafukuzela Week was inaugurated at Ohlange in 1959, as if people felt a need to step back and take stock of his legacy. It is time to do the same here.

Although Dube grew up in a British colony in the late nineteenth century, his upbringing, education, travels, financial support and moral guidance were very largely derived from American life and thought. He followed African Americans' debates about progress and enlightenment, and modelled his efforts on their achievements. From a republican tradition, he developed a strong civic and oppositional politics that set out to win not only individual rights but collective ones too. More conventionally for someone in a British colony, he displayed a ready sympathy for the monarchy. This was based in part on the possibilities he had long seen at home, of a renovated chiefly tradition promoting orderly transition from 'old' to 'new'. He railed against the darkness of heathenism and the dead hand of chiefly rule when the 'old' order failed to come up to scratch, yet he also urged people to defend their birthright and to be proud of their cultural heritage. He thought it entirely possible to harmonise old and new codes of life, although the precise mix proved elusive.

It is hard to know what he felt about the notion of 'British fair play'. In practice, there seemed too much emphasis on perpetual subordination for his liking, and his personal experiences must have made him deeply sceptical. It is possible that he was not involved in the beginnings of the Natal Native Congress because of the excessive allegiance it wanted to demonstrate to empire; he was a harsh critic of Rhodes; the 1914 deputation was a débâcle.

In short, he had been moulded rather more by American than by British influences. The combination from both sides of what Isabel Hofmeyr has called the 'protestant Atlantic' means that the description 'Victorian liberal' does not properly capture the complexity of Dube's outlook. (One also has to add that in America at the time, the term 'liberal' generally connoted 'libertarian', something Dube decidedly was not.)

While the founding of Ohlange in 1900 was undoubtedly a key moment in his public life, Dube could not have reached even that point without the patronage he enjoyed in Inanda among the Qadi rulers, the network of contacts he had created in the AZM in Natal and the support he had won in America among Brooklyn Congregationalists. It was this particular combination that allowed him the relative freedom to operate outside the structures of mission control and established convention, something he had already shown his willingness to try in his work at Incwadi. He never seriously entertained a complete break with this world, however; to do so would have undermined the very attempt to gain greater recognition within it. It was a mode of operation not understood or appreciated by Natal's colonial rulers in the 1890s and it is doubtful whether he would have been able to continue (especially after *Ilanga* was started) without the support of his neighbour Marshall Campbell, not so much in financial terms – though these were important enough – but also because of Campbell's influential position in Natal politics and society.

Yet support came at a price, as the Bhambatha Rebellion soon revealed. Dube's redemption of Africa depended on his observing a rule of law that was quite at odds with the very idea of redemption, and that conflict propelled him towards the sort of political involvement that Campbell had tried so hard to prevent. Bound up in this process were two strands of thought that also, to some extent, came into conflict. In the way that Ohlange was conceived and run, and even in the operation of *Ilanga*, Dube's intellectual debt to Booker Washington is clear; it was acknowledged by him and has been remarked upon frequently ever since. Yet his entry into politics was most un-Washingtonian and points to other intellectual debts, less clear but no less important, to the likes of J.E. Bruce and W.E.B. Du Bois.

While Campbell did not abandon Ohlange or Dube, it is also the case that Ohlange was in many ways the casualty of Dube's presidency of Congress: it was more the conflict of interest than of thought that became destructive. Ultimately, Dube's fate was more closely tied to Ohlange than to Congress. That quality 'which made him endure everything to attain his goal regardless of cost' enabled him to keep the school going as an independent enterprise for two decades before he had to relinquish control. The odds stacked against him were undeniably great: 'friends' turned out to be nothing of the sort and he failed to find support where he most expected to find it, among Africans themselves. It was never quite clear where he laid the blame for failure – possibly even his own weaknesses and transgressions – but having to give up Ohlange was a turning point in his career, as many commentators have noted. Ironically, he admitted defeat in the fundraising efforts that had occupied so much of his time just at the moment that the segregationist state found some use in keeping his school going. Yet his capacity for inventiveness and autonomy had been seriously undermined. He had begun his career in full confidence that the end result of a disciplined and managed transition from tradition to modernity, via a scheme like Ohlange and an organisation like the African National Congress, would be full acceptance in a colour-blind society where no one would be held back by class legislation. He ended it 'milking a dry cow', as Albert Luthuli called the Natives Representative Council.

Although his political alliance with the Zulu royal house dates from the 1920s, he was no newcomer on the scene. It is hard to know precisely when his contacts began, although he was positing a link from the early 1890s in *A familiar talk on my native land*, which may well have been based on dealings between Mqhawe and Cetshwayo, to which his father James had been party. Again, the set of 'inside–outside' relationships that developed at Inanda provided Dube with possibilities that he used to great effect. (It has always been thought that these relationships were unusual, or even unique; one wonders whether further research might not uncover similar ones elsewhere in Natal and beyond.) Dube was certainly in close contact with Dinuzulu at least from 1900, so it is not surprising that he played such an important role in defending the prince after the Rebellion and in discussions about a successor in 1913. By the time he came to need a political alliance with Solomon, therefore, he had a well-established track record with the uSuthu leadership. The point about ethnic politics and an alternative form of authority in the person of the (would-be) king was that *they* could exclude whites, to some degree at least, in the way in which they went about their political business. Moreover, as Paul La Hausse has noted, by the 1920s the sense of race pride that Dube had always articulated 'was not necessarily at variance with the ideology of segregation'.

By this stage, too, Dube was describing himself as a moderate, although he probably never saw himself as anything more or less. While Ohlange and Congress *were* very radical for the early 1900s, in that they challenged the received wisdom of white paternalism by refusing direct white tutelage and held out the promise of incorporation into a common society, Dube had always embraced orderly transition and spoken up for the oppressed 'in terms that smoothed over the conflicts between capital and labour'. (On these points, his various African American intellectual mentors were of exactly the same view.) Until a *more* radical alternative presented itself in the form of the ICU, his moderation was not so very obvious. Yet there was something in his public expression that continued to rub against the grain, to show up the iniquities of segregation and the jagged consequences of unrestrained capitalist expansion. The mix of defiance and compliance, radicalism and moderation, broadness and narrowness of vision, tended to exhibit itself from early in his career until its end. It was a product of his awkward location, 'torn between the expectations of his fellow Africans, the beliefs of the conservative settlers, and the hopes of his Liberal friends at home and abroad', as Phumzile Mlambo put it. It was what Shula Marks called the 'ambiguities of dependence'.

The two phases of his career – first in control of Ohlange and then having lost it – can be loosely but significantly mapped against two phases in the evolution of South Africa's political economy. The first, stretching from the South African War to the immediate post-First World War period, witnessed a contest over the form that a united South African state would take and a settling-in process once Union had been achieved. Leaders like Dube were able to use the flux and fluidity to their advantage, enjoying relatively easy access to the corridors of power in Cape Town and Pretoria (although mostly not getting what they asked for). From the early 1920s, a harsher form of segregation emerged as the state moved more aggressively to consolidate the interests of racial capitalism. As the power of the state grew, so Congress was excluded and Dube's options became ever more proscribed.

These two phases also have a very personal dimension. Each in her own way, Nokutela Dube and Angelina Dube were strong and illustrious female proponents of African redemption. Nokutela Dube's efforts were as significant as John's in the founding and development of Ohlange. What led to the unravelling of that dream was not only John's Congress presidency but also the tragic end to their relationship. She has dropped largely into oblivion these past one hundred years, escaping attention even when the reawakening of the women's movement in South Africa prompted a search for heroic figures in the struggle for emancipation: Charlotte Maxeke, Bertha Mkhize, Dr Goonam, Sibusisiwe Makhanya, Lilian Ngoyi and others. It is surely time to acknowledge her role now, however delayed a recognition this is.

Angelina entered Dube's life just at the time that he was withdrawing from control of Ohlange. Her own race pride, evident in her decision to teach at Wilberforce, continued into her fundraising efforts for Ohlange – she sometimes even had to manage donations in cattle – as well as into the founding of the Daughters of Africa and the Bantu Parents' League (both of which applied for government funding, which both were refused). Importantly, she not only achieved recognition as wife of 'South Africa's most prominent man' but also brought fulfilment as mother of their children. She became a powerful role model as a working mother whose first priority was as a parent: 'her many public and social calls do not in any way interfere with her duty as a mother'.

In the middle of an exam revision session about 'men of magnitude' in history in Athol Fugard's *'Master Harold' … and the boys*, Hally warns Sam, 'Don't confuse historical significance with greatness.' For his many contributions to South African public life, Dube may legitimately claim 'historical significance'. But was he 'great'? H.I.E. Dhlomo had no doubt at all in the obituary he penned in 1946. There were three ways to judge greatness, he said: 'the verdict of the wise and learned', 'the common and spontaneous approval of the Masses' and 'Time'. According to all three, Dube was exceedingly great. That verdict has some validity another six decades on. Dube was a leading figure in the generation of political leaders who helped to bring 'South Africa' into being, in the sense that they understood the profound political possibilities that a modern nation–state could offer to all South Africans (and it is no coincidence that he should have been one of the most widely travelled as well: such a modern vision entailed extensive mobility). It was from him and his supporters that many ordinary people in the Natal countryside first heard the extraordinary proposition that they could and should find a home in a common polity: Africans should be entitled to vote directly for representatives in the central Union parliament since they paid so much in taxes, and they had a right to enough land for their needs, to earn decent wages and to acquire an education. Moreover, it was proper to oppose racial nomination (what we now call discrimination) of any sort. These were remarkably forward-looking ideals, and he kept them alive despite numerous setbacks and shrinking political opportunities. He himself was never able to vote for an MP in his lifetime. It would take another 48 years after his death and a punishing armed struggle before these aspirations began to be realised.

Dube's pre-eminence as a leader came from his ability to speak to (or, more importantly, for) so many different constituents – chiefs, commoners, workers, the educated but squeezed and struggling middle classes – all of them facing increasing oppression, at an early period in the development of nationalism in South Africa. The latter part of his presidency of the SANNC was beset by factionalism and stasis, but his campaigns of the first part did an enormous amount to make ordinary people feel part of a nation and to give them hope. Despite the difficulties of a lack of resources and coordination, ill-formed local structures and so on, he helped to steady this organisation through its first five years. For at the end of the day, Dube was a pragmatist rather than an ideologue. While he was animated by a powerful vision of redemption and representation, his chosen means of realising it was to get on with the practicalities: hence the founding of a newspaper, a school, various cooperative schemes, business leagues and assumption of political leadership.

John Dube's legacy has been contested in the past. He articulated both inclusive and exclusive variants of nationalism. When bitter ideological divisions sharpened into civil war in KwaZulu-Natal in the 1980s, both Inkatha and the ANC claimed his inheritance. It is worth remembering that while allied to the Zulu royal house, campaigning for recognition of the king and working to save folklore, poetry and customs from extinction, Dube also continued to look forward to a day when all South Africans would have representation in a common parliament. He never treated these as mutually exclusive, nor did he promote any other than peaceful, constitutional means for their realisation. While it is not hard to see why his example was called on by both sides, there is something futile in wondering whom he might have supported in *any* of the post-Second World War political struggles in South Africa; these were so different from the ones he had known and from the organisational forms he had helped to create. One imagines, though, that he would have been very satisfied indeed with the realisation of a democratic transition to majority rule. As he himself was often known to say, 'Where there was once a pool, water will collect again.' And Ohlange has survived, despite his disappointments.[1]

Endnotes

Introduction

1 The story of the clearing of John Dube's study was told to me by Lulu Dube, his last-surviving child, in an interview, 2005. She very kindly allowed me to look at the remaining books, on which this list is based. Wolcott's observation is in *London Review of Books*, 3.2.2000, 29. The Mark Twain quote is cited in G. Keillor's review in the *New York Times*, 16.12.2010. Holroyd makes his point in his *Unreceived opinions* (Harmondsworth, 1976), 35. For Hermione Lee's argument, see her *Biography: a very short introduction* (Oxford, 2009), 18. Janet Malcolm's famous verdict on biography is in her *The silent woman: Sylvia Plath and Ted Hughes* (London, 1995), 8, and Hans Magnus Enzensberger delivered his in a radio interview on the occasion of the English publication of his *The silences of Hammerstein* (London, 2009), on 'Night Wave', BBC Radio 3, 24.3.2009. Cannadine's distinction between history and biography is in his *Aspects of aristocracy* (Harmondsworth, 1995), 3. Richard Holmes's 'cheering epistemology' is from his collection *Sidetracks: explorations of a romantic biographer* (London, 2005), 371; see also his *Footsteps: adventures of a romantic biographer* (London, 1995) for what might be called his 'immersion' method of biography-writing. The 'Michelangelo' reference is from L. Borges, *The perpetual race of Achilles and the tortoise* (London, 2010), 64. The version of Nelson Mandela's words was reported by Logie Naidoo in his speech at the unveiling of a sculpture of John Dube, sited on the spot where Mandela voted, in 2010: at http://www.wandahennig.com/2010/05/woza-enanda-heritage-site-hails-south-african-heroes/ [accessed 21.1.2011]. G.G. Nxaba's manuscript biography of Dube is in Houghton Library, Harvard University, and R.R.R. Dhlomo's attempts were recorded an interview with Tom Karis, March 1964, Document 2: XD20: 96/1, Karis-Carter Collection (microform edition). The studies of Dube referred to are: M. Marable, 'African nationalist: the life of John Langalibalele Dube' (PhD thesis, University of Maryland, 1976); E. Roux, *Time longer than rope* (Madison, 1964); R. Hunt Davis, 'John L. Dube: a South African exponent of Booker T. Washington', *Journal of African Studies* 2, 4, 1975/6, 497–528; S. Marks, *The ambiguities of dependence in South Africa: class, nationalism and the state in twentieth-century Natal* (Johannesburg, 1986) – her chapter on Dube synthesises a number of earlier articles. William Gerhardie made his comments on the arbitrariness of segmenting time in his *God's fifth column* (New York, 1991), 92. On terminology and the African middle class, see Paul La Hausse, *Restless identities: signatures of nationalism, Zulu ethnicity and history in the lives of Petros Lamula (c1881–1948) and Lymon Maling (1889–c1936)* (Pietermaritzburg, 2000), 259; and P. Limb, *The ANC's early years: nation, class and place in South Africa before 1940* (Pretoria, 1910), 13. Norman Nembula's testimony is in C. de B. Webb and J. Wright (eds.),

The James Stuart Archive 5 (Durban and Pietermaritzburg, 2001), 15. A useful survey of the shifting composition of the middle class is M. Archer and J. Blau, 'Class formation in nineteenth-century America: the case of the middle class', *Annual Review of Sociology* 19, 1993.

Chapter 1

1 Much has been written about how to approach oral tradition; it is clear that a search for 'literal truth' is both misguided and doomed. Jan Vansina long ago noted that 'a testimony is no more than a mirage of the reality it describes'. See his *Oral tradition: a study in historical methodology* (Harmondsworth, 1973), 76. Others have reminded us of the complex ways in which memory interacts with the context in which telling and retelling occur. For a succinct summary of these issues, see I. Hofmeyr, '"Wailing for purity": oral studies in southern African studies', *African Studies* 54, 2, 1995, 16–31. In addition, several cautionary (and worse) notes have been sounded about using the source material on south-eastern Africa, even though all scholars of precolonial and colonial history in Natal and Zululand will always be deeply dependent on it. Bearing all this in mind, the main sources on Qadi history and tradition are: Madikane Cele in C. de B. Webb and J. Wright (eds.), *The James Stuart Archive 2* (Pietermaritzburg and Durban, 1979), 46–67; M.V. Gumede, 'Umlando wenkosi yesizwe samaQadi' ['History of the Qadi chiefs'], unpublished paper, c.1970; M. Fuze, *The black people and whence they came* (Pietermaritzburg and Durban, 1979); the contributions of V. Ngidi, B. Cele and E.H. Ngcobo to the Zulu Tribal History Competition (hereafter ZTHC), Manuscript Collection, Killie Campbell Africana Library (hereafter KCAL); A. Vilakazi, *Zulu transformations* (Pietermaritzburg, 1965); A.T. Bryant, *Olden times in Zululand and Natal* (London, 1929); J. Wright and C. Hamilton, 'Traditions and transformations: the Phongolo-Mzimkhulu region in the late eighteenth and early nineteenth centuries' in A. Duminy and B. Guest (eds.), *Natal and Zululand from earliest times to 1910* (Pietermaritzburg, 1989); and C. Hamilton, 'Ideology, oral traditions and the struggle for power in the early Zulu kingdom' (MA thesis, University of the Witwatersrand, 1985). On the ways in which Natal and Zululand were united in literature, a particularly lyrical example is H.I.E. Dhlomo's *Valley of a thousand hills* (Durban, 1941). The quote giving a description of the Lindleys' mission surroundings is from Anthony Trollope, *South Africa 1* (Gloucester, [1877] 1987), 201. Lindley's account of Mayembe's arrival is in a letter to Adams, 15.1.1849, File 1849, A/2/27, American Zulu Mission Papers A608 (hereafter AZMP), Pietermaritzburg Depot of the National Archives (hereafter PDNA). Reference to Ukakonina's sister is in J. Dube, *A familiar talk upon my native land and some things found there* (New York, 1892), 18. The word 'chief' has been used here to indicate a position of authority and leadership in the precolonial polities of the region; it is an imperfect translation of *inkosi*, and moreover the status of the incumbent changed dramatically under colonial conditions, but it is used here in the absence of anything more suitable, with these provisos.

2 On the parallel between the Qadi and Boer attacks, see J. Stuart and D. McK. Malcolm (eds.), *The diary of Henry Francis Fynn* (Pietermaritzburg, 1969), 257–9. Fynn estimated about 1,000 Qadi had been killed. On Qadi beliefs in the closeness of Shaka and Dube, see Gumede, 'History of the Qadi chiefs', Gumede interview, Inanda, October 1985, and a performance of the praises of Dube kaSilwane by the official Qadi *imbongi*, Khekhe Ngcobo, Mzinyathi, 2.12.1985. These were of course late-twentieth-century renditions, and need to be situated in that time. The *imbongi* would have had good reason to stress the Shaka–Dube association, for example, in that the then Qadi chief, Mzonjani, was a Cabinet Minister in the KwaZulu government – and connecting that political entity to the founder of the Zulu state would

have been important. It is hard (maybe impossible) to say how far back in Qadi tradition this association is embedded; in that Madikane was able to testify that his father had fought against Zwide, there is likely to be some substance to it. See Webb and Wright, *James Stuart 2*, 61. Evidence of the closeness that Mqhawe felt with his Zulu origins is in Secretary for Native Affairs Papers (hereafter SNA) 1/1/131 (1138/1890), PDNA. As suggested here, it is highly possible, but difficult to prove, that chiefdoms like the Qadi started calling themselves Zulu only after the British defeat of the Zulu in 1879, after which the threat of any possible retribution disappeared. Dube's account of Dingane's attack on his grandfather opens his *A talk upon my native land* (New York, 1892), 5–6. He most likely heard it from his father and Madikane; it was not readily accessible in any published source until much later. Madikane is also the source of the quote about the Nyuswa and Ngcobo: see Webb and Wright, *James Stuart 2*, 52.

3 Madikane's prescient and profound observation about the basis of Qadi wealth in Natal is in his testimony in Webb and Wright, *James Stuart 2*, 56–7. Other sources on the Mawa episode are P. Colenbrander, 'The Zulu kingdom 1828–1879' in Duminy and Guest, *Natal and Zululand from earliest times to 1910*, 99; 'Minute of the import of Panda's message, 11.2.1846' in *Records of the Natal Executive Council, 1846–1848* (Cape Town, 1960), 70; and Mangati's testimony in Webb and Wright, *James Stuart 2*, 216–17. Mqhawe's observation about nursing cattle is in Colony of Natal, *Evidence taken before the Natal Native Commission 1881*, 221–2. On the establishment of the Port, see C.R. Maclean (ed. S. Gray), *The Natal Papers of 'John Ross'* (Durban and Pietermaritzburg, 1992), 51; C. Ballard, 'Traders, trekkers and colonists' in Duminy and Guest, *Natal and Zululand from earliest times to 1910*, 188; and Stuart and Malcolm, *The diary of Henry Francis Fynn*, sketch facing 110. For Biggar's fears about a Zulu attack, see Stuart and Malcolm, *The diary of Henry Francis Fynn*, 260. On the militia's raid of Zulu villages, see Ballard, 'Traders, trekkers', 121. Joseph Kirkman noted the unfit state of the militia, quoted in G.E. Cory (ed.), *The diary of the Rev. Francis Owen* (Cape Town, 1926), 166–7. On the Dlokweni Battle (also called the Battle of the Thukela) see Fuze, *The black people*, 76–7 and 170; the quote about survivors is drawn from 76.

4 On the fertility of the Inanda valley, see 'Report on the Inanda Mission Reserve', SNA 1/1/319 (871/1905). The description of the 'tossed' hills is from A Lady, *Life at Natal a hundred years ago* (Cape Town, [1865] 1972), 126. See also D.L. Niddrie, 'The climate and weather of Natal' in H.R. Burrows (ed.), *The archaeology and natural resources of Natal* (Cape Town, 1951), 49, and Thomas Fayle's diary, 8.2.1890 in SNA 1/1/123 (201/1890). This account of the natural environment is intended to give no more than an impression of conditions in the early colonial period. Many of the sources refer to later times and contemporary sources often presented a misleadingly favourable picture, designed as they were to attract white immigrants. On Qadi settlement in the Mzinyathi valley see J. Bird, *Annals of Natal 1495–1845 volume 1* (Pietermaritzburg, 1888), 32 and G.S. Armstrong, 'Family reminiscences', Armstrong Papers (KCM 25650), KCAL. Bryant has a rather different chronology of Qadi settlement in Natal, in his *Olden times*, 495, which does not accord with other sources. It would appear that the earliest use of the name Inanda was with reference to this Boer farm. Soon, 'Inanda' was to be the name given variously to the lower division of Victoria County, the African location nearby, and the mission station. Less specifically through the twentieth century, the area of the mission reserve and south-east towards the Mgeni and Phoenix came to be known as Inanda. For the Qadi naming of the area, see E.H. Ngcobo, 'The Qadi tribe', ZTHC.

5 John Dube's list of chiefs appears in E. Smith, *The life and times of Daniel Lindley (1801–1880): missionary to the Zulus, pastor to the Voortrekkers, 'Ubebe omhlophe'* (London 1949), 402. On the 'Lala question', C. Hamilton and J. Wright, 'The making of the *Lala*: ethnicity, ideology and class formation in a pre-colonial context', paper to the History Workshop,

University of the Witwatersrand, 1987. Wright was the first to make the suggestion of the positive connotations of Lala in 'Notes on the politics of being "Zulu", 1820–1920', paper to Conference on ethnicity, society and conflict in Natal, University of Natal, Pietermaritzburg, 1992 and reproduced as 'Reflections on the politics of being Zulu' in B. Carton, J. Laband and J.Sithole (eds.), *Zulu identities: being Zulu, past and present* (London, 2009), 35–43. Madikane Cele related Shaka's insults of the Lala in Webb and Wright, *James Stuart 2*, 54–5. Colenso's definition is to be found in his *Zulu–English dictionary* (Pietermaritzburg, 1861), 262. Kirkman's observation is in Cory, *The diary of the Rev. Francis Owen*, 166–7; see also J. Shooter, *The Kafirs of Natal and the Zulu country* (New York, [1857] 1969), 82. On the connection between Lala and iron work, see M. Wilson, 'The Nguni people' in M. Wilson and L. Thompson (eds.), *A history of South Africa to 1870* (Cape Town, 1982), 110–11; S. Marks, 'The traditions of the Natal "Nguni": a second look at the work of A.T. Bryant' in L. Thompson (ed.), *African societies in southern Africa* (London,1969), 136; and D. Hedges, 'Trade and politics in southern Mozambique and Zululand in the 18th and early 19th centuries' (PhD thesis, University of London, 1978), 88. The apparent paradox of blacksmiths being both highly valued and ideologically subordinated has been noted in many parts of Africa. The two most comprehensive accounts of the impacts of Natal's colonial policy on Africans are D. Welsh, *The roots of segregation: native policy in Natal, 1845–1910* (Cape Town, 1971) and J. Lambert, *Betrayed trust: Africans and the state in colonial Natal* (Pietermaritzburg, 1995).

    6 On the founding church members see Smith, *The life and times*, 283; and American Zulu Mission, 'Report for Inanda', June 1897, American Board of Commissioners for Foreign Missions Papers Relating to Southern Africa (hereafter ABCSA) (microfilm version) Reel 188, Volume 13, KCAL. In general and as noted in the introduction, I have not used the term *amakholwa* for the Inanda converts. It tends to focus on the separateness of such communities from, rather than their interaction with, other local groups; while this may have been the case for other convert communities, it does not seem appropriate for the family at the heart of this story. On Joel and Keziah Hawes and their family, see Smith, *The life and times*, 54 and 283; 'Report of the American Zulu Mission', June 1898, ABCSA Reel 188, Volume 13; Verulam Magistrate's Papers, 1/VLM 3/2/5 (719/1888), PDNA. On John Mavuma, see Smith, *The life and times*, 282; Lindley to Tracy, 5.2.1867, Inanda Seminary Papers (hereafter ISP), KCAL; Edwards to Clark, 7.1.1870, ABCSA Reel 178, Volume 6, and 'Report of the American Zulu Mission', June 1898, ABCSA Reel 188, Volume 13. For evidence of links between Bishopstowe and Inanda, see Edwards to Clark, 17.9.1869, ABCSA Reel 178, Volume 6. On Nancy Cane (also Nancy Damon, anglicised form of Ndamane), see Christian Cane in C. de B. Webb and J. Wright (eds.), *The James Stuart archive 1* (Pietermaritzburg and Durban, 1976), 77; Lindley's 'Report of the Inanda Station', June 1853, ABCSA Reel 175, Volume 4; AZM File 806, A608; A.F. Christoferson, *The first one hundred years of the American Board in South Africa*, 17 (copy in AZM Collection); Bryant Lindley in Smith, *The life and times*, 280. The story of Nancy's elopement (and the quote) is from J.W. Colenso, *Ten weeks in Natal: a journal of the first tour of visitation among the colonists and Zulu Kafirs of Natal* (Cambridge, 1855), 240–1. The 'unfathomable glyphs' reference comes from E. Eisenstein, *The printing revolution in early modern Europe* (Cambridge, 1993), 46. On George Champion, see R.R.R. Dhlomo, 'Introduction' in M. Swanson (ed.), *The views of Mahlathi: writings of AWG Champion, a black South African* (Pietermaritzburg, 1983), 6–7. On Jonas Mfeka see Smith, *The life and times*, 283 and SNA 1/1/221 (3096/1896). On Dalida Seme, see A. Wood, *Shine where you are: a history of Inanda Seminary, 1869–1969* (Alice, 1972), 35 and 173–4. Dalida later confessed to having had an affair with the resident missionary while at Inhambane; see Pixley to Judson Smith, 25.12.1889, ABCSA Reel 185, Volume 11. She subsequently married the Rev. Elijah Hlanti and was thereafter based at Mount Silinda in Southern Rhodesia. On

Talitha Hawes, whose aspirations to study abroad were extraordinary for an African woman at that time, and more so due to the fact that she was physically disabled, see Wood, *Shine where you are*, 18, 30–1, 173; and Edwards to Clark, 8.12.1884, ABCSA Reel 183, Volume 9. For her biblical translation, see A.F. Christoferson, *Adventuring with God: the story of the American Board Mission in South Africa* (Durban, 1967), 64 and 120.

7 Background on the Lindleys is from Smith, *The life and times*; E.B. Welsh, *Buckeye Presbyterianism: an account of the seven Presbyterian denominations within the state of Ohio* (Ohio, 1968); M. Dinnerstein, 'The American Board Mission to the Zulu, 1835–1900' (PhD thesis, University of Columbia, 1971). On Natal's colonial land policy, see Welsh, *The roots of segregation*; the 'alphabet of civilisation' quote is also from Smith, *The life and times*, 281, and James Matiwane presented his testimony to the 1881 Natal Native Commission, in the Commission's *Minutes of evidence*, 387. On the Maternal Association, see 'Record Book of the Maternal Association, Lindley Station, 1849–1878', Mary Tyler Papers (A/4/61), AZM. Colenso's conversation with Inanda converts is recorded in his *Ten weeks in Natal*, 232–41. There is a description of the mission at this time in W. Holden, *History of the Colony of Natal* (London, 1855), 206. The description of James Dube's appearance is in Lindley to Clark, 17.12.70, ABCSA Reel 179, Volume 7, and information on his clients is in Armstrong, 'Family reminiscences'. On the Semes, see SNA 1/1/152 (151/1892); SNA 1/1/282 (1897/1898); Wood, *Shine where you are*, 21, 109, 121; R. Rive and T. Couzens, *Seme, the founder of the ANC* (Braamfontein, 1991), 9–23, and J. Ngubane, *An African explains apartheid* (London, 1963), 71. On the Gobas, see SNA 1/1/114 (475/1889); SNA 1/1/152 (149/1892); SNA 1/1/213 (598/1895); SNA 1/1/237 (116/1897); Wood, *Shine where you are*, 21, 50 and 73; Edwards to Clark 17.9.1869, ABCSA Reel 178, Volume 6. In the early days of the mission, daughters were known by either the first name or the surname of their father: thus Lucy Seme was often called Lucy Isaac, Helen Goba was sometimes known as Helen Klaas, and so on. Before Pixley re-Africanised their name, the family all took the surname 'Isaac'. On the agitation to move, see 'Report of the Inanda Station 16 November 1855', ABCSA Reel 175, Volume 4. Lindley's observations on the men's industriousness is from Smith, *The life and times*, 329. See also N. Etherington, *Preachers, peasants and politics in south-eastern Africa, 1835–1880: African Christian communities in Natal, Pondoland and Zululand* (London, 1978), 91. On Pine and his land and labour policy, see Welsh, *The roots of segregation*, 23–5. Evidence that James Dube rented private land is from a statement of Rev. J. Dube in *Minutes of Evidence to the Natives Land Commission* UG22-16 [including UG22-14], 1916, 55; and the story of the £1,000 loan is from G.G. Nxaba's biography of John Dube, Dube File, Houghton Library, Harvard (obtained by the kind offices of Cherif Keita, to whom I am extremely grateful). Nxaba was related to John Dube by marriage and produced the earliest-known biography of him. On the Verulam settlers, see H.M. Robertson, 'The 1849 settlers in Natal', *South African Journal of Economics* 1949, 17; A. Hattersley, *The Natal settlers 1849–51* (Pietermaritzburg, 1949); M. Park, 'The history of early Verulam' in *Archives Yearbook for South African History* 11, 1953. On the demarcation of the Inanda Mission Reserve, see the copy of grant and map, File 1883/4579, AZM.

8 For a brief overview of Elizabeth Dube's life, see *Ilanga*, 5.6.1914. On the Tshangase chiefdom in the Inanda location, see Inanda magistrate to SNA, 3/9/1878 in SNA 1/1/31 (1140/1878). On runaways, see H. Hughes, '"A lighthouse for African womanhood": Inanda Seminary, 1869–1945' in C. Walker (ed.), *Women and gender in southern Africa to 1945* (Cape Town and London, 1990), 97–220. John Dube's passing observation is in his *A talk upon my native land*, 17. On the Lindley household, see Smith, *The life and times*, 281. Among fragments and comments in letters, reports, and other documents on the Dube children, see Nxaba's biography and Mary Edwards to Clark, 17.9.1869, ABCSA Reel 178, Volume 6

('James Dube's oldest daughter Nomagugu is in school … ') and Pixley to SNA, 15.11.1877, SNA 1/1/29 (896/1877) records that 'the elder members of his family are all girls'. In the Dube museum at Ohlange, only three boys, John, Charles and Willie, are recorded as James and Elizabeth's children.

9 Lindley's account of James Dube's ordination is in Lindley to Clark, 17.12.1870, ABCSA Reel 179, Volume 7. On James Dube's initial reluctance, see J. Tyler, *Forty years among the Zulus* (Cape Town, [1891] 1971), 172–3. On general AZM policy with regards to African pastors, see Smith, *The life and times*, 389, and Christoferson, *Adventuring with God*. Rufus Anderson was deposed in 1877 for an illicit affair with a church member and went to live at Inanda, and Nyuswa died in 1876. On the Inanda converts' business dealings, see Smith, *The life and times*, 380 and 398; Lindley, 2.9.1857, ABCSA Reel 175, Volume 4. On the description of the post-1862 church, see J. Robinson, *Notes on Natal: an old colonist's book for new settlers* (Durban and London, 1872), 16–17. On the 1873 rebuild, see Martha Lindley to Governor of Natal, 19.12.1874, SNA 1/1/24 (110/1877). Mqhawe's relations with the mission, and especially the phenomenon of creating functionaries, are explored in H. Hughes, 'Politics and society in Inanda, Natal: the Qadi under Chief Mqhawe, c.1840–1906' (PhD thesis, University of London, 1996), especially chapters 5 and 8. The money to purchase the Qadi farm – or at least pay the deposit – was raised from a levy imposed on all Qadi, the intermediary in this instance being Bishop Colenso, as he was nearby, and by then Lindley had retired. The Qadi named the farm Incwadi, 'The book': by then, they were fully aware of the potency of the written word, of the religious as well as the secular sort. Lindley's role on the Mission Reserve is also covered in Hughes, 'Politics and society in Inanda', 178. On Mqhawe's attendance at services and request for a teacher, see 'Inanda mission report 1864' and 'Inanda tabular view 1865', ABCSA Reel 177, Volume 6. On Mqhawe's wagon, see Lindley to Treat, 30.9.1864, ABCSA Reel 179, Volume 7, and on the expedition to Durban, see Smith, *The life and times*, 184.

Chapter 2

1 The first time John Dube used his formal date of birth was in *A talk upon my native land*, in which he rather proudly presented it in full. Yet when he had first travelled abroad in 1887, he gave his birth as 'about 1870' and later on, in April 1893, he claimed to be 23 years of age: see SNA 1/1/169 (473/1893). Again, in May 1896, he gave his age as 27 (according to *The Telegraph* family history ship's list). On the name John, see *The Oxford names companion*. The information on Hlubi history is from J. Wright and A. Manson, *The Hlubi chiefdom in Zululand–Natal* (Ladysmith, 1983); the quote is from 42. For possible diagnoses of Dube's medical condition on the basis of admittedly scant evidence, I am very grateful to Dr Gilli Procter, who referred me to A. Cilliers, 'Rheumatic fever and its management', *British Medical Journal* 333, 2.12. 2006, 1153–6. Rheumatic fever has long been known as a disease of the poor and endemic in African communities. Dube's family was not poor, but there was what we would now recognise as deprivation round about (e.g. leprosy in the location). In any case, rheumatic fever is no more than a suggestion. The one fact that would seem to run counter to it is Dube's longevity: he was 75 when he died in 1946. Lindley's assessment of James Dube is in Lindley to Clark, 3.7.1871, ABCSA Reel 179, Volume 7. The information that James did not take any church money is from Tyler to Clark, 11.10.1877, ABCSA Reel 182, Volume 8.

2 For a good overview of Indian settlement in South Africa, see S. Bhana and J. Brain, *Setting down roots: Indian migrants in South Africa 1860–1911* (Johannesburg, 1990) and the more recent social history by A. Desai and G. Vahed, *Inside indenture: a South African story, 1860–1914* (Durban, 2007). See also V. Padayachee and R. Morrell, 'Indian merchants and

dukawallahs in the Natal economy, c.1875–1914', *Journal of Southern African Studies* 19, 2, 1993. Figures about Inanda's sugar production are taken from the annual *Blue Books*; the magistrate's quote is from the *Blue Book* of 1876. See also the Inanda magistrate's report of 1888, in SNA 1/1/105 (188/1888) and F.R. Osborn, *Valiant harvest: the founding of the South African sugar industry 1848–1926* (Durban, 1964). Lindley's invective against Indians is cited in Smith, *The life and times*, 378; the source of information about Mary Edwards's acquisition of land is Wood, *Shine where you are*, 56. On African–Indian relations, see H. Hughes, '"We will be elbowed out the country": African responses to Indian indentured immigration to Natal, 1860–1910', *Labour History Review* 72, 2, 2007, 155–68. Matiwane's statement is in *Evidence taken before the Natal Native Commission 1881*, 145–6. On AZM land policy, see Dinnerstein, 'The American Zulu Mission', 241. The account of the destruction of the Hlubi chiefdom is from Wright and Manson, *The Hlubi chiefdom*, chapters 5 and 6. The earliest written source on Mqhawe considering joining Langalibalele is a letter in M.T. Gray, 'Stories of the early American missionaries in South Africa', file 'Centenary 1935', AZMP. Mary Tyler Gray was a missionary's daughter who spent much of her childhood with the Lindleys. Her account is reproduced verbatim (but unattributed) in B. Buchanan, *Natal memories* (Pietermaritzburg, 1941), 92 and is also recalled in Smith, *The life and times*, 417. (If Mqhawe uttered a statement like this, he would clearly have meant *white* men in this context.) The oral version (most unlikely to have derived from the written ones) was told to S. Khumalo and H. Hughes by Baba Khumalo, KwaMashu, Durban, December 1985.

3 Esther Dube's story is from a letter reproduced in Wood, *Shine where you are*, 52. For her correspondence with Americans, see Edwards to Clark, 4.2.1889, ABCSA Reel 183, Volume 9. On AZM educational policy, see Smith, *The life and times*, 388–9, and on reading matter see Christoferson, *Adventuring with God*, 40–1 and N. Etherington, 'The missionary writing machine in nineteenth-century KwaZulu-Natal' in J. Scott and G. Griffiths (eds.), *Mixed messages: materiality, textuality, missions* (New York and Basingstoke, 2005), 37–50. Information on Lindley's replacement, Stephen Pixley, is from Ind Bio 47:35, American Board of Commissioners for Foreign Missions Archives, Houghton Library, Boston (with thanks to the librarians) and Hughes, 'Politics and society in Inanda', 198–200. The account of James's death and funeral relies on Pixley to Clark, 10.11.1877, ABCSA Reel 182, Volume 8 (from which the quotes are drawn). Cherif Keita located, cleared and photographed James's grave in Inanda in 2008. Information on James's legal status and Elizabeth's right to inherit is from Pixley to Acting SNA, 21.11.1877, SNA 1/1/29 (896/1877). For early objections to exemption, see Lambert, *Betrayed trust*, 50. James's participation in the petition is noted in Stephanus Mini, *Evidence taken before the Natal Native Commission 1881*, 135 and discussed in E. Jackson, '"First fruits" at Adams Mission: an investigation into the lives and narratives of the Makhanya/Nembulas, early converts to Christianity at Amanzimtoti, Natal, 1837–1897' (BA Honours dissertation, University of KwaZulu-Natal, 2007). Names of John's siblings are taken from Nxaba's biography. The information that Elizabeth Dube sent three sons abroad is from *Ilanga*, 5.6.1914.

4 Dube, *A talk upon my native land*, 7–17. On Mqhawe and the Qadi in the war, see Inanda magistrate, 31.12.1878, 1/VLM 3/2/1, VM Papers; and P.S. Thompson, *The Natal Native Contingent in the Anglo-Zulu War 1879* (Pietermaritzburg, 1997), 18–20, 63–7, 171–8, 201–8, 370 (on which Mqhawe's 'dancing' quote appears). The anonymous school essay was one of a number presented in a special exercise book by Seminary pupils to Mary Edwards in 1884; sadly, the writers' names were not recorded. The original is in the Inanda Seminary Papers; this essay is reproduced in full, introduced by H. Hughes, as 'The war in Zululand' in M.J. Daymond et al. (eds.), *Women writing Africa: the southern region* (Johannesburg, 2003), 120–3.

For the confederation idea and build-up to war, see J. Guy, *The destruction of the Zulu kingdom* (Johannesburg, 1982), 44–50.

5 The description of 1880s Durban is based on information in B. Kearney, *Architecture in Natal 1824–1893* (Cape Town, 1973). The train journey to Adams is described by Josiah Mapumulo in 'The reminiscences of an old teacher', *Native Teachers' Journal* 1, 4, 1920, 155–8. The Adams building and opening ceremony are described in an undated news clip in the Amanzimtoti section of ABCSA Reel 181, Volume 8. For the idea of estrangement, see E.P. Thompson, *Customs in common* (Harmondsworth, 1993), 7. Dube's reminiscences of the daily Adams routine are contained in his *A talk upon my native land*, 37–40. Other accounts are drawn from 'Report of Amanzimtoti Seminary, 1877' and 'Report of Adams mission church and station, May 1878' in ABCSA Reel 181, Volume 8; Dixon to Judson Smith, 10.5.1886, ABCSA Reel 183, Volume 9; and 'A short historical sketch', MS 65A, File 2, Adams College Papers, KCAL. Information on J.T. Jabavu is from M. Ndletyana (ed.), *African intellectuals in 19th and early 20th century South Africa* (Pretoria, 2008), 34. Information about food at Adams comes from Goodenough to Means, 8.5.1886, ABCSA Reel 184, Volume 10. On food rebellions at school more generally, see B. Hirson, *Year of fire year of ash* (London, 1977). The account of the 1881 'sugar rebellion' is contained in Goodenough to Smith, 8.5.1886, ABCSA Reel 184, Volume 10. Goodenough's detailed and lengthy account of the 1882 episode is in his report to Means, 8.12.1882, ABCSA Reel 184, Volume 10, from which the quotes are drawn, except on the depression, information on which is drawn from Goodenough to Means, 31.3.1883, ABCSA Reel 184, Volume 10. On Africa Dube, see SNA 1/1/48 (427/1881) (from which the quote is drawn), SNA 1/1/139 (1206/1906); *Ilanga*, 25.9.1914. Many years later, John Dube referred to his punishment in a major speech in the Cape Town City Hall, noting that it had left a very unhappy memory and put him off snuff forever: see *Cape Times*, 5.7.1912.

6 The 1886 sugar rebellion and its consequences are related in Goodenough to Smith, 8.5.1886; Goodenough to Smith, 28.2.1887; and Goodenough to Smith, 19.4.1887, all on ABCSA Reel 184, Volume 10. The suggestion that John Dube left the school derives from two pieces of information: that afterwards he was indignant (as the other boys were), and that he was required to make an apology for his behaviour (again, as the other boys were). He may of course have been punished for an unrelated offence, though the timing makes the former possibility distinctly plausible. The physical description of Wilcox (and the quote) is from Marable, 'African nationalist', 60. One of the reasons that this is such a valuable source is that in the early 1970s Marable was able to interview elderly informants who had known Dube since school, such as Gideon Sivetye, whose reminiscences are on 58. Other information on Wilcox is drawn from Rood to Means, 6.6.1883, ABCSA Reel 183, Volume 9; Minutes of the semi-annual meeting of the AZM, 15.12.1886, ABCSA Reel 183, Volume 9; Goodenough to Smith, 20.12.1886, ABCSA Reel 184, Volume 10; Pixley to Smith, 7.2.1887, ABCSA Reel 185, Volume 11; and 'Letter from Miss Day' in *Light and Life for Women* 7, 8, August 1882, 205. Information on the Inhambane mission is drawn from N. Chaudhuri and M. Strobel, *Western women and imperialism: complicity and resistance* (Bloomington, 1992), 209–13. The mission there folded in the mid-1890s. The account of Dube's conversion is in W.C. Wilcox, 'The story of John Dube, the Booker Washington of South Africa', *The Congregationalist* March 1927. It was largely due to Wilcox that this byname was popularised. His accounts of this phase in Dube's life, through his late teens, are virtually the only (and certainly the most complete) extant source. There are elements that we know to have been mis-remembered (Dube served one, not two, terms as ANC president, for example) but it has nevertheless been relied on to fill in missing detail. It was of course written after Dube had become a major public figure; given that Wilcox had been such a key influence in Dube's life, it is entirely

understandable that he would wish not only to give an account of Dube's emergence as a leader, but also to assert his own role in the process. On the broader meanings of conversion, see H. Mokoena, 'Christian converts and the production of *Kholwa* histories in nineteenth-century colonial Natal: the case of Magema Magwaza Fuze and his writings', *Journal of Natal and Zulu History* 23, 2005/6, 1–42. An updated version of the biblical text has been used here, from the *Holy Bible: new international version* (London, 2000), 1075. On Wilcox's decision to return to the US, see Pixley to Smith, 21.6.1887, ABCSA Reel 185, Volume 11. See also Wilcox, 'The story of John Dube', for his account of how he came to take John to America with his family. The various rebellions had clearly taken their toll on Goodenough, whose letter of resignation was submitted to the AZM at much the same time as Wilcox's. See Pixley to Judson Smith, 21.6.1887, ABCSA Reel 185, Volume 11.

Chapter 3

1 On the influence of choral tours as a stimulus to black South Africans to study in the States, see J. Campbell, *Songs of Zion: the African Methodist Episcopal Church in the United States and South Africa* (New York and Oxford, 1995), 252–8. Africans from other parts of Africa, notably Liberia, had begun to study in the United States from the 1870s. See W. Williams, 'Ethnic relations of African students in the United States, with black Americans, 1870–1900', *Journal of Negro History* 65, 3, 1980, 228–49. The quote on the relative openness of colleges is from D. Boorstin, *The democratic experience* (London, 2000), 478. This was the age of university expansion in America, which put colleges under some strain. The essential difference between a college and university was that colleges tended to have a religious foundation, a narrower curriculum based on the traditional subjects of Greek, Latin, natural and moral philosophy, theology and mathematics, offered preparatory courses, and did not possess graduate schools. One of the criticisms to which they were most sensitive was that they offered no 'modern' subjects; Oberlin had in fact introduced a broader curriculum with electives in 1875. See C.L. Waite, *Permission to remain among us: education for blacks in Oberlin, Ohio, 1880–1914* (New York, 2002), 58. The Republican Party at this time was by far the most liberal of the mainstream political parties in the US. The story of the 30 gold sovereigns comes from J. Dube, *The Zulu's appeal for light and England's duty* (London, 1909), 26. Information on John Nembula and his family is drawn from letters that he wrote while in the United States to Judson Smith: 25.7.1886, 15.11.1886, 1.12.1886, 12.4.1887, 12.8.1887, all in ABCSA Reel 185, Volume 11; and Christofersen, *Adventuring with God*, 27, 37, 50–1, 65, 159. Nembula taught at Adams (he had brought a human skeleton back with him, which made a deep impression on the boys) and practised at Amanzimtoti before becoming one of the few Africans in this period to secure a government post, as district surgeon in Msinga, where he served until his death in 1896. See D. Briggs and J. Wing, *The harvest and the hope: the story of Congregationalism in southern Africa* (Johannesburg, 1970), 131 and J. Mapumulo, 'The reminiscences of an old teacher', 156–7. John Dube himself explained he had wanted at this time to study medicine; see the interview in the *Natal Mercury*, 22.9.1936.

2 On missionary attitudes and social distance, see N. Etherington, 'Gender issues in south-east African missions, 1835–1885' in H. Bredekamp and R. Ross (eds.), *Missions and Christianity in South African history* (Johannesburg, 1995), 143–4; also his 'The standard of living question in nineteenth-century missions in KwaZulu-Natal' in J. de Gruchy (ed.), *The London Missionary Society in southern Africa* (Cape Town, 1999), 156–65. The phrase 'benign domination' is from J. and J. Comaroff, *Christianity, colonialism, and consciousness in South Africa, 1* (Chicago and London, 1991), 125. The description of James Dube's appearance is from Lindley to Clark, 17.12.1870, ABCSA Reel 179, Volume 7. On the history of Oberlin,

see W.E. Bigglestone, 'Oberlin College and the Negro student, 1865–1940', *Journal of Negro History* 56, July 1971, 198–219; J.O. Horton, 'Black education at Oberlin College: a controversial commitment', *Journal of Negro Education* 54, 4, 1985, 477–99; and Waite, *Permission to remain among us*. The description of Oberlin's surroundings is from 'Vernon Johns at Oberlin' at http://www.vernonjohns.org/tcal001/vjobrln.html [accessed 2.8.2007]. On the post-Civil War period in America, see H. Brogan, *The Penguin history of the USA* (Harmondsworth, 1999), chapters 16 and 17. The idea of an 'American way of life' is based on F. Braudel, *A history of civilizations* (New York, 1995), 469–76.

3 Dube, *A talk upon my native land*, 25. I am most grateful to Shula Marks for our discussion of the significance of this incident (October 2006). On the costs of transatlantic voyages as well as Boston's population and economy, see E.L. Glaeser, 'Reinventing Boston: 1640–2003', Harvard Institute of Economic Research Paper No. 2017 (2003) , especially 4, 14, 17 and 19, at http://post.economics.harvard/edu/hier/2003papers/2003list.html [accessed 4.12.2006] and Boorstin, *The democratic experience*, 254–5. On the city's inventiveness, see K. Manning, 'The culture of invention in Boston', Queens Borough Public Library resources at http://edison.rutgers.edu/latimer/cultinvt.htm; and Kingwood College, 'American cultural history' at http://kclibrary.nhmccd.edu/19thcentury1880.htm [accessed 28.11.2006]. Steerage conditions are described in Brogan, *The Penguin history of the USA*, 396–7. Many of the passenger lists on these routes have been transcribed and are available online, largely because of the intense interest in Europe and America in tracing migrant forebears. For this reason it has been possible to view the manifest for this voyage online; John Dube's name is clearly visible, searched via www.ancestrey.com [accessed 4.12.2006]. It was possible to trace further details about the *Pavonia*'s movements on http://www.norwayheritage.com/p_ship.asp?sh=pavon [accessed 4.12.2006]. Information on Irish emigration patterns is from R. Foster, *The Oxford illustrated history of Ireland* (Oxford, 2000), 213–14. The following sources were used on 1880s London: on newspaper circulation, C. Cook and B. Keith, *British historical facts 1830–1900* (London and Basingstoke, 1975), 215; on temperance, J. Richardson, *London and its people: a social history from medieval times to the present day* (London, 1995), 242. The remark about the underground, made of 1887, is from John Galsworthy's *The man of property* (London, [1906] 1968), 269 (the first of the Forsyte novels). Information on the jubilee is drawn from *Illustrated London News*, 25.6.1887. The observation about the concentration of powers in London is from D. Cannadine, *The pleasures of the past* (London, 1997), 160. John Dube's overall impressions are remembered in his *A Zulu's appeal for light*, 26, while the story of the lift is from *New York Times*, 9.1.1905. The other sense of London's confusion is from a letter written by Sylvan Pollard to his wife in Guyana, August 1955, recounted in *Guardian Family*, 22.7.2006. Nineteenth-century passenger details for the Cape Town–Southampton–London route are patchy. Natal and Cape newspapers contained 'shipping intelligence' columns which usually listed arrivals and departures, but did not always provide full details of passengers – and then quite often only for those in first class. It has therefore not been possible to pick out John Dube's details for his first sea voyage. General information on the 'mail run' can be found at the Merchant Navy Association at http://www.red-duster.co.uk/UNION.htm [accessed 3.12.2006].

4 John Dube's reflections on the difficulties of this period are contained in *A familiar talk upon my native land*; *The Zulu's appeal for light and England's duty* (from where the quotes come); and *Ilanga*, 18.12.1903. The report of him in the Cleveland court room (including the quotes) is from the *Summit County Beacon*, 5.10.1887. This snippet, as with so many other wonderful and long-forgotten insights, was brought to my attention by Cherif Keita, whose scholarly contributions to this study have been indispensable. Information about Pullman working conditions is from L. Tye, 'The work of a Pullman porter'. The song quoted is 'The

Pullman porter' by William H. Bray, from http://eliillinois.org/30108_87/exhibits/music/ [accessed 5.2.2007].

5 The 'ice cream encounter' is related in Dube, *A talk upon my native land*, 25. Oberlin campus architecture at the time is discussed in G. Blodgett, 'Oberlin College architecture: a short history', at Oberlin College, http://www.oberlin.edu/external/EOG/gbslides/ AShortHistory.html [accessed 4.1.2007] from which the quote describing architectural style is taken. On James Fairchild, see Waite, *Permission to remain among us*, 91. On the numbers and other details of black students at Oberlin, see Bigglestone, 'Oberlin College and the Negro student', 198 and Horton, 'Black education at Oberlin College', 484. Dube's connections with the Fosters are described in Marable, 'African nationalist', 65–6 (which also describes the syllabus he followed); *Ilanga*, 18.12.1903, and in the Oberlin archive 'Foster' finding aid at http://www.oberlin.edu/archive/holdings/finding/RG30/SG103/biography.html. On Cicero's oratory see F. Tinkler, 'Cicero on the genres of rhetoric' (1995) at http://rhetoric. eserver.org/categories/history/classical/genres-of-rhetoric.html [accessed 11.1.2008]. Since Barack Obama's election as US President in 2008, there has been a renewed interest in oratory, because of his own impressive command of this art. Rood's commendation is reproduced in *A familiar talk upon my native land*, 35. In recent years, Oberlin has taken a great interest in their alumnus John Dube, largely due to the efforts of Cherif Keita. A dedicated research project was launched in 2001. Despite the fact that there is very little in the official college record concerning his enrolment, a valuable finding aid as well as several files of biographical information has been assembled. See http://www.oberlin.edu/archive/holdings/finding/ RG30/SG250/accessions.html and http://www.oberlin.edu/external/EOG/Dube/Dube Contents.htm. Wilcox recounted Dube's entrée to public speaking in 'The Booker T. Washington of South Africa'. The identity of Dube's patron is unknown; the information about Olivia Phelps-Stokes in from Marable, 'African nationalist', 105. Dube makes clear his purpose of returning to Oberlin in *A talk upon my native land*, 18.

6 The two editions were both printed by Swinburne and Co., Rochester, New York. *A talk* is dated as 1892, but there is no date on *A familiar talk*. Since Dube makes clear his intention of continuing his education at Oberlin in both editions, they are likely to have come out in quick succession. The passage on Dube's views on education is from *A talk*, 41; that on industrial education is from *A familiar talk*, 27. For a full list of the books and pamphlets submitted for the 'Negro exhibit', see http://www.education.miami.edu/ep/paris/home. htm [accessed 4.4.2008].

7 On Durban in the early 1890s, see J. Lambert and R. Morrell, 'Domination and subordination in Natal, 1890–1920' in R. Morrell (ed.), *Political economy and identities in KwaZulu-Natal* (Durban, 1996), 65; K. Atkins, *The moon is dead! Give us our money!* (Portsmouth and London, 1993), 123–9. On the establishment of the Beatrice Street church, see Briggs and Wing, *The harvest and the hope*, 131. Dube's role in the AZM at this time is mentioned in 'General letter of the Zulu Mission, 1893', ABCSA Reel 188, Volume 13 (from which the quotes are taken about the dangers of city life and of his still being primarily known as James's son) and 'Report of mission work 1892–3', ABCSA Reel 188, Volume 13 (which describes his enthusiasm and the well-attended services). On the matter of exemptions, see J. Lambert, 'From independence to rebellion: African society in crisis c.1880–1910', 384 and Welsh, *The roots of segregation*, 235–42. The issue of medals is discussed in SNA 1/1/128 (236/1891). Dube's exemption application is at SNA 1/1/169 (473/1893). See *Ilanga*, 26.9.1926 for information on his time at Groutville and Maphumulo. It may have been for financial reasons that John Dube lost his AZM appointment, as the mission was complaining at this time of a shortage of funds. The 'Rules for the regulation of the churches connected with the AZM' (or Umsunduze Rules) can be found at A/1/7, AZMP. The quote about

the way the term *Amakholwa* was being used is from S. Meintjes, 'Edendale 1850–1906: a case study of rural transformation and class formation in an African mission in Natal' (PhD thesis, University of London, 1988), 283. On Klaas's position at Inanda, see 'Inanda Magistrate's Report for 1878' in SNA 1/1/35 (872/1879). On the growing tension between Pixley, Goba and Mqhawe, see SNA 1/1/131 (1177/1890); statements of Mankuza and Kaba and minute from F. Foxon, Administrator of Native Law at Ndwedwe, to SNA, all in SNA 1/1/193 (1306/1894). As the dispute worsened and Mqhawe threatened legal action, the Inanda magistrate, W.H. Beaumont, testily told Pixley, 'I shall deem it a favour if you will consult Mqhawe over newcomers': see letter to Pixley, 9.10.1894, 1/NWE 3/1/1, Ndwedwe Magistrate's Papers, PDNA. On families and alignments at Inanda, see Hughes, 'Politics and society in Inanda, Natal', 201–15.

8 Marable suggests that Dube and Wilcox consulted over the idea of Dube going independent; see 'African nationalist', 70. On the Mdima family, see Wood, *Shine where you are*, 47, 50, 69–70; SNA letter, 27.7.1905, File A/2/24, AZM Collection A608; 'General letter of the AZM 1893', ABCSA Reel 188, Volume 13; *Ilanga*, 10.3.1911 (on John) and *Ilanga*, 16.3.1917 (on Willett and Richard). A cutting from the *Los Angeles Times*, 13.1.1899 (in which Nokutela explained her name) was sent to me by Bob Edgar, to whom I am very grateful. There is also useful information on the Mdimas in Marable, 'African nationalist', 70, 122, 124. Nokutela's essay was printed as part of a letter from Mrs Wilcox, dated 2.5.1882, in the *Rice County Journal* at the end of June 1882. For this cutting I am deeply grateful to Cherif Keita, who sent me an electronic version; unfortunately, the date is difficult to read. For evidence that she taught at Amatata, see Pixley to USNA, 14.8.1903, SNA 1/1/289 (1161/1900). Nokutela left a brief account of her family as 'The story of my life', published in something called the *American Evangelical Journal* in May 1898. It has been very difficult to trace this publication because the given title of the journal is probably generic rather than specific, and the copy that was once housed in Killie Campbell Library has gone missing. This has meant having to rely on brief notes taken from this document many years ago, as well as references to it in other sources. I am nevertheless grateful to Nellie Somers for trying extremely hard to locate it. On Mqhawe's intentions for John Dube, see Wood, *Shine where you are*, 50. In *Ilanga*, 10.3.1911, John Mdima's father is noted as Simon Mdima. John's notice of dismissal can be found at '59th Annual Meeting of the AZM', ABCSA Reel 189, Volume 14. Nokutela's first impressions of Incwadi are contained in her 'The story of my life'. For a report of their work at Incwadi, see Marable, 'African nationalist', 70–3. On the naming of the area of the church, see M. Ngcobo, 'Private land purchase and tribal security in Natal: the case of the Qadi and Nooitgedacht [Incwadi] farm from 1878–1948' (Undergraduate research project, University of Natal, Durban, 1992). For Mary Edwards's attempts to open a school at Incwadi, see Secretary of the Board of the Natal Native Trust to Edwards, 29.10.1879, SNA 1/1/33 (112/1879), and on government funding, see *Report of Inspector of Native Education for 1896* and following years, copies of which are in the ISP. As a result of hardship caused by rinderpest in the mid-1890s, many returned from Incwadi to Inanda, resulting in a considerable decrease in school attendance. This stabilised at around 58 from 1898. The AZM and other mission bodies were highly sensitive by the mid-1890s to the issue of 'Ethiopianism', manifesting itself in breakaways from the mainstream churches; this is discussed in later chapters.

9 Dube's first published letter was in *Inkanyiso*, 11.5.1894; see 22.6.1894 for support, and Welsh, *The Roots of segregation*, 297. On his other contributions, see Limb, *The ANC's early years*, 93. His petition is in a letter, John Dube and others to Kilbon, 16.1.1896, A/1/10, AZMP. For the origins of Funamalungelo, see A. Odendaal, *Vukani bantu! The beginnings of black protest politics in South Africa to 1912* (Cape Town, 1984), 17. On Ekukhanyeni, see

V. Khumalo, 'Ekukhanyeni letter-writers: a historical inquiry into epistolary network(s) and political imagination in KwaZulu-Natal' in Karin Barber (ed.), *Africa's hidden histories: everyday literacy and the making of self* (Bloomington, 2006), 113–42, and Jeff Guy, 'Class, imperialism and literary criticism: William Ngidi, John Colenso and Matthew Arnold', *Journal of Southern African Studies* 23, 2, 1997, 219–41.

10 This last reference is to Bunyan's *Pilgrim's progress*, to a point very early into Christian's journey. Dube's recollection is in 'Report of meeting regarding disposal of mission reserve funds', ABCSA Reel 196, Volume 22. The contest over the pastorate went on and on: see *Evidence given before the Lands Commission 1900–1902*, 238 (Klaas's evidence) and 241 (Cetywayo's evidence). Also on divisions between Inanda residents, see Bigelow to Smith, 15.10.1895, ABCSA Reel 190, Volume 15. On the outcome of the ballot, subsequent divisions and Pixley's attitude, see Pixley to Smith, 8.9.1896, ABCSA Reel 192, Volume 18. The meaning of Mafukuzela as 'Energetic and industrious' is T. Cope's; see note in Swanson, *The views of Mahlathi*, 179. 'The trailblazer' meaning is in L. Gunner, 'Zulu writing, the constraints and possibilities, with special reference to *Osibindigidi Bongqondongqondo* and *Ikhiwane Elihle* by Lawrence Molefe', *African Languages and Cultures* 1, 2, 1988, 150.

Chapter 4

1 Information about the Union Missionary Training Institute is from the *New York Times*, 8.11.1895 and the *Brooklyn Eagle*, 15.4.1898 and 26.5.1898. On early Zulu speakers in Brooklyn, see the *Brooklyn Eagle*, 2.9.1881, 14.9.1881, 8.5.1892 and 27.2.1897; B. Lindfors, 'Introduction' and S. Peacock, 'Africa meets the great Farini', both in B. Lindfors (ed.), *Africans on stage: studies in ethnological show business* (Bloomington and Cape Town, 1999), ix and 85; and R. Vinson and R. Edgar, 'Zulus abroad: cultural representations and educational experiences of Zulus in America', *Journal of Southern African Studies* 33, 1, 2007, 43–62. On 1890s Brooklyn, see E. Snyder-Grenier, *Brooklyn! An illustrated history* (Philadelphia, 1996); the Virtual Dime Museum, Brooklyn at http://thevirtualdimemuseum. blogspot.com/2008/12/christmas-tree-grows-in-brooklyn.html [accessed 2.2.2009] and E. Fortmeyer for the Boerum Hill History Association, at http://www.boerumhillbrooklyn.org/ archives/000035.html [accessed 2.2.2009]. Dube's quote about the ice is from the *New York Times*, 13.4.1899 – grateful thanks to Bob Edgar for the reference, as for that to the *New York Tribune* at the start of the chapter. Evidence of the Dubes' addresses is drawn from Rive and Couzens, *Seme the founder of the ANC*, 33 (where the name has been transcribed as Herkerman, but is most likely to be Herkimer), and Dube's letter to J.E. Bruce (discussed later in the chapter). The insight that this trip would give Dube an intellectual rationale is Marable's, in 'African nationalist', 93. Details of the *St Paul* passenger list can be found on the 'Telegraph family history' site at http://familyhistory.telegraph.co.uk/passengerListShowTranscript. action?uvn=227000006&vsn=466&_zga_s=1 [accessed 2.2.2009].

2 Dube's Hampton talk was published as 'The need for industrial education in Africa', *Southern Workman* 27, 7, 1897, 141–2. The 'Sun of Righteousness' quote is taken from M.O. West, 'The Tuskegee model of development in Africa: another dimension of the African/ African-American connection', *Diplomatic History* 16, 3, 2007, 378. See also Marable, 'African nationalist', 101–3 for details of this visit. The report of Washington's address to the Lafayette Avenue church is in the *Brooklyn Eagle*, 8.3.1897. Dube's letter to Washington on missing it, written on 7.3.1897, is in the Booker T. Washington Papers online, Volume 4, 262–3, at http://www.press.uillinois.edu. Selope Thema's statement is in L. Switzer and E. Ceiriog Jones, 'Other voices: the ambiguities of resistance in South Africa's resistance press', *South African Historical Journal* 32, May 1995, 73. The full text of Washington's 'Atlanta

compromise' speech was consulted in J. Daley (ed.), *Great speeches by African Americans* (New York, 2006), 81–4. See also L. Harlan, *Booker T. Washington: the making of a black leader 1856–1901* (Oxford, 1974), 204. Quotes from Washington on his early life and work are taken from his 'The awakening of the Negro', *Atlantic Monthly* 78, 1896. This is the source which famously begins with the image of a ragged African American boy, in miserable, degraded surroundings, trying to teach himself French. Washington would publish his autobiography *Up from slavery* in 1901 (and Zulu was among the many languages into which it was translated). Du Bois's observation on Washington's national leadership is from 'On Mr Booker T. Washington and others' in his classic *The souls of the black folk* (Greenwich, Conn., 1961), 42.

3 Information on Bruce and his mentors is largely drawn from R.L. Crowder, *John Edward Bruce: politician, journalist and self-trained historian of the African diaspora* (New York, 2004), 41 (for his views on 'black thinking'), 15 (on intermarriage), 76 (on his reaction to Douglass's marriage). On Bruce's Christianity and view of industrial education, see T.E. Smith, 'Reform and empire: the British and American transnational search for the rights of black people in the late nineteenth and early twentieth centuries' (PhD thesis, University of Nebraska, Lincoln, 2006), 125, 138 and 159. See also G. Shepperson, 'Notes on Negro American influences on the emergence of African nationalism', *Journal of African History* 1, 2, 1960, 309. Blyden's view on Ethiopia is from his 'Evolution of an Africanist perspective', Edward Blyden Virtual Museum, Columbia University, at http://www.columbia.edu/~hcb8/EWB_Museum/Evolution.html [accessed 7.1.2009] and his view on slavery and Africa's redemption is from Campbell, *Songs of Zion*, 75. On Crummell, see C.J. La Rue, *The heart of black preaching* (Westminster, 2000), 38. For an excellent analysis of Crummell and Washington (and others), see W.J. Moses, *Creative conflict in African American thought: Frederick Douglass, Alexander Crummell, Booker T. Washington, W.E.B. Du Bois and Marcus Garvey* (Cambridge, 2004), 100–1 (for the idea of 'civilisation from the top down') and 129 (for Crummell's views of a separate nation). The observation about imagining Africa from a distance is cited in R. Rathbone, *African history: a very short introduction* (Oxford, 2007), 7. On early Pan-Africanism, see Hill's observations in R.B. Turner, *Islam in the African American experience* (Bloomington, 2003), 85. For the centrality of political submission, rather than industrial education, in Washington's thought, see West, 'The Tuskegee model of development in Africa', 371–87.

4 Unfortunately, Dube's letter to Bruce is incompletely dated. See Group E, Miscellaneous: 13/41–107, John Edward Bruce Collection, Schomburg Center, New York Public Library. The Finding Aid for the Bruce Collection gives the date as 1894–5?, which is unlikely, as the Dubes' Brooklyn address is printed on the notepaper. An assumption has been made accordingly that the letter was written between 1896 and 1899. On the *Cleveland Gazette*, see Crowder, *John Edward Bruce*, 20 and 95–6 and the Booker T. Washington Papers, Volume 5, note 3, 123. The most penetrating analysis of Dube's ambiguity is Marks, *The ambiguities of dependence*, particularly chapter 2. On Plaatje's correspondence with Bruce, see B. Willan, *Sol Plaatje: a biography* (Johannesburg, 1984), 110.

5 Information on Booth and Chilembwe is drawn from H. Langworthy, *Africa for the African: the life of Joseph Booth* (Zomba, n.d.); G.S. Mwase, *Strike a blow and die* (London, 1975), 25–7; and G. Shepperson and T. Price, *Independent African* (Edinburgh, 1958 [also 1987]), especially 92–114; the quote is from 92.

6 For the history of the Lewis Avenue Congregational Church, see the *New York Times*, 11.3.1880 and 21.5.1894; it was later sold to the Cornerstone Baptist Church in 1944. For information on Robert Kent, see the *New York Times*, 8.12.1893 and 11.1.1896, and the *Brooklyn Eagle*, 3.12.1896. For church activities, see the *Brooklyn Eagle*, 14.12.1897, 5.6.1898 and 1.10.1898. For Brooklyn churches generally, see the *Brooklyn Eagle*, 5.2.1898.

7 On the significance of the transatlantic connection, see D. Anthony and R. Edgar 'Religion and the black (south) Atlantic', *Annotations* 30, 1, 2002 at http://www.archives. gov/nhprc/annotation/march-2002/black-south-atlantic.html, which also contains the story of Qandeyana Cele. On Charles Dube's education, see *Ilanga*, 18.11.1904; Campbell, *Songs of Zion*, 254; and Marable 'African nationalist', 106. On other African students at Wilberforce, see R.R. Wright (ed.), *Encyclopaedia of African Methodism* (Philadelphia, 1947), 533 and Campbell, *Songs of Zion*, 267–71. For a contemporary description of Wilberforce, see H. Talbert, *The sons of Allen, together with a sketch of the history of Wilberforce University, Wilberforce, Ohio* (electronic edition at http://docsouth.unc.edu/church/talbert/talbert. html, originally published 1905). On Pixley Seme in America, see M.V. Gumede to H. Hughes, 30.1.1987; Rive and Couzens, *Seme the founder of the ANC*, 13–19 and letters they reproduce from the Mount Hermon School File; and Marable, 'African nationalist', 170–1. Apart from the brother enrolled at Benedict College, Pixley's older brother, Lindley, studied medicine in New York and Canada in the later 1900s. Mqhawe's concerns as to Mandlakayise's fitness to rule were expressed to Mary Edwards; see Edwards to Smith, 27.8.1897, ABCSA Reel 191, Volume 16. Details of the financing of Mandlakayise's trip are from 'Report of Native Intelligence Officer', 7.11.1898 in SNA 1/4/5 (34/1898) and Colony of Natal, *Blue Book on Native Affairs 1898*, B39. In reports at the time (for example in the *Brooklyn Eagle*, 9.1.1898 and 28.2.1899), Mandlakayise and Mabhelubhelu were both described as sons of Chief Mqhawe, yet Madikane was quite clear that his son had accompanied Mandlakayise: see Webb and Wright, *The James Stuart archive 2*, 47. The two visitors may have been described as 'sons of Mqhawe' (as Dube himself did) so that both could qualify as minor Zulu royalty. Pixley's letter to Washington is in Booker T. Washington Papers, Volume 9, 204. Madikane's story is more fully told in Hughes, 'Politics and society in the Qadi chiefdom', 189–93. The magistrate's description of Mandlakayise (and the question of his citizenship) is in SNA 1/1/310 (393/1904); on this issue see also evidence of S.O. Samuelson to *Natal Native Affairs Commission*, 1906–7, 19.

8 The Union Missionary Training Institute graduation was reported in the *Brooklyn Eagle*, 26.5.1898. Nokutela's and John's fundraising efforts were covered in the *Brooklyn Eagle*, 11.3.1899. Evidence of the Seneca Castle connection is from Rive and Couzens, *Seme founder of the ANC*, letter from John Dube to Cutler, 8.9.1898, 41. On the early connection with the Phelps-Stokes family, see Marable, 'African nationalist', 105. The news stories and interviews that the Dubes gave appeared in the following papers; I am deeply grateful to Bob Edgar for many of these references: *Los Angeles Times*, 30.6.1896 and 13.1.1899; *New York Observer*, 9.3.1899; *New York Times*, 17.8.1898 and 13.4.1899; *Brooklyn Eagle*, 30.3.1899. Emphasis has been added to the quote about Zulu people respecting whites, *New York Times*, 17.8.1898. Washington's comments are in a letter of December 1896 in L. Harlan (ed.), The Booker T. Washington Papers 4, 251 of Open Book Edition at http://www.historycooperative.org/ btw/Vol.4/html/251.html. An article on the subject of 'Language of the Zulus' appeared in the *New York Times*, 14.3.1897, which also contained some strident anti-colonial remarks. This article has sometimes been attributed to Dube but his name neither appears in it nor is he given as author of it, and it has been omitted from discussion here on grounds that there is little internal evidence to support Dube's involvement. See also J. Dube, 'Zululand and the Zulus', *Missionary Review of the World* 21, 1898. The theme of precedence has recently been explored from the perspective of missionary history in Jackson, '"First fruits" at Adams Mission'; insights developed there have been applied here to the way Dube used the idea. On Arthur T. Pierson, see D.L. Robert, *Occupy until I come: A.T. Pierson and the evangelization of the world* (Grand Rapids, 2003). On the notion of false progress, see Moses, *Creative conflict in African American thought*, 151. Grateful thanks to Cherif Keita for drawing my attention to the Ousley–Rhodes incident (email communication, 16.8.2009). Booker Washington's allusion to Rhodes is in a letter to the editor of the *Colored American*, 20.7.1899; see Booker T. Washington Papers, Volume 5, 164.

9 Dube's ordination service was covered in the *Brooklyn Eagle*, 11.3.1899. For information on Louis Stoiber and the Legal Aid Society, see *New York Times*, 23.1.1898, the Arthur von Briesen Papers [Series 2], Princeton University Library; and Lain's Directory, Brooklyn Genealogy Information at http://www.bklyn-genealogy-info.com/Directory/1897/k.html (which also contains information on Kniffen). On other members of the American Committee, see Marable, 'African nationalist', 176 and the *New York Times*, 19.12.1897 and 24.5.1902. On details of the Dubes' departure, see the *Brooklyn Eagle*, 12.4.1899.

Chapter 5

1 John L. Dube to H. Colenso, 22.4.1908, Volume 45, Colenso Papers, A204, PDNA. The quote from Smuts's *A century of wrong* is in the Conclusion. See the Gutenberg Project version at http://www.archive.org/details/ACenturyOfWrong [accessed 27.7.2009]. For Wilcox's views on the war, see 'Minutes of the semi-annual meeting of the American Zulu Mission, 6–15 February 1900', ABCSA Reel 195, Volume 21. The account of the Zulu workers' long march to Natal is based on P. Warwick, *Black people and the South African war, 1899–1902* (Johannesburg, 1983), 128. The American flag referred to is discussed in Wood, *Shine where you are*, 58. It is now stored with other archival items in the ISP, KCAL. The information on the AZM temporarily housing Rand-based missionaries is in 'General letter of the AZM, 1899–1900', ABCSA Reel 196, Volume 22. The description of Natal's white population as 'nervous' was originally made by W.M. Macmillan in his *Africa emergent* (Harmondsworth, 1949), 118, and has been noted many times since. The account of the dedication ceremony to mark the establishment of the Dubes' school is from Marable, 'African nationalist', 122–3. The title of the chapter is taken from an interview with the Dubes in the *Los Angeles Times*, 13.1.1899.

2 The report on Incwadi school is from 'Report of the Inspector of Native Education (Mr R. Plant)', Departmental Reports, *Natal Blue Book 1900*, G45. Information on the first meeting Dube called to plan for the school (and the quote) is from his 'The opening of a native school' in SNA 1/1/294 (2818/1901). On Dube becoming pastor of Inanda church, see 'General letter of the AZM 1899–1900', 'General letter of the AZM 1900–1901' and 'AZM annual letter 1901–2', all on ABCSA Reel 198, Volume 22; testimony of Klaas Goba in Colony of Natal, *Evidence given before the Lands Commission (1900-01-02)*, 238; and 'Annual Statement (no. 4) by the American Committee' (1902), in Dube File, University of Hampton Archives, Virginia (with thanks to Bob Edgar for this reference). Bokwe's quote comes from Tim Couzens, 'Widening horizons of African literature, 1870–1900' in L. White and T. Couzens (eds.), *Literature and society in South Africa* (Longman, 1984), 63. See also L. Switzer, 'American missionaries and the making of an African church in colonial Natal' in De Gruchy, *The London Missionary Society in Southern Africa*, 166–88, on the status of African pastors.

3 Robert Grendon has been a sadly neglected figure in South African literature and journalism – he later edited the African National Congress paper, *Abantu-Batho* – but there is now an excellent study by Grant Christison, 'African Jerusalem: the vision of Robert Grendon' (PhD thesis, University of KwaZulu-Natal, Pietermaritzburg, 2007). Grateful thanks to the author for sending me a copy and for permission to use it; this material is largely drawn from chapter 7. On other early staff members and trustees, see *Ilanga*, 18.12.1903; SNA 1/1/140 (370/1891); La Hausse, *Restless identities*, 51. On the Dubes' early fundraising

and recruiting activities, see John Dube, 'On the opening of an African school', 4.7.1901; copy in SNA 1/1/294 (2818/1901); and *Ilanga*, 8.8.1903.The amount raised for 1903 is noted in *Ilanga*, 28.8.1903. His later reflections are in *Ukuziphatha kahle* ('Good manners'), translated by N.N. Dhlomo. See her 'The theory, value and practice of translation with reference to John L. Dube's texts *Isita somuntu nguye* (1928) and *Ukuziphatha kahle* (1935)' (MA thesis, University of Durban-Westville, 1996), 122. Dube's views on atheism are contained in E. Smith, *The Christian mission in Africa* (International Missionary Council, 1926), 42. On the meaning of *uhlanga*, see Khaba Mkhize in Cherif Keita's documentary film, *Oberlin-Inanda* (Mogoya Productions, 2008); J. Guy, *The Maphumulo uprising* (Pietermaritzburg, 2007), 250; and Joe Matthews's interview with G. Carter, March 1964, 2:XD20:96/1, Karis-Carter Papers (microform edition).

4 Crutcher's observation is cited in M.L. Kremm, *Race and U.S. foreign policy in the ages of territorial and market expansion 1840–1900* (London, 1998), 406. On revivals at Inanda, see 'Annual Statement (no. 4) by the American Committee' (1902), Dube File, University of Hampton Archives, and Wood, *Shine where you are*, 175. Albert Luthuli's recollections are in his *Let my people go* (London, 1974), 26. On daily school life, see Marable, 'African nationalist', 149; *Ilanga*, 5.6.1903 and 28.8.1903; John Dube, 'Opening of the people's school, 4 July 1901', in SNA 1/1/294 (2818/1901); John Dube, 'Practical Christianity among the Zulus', *Missionary Review of the World* 20, 5, May 1907; and Hunt Davis, 'John L. Dube', 497–528. The reference to boys giving up their liberty is in L. Switzer, 'American Congregational schools in colonial Natal', paper to the Conference of the African Studies Association of Australasia and the Pacific, University of Western Australia, November 1999, 4.

5 *Amagama abantu* was originally published on the Ohlange press in 1911; it was reissued as *A Zulu songbook*, transliterated, translated and edited by David Rycroft (Durban and Pietermaritzburg, 1996). The songs mentioned here have been drawn from the later version. Grateful thanks to Muzi Hadebe for assistance with the translation of the full title. On the minstrel tradition, see J. Kenrick, 'A history of the musical minstrel shows' (2003) at http://www.musicals101.com/minstrel.htm [accessed 10.2.2010]. The reference to minstrelsy at Ohlange is from V. Erlmann, 'Reuben T. Caluza and early popular music' in C. Lucia (ed.), *The world of South African music: a reader* (Newcastle, 2005), 177. Veit Erlmann has written in depth about the Virginia Jubilee Singers: see his *African stars: studies in black South African performance* (Chicago, 1991), chapter 2. On the Inanda Native Singers, see *Ilanga*, 20.4.1904 and 15.5.1905.

6 Background on Samuelson is from the Samuelson Papers (A639), Historical Papers, William Cullen Library, University of the Witwatersrand (HPCW), especially his own youthful diary. On his role and the period during which he was in office, see S. Marks, *Reluctant rebellion: the 1906–1908 disturbances in Natal* (Oxford, 1970), 24–6; and S. Meintjies, 'The ambiguities of ideological change: the impact of settler hegemony on the Amakholwa in the 1880s and 1890s', paper to the Conference on the history of Natal and Zululand, University of Natal, Durban, 1985, 11. The record of his interview with Dube is in SNA 1/4/9 (31/1901) and SNA 1/4/12 (6/1903). His note of support is in SNA 1/1/324 (1915/1905). Police reports on Dube and his first arrest are detailed in SNA 1/4/9 (31/1901); see particularly Officer Pook's notes, 29.1.1903, on the issue of inducing 'wholesome fear'. See also *Ilanga*, 7.8.1903. For background on Simungu Shibe and Dube's role in trying to heal divisions, see SNA 1/1/278 (1029/1897); 'General letter of the AZM, 1899–1900', ABCSA Reel 196, Volume 22, 10; 'Semi-annual meeting of the AZM, 5–6 February 1900', ABCSA Reel 195, Volume 21; Christoferson, *Adventuring with God*, 110; Switzer, 'American missionaries and the making of an African church in colonial Natal'. On official attitudes to independent churches generally, see Marks, *Reluctant rebellion*, 62–82. The best study of the AME in

South Africa is Campbell, *Songs of Zion*. Bridgman's observation was made in the *Christian Express*, 1.10.1903. On the AZM's general attitude to state control of mission reserves, see H. Goodenough, 'Reply of the American Mission Reserve Trustees to Lands Commission Report', copy in A/3/49, File 1901, AZMP. Evidence for Dube's gun ownership and hunting activities is in SNA 1/1/324 (1915/1905), SNA 1/1/401 (1759/1908) and the interview with Dumi Zondi in Cherif Keita's documentary film, *Oberlin-Inanda* (Villon Films, Vancouver, 2006). For hunting more generally, see Smith, *The life and times*, 442 and A.T. Bryant, *The Zulu people* (Pietermaritzburg, 1967), 683–6.

7 Dube's comments about the Natal Native Congress are from *Ilanga*, 19.6.1903, 7.8.1903 and 25.11.1904 ('Restriction' by Mafukuzela; copy in SNA 1/1/315 (2468/1904)). The report of the inaugural meeting in *Natal Mercury*, 8.6.1900, is the most detailed available; see also *Christian Express*, 1.10.1900. Martin Lutuli's evidence to the South African Native Affairs Commission gives invaluable insights into the very early years of the Congress; excerpts are reproduced in Johns III, *Protest and hope 1882–1934*, 29–34. Mark Radebe's statement, as well as information about other early Congress officials, is to be found in Marks, *Reluctant rebellion*, 69–73. See also Odendaal, *Vukani bantu!*, 59–62. Hamilton suggests that James Stuart, the Natal official better known for his prodigious collection of African oral testimony, might also have been supportive of Congress. See C. Hamilton, *Terrific majesty: the powers of Shaka Zulu and the limits of historical invention* (Cape Town, 1998), 133–5. On Zacharias Goba's son, see 'Verulam Register of Births 1868–1897', PDNA. Information on land ownership is taken from Natal Government, *Blue Book on Native Affairs*, 1894. Dube's visit to Driefontein is described in Christison, 'African Jerusalem', 499–500. The most useful history of the black press in South Africa is L. Switzer (ed.), *South Africa's alternative press: voices of protest and resistance 1880–1960* (Cambridge, 1997). See especially the contributions by R. Hunt Davis, '"Qude maniki!" John L. Dube, pioneer editor of *Ilanga lase Natal*' and U. Shashikant-Mesthrie, 'From advocacy to mobilisation: *Indian Opinion*, 1903–1923'. The observation on the weighting of votes in the Cape parliament is from C.W. de Kiewiet, *The imperial factor in South Africa* (Cambridge, 1937), 62. I am grateful to Paul La Hausse for the information that *Ilanga* was registered as a newspaper in 1902. The arrival of the printing press was celebrated in *Ilanga*, 19.6.1903; see also the edition of 7.8.1903. Dube's hope that his press would spawn a great Zulu literature was expressed in his 'Practical Christianity among the Zulus', *Missionary Review of the World* 20, 5, 1907, 371. Grendon's poem appeared in the 15.5.1903 edition of *Ilanga*. Walter Rubusana explained that the term *abelungu* derived from *ubulunga*, a necklace of hair worn by African women as a charm to ward off danger. It was applied to whites because of their long hair. W.B. Rubusana, 'Cooperation from the West' in M. Stauffer (ed.), *Thinking with Africa* (Missionary Education Movement of the US and Canada, 1927), 148.

8 There is a wide literature on Gandhi in South Africa, enriched since 1994 by the engagement of scholars from India with this period of the Mahatma's life. Sources used here are A.J. Parel, 'The origins of *Hind Swaraj*' in J.M. Brown and M. Prozesky (eds.), *Gandhi and South Africa* (Pietermaritzburg, 1996), 35–66 (which cites Gandhi's letter to Polak, 46); M. Swan, *Gandhi: the South African experience* (Johannesburg, 1985), in which is cited Gandhi's views on Indians' post-war position in the Transvaal (58) and his observations on Johannesburg mixing (113); A. Nauriya, *The African element in Gandhi* (New Delhi, 2006), from which is drawn the example of African cyclists. Nazar's letter to Gandhi is quoted in Mesthrie, 'From advocacy to mobilisation: *Indian Opinion*, 1903–1923', 102. For an excellent study of the history of Phoenix, see U. Dhupelia-Mesthrie, *Gandhi's prisoner? The life of Gandhi's son Manilal* (Cape Town, 2004), especially chapter 2. Gandhi's account of this period is in his *An autobiography, or The story of my experiments with truth* (Ahmedabad, 1927), 250–6.

On linking Gandhi and Dube, see E.S. Reddy, 'Mahatma Gandhi and John Dube' at http://www.anc.org.za/ancdocs/history/people/gandhi/4.html) [accessed 19.12.2009]. *Ahimsa-Ubuntu*, devised by Fatima Meer with Jay Pather and Jurgen Brauninger, was staged at the Durban Playhouse, October 1996. The point about their contradictory outlooks is based on an idea about Thomas Carlyle developed by E.P. Thompson in his *William Morris: romantic to revolutionary* (New York, 1975), 30. Examples of *Ilanga*'s anti-Indian pronouncements are from the editions of 20.11.1903 and 11.12.1903. For attempts to focus more on interaction between Africans and Indians, rather than their separate realities, see S. Bhana and G. Vahed, *The making of a political reformer: Gandhi in South Africa, 1893–1914* (New Delhi, 2005), especially chapter 1. See also Hughes, '"We will be elbowed out the country"', H. Hughes, 'Violence in Inanda, August 1985', *Journal of Southern African Studies* 13, 3, 1987, 331–54; and E. Webster, 'The 1949 Durban "riots": a study in race and class' in P. Bonner (ed.), *Working papers in Southern African Studies 1* (Johannesburg, 1977). Information on Marshall Campbell is based on 'A short sketch of the life of Marshall Campbell' by his niece, Ellen Campbell, KCM 32848, Marshall Campbell Papers, KCAL. For his own views on African government, see Colony of Natal, *Evidence taken before the Natal Native Affairs Commission 1906–7*, 478–82. His relations with the Qadi are dealt with in his correspondence, KCM 32631 and KCM 32632, all in Marshall Campbell Papers, KCAL. See also Osborn, *Valiant harvest*, 238, 243–4 and 252–4. Dube expressed his indebtedness in a letter to Killie Campbell, 24.9.1936, KCM 4330, Correspondence File 12d, Killie Campbell Papers, KCAL. The account of the 1905 conference of the British Association for the Advancement of Science is drawn from *Natal Mercury*, 24.8.1905 and E. Bradlow, 'The British Association's South African meeting, 1905: "the flight to the colonies" and some post Anglo-Boer War problems', *South African Historical Journal* 14, 2002, 42–62. Reports of Qadi participation at Mount Edgecombe are in SNA1/1/229 (2844/1905). It is an informed guess (though highly likely) that the African singer referred to in reports was Nokutela, given Dube's involvement in the event and the fact that no other singer from the area consistently attracted this kind of praise. Gandhi's report of Dube's speech is in *Indian Opinion*, 2.9.1905, although I have had to depend on E.S. Reddy's translation, and not the original, here.

Chapter 6

1 On Sidney Strong's visit to Ohlange, see *Report of the deputation sent by the American Board to its mission in South Eastern Africa in 1903*, AZMP A608, PDNA: *Ilanga*, 12.6. 1903. Information on the Piersons and *Missionary Review* is from D. Robert, *Occupy until I come: A.T. Pierson and the evangelism of the world* (Grand Rapids, 2003), 286. Dube's article, 'Are Negroes better off in Africa?' appeared in *Missionary Review of the World* August 1904, 583–6. Information on S. Parkes Cadman is from Marable, 'African nationalist', 170; there is a biography of Cadman by Fred Hamlin, *S. Parkes Cadman, pioneer radio minister* (New York and London, 1930); however, it is sketchy on dates and events, preferring to focus on ideas and sweeping claims. It does not mention his work on the American Committee. On his role in the eugenics movement, see Christine Rosen, *Preaching eugenics: religious leaders and the American eugenics movement* (New York and Oxford, 2004). Marable has undertaken a most detailed analysis of the role of the American Committee in the survival of Ohlange: see 'African nationalist', chapter 5. Qandeyana Cele's story features in D. Anthony and R. Edgar, 'Religion and the (black) South Atlantic', *Annotation* 30, 1, March 2002, at http://www.archives.gov/nhprc/annotation/march-2002/black-south-atlantic.html. On Lindley Seme, see T.D. Mweli Skota, *The African yearly register* (Johannesburg, 1932), 253. As noted before, it is often extremely difficult to work out the exact dates of many of these periods of study

in America. On Grendon and the editorship of *Ilanga*, see Christison, 'African Jerusalem'. Christison has undertaken a careful textual analysis of *Ilanga*'s English copy during this period. See especially 544–7; the quote is from 545; see also 518. One can only agree with him that there remains the important task of analysing the paper's Zulu editorial copy over a longer period – this has now begun to be addressed in the research of Muzi Hadebe. As far as can be ascertained, R.R.R. Dhlomo, editor of *Ilanga* 1944–63, was the first to name John Mdima as an early editor of the paper: see his interview with Tom Karis, 27.3.1964, 2:XD 20, Reel 9A, Karis-Carter Collection. The *Campania*'s passenger list for the Dubes' voyage is at Ellis Island Records, http://www.ellisisland.org/search/passRecord.asp?MID=0213469589 0137538336&FNM=N&LNM=DUBE&PLNM=DUBE&first_kind=1&last_kind=0&TO WN=null&SHIP=null&RF=2&pID=102505120212 [accessed 22.1.2009].

   2 On the role of transport in Chicago's history (and also the source of the quote about the thunderous city sounds), see 'Chicago, the transit metropolis' at http://americanhistory. si.edu/onthemove/themes/story_45_1.html [accessed 2.4.2010]. On Oak Park, see http:// www.oppl.org/research/ophistory.htm [accessed 2.4.2010]. I am most grateful to Bill Jerousek of the Oak Park Public Library, who sent me much helpful material on the Smiths and their life in Oak Park. See *Oak Leaves*, 1.5.1941, 68 and 26.6.1952, 94; and *Chicago Daily Tribune*, 22.2.1890 and 9.3.1928. On the Smiths' support for Ohlange, see Marable, 'African nationalist', 170 and 178–9. Information on Hull House is from http://www.encyclopedia. chicagohistory.org/pages/615.html [accessed 9.4.2010]. Charles's time at Wilberforce is described in *Ilanga*, 18.11.1904. Dube's correspondence regarding possible African American teachers is at Restriction Department Minute Papers, Volume 32, 1166/1904, National Archives, Pretoria (NAP) – he gave his address on this occasion as 617 Jefferson Avenue, Brooklyn; and Dube to Washington, 21.9.1907, Booker T. Washington Papers online edition, Volume 9, 338–9, at http://www.historycooperative.org/btw/Vol.9/html/338.html. Dube's YMCA talk was reported in the *New York Times*, 9.1.1905; his views on women's status are in 'Practical Christianity among the Zulu', *Monthly Review of the World* 20, 5, May 1907, 371. Sources used on manliness as ideology are J.A. Mangan and J. Walvin (eds.), *Manliness and morality: middle class masculinity in Britain and America, 1800–1940* (New York, 1987) (in which the significance of hunting is discussed) and John Tosh, *Manliness and masculinities in nineteenth-century Britain: essays on gender, family and empire* (Harlow, 2004). Dube's Boston meetings were reported in the *Boston Daily Globe*, 27.2.1905; thanks to Bob Edgar for finding this reference. W.E.B. Du Bois's contact with black South Africans at Wilberforce is recorded in Anthony and Edgar, 'Religion and the (black) South Atlantic'. His 'race' observation is in his 'Of the dawn of freedom' in *The souls of black folk*, 23, and his impatience with Washington is discussed in Moses, *Creative conflict in African American thought*, 203. See *Ilanga*, 18.2.1910 for reference to *The souls of black folk*.

   3 Material on conditions in Natal in the early twentieth century is drawn from Lambert, *Betrayed trust* (the reference to Leuchars is cited on 166) and Marks, *Reluctant rebellion*. A copy of the Mission Reserve Act No. 49 of 1903 is in File 1903, A/2/24, AZMP A608, PDNA. On Mqhawe's refusal to pay the new rent, see SNA I/1/314 (2184/1904) and on his *isibhalo* arrears, see report of Ndwedwe magistrate, 26.10.1905, SNA I/1/329 (2844/1905). Harriette Colenso's commendation is in *Minutes of evidence to the South African Native Affairs Commission 1903–5 Volume 3*, 418. The American Board's criticisms of the Act and rent are expressed in a letter from the Commissioners to the Governor of Natal, 4.5.1906, File 'Correspondence on Report of Under-SNA and the Mission', ISP. Dube's criticisms of the rent are in 'Report of a meeting regarding the disposal of mission reserve funds', ABCSA Volume 22, Reel 196. See also SNA I/1/340 (1617/1906) for evidence of widespread indebtedness on the Inanda Mission Reserve. The Supervisor's attitude to glebe residents is

in 'Weekly report of Mission Reserve Supervisor', 21.1.1905, SNA I/1/316 (191/1905) and the matter of destruction of churches is in Colonial Office Papers, 179/235 (24595), PDNA. Inanda reserve's value is noted in 'Report of Inanda Mission Reserve', 16.3.1904, SNA I/1/319 (871/1905). Madikane's sense of foreboding is taken from his interview with Stuart, 27.5.1905, in Webb and Wright, *The James Stuart Archive 2*, 54. Campbell's and Samuelson's attitude to the poll tax is from Marks, *Reluctant rebellion*, 141 and File 4, 'Bantu Section', Marshall Campbell Papers. Gandhi's views are in *Indian Opinion*, 9.9.1905. Dube's visit to Samuelson is recorded in SNA I/1/345 (2157/1906) and in Annual Report No. 7 to the American Committee. *Ilanga*'s reports of poll tax meetings are from 10.11.1905, translations in SNA I/1/329 (3052/1905).

4 The two works most heavily drawn upon for an overview of the rebellion are Marks, *Reluctant rebellion* and Jeff Guy, *Remembering the rebellion: the Zulu uprising of 1906* (Pietermaritzburg, 2006). Suspected involvement of men on the Qadi farm is recorded in a letter from Charles Colville to SNA, 14.2.1906, SNA I/1/336 (507/1096). Resistance to paying the tax, except to acquire labour passes, is noted in 'Ndwedwe Magistrate's report, February 1906', SNA I/1/283 (119/1906), also the source of the quote. Dube's exhortation to Christians appeared in *Ilanga*, 16.2.1906, as did his report of the meeting between Mqhawe, Winter and Samuelson. Further information on this meeting and its outcome is in SNA I/1/336 (568/1906), SNA I/1/349 (2806/1906) and evidence of George Armstrong to the Natal Native Affairs Commission, 484. On Dube's attitude to the poll tax, see also M. Hadebe, 'Contradictions and perspectives in interpretations: reporting on the *Isidumo sokulwa e Richmond*'. I am grateful to the author for allowing me to see this work in progress. On the Edendale levies, see R.C.A. Samuelson, 'History of the Natal Native Horse' [introduced by S. Spencer], *Natalia* 35, 2005, 1–9. For Dube's views of the levies, see Marks, *Reluctant rebellion*, 335, and confidential correspondence between the Governor of Natal and Lord Selborne, 6.8.1906, GH 579 C.807/1906, Government House Papers, PDNA. Dube's request to Samuelson for assistance in forming a new congress was dated 29.3.1906; this and further correspondence are in SNA I/1/338 (991/1906); his letter requesting a list of chiefs (12.8.1907) is in SNA I/1/375 (2333/1907). The 'Vukani bantu!' editorial appeared in *Ilanga* on 4.5.1906. The whole record of Dube's interview with McCallum and other Natal politicians is in Governor to Secretary of State for the Colonies, Despatch no. 103, 30.5.1906 and Enclosure, CO 179/235 (22646). The follow-up is in Governor to Secretary of State for the Colonies, Despatch no. 128, 21.6.1906 and Enclosure, CO 179/235 (25728). See Odendaal, *Vukani bantu!*, 70, for the reaction of *Izwi Labantu*; and *Natal Mercury*, 6.7.1907 for an impression of *Ilanga*'s circulation. Bryant's account of the devastation in Natal is in a letter to SNA, 8.8.1906, SNA I/1/348 (2635/1906). See also Cd. 3247, SNA I/1/353 (2352/1906), SNA I/1/349 (2806/1906). The effects of the army's behaviour on Gandhi is recorded in his *An autobiography*, 263–4. On the Qwabe role in the rebellion see also M. Mahoney, 'Racial formation and ethnogenesis from below: the Zulu case, 1879–1906', *International Journal of African Historical Studies* 36, 3, 2003, 559–83. Dube's plea for mercy for the Richmond accused is the subject of M. Hadebe, 'Pleading for clemency through poetry: discursive issues in the 1906 poll tax rebellion', Unpublished paper; as before, thanks to the author for permission to use.

5 See Dube, 'Practical Christianity among the Zulus', 372, for his views on the Zulu and salvation, and also *Ilanga*, 14.9.1906, cited in Marks, *Reluctant rebellion*, 358. The quote on different sorts of alliances in early Zulu nationalism is from Wright, 'Reflections on the politics of being Zulu', 38. See also P. La Hausse, '"Death is not the end": Zulu cosmopolitanism and the politics of Zulu cultural revival' in Carton, Laband and Sithole, *Zulu identities*, 256–72. The biographical work of Nxaba, Dhlomo and Zondi is discussed in the Introduction. The

meaning of Mbokodwebomvu is from A. Koopman, *Zulu names* (Pietermaritzburg, 2002), 97 and 105; Muzi Hadebe cautions, however, that the inference of 'blood' may be misleading; a grinding stone could be red for other reasons too, such as the kinds of herbs ground to make medicine (email communication, 10.10.2010). The quote about age-sets is from Bryant, *The Zulu people*, 496. Chief Mangosuthu Buthelezi also noted Dube's and Dinuzulu's membership of this age-set in an address in October 1974 (notes by Reggie Zondi, Uncat MS file, Dube Papers, KCAL). On relations between Dinuzulu and the Qadi chiefs, see 'Report on behaviour of Acting Chief Mandlakayise', 15.8.1911 in CNC 28 (1921/1911) and 'Report of Native Intelligence Officer 1', SNA I/4/5 (28/1898). On the pupil Dinuzulu allegedly sent to Ohlange, see 'Secret report re. John Dube of Inanda Mission Station', December 1902, SNA I/4/12 (6/1903). There is a copy of *The Zulu orthography conference* [report] (Dundee, Natal, 1906) in Box 140 (C1276/15), Colenso Papers A204, PDNA. On this conference see also *Natal Mercury*, 24.8.1905. Rumours about Dube, Mqhawe and Dinuzulu are in *Ilanga*, 2.3.1906, and Guy, *Remembering the rebellion*, 174–5. The closeness between Dube and Dinuzulu is discussed in M. Hadebe, 'A contextualisation and examination of the *impi yamakhanda* (1906 uprising) as reported by J.L. Dube in *Ilanga Lase Natal …*' (MA dissertation, University of Natal, Durban, 2003), 94, and 98–101 on the progress of the entourage. Dinuzulu's reluctance to visit the capital is discussed in Marks, *Reluctant rebellion*, 255–6. There is more detail on the Colensos and the Zulu royal house in Jeff Guy's *The view across the river: Harriette Colenso and the Zulu struggle against imperialism* (London, 2002), and S. Marks, 'Harriette Colenso and the Zulus, 1874–1913', *Journal of African History* 4, 3, 403–11. The account of Siyekiwe's and Mangathi's testimonies is from Guy, *Remembering the rebellion*, 176. Dube's reassurance to Campbell is in an undated letter, KCM32589, File 4, Marshall Campbell Papers. Internal evidence suggests this was written in 1907, rather than at the height of the rebellion; he was possibly referring to agitation for self-government in the Transvaal and OFS. Dube's letter to Dinuzulu, 4.12.1907, is in MJC96/1907, Box 1/7/53, Attorney-General's Office Papers, NAP. It is not clear how this came to be in official files; it may have been intercepted en route, or possibly found among Dinuzulu's possessions when his house was later searched. Information on Dube's fundraising efforts is in his letter to H. Colenso, 16.8.1908, 'Correspondence 1908', Volume 46, Colenso Papers A204, PDNA. On Sir Matthew Nathan, see Marks, *Reluctant rebellion*, 341 and *Australian dictionary of national biography online* at http://adb.online.anu.edu.au/biogs/A100646b.htm. Nathan's visit to Ohlange is related in Cherif Keita's documentary film, *Oberlin-Inanda*; see *Ilanga*, 29.11.1907 for the song composed in his honour. Dube's letter to Washington, 21.9.1907, is in Booker Washington Papers online edition, Volume 9, 338–9. See Dube's testimony in *Evidence taken before the Natal Native Affairs Commission*, 957–63. See also Marks, *Reluctant rebellion*, 358. Dube's article in *Missionary Review of the World* (March 1907) is cited in Marable, 'African nationalist', 214. On Gideon Mvakwendlu Sivetye, see Cd. 3s888, Colonial Office Papers, National Archives, Kew (NAK); on wider effects of the rebellion on Christian communities, see *Ilanga*, 17.8.1906. Mqhawe's death was reported in *Ilanga*, 23.11.1906 and in SNA I/1/356 (3905/1906).

6 On the self-help schemes, see La Hausse, *Restless identities*, 18; and Odendaal, *Vukani bantu!*, 82. On the Zulu Industrial Improvement Company in particular, see *Ilanga*, 24.9.1909, 1.10.1909, 7.10.1910 (in which Wilcox announces he has secured backing in America) and 4.11.1910 as examples. The notion of defence against total hire is Raymond Williams's in *The country and the city* (London, 1973), 102. There is a growing literature on the organisation of the press in the British Empire; see for example S. Potter, *News and the British world: the emergence of an imperial press system, 1876–1922* (Oxford, 2004). This work, however, discusses only the English-language press, and so does not examine the so-called 'alternative [black]

press' in South Africa. On the first attempt to form a press association, see Willan, *Sol Plaatje*, 110 and 119, and Les Switzer, 'The beginnings of African protest journalism at the Cape' in his edited volume *South Africa's alternative press*, 67. Dube's account of his involvement in the later attempt is in a letter to Harriette Colenso, 22.4.1908, Volume 45, Correspondence 1908, Colenso Papers; see also Odendaal, *Vukani bantu!*, 104–5 and Les Switzer and Donna Switzer, *The black press in South Africa and Lesotho: a descriptive bibliographic guide to African, Coloured and Indian newspapers, newsletters and magazines, 1836–1976* (Boston, 1979), available at http://icon.crl.edu/guides/Switzer.pdf). Dube's resignation from the pastorate is in 'General letter for 1908', ABCSA Reel 196, Volume 22; and his call for a walk-out is in *Ilanga*, 15.11.1907, which was discussed by the AZM in a document titled 'Governmental difficulties 1907–8', ABCSA Reel 198, Volume 22. Dube acquired a large, 300-acre block of the farm Piezang River, Inanda, in 1906: see his estate at MSCE 465/46, PDNA. The tension between Dube and Mandlakayise is noted in 'Intelligence Officer Statement', 2.3.1908, SNA I/4/20 (39/1908). On Mandlakayise's status, see CNC 28 (1921/1911). Information on Charles Dube is drawn from his application for exemption, March 1908, SNA I/1/393 (733/1908). John Mdima's photo appeared in *Ilanga*, 10.3.1911. The court case with Tatham was reported in the *Natal Mercury*, 6.7.1907.

Chapter 7

1 There is a succinct list of the recommendations of the Natal Native Affairs Commission 1906 in E. Brookes, *White rule in South Africa 1830–1910* (Pietermaritzburg, 1974), 68–9. Analysis of the ensuing legislation can be found in A. Duminy, 'Towards Union, 1900–1910' in Duminy and Guest, *Natal and Zululand from earliest times to 1910*, 417. On the activities of the Natal Native Congress regarding this legislation, see correspondence and petition in CO179/248 and 'Report of what took place at a meeting of Natives, Kolwas, and others, held at Ladysmith, Thursday 23 July 1908' in SNA I/4/20 (92/1908). On scholars' treatment of early political strategy and tactics, see Limb, *The ANC's early years*, 75. Dube's letter to F.R. Moor, 4.9.1908, as well as follow-up correspondence, is in SNA I/1/411 (2812/1098). The quote about 'combination' is from the Chief Native Commissioner in 1912, cited in P. La Hausse, *Restless identities* (Pietermaritzburg, 2000), 29 (fn 63). On visits to Ohlange arranged by Campbell, see *Ilanga*, 30.10.1908; Dube to Campbell, 29.10.1908, Marshall Campbell Papers, File 4, KCM 32623; and diary entry for 25.10.1908 in P. Lewsen (ed.), *Selections from the correspondence of John X. Merriman 1905–1924 Volume 4* (Cape Town, 1969), 97.

2 Dube's observation about black British subjects as aliens is from *Ilanga*, 2.10.1908, and the Congress petition to the National Convention was printed in *Ilanga*, 13.11.1908. Representatives to the South African Native Convention in May 1909 were listed in *Ilanga*, 2.4.1909; Dube's friendship with Kambule is noted in Christison, 'African Jerusalem', 499–500. The observation that the Bloemfontein Convention was a major step is from Odendaal, *Vukani bantu!*, 168. On Waaihoek, see J. Wells, *We have done with pleading: the women's 1913 anti-pass campaign* (Johannesburg, 1991), 7–9. Dube's speech was reported in *Bloemfontein Post*, 27.3.1909; the same paper carried the resolutions on 29.3.1909. On the election of office-bearers, see *Ilanga*, 9.4.1909; see also Odendaal, *Vukani bantu!*, 198, which is also the source for information on Rubusana (41–3, 262), as are S.J. Ngqongqo, 'Rubusana, one of the greatest', *Daily Dispatch*, 20.4.1998 and his 'Mpilo Walter Benson Rubusana' in Ndletyana, *African intellectuals in 19th and early 20th century South Africa*, 45–54. On Dube's relations with Campbell after his election, see Marable, 'African nationalist', 138–9; and the following correspondence: Dube to Campbell, 10.6.1909, KCM 32602; Tatham, Wilkes and Shaw to Campbell, 29.6.1909, KCM 32631; Campbell to Charles Dube, 15.8.1909, KCM 32605,

all in File 4, Marshall Campbell Papers. On W.P. Schreiner and Union, see E. Walker, *W.P. Schreiner, a South African* (Oxford, 1969), 310–17. Dube's role in the delegation is constructed from Odendaal, *Vukani bantu!*, 185; SNA I/1/435 (1931/1909); and *Cape Times*, 1.7.1909. A copy of Campbell's testimonial, dated 3.7.1909, is at KCM 32604, File 4, Marshall Campbell Papers. Dube's *The Zulu's appeal for light and England's duty* was published in London in 1909. His explanation of its purpose is in Dube to Campbell, 15.6.1909, KCM 32603, File 4, Marshall Campbell Papers (there is a page of this letter missing).

3 The Dubes' departure for London was reported in *Ilanga*, 13.8.1909. For a fuller account of the delegation, see Odendaal, *Vukani bantu!*, chapter 9. On Mangena, see Marks, *Reluctant rebellion*, 363–4; Seme's sketch appeared in *Ilanga*, 14.8.1908. C. Swaisland, 'The Aborigines' Protection Society, 1837–1909', *Slavery and Abolition* 21, 2, 2000, gives a good explanation of its work; the quote is from 265. Information on the church leaders to whom Dube was introduced is taken from the *Oxford dictionary of national biography* (online edition) and Testimonials, C80/94 and C80/95, in MSS Brit Emp S18, ASAPS, Rhodes House, Oxford. The breakfast meeting was reported in *The Times*, 28.7.1909; the quote about the forfeiture of rights is from a letter by Schreiner, published in the same edition. Merriman's attempt to discredit his delegation is cited in Odendaal, *Vukani bantu!*, 219. Schreiner's description of Dube is from Marable, 'African nationalist', 256. See C80/93 and C80/99, MSS Brit Emp S18, for details of the publication of Dube's pamphlet and further support for the Dubes. The report on Olive Schreiner appeared in *Ilanga*, 29.1.1909. Betty Molteno's explanation for her absence from South Africa, as well as her description of Phoenix and the encounter between Schreiner and Gandhi in Cape Town, is from E.S. Reddy, 'Some remarkable European women who helped Gandhiji in South Africa' at http://www.sahistory. org.za/pages/library-resources/articles_papers/remarkable-women-gandhi.html [accessed 11.11.2009]. See also the letter from Alice Greene to Eva Greene, 8.9.1909, in J. Barham (ed.), *The mother and the maiden aunt: letters of Eva and Alice Greene 1909–1912* (Leicester, 2010), 31, for evidence of Molteno's activities in London at this time. The Transvaal re-registration legislation is discussed in S. Bhana, *Gandhi's legacy: the Natal Indian Congress 1894–1994* (Pietermaritzburg, 1997), 22–3, and the *satyagraha* principles are from A.J. Parel, 'The origins of *Hind Swaraj*' in Brown and Prozesky, *Gandhi in South Africa*, 41. The collapse of the campaign is covered in Swan, *Gandhi*, chapter 4. Evidence of Molteno's and Greene's support for Ohlange is in Harris to Buxton, 10.11.1914, D5/1-3, MSS Brit Emp S22. Mrs Dube's record as a passive resistance supporter is in *Indian Opinion*, 5.3.1910. On the Dubes' other fundraising activities in England, see the shortened version of 'The Zulu's appeal' printed by the Anti-Slavery and Aborigines' Protection Society (ASAPS), December 1909, C80/95, MSS Brit Emp S18, ASAPS; *Ilanga*, 29.10.1909, 12.11.1909 and 31.12.1909. For the American leg of this journey, see C80/97, MSS Brit Emp S18, and the Ellis Island passenger list at http://www.ellisisland.org/search/matchMore.asp?FNM=N&LNM=D UBE&PLNM=DUBE&first_kind=1&kind=exact&offset=0&dwpdone=1 for their arrival. *Ilanga*, 2.9.1910, 9.12.1910, 20.1.1911, 3.3.1911 carried information on places they visited (the last-mentioned suggested that Nokutela had not been abroad as long as he, but it is difficult to work out the exact dates of comings and goings: they were certainly fundraising in London together, travelled to America together and returned to Durban together) and Dube's address in Washington was published in W. Hartshorn (ed.), *World-wide Sunday School work: the official report of the World's Sixth Sunday School Convention, held in the city of Washington, USA., May 19–24, 1910* (Chicago, 1910), 297, available from http://www.archive.org/stream/worldwidesundays00worl#page/n3/mode/2up [accessed 31.10.2010]. The incident over discrimination was reported in *Washington Post*, 23.5.1910; many thanks for Bob Edgar for this reference. The suggestion that the American Committee was not quite as active as in

previous years is made in Marable, 'African nationalist', 181–2. The information that Booker Washington finally gave his approval is in Hunt Davis, 'John L. Dube', 508.

4 On Dinuzulu and Botha, see C. de B. Webb and J. Wright (eds.), *A Zulu king speaks: statements made by Cetshwayo kaMpande on the history and customs of his people* (Pietermaritzburg and Durban, 1987), xxix–xxx; Guy, *The view across the river*, 95–101; and J. Laband and P. Thompson, 'The reduction of Zululand, 1878–1904' in Duminy and Guest, *Natal and Zululand from earliest times to 1910*, 211–16. Dube's reaction to Dinuzulu's release was expressed in *Ilanga*, 2.9.1910 and 24.6.1910. Burton's visit to Ohlange was reported in *Ilanga*, 7.10.1910; the quote from his speech is taken from Odendaal, *Vukani bantu!*, 238. Rubusana's election victory and Durban visit were covered in *Ilanga*, 7.10.1910, 28.10.1910 and 11.11.1910. Details of the second and third meetings of the Native Convention are from Odendaal, *Vukani bantu!*, 233–5, 256, 258–9. The reference to land dispossession is from T. Keegan, *Facing the storm: portraits of black lives in rural South Africa* (Cape Town, 1988), 132. Information on Cleopas Kunene's background is from Limb, *The ANC's early years*, 96. On the Universal Races Congress, see S. Pennybacker, 'The Universal Races Congress, London political culture and imperial dissent, 1900–1939', *Radical History Review* 92, 2005, 103–17. On Seme's overseas experiences, see *Ilanga*, 7.10.1910, 20.1.1911 (from which is drawn the 'thrill of happiness' quote) and 3.11.1911, as well as *New York Times*, 15.4.1906. His 'Regeneration' speech is available at http://www.anc.org.za/ancdocs/history/early/regeneration.htm [accessed 20.7.2009]. H. Selby Msimang's early memories are in his manuscript autobiography, 'H. Selby Msimang looks back', SAMP Box 13, SOAS Special Collections. The connections between law and political leadership are explored in L. Kuper, *An African bourgeoisie* (New Haven, 1965), 234; Mangena's early career is covered in *Ilanga*, 22.07.1910; for information on Msimang and Montsioa, see P. Walshe, *The rise of African nationalism in South Africa* (London, 1970), 32, and Skota, *The African yearly register*, 213. Tim Couzens's path-breaking work on H.I.E. Dhlomo, titled *The New African* (Johannesburg, 1985), was the first full discussion of the concept (in a South African setting) of the 'New African' as an expression of cultural modernity. The description of life in Johannesburg in 1910 experienced as a 'maelstrom' is Jonathan Hyslop's, in his 'Gandhi, Mandela and the African modern' in S. Nuttall and A. Mbembe (eds.), *Johannesburg, the elusive metropolis* (Durham, N.C., 2008), 122. The quote about queues at taps is from M. McCord, *The calling of Katie Makanya* (Cape Town, 1995), 203. Schreiner's description is in R. First and A. Scott, *Olive Schreiner* (London, 1980), 234. Other information on living conditions is taken from S. Parnell, 'Race, power and urban control: Johannesburg's inner city slum-yards, 1910–1923', *Journal of Southern African Studies* 29, 3, 2003, 616, from which the description of the city as an industrial hub is drawn, and D. Goodhew, *Respectability and resistance: a history of Sophiatown* (London, 2004), 2–3. On passes, see also Saul Msane and colleagues' evidence to the South African Native Affairs Commission 1904, reproduced in J. Williams, *From the South African past: narratives, documents, and debates* (Boston, 1997), 190–6. The Native Convention's record of thanks for the repatriation of Chinese workers is noted in Odendaal, *Vukani bantu!*, 235.

5 For reports of the Convention's committee meetings, see *Ilanga*, 2.6.1911 and Odendaal, *Vukani bantu!*, 259, which also quotes from Seme's prospectus, 260. On Seme's convening of Congress, see Jordan Ngubane, *Inkundla ya Bantu*, 30.6.1951, item 2:X514:91/2, Seme file, Karis-Carter Papers, and R.V. Selope Thema, 'How Congress began', *Drum* July 1953. For Seme's speech, see Odendaal, *Vukani bantu!*, 273, which also contains the most complete account of the election of office-bearers, 275–6; backgrounds of delegates are from 241–2, and the closing 'trees' remark from 277. See also Skota, *The African yearly register*, 423. The purposes of Congress, as agreed by delegates, are summarised from Willan, *Sol Plaatje*,

155. Dube's visit to Johannesburg was reported in *Ilanga*, 12.1.1912. The quote concerning substance and show, though not about Seme, seems apt under the circumstances; it is from Walker, *W.P. Schreiner*, 111. Dube's reasons for non-attendance are in his acceptance address; the copy consulted here is in CNC 59 (214/1912). Some sources give the reason that he had fallen from a horse – this in fact happened some weeks later (*Ilanga*, 24.5.1912). Nokutela's participation in the AZM anniversary is in Wood, *Shine where you are*, 70.

Chapter 8

1 For Dube's campaign meetings in Natal, see *Natal Mercury*, 12.4.1912 (Union Theatre meeting); Statement by James Majozi, 6.5.1912 (Pietermaritzburg meeting) and Magistrate to CNC, 7.5.1912 (Mthwalume meeting); 'Report of meeting at Mazihila's Kraal', 12.4.1913 (Ngwenya's meeting), all in CNC 62 (338/1912). On Zibisi, see CNC to SNA, 21.3.1913. His description of Dube being their gate post is in Informer to C. Faye, Eshowe, 8.7.1912 – all in CNC 62 (338/1912). Accusations that Dube was misusing meetings are in Acting CNC to Dube, 20.6.1912; his denial is in Dube to Acting CNC, 21.6.1913 and Dube to Burton, 18.6.1912; and the quote that he was threatening whites' safety is from Memo, 'Re Dube's meetings', all of these in CNC 62 (338/1912). The poem on Dube's fall, by a pupil of Ohlange, is in *Ilanga*, 24.5.1912, and the fact that it interfered with his attending the Select Committee is recorded in Memo to CNC, via Empangeni, 5.5.1912, CNC 62 (338/1912). On the Natal Native Congress 'unity' meeting, see *Ilanga*, 26.4.1913. Evidence of subsequent tension between Dube and Lutuli is in Dube to Acting CNC, 24.2.1912 and 21.5.1912, in CNC 62 (338/1912). Their church work is noted in 'General letter of the AZM, 1899–1900', ABCSA Reel 196, Volume 22. On Congress's delegation to Burton and Dower, see Willan, *Sol Plaatje*, 155–7, which also notes Plaatje's contacts in government (48–9, 147). For issues they discussed, see C. Walker, *Women and resistance in South Africa* (London, 1982), 27, on passes for women; and on the 'black peril', see C. van Onselen, *Studies in the social and economic history of the Witwatersrand 1886–1914, Volume 2: New Nineveh* (Johannesburg, 1982), 45–54; and on train conditions, see G. Pirie, 'Racial segregation on South African trains, 1910–1928: entrenchment and protest', *South African Historical Journal* 20, 1988, 75–93. Dube's permission to hold meetings is in CNC 56 (151/1912). Merriman's description is in his diary entry for 14.3.1912 in Lewsen, *Selections from the correspondence of John X. Merriman*, 217.

2 The quote on the significance of the Land Act is from W. Beinart and S. Dubow, 'Introduction' in their (eds.), *Segregation and apartheid in twentieth century South Africa* (London, 1995), 3. It was Rubusana's view that the purpose of the Land Act was to mollify Hertzog supporters: see S. Plaatje, *Native life in South Africa* (Johannesburg, 1982), 201, also in which the Act is reproduced in full, 61–9. The Act's rapid passage through parliament is noted in H. Feinberg, 'The 1913 Natives Land Act in South Africa: politics, race and segregation in the early 20th century', *International Journal of African Historical Studies* 26, 1, 1993, 68. Schreiner's reaction is recorded in 'Natives Land Act No. 27 of 1913 – Native protest', in G203, S22, ASAPS Papers; and *Indian Opinion*'s response is noted in Dhupelia-Mesthrie, *Gandhi's prisoner?*, 111. On other aspects of the Act, see 'Natives' Land Act 1913', Circular letter SNA to Magistrates and Native Commissioners, CO 551/65/20147, NAK. Possessory segregation was a term coined by Edgar Brookes in *The history of native policy in South Africa* (Pretoria, 1927). The quote about Van Riebeeck's hedge is from T.R.H. Davenport and K. Hunt, *The right to the land* (Cape Town, 1974), 32. Dube's views on separation are in his 'Segregation', in *A national symposium: special articles on South African subjects* (Durban, 1912), copy in News Cuttings Book 23, KCAL. Burton's reply to his query is in Feinberg, 'The 1913 Land Act', 88; and Schreiner's and Solomon's views are cited in Walker, *W.P.*

Schreiner, 345. The record of Dube's Eshowe meeting is to be found in C. Faye, *Zulu references for interpreters and students* (Pietermaritzburg, 1922). The uSuthu presence is noted in District Native Commissioner to CNC, 10.12.1912, CNC 62 (338/1912). Information on Gokhale is taken from S.A. Wolpert, *Tilak and Gokhale: revolution and reform in the making of modern India* (Los Angeles, 1962). His visit to Ohlange and other activities in South Africa are documented in Dhupelia-Mesthrie, *Gandhi's prisoner?*, 104, and Swan, *Gandhi*, 235. Other information on Ohlange is from *Ilanga*, 26.12.1912; *Diamond Fields Advertiser*, 26.2.1914. Merriman's impressions are in Lewsen, *Selections*, 220. Dube's address in Cape Town was reported in detail in *Cape Times*, 5.7.1912.

3 Dinuzulu's death and funeral are discussed in Cope, *To bind the nation*, 38–41 and 50. Dube's reports to Durban workers are recorded in Grimaldi to Chief Magistrate, Durban, 29.10.1913, CNC 62 (338/1912). On preparations for the Congress deputation in May, see *Ilanga*, 7.2.1913, which notes Dube's detention at Van Reenen; see also CNC 107 (160/1913). (On the Inter-State Native College, see Odendaal, *Vukani bantu!*, 66–7, 269–70.) Dube's Ixopo meeting and the source of the 'greyhound' quote are in 'Report of meeting at Ixopo, 11.3.1913', CNC 62 (338/1912). Attempts to prevail on Lord Gladstone are noted in Plaatje, *Native life*, 201 and Westermeyer to Wanless, 26.7.1913, CNC 62 (338/1912). On the Cape Town meetings, see H. Selby Msimang to Harris, 13.10.1913, G203/S22 and Plaatje, *Native life*, 200–1. Merriman's impressions of Dube are in Lewsen, *Selections*, 252, and of the deputation's response of the Act on 252. On Congress information-gathering on the effects of the Land Act, the best source is of course Plaatje's *Native life*. See also 'H. Selby Msimang looks back', an autobiographical reminiscence, MS380241, Box 13, Southern African Materials Project (SAMP), School of Oriental and African Studies, London. Dube's own efforts to list cases of hardship are noted in there (205–7), which is also the source of the quote regarding his views on the eviction of tenants. Charles van Onselen's remarkable biography of Kas Maine, *The seed is mine: the life of Kas Maine* (Cape Town, 1996), also discusses the 'great rural spasm' (50) of mass evictions in some detail. The deputation to F.S. Malan is discussed in Willan, *Sol Plaatje*, 163–4. Harriette Colenso's caveat is in H. Colenso to Dube, 30.8.1913, Box 138, Colenso Papers, PDNA; on the Swazi Queen's involvement in *Abantu-Batho* see Limb, *The ANC's early years*, 118. My source of information on the white workers' strike of 1913–14 is J. Hyslop, *Notorious syndicalist: J.T. Bain, a Scottish rebel in colonial South Africa* (Johannesburg, 2004), chapter 17, and for Congress's reaction, see Willan, *Sol Plaatje*, 162–3 and Limb, *The ANC's early years*, 127–8. Dube's views on white miners were in an article he wrote for *Missionary Review of the World*, cited in A. Gerard, *Four African literatures* (Berkeley, 1971), 206. Gandhi's 1913–14 *satyagraha* campaign is covered in S. Bhana and G. Vahed, *The making of a political reformer: Gandhi in South Africa 1893–1914* (New Delhi, 2005), chapter 5; strikers' actions at Mount Edgecombe and the Verulam areas are recorded in William Campbell to Marshall Campbell, 1.12.1913, KCM 32528, File 3, Marshall Campbell Papers. Dube's account of and reactions to the Phoenix incident are cited in E.S. Reddy, *Gandhiji's Vision of a Free South Africa* (New Delhi, 1995), chapter 4. Reddy used an account which Dube gave to W. Pearson, who visited him at Ohlange in early 1914, accompanied by Phoenix resident R.M. Patel. Patel later published this conversation in his *Gandhijini Sadhana*, published in Gujarati in India in 1939.

4 A copy of 'Petition to the Prime Minister, from the Rev. John L. Dube, President of the South African Native National Congress, 14 February, 1914', as well as Dower's response, can be found in CO 551/64 (20147), NAK. Dube's 'root and branch' expression is in Dube to Buxton, 1.9.1913, D2/4, S22, ASAPS. Mini's advocacy of a separation of the 'black house' is in CNC to SNA 21.2.1914, CNC 62 (338/1912); other evidence can be found in La Hausse, *Restless identities*, 15–16 and Cope, *To bind the nation*, 34. Preparations for the London trip

are detailed in Dube to Buxton, 1.9.1913 and 24.10.1913; Buxton to Schreiner, 13.11.1913 and Buxton to H.S. Msimang, 2.1.1914, all in G203,S22, ASAPS (on seeking the help of the ASAPS: for a clear explanation of the Society's position, see B. Willan, 'The Anti-Slavery and Aborigines' Protection Society and the South African Natives' Land Act of 1913', *Journal of African History* 20, 1, 1979, 83–102); Plaatje, *Native life*, 217 (for Dower's visit to Kimberley) and *Diamond Fields Advertiser*, 2.3.1914 (for Dube's views on acceptable land separation). For other aspects of the Kimberley meeting, see *Diamond Fields Advertiser*, 18.2.1914 (Plaatje's letter) and 3.3.1914 (Cele's account of money raised); the Reuter's report, 27.2. 1914 is in G203/S22. For more on Elka Cele, see the obituary in *Ilanga*, 17.8.1923. Dube's doubts about the deputation are recorded in Dube to Merriman, 6.5.1914, Item 236, Merriman Papers, National Library, Cape Town (NLCT). Botha's impressions are in Botha to Merriman, 8.5.1914, Item 241, Merriman Papers; and Merriman's notes on his interview with Dube are enclosed with Merriman to Botha, 11.5.1914, Item 244, Merriman Papers. I am extremely grateful to Melanie Geustyn for arranging copies of all these documents. See Bole, Prime Minister's Office, to Stanley, Government House, 4.3.1914, GG 1542 (50/403), NAP, for Dube's confidence to Dower. For official last-minute attempts to pressure Congress to call off the deputation, see Dube to Merriman, 6.6.1914, Item 236, Merriman Papers; *Cape Times*, 16.5.1914; and Plaatje, *Native life*, 220–2. Rider Haggard's record of his interview with Dube is in his *Diary of an African journey: the return of Rider Haggard*, edited with an Introduction by S. Coan (Pietermaritzburg, 2000), 229–30; see Coan's 'Introduction' to this volume for background information. On Dube's YMCA meeting, see report of C. Faye, 14.4.1914, CNC 62 (338/1912); and evidence of the willingness of ordinary people to give money towards the deputation is in CNC to SNA 9.7.1914, NTS 7664 (40/332), NAP.

5 The support of the South African Society for the deputation is recorded in White to Buxton, 16.5.1914, G203/S22. On the deputation's main business of pleading with Harcourt, see Dube to Buxton, 22.10.1913, Dube and Rubusana, 'Natives' Land Act – No. 27 of 1913: Native protest'; Dube and others to Harcourt, 15.6.1914; Buxton to Dube, 30.6.1914; Harris to Dube, 22.6.1914; Harris to Under-Secretary of State, 6.7.1914, all in G203, S22, ASAPS, as well as Plaatje, *Native life*, chapter 16. On their dealings with the press, see Harris to Dube, 29.6.1914, 2.7.1914, 9.7.1914 and 14.7.1914; and Dube to Buxton, 1.7.1914 (for the Reuters statement), all in G203, S22, ASAPS. Examples of press coverage can be found in the *Daily Chronicle*, 6.7.1914 and the *Manchester Guardian*, 6.7.1914; Harris's congratulatory note is in Harris to Dube, 14.7.1914, D3/11, S22, ASAPS. On Dube's sudden departure, see Dube to Buxton, 22.7.1914, G203, S22, ASAPS, and Plaatje to S.J. Colenso, 31.8.1914, Box 54, Colenso Papers, PDNA; Plaatje also discusses the others' fate in this letter. Their position is also raised in Harris to Dube, 16.10.1914; Harris to Wynne, 28.8.1914, Buxton to Dube, 19.10.1914 and Bradford to Buxton, 19.10.1916, all in G203, S22, ASAPS. On the 'Rhodesian business', see Buxton to Morgan, 9.9.1914, D3/11, S22, ASAPS; Harris to Buxton, 10.11.1914, D5/1-3, S22, ASAPS; and Harris to Dube, 9.10.1914, G203, S22, ASAPS. See also T. Ranger, *The African voice in Southern Rhodesia* (London, 1970), 64–6 and Willan, 'The Anti-Slavery and Aborigines' Protection Society', 90–2. *The struggle for mastery in Europe* is of course the title of A.J. P. Taylor's classic work (Oxford, 1954) and the other useful source on the outbreak of the First World War consulted is K. Robbins, *The First World War: the outbreak, events and aftermath* (Oxford, 1984). Congress's decision to suspend agitation is in Dube and Seme, telegram to Minister for Native Affairs, 6.8.1914, file 187/1217/14, Government Native Labour Bureau (GNLB), NAP. On Dube's post-London meetings, see reports of 4.9.1914 and 7.11.1914, and his attempt to explain how far away the war was is in CNC to SNA, 11.9.1914, all in CNC 62 (338/1912).

6 The account of the female student and the baby at Ohlange is in Harris to Buxton, 10.11.1914, 11.11.1914 and 15.11.1914, all in D5/1-3, S22, ASAPS. The version of *The history of Rasselas* consulted is D. Greene (ed.), *The Oxford authors: Samuel Johnson* (Oxford, 1984); the quote is from 366. Nokutela's essay was the one published in *Rice County Journal*, June 1882. Marable thought the adopted girls were called Lillian and Norah, but it seems one was called Violet: see *Ilanga*, 12.2.1904. The earlier rumour about Dube is in SNA 1/4/12 (9/1903). The phrase 'code of privacy' is Michael Holroyd's, from his *Basil Street Blues* (London, 1999), 142. Information on 1914 Sophiatown is from M. Hart and G. Pirie, 'The sight and soul of Sophiatown', *Geographical Review* 74, 1, 1984, 39. Dube's application for extension of his exemption certificate is in file 247 (257/16), GNLB; his office address is in a notice regularly appearing in *Ilanga* in these years; see for example 28.7.1916. An overview of the problems confronting Congress in the war years can be found in Walshe, *The rise of African nationalism in South Africa*, 205. A more nuanced examination can be found in J. Starfield, '"Not quite history": the autobiographies of H. Selby Msimang and R.V. Selope Thema and the writing of South African history', *Social Dynamics* 14, 2, 1988, 26–7. The ANC's 1919 constitution is reproduced in Johns III, *Protest and hope 1883–1934*, 76–82. For Seme's Farmers' Association, see interview with H. Selby Msimang, MS380077, Box 3, SAMP; *Cape Times*, 17.3.1917; H. Feinberg and A. Horn, 'South African territorial segregation: new data on African farm purchases, 1913–1936', *Journal of African History* 50, 2009, 41–60; R. Morrell, '"Pipping a little game in the bud": Pixley kaIsaka Seme, land purchase and rural differentiation in the eastern Transvaal', paper to History Workshop, University of the Witwatersrand, 1987; La Hausse, *Restless identities*, 18; and notices that appeared in *Ilanga* through these years, e.g. 18.6.1916. Ngazana Luthuli featured in a story in *Ilanga*, 16.11.1911; his background is also detailed in Skota, *The African yearly register*, 174, and Jordan Ngubane, 'Three famous African journalists I knew', *Inkundla yabantu* 121, 1946 (from which the 'loyalty' quote comes). His career on the paper is discussed by R.R.R. Dhlomo in his interview with Tom Karis, Edendale, 27.3.1964, 2:XD 20: 96/2 and Jordan Ngubane in *Inkundla yaBantu*, February 1946, 2: XD 20: 91/2; both these sources are on Reel 9A of the Karis-Carter Papers. See Couzens, *The New African*, 48, for a schoolboy reminiscence of having helped in the production of *Ilanga*. The arrival of white teachers is covered in *Ilanga*, 21.1.1916 and 28.1.1916; intentions for the school are discussed in Pim to Harris, 31.1.1922, G190, S22, ASAPS. Information on Reuben Caluza is in Erlmann, 'Reuben T. Caluza and early popular music', 176. Dube's recruitment efforts are discussed in A. Grundlingh, *Fighting their own war: South African blacks and the First World War* (Johannesburg, 1987), 58, 61. Cope, *To bind the nation*, 75–8, discusses Solomon's status in relation to recruitment. See Dube's appeal in *Ilanga*, 20.10.1916. The rumour concerning a German landing in St Lucia is in Limb, *The ANC's early years*, 216, which also contains information on Dube's recruitment efforts.

7 Dube's evidence to the Beaumont Commission is in *Minutes of evidence to the Natives Land Commission*, UG22-16 [including UG22-14], 555–62. Congress's official response to its report, 'Resolution against the Natives Land Act 1913 and the Report of the Natives Land Commission', can be found in G203/S22. Reports of the rowdy Natal Congress meeting are in Statement by Induna, 5.6.1914 and CNC to SNA, 19.6.1914, in CNC 62 (338/1912). On Gumede's action, see CNC 219 (1493/1915) and on a united front restored, see *Ilanga*, 12.5.1916. Dube's likening his lateness to a dog's tail is in NAD to CNC, 1.11.1916, CNC 47 (1179/1916), and his remarks concerning his exclusion from the City Hall are in a Report of 15.8.1916, CNC 247 (1170.1916); the description of the building is Haggard's, *African journey*, 234. On the Council's new advisory committee, see file 1/2/9/1/1, 3/DBN (Town Clerk's Records), DDNA and La Hausse, *Restless identities*, 54–6. Nokutela's death and funeral were covered in *Ilanga*, 2.2.1917; the record of her burial plot is in the Brixton Cemetery Burial Register, held at the Braamfontein Cemetery; many thanks to the Manager of Johannesburg's Parks and Gardens, Alan Buff, for generous help in locating this as well as attempts to locate the site itself. Lessing's observation is from her *Under my skin: volume one of my autobiography, to 1949* (London, 1995), 12. Dube's oration against the 1917 Bill was issued as a pamphlet, 'Extraordinary meeting of the South African Native National Congress, 16 February 1917 in Pretoria'; it was reproduced in full in *Ilanga*, 23.2.1917. The letter that Selope Thema read out was from Buxton, 29.3.1917. This and his reply to Buxton detailing its effects as well as Congress's final word on the 1917 Bill, 15.8.1917, are in G203, S22, ASAPS. See J. Harris, 'General Botha's native land policy', *Journal of the Royal African Society* 16, 61, 1916, 7–15, for Harris's position. Dube's request for funds was published on a number of occasions; see, for example, 15.6.1917, and notice of the special meeting to elect new office-bearers appeared in *Ilanga*, 8.6.1917.

Chapter 9

1 Paul La Hausse has written extensively on Durban in the early twentieth century. On the Durban System and the city's population growth, see especially P. La Hausse, 'The message of the warriors: the ICU, the labouring poor and the making of a popular political culture in Durban, 1925–1930' in P. Bonner et al. (eds.), *Holding their ground* (Johannesburg, 1989), 19–58; and P. La Hausse, 'The struggle for the city: alcohol, the Ematsheni and popular culture in Durban, 1902–1936' in Maylam and Edwards, *The people's city*. On Durban's growth, see also M.H. Alsop, *The population of Natal* (London, 1952), 80. Women servants' behaviour at the beachfront is discussed in Beach Superintendent to Town Clerk, 12.2.1914, File 4/1/2/426, 3/DBN, DDNA. Marwick's efforts to enforce regulations, especially against typhus, are described in Marwick to Town Clerk, 12.3.1918, File 467a, 4/1/2/1223, 3/DBN. Reconstruction of the incident that led to Dube's naming Marwick 'Mubi' has been based on information in 'Marwick versus Dube, Judgment of the Court' in File 467a, 4/1/2/1223, 3/DBN; *Ilanga*, 16.2.1917 (a copy of Bryant's translation is in the court judgment); Marwick to Town Clerk, 9.3.1917, File 467a, 4/1/2/1223, 3/DBN; and KwaMuhle Museum, 'Phikankani kaSitheku kaMpande' [pamphlet] (Durban, n.d.). An example of lists of donations to Dube's fine fund can be found in *Ilanga*, 12.10.1917. The follow-up incident, in which Dube likened Marwick to a snake, was reported in the *Natal Advertiser*, 26.2.1918; his letter to its editor appeared in *Natal Advertiser*, 5.3.1918 and the denial in *Ilanga* appeared on 8.3.1918. Marwick's attempt to pursue another case is noted in Marwick to Town Clerk, 12.3.1918, File 467a, 4/1/2/1223, 3/DBN. On the countrywide anti-pass campaigns at this time, see Roux, *Time longer than rope*, 113–21, and Limb, *The ANC's early years*, 213. Dube's attack on the Land Act is in *Minutes of evidence of the Natal Natives Land Committee* (UG 35-18), 99–101; information on Wilcox's last South African scheme and his departure is from *Ilanga*, 19.4.1918 and email communication with Cherif Keita, 19.9.2006, for which I am most grateful. See also Cherif Keita's film, *Cemetery stories: a rebel missionary in South Africa* (2009), a documentary charting William and Ida Belle Wilcox's work in southern Africa.

2 Dube's national roles in Congress are noted in *Ilanga*, 10.6.1921 and 9.6.1922. Since its publication in 1930, there have been a number of editions of *Mhudi*. See for example the edition with an introduction by Tim Couzens (Cape Town, 1996). On the 1919 Congress delegation, see Willan, *Sol Plaatje*, 233–46. On relations between Dube and Gumede, see R. van Diemel, *In search of 'freedom, justice and fair play': Josiah Tshangana Gumede 1867–1946* (Belhar, 2001), 43–5, and for an excellent overview of Congress politics in Natal through these years, see Marks, *The ambiguities of dependence in South Africa*, especially chapter 2.

On the *Mendi* disaster, see Grundlingh, *Fighting their own war*, 93–6. The cabinet minister's undertaking to Plaatje is recorded by Walshe, *The rise of African nationalism in South Africa*, 62; Woodrow Wilson's famous pledge is taken from Gerhardie, *God's fifth column*, 264. For the ricksha pullers and their dispute, I have depended heavily on R. Posel, 'The Durban ricksha pullers' "strikes" of 1918 and 1930', paper presented to the Conference of the History of Natal and Zululand, University of Natal, 1985, 1–4, and Posel's 'Amahashi: the ricksha-pullers of Durban' in Maylam and Edwards, *The people's city*, 202–21. The close connection between Nonconformism and socialism was posited by Yvonne Kapp in her *Eleanor Marx 1* (London, 1972), 267. For Dube's later campaigns on behalf of workers, see Cope, *To bind the nation*, 98–9; P. Maylam, 'The struggle for space in twentieth-century Durban' in Maylam and Edwards, *The people's city*, 10; Limb, *The ANC's early years*, 135 and 214; and T. Nuttall, 'The leaves in the trees are proclaiming our slavery: African trade-union organisation, 1937–1949' in Maylam and Edwards, *The people's city*, 181. The generally more radical post-war atmosphere is well captured in D. Hemson, 'In the eye of the storm: dock workers in Durban' in Maylam and Edwards, *The people's city* (from which the term 'extra-contractual element' is drawn, 151); B. Hirson and G.A. Williams, *The delegate for Africa: David Ivon Jones 1883–1924* (London, 1995), 171–7; and P. Bonner, 'The Transvaal Native Congress, 1917–1920: the radicalisation of the black petty bourgeoisie on the Rand' in S. Marks and R. Rathbone, *Industrialisation and social change in South Africa: African class formation, culture and consciousness 1870–1930* (London, 1982), 270–313.

3 For the expansion and development of the Ohlange campus, see R.T. Bokwe, 'Our high schools: Ohlange', *Natal Native Teachers' Journal* 4, 4, 1925, 201–2 and on financial constraints preventing the enrolment of girls, see *Ilanga*, 21.1.1921. Its wartime finances are discussed in Pim to Harris, 31.1.1922, G191A, S22, ASAPS, and the quote about Campbell balancing the budget is Dube's own words, in *Ilanga*, 5.6.1937. Information on fees is from Charles Dube, 'Difficulties of boarding masters', *Natal Native Teachers' Journal* October 1921, 5. The later work of the American Committee is discussed in Marable, 'African nationalist', 171. Dube's call for assistance, 'Mafukuzela's request', began in *Ilanga*, 5.12.1919. Dube's protest against the 'intolerable' 1917 Bill is in 'Extraordinary meeting of the South African Native National Congress, 16 February 1917 in Pretoria'. The 'highpoint' description of the 1920 Act is Saul Dubow's, cited in C. Higgs, *The ghost of equality: the public lives of D.D.T. Jabavu of South Africa, 1885–1959* (Athens, Ohio University Press, 1997), 95. Its key provisions are taken from the description in Walshe, *The rise of African nationalism*, 100. Dube's enthusiastic welcome for the Act is in his evidence, 14.6.1920, in *Evidence taken before the Select Committee on Native Affairs* [SC6A-20]. UNIA's constitution is cited in Moses, *Creative conflict in African American thought*, 244. The significance of the 'Look up' injunction is discussed in Hill, 'General introduction', xli–xlvi. Discussion of the Black Star Steamship Line (including its financial difficulties) and Garvey's appointment as 'Provisional President' is in T. Martin, *Race first: the ideological and organisational struggles of Marcus Garvey and the Universal Negro Improvement Association* (Dover, Mass., 1976), 151–73 and 12. Martin is also the source of information on Bruce's role in UNIA, 43 and 93. The best overview of the reception of Garveyism in South Africa remains R. Hill and G. Pirio, '"Africa for the Africans": the Garvey movement in South Africa, 1920–1940' in S. Marks and S. Trapido (eds.), *The politics of race, class and nationalism in twentieth century South Africa* (London, 1987), 209–53; the 'black government' quote is on 236. The most complete treatment of James Thaele is A. Kemp and R. Vinson, '"Poking holes in the sky": Professor James Thaele, American Negroes and modernity in 1920s segregationist South Africa', *African Studies Review* 43, 1, 141–59. On the Israelites at Bulhoek see also R. Edgar, *Because they chose the plan of God: the story of the Bulhoek massacre* (Johannesburg, 1988). The Natal Congress meeting addressed by Moses is

covered in Hill and Pirio, '"Africa for the Africans"', 211–12 (they discuss Wallace on 239) and La Hausse, *Restless identities*, 69. The Dundee meeting is noted at 'Report of meeting 4.2.1921', CNC 344 (21/1919). See David Cannadine's *Ornamentalism: how the British saw their Empire* (London, 2002) for his elaboration of this concept. Still an indispensable study of J.E.K. Aggrey is Edwin Smith's *Aggrey of Africa* (London, 1929); the piano quote is cited on 123. There is an example of his correspondence with Bruce, 28.6.1922, in P. Newkirk (ed.), *Letters from black America: intimate portraits of the African American experience* (Boston, 2009), 332–4. His anti-Garvey remarks are cited in Martin, *Race first*, 138 and his visits to Inanda, Ohlange and Durban were reported in *Ilanga*, 21.4.1921. The description of Aggrey as a 'luminary' is from Skota, *The African yearly register*, 3. The quote from C.T. Loram's *The education of the South African Native* (London, 1917) is on 127. Dube's approach to him is noted in Pim to Harris, 31.1.1922, G190, S22, ASAPS. See also R. Hunt Davis, 'Charles T. Loram and an American model for African education in South Africa', *African Studies Review* 19, 2, 1976, 87–99, and A. Cobley, *Class and consciousness: the black petty bourgeoisie in South Africa, 1924–1950* (New York, 1990), 84–5. Charles Dube's presidential address is from the *Natal Native Teachers' Journal* October 1920, 4–6. The Commission's report was published as Thomas Jesse Jones, *Education in Africa: a study of West, South, and Equatorial Africa by the African Education Commission, under the auspices of the Phelps–Stokes Fund and Foreign Mission Societies of North America and Europe* (New York, 1922), and is available from http:// openlibrary.org/books/OL7078088M/Education_in_Africa [accessed 13.2.2011]; the quote is from 194. Luthuli's accusation comes from his *Let my people go*, 34; and *Ilanga's* verdict appeared in the edition of 17.6.1921.

4 Du Bois's denunciation of Garveyism is cited in Martin, *Race first*, 289. For an overview of Du Bois's organisation of the 1921 Congress, see I. Geiss, *The Pan-African movement* (London, 1968), 237–48. (There is a note on 241 about the presence of wives of male delegates.) Plaatje's connections to Du Bois are explored in Willan, *Sol Plaatje*, 271–3. The resolutions of the London Congress were reproduced in the NAACP's *Crisis*, 23, 1, November 1921 and can be found at http://www.archive.org/stream/crisis2324dubo#page/n17/mode/2up [accessed 1.3.2011]; see also Geiss, *The Pan-African movement*, 244–5. Dube explained his invitation in a letter to Merriman, 24.8.1921, doc. 354, Merriman Papers; the poem wishing him well on his journey by A.F. Matibela appeared in *Ilanga*, 2.12.1921. John and Angelina's marriage year was given as 1919 in their will, but was reported in *Ilanga* on 6.8.1920; on the ground that the paper is unlikely to have been a year out, its date has been adopted here. The report on Roosboom as a 'black spot' appeared in *Sunday Tribune*, 19.5.1985. On Angelina's background, see J. Ngubane, *An African explains apartheid* (London 1963), 36; A. Manson and D. Collins, interview with Angelina Dube, Inanda, 8.3.1979, KCAV116, KCAL; H. Hughes interview with Angelina Dube, Inanda, 5.8.1979; H. Hughes interview with Junerose Nala, Durban, 7.2.1999; H. Hughes interview with Zenzele Dube, Durban, 3.7.2004; and H. Hughes interview with Lulu Dube, Inanda, 5.9.2005. Information on Ivy Goba supplied by Trueman Goba in Prologue to Presidential Address, SA Institution of Civil Engineering, 2002, at www.civils.org.tgpa.pdf [accessed 23.6.2003]. The details of their children are drawn from their will at MSCE 465/46 (Deceased Estates), PDNA. Sources consulted on Wilberforce Institute are H. Hughes, 'Black mission to South Africa' (Honours dissertation, University of the Witwatersrand, 1976); and G.Z. Lethoba, 'The African Methodist Episcopal Church in South Africa', unpub. MS (Evaton, c.1967). On David Opperman at Ohlange, see *Ilanga*, 8.1.1915; on the Opperman family, see H. Hughes, 'Black mission'. In a speech in 1926, Dube alluded to a trip to Holland and Norway: 'Address by the Rev. John L. Dube as representing the Native viewpoint' in *The clash of colour* (Amanzimtoti, 1926), 8. Dube's initial letter to Harris concerning Ohlange is 6.10.1921 (his pamphlet is enclosed); Harris's investigations

are in his letter to Pim, March 1922; Pim's report is in Pim to Harris, 31.1.1922, which also contains the 'few Europeans' reference to Le Roy. Pim to Dube, 5.6.1922, contains the first set of proposals put to him. Dube's response is in Dube to Wheelwright, 14.6.1922, from which the 'top dog' and 'disintegrate the only institution' quotes are drawn. Pim to Harris, 21.1.1922, discusses reference councils. Pim's description of Dube's character is in Pim to Harris, 4.12.1923. The quote about 'weakness in money matters' is in Harris to Buxton, 10.1.1922. All the aforementioned correspondence is in G191A, S22, ASAPS, as is the deed of trust, 26.2.1924. The observation that the property was mortgage-free is in 'Statement adopted by the committee meeting, 8.12.1925' in G191B, S22, ASAPS. The full list of members of the London reference committee is in Harris to Dube, 13.10.1926 and the donation from the Rhodes Trust is noted in Harris to Loring, 7.9.1926, both in G192, S22, ASAPS. Information on Charles Dube is from Skota, *The African yearly register*, 147 and K. E. Flint, *Healing traditions: African medicine, cultural exchange and competition in South Africa, 1820–1948* (Athens, Ohio, 2008), 172. Information on A.C. Maseko is in Karis interview with R.R.R. Dhlomo, March 1964, 2:XD20:96/1, Karis-Carter Papers. (Maseko had been boarding master and choir master at Ohlange; in the 1960s, he was working for a government parastatal in Durban.) The 'Great Bantu Institution' advertisement appeared regularly in *Ilanga*; see for example 11.12.1931. Doke acknowledges Dube's assistance with his research in the 'Introduction' to his *The phonetics of the Zulu language* [Special edition of *Bantu Studies* 11, July 1926], 12–13. The Dubes' welcome reception was reported in *Ilanga*, 12.5.1922. On Sibusisiwe Makhanya, see S. Marks, *Not either an experimental doll: the separate worlds of three South African women* (Durban and Pietermaritzburg, 1987); information on Bertha Mkhize is drawn from interview H. Hughes with Bertha Mkhize, Inanda, 2.5.1981. The 'Isita' editorial in *Ilanga* appeared on 15.6.1917. It is now extremely hard to locate a first edition of *Isita somuntu nguye uqobo lwakhe* (Pietermaritzburg, 1922). A second edition was published under the same name (Mariannhill, 1928) and has been used here. See N.N. Dhlomo, 'The theory, value and practice of translation with reference to John L. Dube's texts *Isita somuntu nguye uqobo lwakhe* (1928) and *Ukuziphatha kahle* (1935)' (MA thesis, University of Durban-Westville, 1996). La Hausse argues a forceful case that *Isita* was a reaction to Petros Lamula's recently published guide to redemptive self-help, *Ukuzaka kwaBantu*, to quash any pretentions to influence that Lamula might have had. See his *Restless identities*, especially chapter 2.

5 On the Durban Joint Council, see 'Report of the Durban Joint Council of Europeans and Natives from its formation to 1925', File Cd. 3.2, Joint Council Papers, AD1433, HPCW. On the Native Affairs Reform Association, see *Ilanga*, 28.1.1921 and 4.3.1921. Dube's report on the London Congress is in 'Confidential police report', 6.7.1922, 359 (142/24/110) GNLB. On Samuel Simelane and the meaning of the term Inkatha, see Cope, *To bind the nation*, 105–8; and Marks, *The ambiguities of dependence*, 69. Gumede's dealings with Solomon are discussed in Van Diemel, *In search of 'freedom, justice and fair play'*, 79–86, which also deals with his wider political affiliations; Cope, *To bind the nation*, 104; and La Hausse, *Restless identities*, 88. La Hausse, *Restless identities*, discusses the awakening of ethnic consciousness on the Reef, 21–4. Fuze's *Abantu Abamnyama* was originally privately published; it was reissued as T. Cope (ed.), *The black people and whence they came* (Pietermaritzburg and Durban, 1979). Congress's constitution is reproduced in Karis and Carter, *From Protest to challenge, Volume 1: Protest and hope*, 79–82. The proceedings of the meeting at which Solomon's representative had attended were reported in *Ilanga*, 18.4.1921. Solomon's attempts to fashion an appropriate style are best described in Cope, *To bind the nation*, 120–30. The agenda for the Estcourt meeting of Congress was publicised in *Ilanga*, 18.4.1924. The results of the election were covered in some detail in the edition of 25.4.1924. Reports of discontent with Dube appeared in *Ilanga*, 6.4.1923. The cost of cars is noted in W.H. Bizley, 'A horse, a singer and a prince – two busy

months in the life of Pietermaritzburg', *Natalia* 38, 2008, 43. The 1924 launch of Inkatha is detailed in Cope, *To bind the nation*, 110–13.

Chapter 10

1 Edward Roux's account of Dube is in his *Time longer than rope*, 250. For the pass burnings and the significance of Dingane's Day, see S.M. Ndlovu, 'Johannes Nkosi and the Communist Party of South Africa: images of "Blood River" and King Dingane, late 1920s–1930', *History and Theory* 39, 4, 111–32. On Congress policy at this time, see Walshe, *The rise of African nationalism*, 104. Dube's interventions in the 1924 Native Conference are taken from 'Proceedings and resolutions of the Governor-General's Native Conference, 1924 [Extracts]' in Johns, *Protest and Hope, Volume 1*, 166–8. For 1925, see *Report of the Native Affairs Commission for the Years 1925–6* [U.G. 17-27]; copy in File 9, Marwick Papers, KCAL. The 'retribalisation' quote is from S. Dubow, '"Holding a just balance between white and black": the Native Affairs Department in South Africa, c.1920–1933', *Journal of Southern African Studies* 12, 2, 1986, 217. Dube's criticism of this forum is contained in his 'Native political and industrial organisations in South Africa' in J. Dexter Taylor (ed.), *Christianity and the Natives of South Africa* (Lovedale, 1928), 58. The account of the Prince of Wales's visit has drawn on the following: Marks, *The ambiguities of dependence*, 20: Cope, *To bind the nation*, 133–6; Bizley, 'A horse, a singer and a prince', 44; and W.H. Bizley, 'Interview: a trip to see the Prince of Wales' [S.W. Bizley and N.W. Ormond to W.H. Bizley], *Natalia* 25, 1995, 24. Dube's note that he had been involved in other celebrations is from his 'Address by the Rev. John L. Dube as representing the native viewpoint' in Natal Missionary Conference, *The clash of colour* (Durban, 1926); copy in Box 141, Colenso Papers. On the Zulu National Training Institute, see Cope, *To bind the nation*, 82–3.

2 The overview of Europe is extracted from T.C.W. Blanning (ed.), *The Oxford illustrated history of modern Europe* (Oxford, 1996). Dube's interview appeared in the *Christian Science Monitor*, 8.9.1926; the 'powerful yet subtle' quote is W.H. Hutt's, cited in T.R.H. Davenport, *South Africa: a modern history* (Johannesburg, 1978), 361. On Max Yergan, see D.H. Anthony III, 'Max Yergan encounters South Africa: theological perspectives on race', *Journal of Religion in Africa*, 34, 3, 2004, 235–65. Dube's statement on what Le Zoute had meant to him and the description of him leading prayers are from E. Smith, *The Christian Mission in Africa: a study based on the work of the International Conference at Le Zoute, Belgium, September 14th to 21st, 1926* (London and New York, 1926), 33–4. Oldham's reflections (which also contain the resolutions) are in J.H. Oldham, 'Developments in the relations between White and Black in Africa (1911–1931)', *Journal of the Royal African Society* 32, 127, 1933; the quote about Dube, Hope and Mahabane is on 169. See also J. Davis, 'The Christian Mission in Africa: International Conference held at Le Zoute Belgium September 14–20 1926', *Social Forces* 5, 3, 1927, 483–7. On the origins of the South African Institute of International Relations, see Higgs, *The Ghost of Equality*, 108. His name is on the *Majestic* passenger list found through a search at http://search.ancestry.com [accessed 12.12.2006]. The priority of an industrial building is discussed in Dube to Harris, 29.7.1926, G192, S22, ASAPS. On the American leg of Dube's journey, see Dube to Harris, 11.1.1927 and Harris to Dube, 24.1.1927, G192, S22, ASAPS. His visit to Penn State is recorded in Hunt Davis, 'John L. Dube', 509 – this is also the source for information on Frederick Dube. The Smiths' donation is noted in Smith to Dube, 18.1.1927 and Dube to Harris, 18.1.1927, G192, S22, ASAPS. Dube's illness was confirmed by Dr M.V. Gumede, the son of Dr I.B. Gumede who had been Dube's personal doctor; interview H. Hughes with M.V. Gumede. His trip to see the Wilcoxes is mentioned in Dube to Harris, 11.1.1927, G192, S22, ASAPS; the details of Wilcox's article are 'John

L. Dube, the Booker T. Washington of South Africa', *The Congregationalist*, 10.3.1927; there is a copy in KC Cuttings Book 4, 131, KCAL. He discusses his return travel arrangements in Dube to Harris, 11.1.1927, G192, S22, ASAPS. Angelina's fundraising activities are detailed in interview H. Hughes with M.V. Gumede, Inanda; Manson Collins interview with A. Dube, 8.3.1979, KCAV116; and *Bantu World*, 27.11.1937. On the London reference committee, the accusation that he might not be ill is in Harris to Buxton, 14.3.1927, and that he had prejudiced his work is in Harris to Pim, 28.4.1927; the winding up of its business is in Statement 9.1.1929, all in G192 S22, ASAPS.

3 Background information on Champion is from R.R.R. Dhlomo, 'Biography of Mahlathi' in M. Swanson (ed.), *The views of Mahlathi* (Pietermaritzburg and Durban, 1982), 6–17. For their early, courteous exchange of letters, see for example Champion to Dube, 8.12.1925 and 18.12.1925, Champion Papers A922, HPCW. The ICU's approach to organisation and its early Durban successes are detailed in T. Nuttall, 'Class, race and nation: African politics in Durban, 1929–1949' (PhD thesis, University of Oxford, 1991), especially 37. The leading source on the ICU's rural campaigns remains H. Bradford's *A taste of freedom: the ICU in rural South Africa 1924–1930* (Johannesburg, 1987); see 188–95 on Natal. The quote about the crowded roads is from 196. For Dube's farming pursuits, including his rates of pay, see interview with Mr A. Ngcobo, 8.3.1979, KCAV116 and CNC 17 (4/38) and CNC 32 (22/275) for the state of the roads. Possett Gumede's attempts to secure title to his land are detailed in CNC 40 (36/7); information also obtained from personal communication Dr M.V. Gumede. The precariousness of an agrarian-based middle class is well captured in Cobley, *Class and consciousness*; see especially 156–7. The quote capturing the aims of the Inanda Show is from *Ilanga*, 24.9.1926; Couzens suggests that Amicus was H.I.E. Dhlomo's pen name in *The New African*, 64. The 'progressive community' description is in Carter to Msimang, 3.6.1929, CNC 62 (49/8); that of the first show is in Walbridge letter, 30.6.1925, in C.K. Walbridge (ed.), *Thokozile* (Topeka, 1978) and CNC 62 (49/8), while the 1927 show is described in *Weekend Advertiser*, 2.7.1927 and *Ilanga*, 1.7.1927. See CNC 62 (49/6) and (49/88) for other shows in the region. Solomon's visit to the Seminary is noted in Walbridge letter, 15.5.1927 in Walbridge, *Thokozile*. Dube's criticism of what he considered the ICU's unrealistic demands is in *Ilanga*, 12.8.1927. La Hausse is of the opinion that Dube wrote Solomon's piece, on the basis of an allegation made by Champion; see *Restless identities*, 213, which is also the source of the 'Elephant of Inanda' quote. Champion's pamphlet was called *Champion, Kadalie, Dube: three names*; see Dhlomo, 'Biography of Mahlathi', 47. For an overview of the Dube–Champion contest, see La Hausse, *Restless identities*, 115; Nuttall, 'Class, race and nation', 43–7 (the quote about the NNC is on 96) and Selby Msimang, Box 3, SAMP. Dividing lines, however, were sometimes not at all clear: Gumede attended the first Non-European Conference in June 1927, convened by Abdullah Abdurahman, as a delegate of the 'Natal Native Congress'. See *Minutes of the first Non-European Conference held in the City Hall, Kimberley, 23rd, 24th and 25th June 1927* (Wynberg, n.d.), 4. Dube's letter to Marwick, 24.2.1928, is in File 74, Marwick Papers, KCAL, and his letter to Rheinallt Jones, 28.2.1928 is in File Cj 2.1.8a, Joint Council Papers, AD1433, HPCW. See P. Limb, *The ANC's early years*, 297, for evidence of increasing donations to Ohlange. The problems of the ICU are discussed in Bradford, *A taste of freedom*, 206–12; Marks, *Ambiguities of dependence*, 76; and Nuttall, 'Class, race and nation', 43. On Inkatha in the late 1920s, see Cope, *To bind the nation*, 201–2 and 224, and La Hausse, *Restless identities*, 223.

4 The account of the beerhall boycotts and subsequent events is drawn from La Hausse, 'The struggle for the city: alcohol, the Ematsheni and popular culture in Durban 1902–36' in Maylam and Edwards, *The people's city*, especially 52–6; the fall in revenues is noted on 57. The quote about the impossibility of forcing people into beerhalls is from Nuttall, 'Class, race

and nation', 73, which also discusses the impact on the ICU's leadership (67), Champion's attempt to build an alliance with chiefs (78–9), his return to Durban after his banishment (92) and the local Congress wrangles at the time (97–8). The disruption of Dube's meeting is noted in Cope, *To bind the nation*, 212. See 233–4 for Dube's attempts to have Solomon recognised as king, as well as *Ilanga*, 6.9.1929 and 13.9.1929. Dube's statement about Africans' treatment is in Minutes of Native Administration Committee, 3.10.1929, File 1/2/11/1/1, 3/DBN. Dube's view that the ICU served a useful purpose is in his 'Native political and industrial organisations in South Africa' in J. Dexter Taylor (ed.), *Christianity and the Natives of South Africa: a year-book of South African missions* (Lovedale, 1928), 53–9. His blaming the government for the rise of the ICU is argued in his contribution to *Report of the National European–Bantu Conference, Cape Town, February 6–9, 1929* (Lovedale, 1929), 146. Champion's exclusion from the Joint Council is noted in Marks, *Ambiguities of dependence*, 7. Champion's alternative Social Centre is discussed in M. Cele, 'Co-opting Durban's black African urban dwellers: the establishment of the Durban Bantu Social Centre', unpublished seminar paper (I am grateful to the author for permission to quote). The 'secret caucus' quote is from J. Ngubane, 'Three famous journalists I knew', *Inkundla yaBantu* 9, 121, June 1946, Uncat. MSS, KCAL. La Hausse discusses the 'personality-centred nature of nationalism' in *Restless identities*, 265, and Champion's entry is in Skota, *Who's who*, 138. Dube's trial was reported in the *Natal Mercury*, 10.1.1934.

Chapter 11

1 On the various organisations seeking to promote order, see Marks, *Not either an experimental doll* for the Bantu Purity League; Couzens, *The New African* on the Bantu Men's Social Centre in Johannesburg; and Cele, 'Co-opting Durban's black African urban dwellers' for the Durban equivalent; CNC (Series 2) 100 (73/12) for Daughters of Africa; and R. Elphick, *Christianity in South Africa: a political, social and cultural history* (Berkeley, 1997), 203 for the Catholic African Union. Couzens's *The New African* remains a central study of the topic, as is N. Masilela's 'New African Movement' website at http://www. pzacad.pitzer.edu/NAM/. *Ukuziphatha* was originally published in 1928 at Mariannhill; the translation upon which I have depended here is by N.N. Dhlomo, 'The theory, value and practice of translation', 79–122, which uses the 1935 edition published in Pietermaritzburg. Selope Thema is cited in A. Cobley, 'The "African National Church": self-determination and political struggle among black Christians in South Africa to 1948', *Church History* 60, 3, 1991, 358. Insights into the Dube children's early home life are from interview H. Hughes with Lulu Dube, 5.9.2005 and J. Ngubane, 'Three famous journalists I knew', *Inkundla yaBantu* second fortnight, 1946; copy in Uncat. MSS, KCAL. R. Waldo Emerson's *Conduct of life* was published in Boston in 1860; on Garvey's interpretation, see Hill, 'General Introduction', lvii. Dube's conference paper, 'The reintegration of native social and religious life through education' appeared in *The realignment of Native life on a Christian basis* (Lovedale, 1928), 42–7. Couzens, in *New African*, connects Plomer to the acronym, 58. Dube's *Insila kaShaka* was first published in 1930 in Mariannhill; there have been several subsequent editions, as there have been of Boxwell's English translation. The first edition was published in 1951 at Lovedale; it was recently reissued as a Penguin Modern Classic (Johannesburg, 2008). Ntuli's *Umbuso kaShaka* was published in 1930; see preface to the Penguin edition of *Insila*. The 'modernised subject' quote is from D. Attwell, *Rewriting modernity: studies in black South African literary history* (Pietermaritzburg, 2005), 76. Gerard, *Four African literatures*, 216, corroborates Lulu Dube's memory of hunting trips in Swaziland: H. Hughes interview with Lulu Dube, 5.9.2005.

2 Heaton Nicholls's background is summarised from his autobiography, *South Africa in my time* (London, 1961); the story of why Hertzog's bills took so long to develop is from 285–90 and the quotes on communalism and the 'civilised advance' of the Zulu are on 282–3. *Bayete!* was published in London in 1923. For an analysis of the timing of its writing and publication, see H. Hughes, 'G.H. Nicholls and his novel *Bayete!*', *Inspan* 1, 2, 1978, 51–9. The 'Chakas' quote is from 371. Dube's consultative trip is set out in Dube to Heaton Nicholls, 6.2.1931 and 13.5.1931; the proposals he and his colleagues suggested are in the enclosure with Heaton Nicholls to Dube, 9.2.1931. Heaton Nicholls's compromises are noted in letter to Dube, 9.7.1931, all in File 5, Heaton Nicholls Papers, KCAL. Jabavu's reaction is described in Higgs, *The ghost of equality*, 113. On Dube's dispute with Seme, see Seme to Champion, 31.7.1930, Folder Da1, Champion Papers, A922; and Walshe, *The rise of African nationalism*, 230. The claim of Africans' full support is in *South Africa in my time*, 290. This entire episode was first analysed in S. Marks, 'Natal, the Zulu royal family and the ideology of segregation', *Journal of Southern African Studies* 4, 2, 1978, 172–94. The full transcript of Dube's evidence to the Natives Economic Commission, April 1931, is in Box 6, 6228–76, NEC Evidence, AD1438, HPCW. Quotes are from the following pages: the land allocation 6245–6; on carpenters knowing arithmetic 6249; the 'black ox' and attempting to make point clear 6241, 6247; the serfdom of farm workers, 6229; wages contributing to white supremacy, 6271; on the Urban Areas Act, 6263–4 and on trade union rights, 6275; requests for representation, 6252; on health and declining fertility, 6243–4; and on a 'place in the sun', 6255. The 'apex of subordination' is from L. Kuper, *An African bourgeoisie: race, class and politics in South Africa* (New Haven, 1965), 8.

3 Cope, *To bind the nation*, is the most detailed source on the collapse of the first Inkatha and the Shaka Memorial Fund; see especially 256. The 'abstemious' description of Mshiyeni is cited in A.K. Buverud, 'The king and the honeybirds: Cyprian Bhekuzulu, Zulu nationalism and the implementation of the Bantu Authorities System in Zululand, 1948–57' (PhD thesis, University of Oslo, 2007), 30. Dube's speech at the purification ceremony in 1934 is cited in Marks, *Ambiguities of dependence*, 44. The description of the 1936 bills is from Walshe, *The rise of African nationalism*, 188–9. Information on Mtimkulu is from R. Edgar (ed.), *An African American in South Africa: the travel notes of Ralph J. Bunche, 28 September 1937 to 1 January 1938* (Athens, Ohio, 2001), 368. On Luthuli and Matthews, see Marks, *Not either an experimental doll*, 19; see also Nuttall, 'Class, race and nation', 129. The Natal consultation is recorded in 'Proceedings in Pietermaritzburg of representatives of the Department of Native Affairs and leading Zulus on 3rd and 4th September, 1935', CNC 110A (N1/15/5 Pt1). The incident in Shepstone's office is recounted in Z.K. Matthews in an interview with G. Carter, March 1964, 2:XD20:96/1, Karis-Carter Papers. The follow-up meeting, 'Bantu Conference held in the Umgeni Court, Pietermaritzburg, on Tuesday to Friday, 22nd – 25th October, 1935' is in CNC 110A (N1/15/5 Pt1). The poor turnout for the ANC's annual conference in 1933 is noted in Walshe, *The rise of African nationalism*, 255. On the All-African Convention, see D.D.T. Jabavu, *The findings of the All African Convention* (Lovedale, n.d.); Dube's hopes are on 28; and C. Higgs, *The ghost of equality*, 118–20; Dube's reflections are cited on 119. See Grobler to Heaton Nicholls, 13.12.35, File 5, Heaton Nicholls Papers, for attempts to use Dube to block opposition. On Dube's growing influence in white circles, see CNC 108 (94/4) and *Natal Mercury*, 25.12.1934 and 22.9.1936; his selection for the Jubilee Medal is recorded in CNC to Comptroller King's House, 16.6.1935, CNC 87 (58/77); and NTS 7322 (137/326). On the Empire Press Union, see D. Cryle, 'A British legacy? The Empire Press Union and freedom of the press, 1940–1950', *History of Intellectual Culture* 4, 1, 2004, at http://www.ucalgary.ca/hic [accessed 10.2.2011]. Astor's details are from his entry in the *Oxford dictionary of national biography* (online version) [accessed 10.2.2011]. Dube's address was reported in the *Natal Mercury*, 13.2.1935. The record of Dube's nomination for an Honorary PhD is in 'Meeting of Honorary Degrees Committee Friday 26 June 1936', University Council Minute Book 1934–8, University of South Africa; I am grateful to Herma van Niekerk of the Unisa archives for assistance in locating this item.

4 Some sources claim that *uShembe* was published in 1930, but 1936 is the correct date; it was published in Pietermaritzburg. I have used a translation produced by Mandla Ngcobo (personal copy). See A. Vilakazi with B. Mthethwa and M. Mpanza, *Shembe: the revitalization of African society* (Johannesburg, 1986), which is the source of much of the background information, as well as the quotes on the establishment of a new African society (73) and release from bondage, 40. See also R. Papini, 'Carl Faye's transcript of Isaiah Shembe's testimony of his early life and calling', *Journal of Religion in Africa* 29, 3, 1999, 243–84, which provides an account of those who had previously interviewed Shembe, 254. On this issue see also *Natal Mercury*, 26.7.1927. The insight on the significance of *uShembe* as written word is L. Gunner's, 'Zulu writing, the constraints and possibilities, with special reference to *Osibindigidi Bongqondongqondo* and *Ikhiwane Elihle* by Lawrence Molefe', *African Languages and Cultures* 1, 2, 1988, 151. On the Zulu Society, see 'Charter of Zulu Society' (the source of the brief statement of its aims); CNC to SNA, 'Report on the Zulu Society', 30.3.1937; and CNC to NC Nongoma, 5.2.1938, all in NTS 7322 (137/326). The quote about its being an arcane society is from La Hausse, *Restless identities*, 145. See *Ilanga*, 19.3.1938 for the inauguration of Shaka–Moshoeshoe Day. Mapumulo's letter to the editor on the NRC appeared in *Natal Mercury*, 2.8.1937. Dube's metaphor of the beast grazing at the edges is from 'Meeting of chiefs and others', 28.7.1937 in CNC 110A (N1/15/5 Pt 1). Dube's choice as leader of the African caucus is recalled in Z.K. Matthews's life of Dube, in *Imvo Zabantsundu*, 22.7.1961. Bunche's account of the NRC opening session is in Edgar, *An African American in South Africa*, 229–34; the impossibility of frank debate is noted on 232 and Dube's old age is noted on 268. Dube's communications with officialdom regarding Mshiyeni are in 'Meeting of Chiefs and other representatives, Eshowe, 28.7.1937' in CNC 110A (N1/15/5 Pt 4); and Deputation to CNC, 1.8.1939 in CNC 110A (N1/15/5 Pt 2). Seme's letter was published in *Ilanga*, 16.9.1939. On Phikokwaziwayo's status, see Confidential Minute, NC Nongoma to CNC, 20.3.1933 and 'Precis of correspondence relating to the succession', both in NTS 248 (78/53/2); also Buverud, 'The king and the honeybirds', 31–2 and R. Reyher, *Zulu woman: the life of Christina Sibiya* (Pietermaritzburg, 1999), 197–8. On Dube's role in the ANC in the late 1930s, see Dube to Champion, n.d. [1937], 2:XD20:96/1; Calata to Champion, 19.7.1938, 2:XC3:41/9 (which notes the need to close ranks); and James Calata's interview with Karis and Carter, March 1964, 2:XD20:96/1 (which notes that Dube 'came in'), all in the Karis-Carter Papers. The workers' rally was reported in the *Natal Mercury*, 10.8.1937 and is discussed in Nuttall, 'The leaves in the trees', 181–2. The 1939 conference resolutions are reproduced in T. Karis (ed.), *Hope and Challenge 1935–1952*, Volume 2 of T. Karis and G. Carter (eds.), *From protest to challenge: a documentary history of African politics in South Africa 1882–1964* (Stanford, 1973), 154–5. Dube's welcome for Mshiyeni is described in M. Benson, *The African patriots: the story of the African National Congress of South Africa* (London, 1963), 93. (Others similarly referred to his emotional outbursts in old age: see J. Ngubane, 'Three famous journalists I knew', *Inkundla ya Bantu* 9, 121, second fortnight, June 1946.) For Dube's honorary life presidency, see Xuma to Dube, 12.3.1943, ABX 430312a, Xuma Papers, HPCW; and the Natal leadership contest, see Walshe, *The rise of African nationalism*, 393–4. Gerard, *Four African literatures*, 219, notes his illness at his last NRC meeting. On the Charter Committee, see Karis, *Hope and Challenge*, 88. The Dubes' will is at MSCE 465/46, PDNA. For the Champion–Mtimkulu contest, see Walshe, *The rise of African nationalism*, 394. Dube's death was widely reported in the press; see *Ilanga*, 16.2.1946. The fullest report of the funeral

is J. Ngubane, *Inkundla yaBantu* 8, 114, first fortnight, February 1946. Dhlomo's valediction was originally published in *Ilanga*, 23.11.1946; it is reproduced in N. Visser and T. Couzens (eds.), *H.I.E. Dhlomo Collected Works* (Johannesburg, 1985), 341–3. See *Ilanga*, 23.2.1946 for Charles Dube's speech. There was a far bigger memorial service the week following the funeral, which had a more national character.

Chapter 12

1 The story of Mafukuzela Week was told me by the Rev. Bheki Dludla, who was instrumental in its inauguration (interview, 20.10.1999). Isabel Hofmeyr developed the idea of the 'protestant Atlantic' in her *The portable Bunyan: a transnational history of* The Pilgrim's Progress (Princeton, 2004). The quote about Dube's endurance is from Jordan Ngubane, 'Three famous journalists', and Albert Luthuli's views of the NRC are in his *Let my people go*, 93–6. The idea of segregation and race pride being compatible is in La Hausse, *Restless identities*, 231. The quote about harmonising the interests of workers and capital is from Moses, *Creative conflict in African American thought*, 164 (and was used in relation to Booker Washington). Mlambo's observation is in her 'John. L. Dube First President of the SANNC (ANC) and the Natives' Land Act of 1913' (BA dissertation, National University of Lesotho, 1980), v. The descriptions of Angelina Dube are from *Bantu World*, 27.11.1937 and of Dube's greatness (according to H.I.E. Dhlomo) in *Ilanga*, 23.2.1946. The exchange between Hally and Sam is in A. Fugard, '*Master Harold*' ... *and the boys* (New York, 1982), 21. The 'pool' saying is cited in Kuper, *An African bourgeoisie*, 370.

Index